THE MEMOIRS OF

ETHEL SMYTH

ABRIDGED AND INTRODUCED BY
RONALD CRICHTON

With a list of works by
Jory Bennett

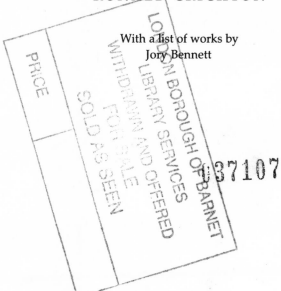
VIKING

VIKING

Penguin Books Ltd, Harmondsworth, Middlesex, England
Viking Penguin Inc., 40 West 23rd Street, New York, New York 10010, U.S.A.
Penguin Books Australia Ltd, Ringwood, Victoria, Australia
Penguin Books Canada Limited, 2801 John Street, Markham, Ontario, Canada L3R 1B4
Penguin Books (N.Z.) Ltd, 182–190 Wairau Road, Auckland 10, New Zealand

Impressions that Remained first published by Longmans, Green 1919, *Streaks of Life* by Longmans, Green 1921, *A Final Burning of Boats Etc* by Longmans, Green 1928, *Female Pipings in Eden* by Peter Davies 1933, *Beecham and Pharaoh* by Chapman & Hall 1935, *As Time Went On . . .* by Longmans, Green 1936, *Inordinate (?) Affection* by Cresset Press 1936, *What Happened Next* by Longmans, Green 1940
This abridged collection first published 1987

Typeset in 10 on 13pt Linotron 202 Palatino
Filmset, printed and bound in Great Britain by
Hazell, Watson & Viney Limited,
Member of the BPCC group,
Aylesbury, Bucks

British Library Cataloguing in Publication Data

Smyth, Ethel
The memoirs of Ethel Smyth.
1. Smyth, Ethel   2. Composers — Great
Britain — Biography
I. Title   II. Crichton, Ronald
780'.92'4   ML410.S5/

ISBN 0–670–80655–2

Library of Congress Catalog Card Number 86–50802

Contents

Introduction 7
Acknowledgements 15
Editor's Note 17

ONE
1858–77

A Soldier's Child 21
My Father 29
My Mother 34
Musical Stirrings 39

TWO
1877–9

Music at Leipzig 63
Lisl von Herzogenberg 87
Brahms 99

THREE
1879–91

Henry and Julia Brewster 111
The Break with Lisl 129
In the Desert 144

FOUR
1891–4

Lady Ponsonby 177
Balmoral 184
Launching the Mass 193
One Oak 206

FIVE
1894–1903

Fantasio 213
Der Wald 235

SIX
1903–9

The Wreckers 259
The Illness and Death of H. B. 273
Thomas Beecham 284

SEVEN
1910–25

Women's Suffrage 293

EIGHT

Recollections of the Empress Eugénie 321

NINE

Women in Music 339
Pan the Fourth 346
A Life Summed Up 353

Epilogue 363
Biographical Notes 365
Sources 371
List of Works 373
Index 381

Introduction

THE WRITER

Ethel Smyth wrote ten books. Since they are out of print, a list in order of publication may be useful:

Impressions that Remained (two volumes, Longmans, Green, 1919)
Streaks of Life (Longmans, Green, 1921)
A Three-Legged Tour in Greece (Heinemann, 1927)
A Final Burning of Boats Etc (Longmans, Green, 1928)
Female Pipings in Eden (Peter Davies, 1933)
Beecham and Pharaoh (Chapman and Hall, 1935)
As Time Went On . . . (Longmans, Green, 1936)
Inordinate (?) Affection (Cresset Press, 1936)
Maurice Baring (Heinemann, 1938)
What Happened Next (Longmans, Green, 1940)

She also wrote, and received, a huge quantity of letters, and in the second half of her career she kept a diary. Her last piece of writing, according to her first biographer, Christopher St John,* was the memoir of Louisa, Lady Sitwell, written in the form of a letter to Lady Sitwell's grandson Osbert and reprinted by him as an appendix to *Left Hand, Right Hand!*. Perhaps she would have included this in a further autobiographical volume, *A Fresh Start*, which was unfinished at her death in 1944.

Impressions, As Time Went On . . . and *What Happened Next* are discursively autobiographical, with interludes consisting of letters to and from the author. They overlap and, in the case of later volumes, sometimes recapitulate for the benefit of new readers. The lapse of time allowed more to be said about people and incidents. In between came the miscellaneous volumes *Streaks of Life, A Final Burning of Boats Etc* and *Female Pipings in Eden*. They are uneven, but they contain some of her best writing, including the extended portraits of Brahms, the

* *Ethel Smyth: A Biography* (Longmans, Green, 1959).

ex-Empress Eugénie of France and Mrs Pankhurst. There are also book reviews, a couple of lectures and assorted polemical writing about the status of women. *Beecham and Pharaoh* is a literary equivalent of the operatic double bill, an extended character sketch which is also autobiography, followed by a description of a holiday which, unlike some of her travel writing, is not detached from other events in her life. *Inordinate (?) Affection* concerns an essential element in her personality, one that ran parallel to her musical career – her love of big dogs.

All the above have been drawn on for this abridgement, and as far as possible the extracts are arranged in chronological order. Two of her books remain unpillaged, for different reasons: *A Three-Legged Tour in Greece*, an entertaining, observant account of a tough walking holiday in Thessaly and the Peloponnese which is in no way connected with surrounding events; and *Maurice Baring*, a full-length tribute to a friend in the form of an excursion through his writings that, alas, provokes little desire to read them. In the latter volume a combination of perpetually youthful enthusiasm (she was close on eighty when she wrote it) and drawing-room slang ('killingly funny') has not worn well.

Ethel Smyth was first and foremost a composer of music, but her books are so readable that people argue whether or not they are 'better' than her music. Since there is no common measure by which the value of, say, a volume of memoirs and a string quartet may be weighed, this is surely a pointless exercise. At the moment her books are, or appear to be, of greater interest, but if the revival of interest in British music of the earlier part of this century turns out to be more than a fresh fit of parish pumpery, the position may be reversed. She knew all about the parish pump in real life but (like Elgar, whom she very much disliked) she did not bring it into her music. Her books are readable for the revelation of an exceptional personality and for descriptions of musical life in more than one important European centre a hundred years ago.

Christopher St John notes a letter from Virginia Woolf praising the 'long, rolling breakers' and 'easy, large stride' of Ethel Smyth's prose. The surge and the stride can be seen in the three portraits mentioned above and in those of two remarkable women who have a prominent place in her gallery of female friendships – Mrs Benson, wife of the Archbishop of Canterbury, and Lady Ponsonby, wife of Queen Victoria's private secretary. Christopher St John also quotes a revealing passage from Ethel Smyth's diary about the beginning of her passion, when in her seventies, for Virginia Woolf:

. . . for many women, anyhow for me, passion is independent of the sex machine. Of course when you are young, it will not be gainsaid. (Nor indeed, if I am frank, did it cease to play any part with me when I should have done with all things physical . . . But I have remained capable of a love as deep and absorbing as one or two major loves of my youth.)

Virginia Woolf was much younger, Emmeline Pankhurst and Edith Somerville were the same age as Ethel Smyth, but they were exceptions. On the whole it seems that the greatest and most enduring of her 'passions' were for older women with whom, through character or circumstance or both, physical gratification was out of the question even to one of her on-coming disposition. Though much was written to them in the form of letters, there is little of Edith Somerville and Virginia Woolf in the autobiographies for they came into her life too late.

By a nice stroke of irony the introduction of Henry Brewster ('Harry' or 'H.B.'), the only man she loved and the greatest single influence of her life, follows closely on the remarkable passage on friendships with women in the second volume of *Impressions*. Brewster, a writer and philosopher of American-English extraction, was born in France in 1850 and educated there. He lived in Europe, preferring Rome. His writings, in French and English, included *L'Âme païenne*, *The Statue and the Background*, *Anarchy and Law* and *The Prison: a Dialogue*. He is poised between the various worlds Ethel Smyth inhabited, family, musical and social, like a figure out of Henry James – handsome, cosmopolitan, understanding, not so much an outsider as an onlooker. Maurice Baring, who became Ethel's closest man friend after H.B., once heard someone say it was a pity Brewster was 'such an idle and ignorant man'. Baring rather considered that 'his ignorance was more suggestive than the knowledge of others, for he ignored not what he was unable to learn, but what he had no wish to learn, and his idleness was a benefit to others as well as to himself'. In his autobiography, *The Puppet Show of Memory* (Heinemann, 1922), Baring described him thus:

His appearance was striking; he had a fair beard and the eyes of a seer; *à contre jour*, someone said he looked like a Rembrandt. His manner was suave, and at first one thought him inscrutable – a person whom one could never know, surrounded as it were by a hedge of roses. When I got to know him better I found the whole secret of Brewster was this: he was absolutely himself; he said quite simply and calmly what he thought, and the truth is sometimes disconcerting when calmly expressed.

Brewster tamed Ethel without bruising her spirit and corrected what he saw as barbarous Germanic influence with a wider appreciation of French civilization. The ground was fertile but not, except by her mother in childhood, tilled, and Ethel's affection for Germany, even where music was concerned, was never blinkered. She befriended Brewster's two children (his wife was Julia von Stockhausen, sister of Lisl von Herzogenberg), Clotilde, who studied architecture in London and married a fellow student, Percy Feilding, and Christopher, who married a daughter of the sculptor Hildebrand.

Of the profoundest events in their friendship, the moment when H. B. finally became her lover, and his death at the age of fifty-eight, she writes with a reticence in strange contrast with the outspokenness of pen and speech that caused justifiable alarm to family and friends. In spite of her frankness she was neither uncharitable nor prurient. She did not believe, for instance, what others assumed, that the painter Sargent and her sister Mary Hunter were lovers. This was not due to unworldliness or impercipience, for she had a keen eye, indeed a relish, for the quirks of human nature and for details of physical behaviour. With the forward sweep of her writing there goes a rarer gift, an ability to draw a character swiftly and sharply comparable to Sargent's skill with the charcoal stick, shown brilliantly in his sketch of her singing at the piano. Her subject may be an eccentric neighbour in the heath country round Aldershot which was her English home all her life, a Leipzig worthy or a half-forgotten figure from the world of music such as the Franco-Irish composer Augusta Holmès, often encountered in books about nineteenth-century Paris but surely never brought to life as here.

The only feature of her background against which Ethel Smyth reacted with real fury was her father's refusal, while it lasted, to let her study music in Germany. For the rest she fitted into garrison life with its hunting, sport and ceaseless entertaining, more comfortably than did her bored and frustrated mother. That life, for all its conventions and shibboleths, narrowness, philistinism and xenophobia, was more adaptable and less impregnable in reality than it seemed from outside. A world where class counted but not rigidly, where wealth was not essential though financial security was expected if not always achieved, where ostentation was deplored and economy practised with absurd inefficiency, and where the worship of conformity never excluded eccentricity, it survived until the Second World War and no doubt, in pockets here and there, is still to be found.

With her quick wits, resourcefulness and push, Ethel Smyth would have found her feet in the wider world without assistance, but the chance arrival of the Empress Eugénie as her neighbour greatly hastened the process. She was introduced by the Empress to reigning royalties from Queen Victoria downwards, bringing support of various kinds for her musical projects which she had no false modesty about accepting. She was not a snob in the conventional sense, and was incapable of fawning or pretence; indeed her lack of obsequiousness seems to have been an advantage rather than otherwise. Lady Ponsonby, a loyal and devoted courtier with a grain of Whiggish cynicism, used to chaff her about her 'royal *culte'*, to which her sensible response was that 'all closed communities are interesting as study – the small bourgeois world of Leipzig, the episcopal one at Lambeth, the far more curious genus, Royalty'.

THE MUSICIAN

Ethel Smyth wrote a respectable amount of music though her *œuvre* was not large for a composer who died in her eighties. Fauré and Vaughan Williams, respectively a generation older and younger, both lived long and wrote much more. In later life, in her fifties, deafness began to slow her down and she did not have the kind of inner ear that could defeat it; unlike Fauré, who went deaf at much the same age, she needed to hear what she wrote. Besides, there were always too many distractions: sport, travel (some, though not all, in pursuit of performances of her operas), friendships and the letter-writing that went with them. Lisl von Herzogenberg, Henry Brewster's sister-in-law and Ethel's mentor in Leipzig, was incapable of understanding this duality in her protégée's character, yet she was right to scent danger and warn her. Lisl could not have foreseen that the pull between circumstance (upper-class military life) and the chosen profession would become one of the things that made Ethel Smyth the extraordinary person she was.

Of her now neglected Mass in D, the product of a religious crisis, Donald Francis Tovey wrote, 'There is no "religiosity" about it; and the prayers of the Kyrie and Agnus Dei are far from expressing a mood of resignation. But the music is throughout, like Spinoza, God-intoxicated.' In a note prefixed to the score the composer asks for the Gloria to be played at the end, after the Agnus Dei, and though Tovey implies that the unusual order is for concert performance only, it is typical of her to prefer to end in a blaze of triumph rather than with a prayer.

It is not strange that a British composer, even one whose connections with the Anglican church music tradition were only intermittent, should write a major choral work. It is on the other hand surprising that she should have written six operas. When she began the series the only swallow of the English operatic summer that was somehow delayed for half a century was Stanford's *Shamus O'Brien* (1896). The Leipzig circle she frequented had little use for opera, but in Munich the Wagner conductor Hermann Levi, struck by the dramatic possibilities he detected in the Mass, cried, 'You must at once sit down and write an opera.'

The Wreckers, her only full-length opera, comes up from time to time in student or semi-professional productions, but the score deserves the full-scale treatment it has not been given since the Sadler's Wells revival of 1939. Thomas Beecham wrote of his admiration for it in his autobiography, *A Mingled Chime* (Hutchinson, 1944), in which he also gives as vivid a portrait of her as she gave of him in *Beecham and Pharoah*:

This fine piece has never had a convincing representation owing to the apparent impossibility of finding an Anglo-Saxon soprano who can interpret revealingly that splendid and original figure, the tragic heroine Thirza. Neither in this part nor that of Mark, the tenor, have I heard or seen more than a tithe of that intensity and spiritual exaltation without which these two characters must fail to make their mark.

Forty years on one might find the singers.

The libretto for *The Wreckers* was written by Harry Brewster, in French, as *Les Naufrageurs* – he liked that language, and at the time the Frenchman Messager was in charge at Covent Garden. For four of her operas, a varied bunch, Ethel Smyth herself provided the librettos, Harry advising in the background for the first two. *Fantasio*, a fantastic comedy in two acts in German, is based on the play of the same name by Musset. *Der Wald*, a music-drama in one act with prologue and epilogue, also in German, is *verismo* in medieval-romantic costume.

During the 1914–18 war, with the establishment of Beecham as opera conductor and impresario, and the growth of opera at the Old Vic, Ethel Smyth turned to English. *The Boatswain's Mate* (one act, two scenes, with optional intermezzo), in which the heroine is a masterful woman inn-keeper, is based on the comedy by W. W. Jacobs. *Fête Galante*, a 'dance dream' in one act with dancers as well as soloists and chorus, is a versification by Edward Shanks of a story by Maurice Baring, returning to the courtly world of *Fantasio* but with a bitter twist. *Entente Cordiale*, a 'post-war comedy in one act' dedicated to 'my own Branch, the Army', has songs interspersed with dialogue in stage cockney and soldiers' parley-voo. The *Two Interlinked French Folk Melodies* for orchestra derive from this opera. She did not aim high in her English comic operas; just as she claimed to write her books for 'Mr and Mrs Everybody', she confessed to hankering after the musical-comedy public. She overlooked the strong British prejudice against one-act operas. What she wanted most of all was the permanent light opera company that did not, and still does not, exist in this country.

What she refers to as her 'chamber music songs' of 1908 consist of three poems by Henri de Régnier, *Odelette, La Danse* and *Chrysilla*, to which she added an *Anacreontic Ode*, in a French translation by Leconte de Lisle. Her last work, *The Prison* (1930), described as a symphony, is a two-part cantata for soprano, bass-baritone, chorus and orchestra, based on the philosophical dialogue of that name by Harry Brewster. The composer's affection for this late love-child has not been rewarded by frequent performance. A more likely and simpler candidate for revival is the earlier *Hey Nonny No* for chorus and orchestra (1911), a sixteenth-century drinking song set in clumping waltz rhythm. Though the words are in no way feminist, the composer emphasizes the phrase 'men are fools'. A late work now fallen into oblivion is the three-movement Concerto for violin, horn and orchestra (1927) which the composer also arranged as a Trio in A for the two solo instruments with piano.

Ethel Smyth's autobiographies are full of references to her singing, usually to her own piano accompaniment – an art much practised in the days of drawing-room music, of which her friend Sir George Henschel was a notable exponent. She charmed and excited amateur listeners and fired professionals with a determination, unfortunately not always carried through, to produce the operas she sang and played to them. In *The Puppet Show of Memory*, Maurice Baring describes 'the rare and exquisite quality and delicacy of her voice, the strange thrill and wail, the distinction and distinct, clear utterance'. Another friend, Sylvia Pankhurst (in *The Suffragette Movement*, Longmans, Green, 1931) was also impressed by a note of strangeness in Ethel's singing:

'Hey Nonny No!' . . . was never heard with such great power and weirdness as when she gave it, playing to some casual group of Suffragettes in [her] small cottage. Voices of sailors drinking in a tavern, rude, rough fellows, wild adventurous spirits; voices of merriment; coarse, large laughter; voices of women, foolish, fierce, merry, sad and grieving; voices of horror; voices of Death – all these enwrapt in the rude, wild blast of the storm one heard in that chorus, given by that one magic being.

Summing up her career, Edward J. Dent, writing in *A Theatre for Everybody* (T. V. Boardman, 1945) about the history of the Old Vic and Sadler's Wells, the two theatres Ethel Smyth admired so much, had this to say:

It does not matter whether she was really a great composer or not, nor does it matter that she was a woman and had, or thought she had, all sorts of sex-prejudice to contend with. The same fate might have befallen any male composer. Ethel Smyth's autobiography . . . is a chapter of general social and operatic history.

RONALD CRICHTON
Eastbourne

Acknowledgements

I am indebted to *Ethel Smyth: a Biography* by Christopher St John, with additional chapters by Victoria Sackville-West, Edward Sackville-West and Kathleen Dale, and to *Impetuous Heart: the Story of Ethel Smyth* by Louise Collis (William Kimber, 1984). The latter includes a short bibliography. My Introduction is partly based on one written by me for the New York reprint of *Impressions that Remained* (Da Capo Press, 1981). Other sources are given in the text or in notes.

I gratefully acknowledge assistance from the Service Culturel of the French Embassy (London); the music department of the Bibliothèque Nationale (Paris); *Le Figaro* (Paris); the Opéra du Rhin (Strasbourg); the Deutsche Staatsoper (Berlin); and the Historisches Archiv of Cologne. In Great Britain assistance has been received from Breitkopf and Härtel; William Elkin; Faber Music; Novello & Co.; Universal Edition; Camden Festival; the Performing Right Society; and Letcher & Sons (Ringwood, Hampshire). My thanks are due also to Robert A. Cecil; Dr Michael de Cossart; Tom Eastwood; Mrs J. C. Elwes; Frederick Fuller; Charles Jahant; Dr Robert Orledge; Richard Ormond; the late Nicolas Powell; Harold Rosenthal (former editor of *Opera* magazine); and Dietrich Voss. I owe special thanks to my assistant, Juan Soriano for his unfailing support and patience; to Jory Bennett for undertaking what we believe to be the most informative work-list yet compiled of Ethel Smyth's compositions, and for correcting her sometimes unreliable dates; and finally to John Denny, formerly of Penguin Books, who at every stage has advised, assisted and encouraged the paring down and putting together of the Memoirs.

R. C.

24 JULY 1986

Editor's Note

In editing this abridgement it has proved necessary to make minor adjustments to the text in the interests of clarity and continuity. In addition, dates have been inserted where the lapse of time between extracts may be confusing, inaccurate performance dates and misspellings of proper names have been corrected, and inconsistencies of spelling and styling have been made uniform where appropriate. These adjustments are not indicated in the text; the frequent occurrence of three full points is therefore an indication not of editorial excision but of an addiction to them which Ethel Smyth shared with many writers of her period.

The origin of each extract can be traced in a list of sources at the end of the book, numerical references to which appear in the text at the end of each extract or group of extracts from a single volume. Also to be found at the end of the book are brief biographical notes on many of the people referred to, and a complete list of Ethel Smyth's compositions.

Ethel Smyth wrote for a public whose working knowledge of French could be taken for granted; only rarely does she provide translations of quotations in French. Of the remaining passages it has proved impracticable to translate in footnotes any but the most important. These and other footnotes are editorial except where marked 'E.S.'. Further editorial commentary appears within the text in the form of linking passages in italics.

R. C.

ONE

1858–77

A SOLDIER'S CHILD

MY FATHER

MY MOTHER

MUSICAL STIRRINGS

A Soldier's Child

One day during the lifetime of my brother Johnny, who had a turn for mathematics, and whose memory was accurate, we children started trying to fix the date of our earliest recollections, but it was found impossible to decide exactly when the first event I recall took place; namely an attempt to jump out of the low pony-carriage as it was crawling up St Mary Cray's hill, which ended in my falling on my back in the road, having failed to observe that Johnny and the groom always jumped in the direction the carriage was moving in. Thus my conscious life began with the first of a long series of croppers – not a bad beginning.

We lived in those days at Sidcup, then quite a country place, selected by my father as not too far from Woolwich, where, on his return to England after the Indian Mutiny, he took up the command of the Artillery Depot. The Indian forces to which he belonged were then in course of fusion with the regular army, and being very popular, and having served with distinction, he was considered the right man for a task requiring both tact and common sense. I can see him now, starting for the daily ride to his office mounted on his eighteen-hand charger Paddy, who later filled the parts of hunter, brougham horse and coal-cart horse with good humour and propriety. I have even ridden him myself, and an old friend once told us his first sight of me was wrong end upwards, suspended by the foot on Paddy's off side with my long hair sweeping the grass, the saddle having slipped round in Bramshill Park. As a tiny child I firmly believed the horse-radish served with the Sunday joint was plucked from the white saddle-marks on Paddy's high withers, and for this reason had an aversion to horse-radish sauce years after I knew the truth about it.

At the time of that leap from the pony-carriage the Sidcup household consisted of my paternal grandparents, who came to live with us after the Mutiny, my parents, and five children – four girls and a boy. As time went on two more girls arrived on the scene, Bob my youngest brother being born the year after we left Sidcup; in fact we eventually blossomed into one of the large families that in those days were rather the rule than the exception.

Looking at the portrait of what our friend George Henschel called my grandfather's 'dear old port-wine face', one remembers the legend that his last action before he died was to stroke his stomach and remark with a chuckle, 'To think of the hogsheads of port I have consoomed in my time!' He might well say so, for he lived to be ninety-six – a splendid, intensely alive old man whom I should have worshipped in later years, whereas then, alas! I only felt a child's repulsion to extreme old age. He always wore a black velvet skull-cap which was associated in my mind with wizards, and I disliked having to kiss his scrubby apple-red old cheek, wondering uneasily why there was always white powder on the lapels of his coat. Again I detested a favourite joke of his, which was to say very slowly, when a certain dreaded hour struck, 'Shadrach . . . Meschach . . . and . . . TO BED WE GO!' – the last words with a sudden roar. But what chiefly roused my disapproval was his comment when Johnny, who had put something very hot into his mouth, instantly spat it out: 'Well done, my boy,' cried grandpapa, 'a fool would have swallowed it!' Being imbued with nursery notions of pretty behaviour I was shocked at the coarseness of the males of the family.

My grandmother left no impression on my mind; and as my father and mother will be described later, I will pass on to my own generation, beginning with the eldest, Alice, supposed never to have been naughty in her life, and whose goodness one governess said was 'positively monotonous'. Of this specially beloved sister I chiefly remember that she said her Catechism in what we used to call a squeaky voice, that is a voice to which she has been prone all her life when reading family prayers. I also remember that she once said to me, 'You have a very strong will; *why not will to be good?*' and that this tribute to my strength of character secretly delighted me. Whether the advice was followed I cannot say, but to harness the pride of a child to the cart is a good receipt.

Johnny, the next of the family, was at that time my model, my tastes being essentially boyish – a trait he met with mingled disapproval and patronage. I soon noticed that I climbed higher and was generally more daring than he, and no doubt dwelt on the fact, which would partly account for a certain lack of sympathy between us. Being himself of a quiet, orderly disposition, perhaps too he disliked the violent ways that made my mother call me 'the stormy petrel'; anyhow I always thought he judged me severely.

After Johnny came Mary; two years later I arrived – the first of the bunch to be born in England, all the rest being little Indians. When the Mutiny broke out our parents were at home on leave, having brought with them Alice and Johnny, who were getting too old for the climate. As often happened in those days the baby, Mary, had been left behind in charge of a cousin, the idea being to return to her in a few months; and while my father was hurrying back alone to India, Mary went through all sorts of vicissitudes, was carried off to a place of safety by her ayah, hidden behind a haystack, and so on, till arrangements could be made for sending her home.

My father left England on 30 June 1857, and I was born on the 23rd day of the following April – a ten months' child.* In pre-Suffragette days I was proud of this fact, having heard that such children are generally boys and always remarkable! Since then I have ascertained that no one but the most benighted old Gamps ever held such a theory.

There were four years between me and the next child, Nina, a gap accounted for, as I used innocently to explain to inquirers, by my father's absence in India. I well remember the change when I ceased being the spoiled baby; details escape me but not the ache and fury of it. The births of the other two Sidcup children, Violet and Nelly, evidently took place, but I remember nothing about those events; indeed my early recollections, when not concerning myself only, are chiefly connected with Johnny and Mary.

Sidcup Place, in the parish of Footscray, Kent, was originally a small, square, Queen Anne house, separated from the main road by a high wall covered with ivy, between the two a strip of garden. A wing had been added later, along the first storey of which, facing the real garden which was at the back, ran what seemed to me then an endless gallery, the most ideal of places for children to rush up and down and yell in. There were roomy stables and a big old-fashioned granary mounted on stone pillars, yet none the less infested, so they told me, by rats – a useful legend. The grounds were charming; on one side of the croquet lawn was the most enormous acacia I have ever seen, the bloom of which never failed, and on the other a fine cedar. Beyond was a walled kitchen garden with flowery borders and rose patches, and the object of our lives was to mount the walls, unobserved, from the far side in quest of forbidden fruit. Once I remember the gardener, who

* The birth certificate gives the date 22 April.

had stealthily removed the ladder, suddenly appearing with a long switch; we flew along the top, he at the bottom of the wall, calling out as we reached the spot where the ladder should have been, 'Now I've got yer, yer little warmints,' and I am glad to say I followed Johnny's lead and took a flying leap down into safety, a drop of eight or nine feet – not a mean performance for a child of less than that number of years.

Beyond the kitchen garden was a shrubbery that seemed to me then what the woods in Rossetti's sonnets seem to me now – a vast mysterious place full of glades and birds, wild flowers and bracken; beyond that again, not on our property, I think, was a nut-wood intersected by green paths one exactly like the other, in which I never strayed far from my elders for fear of getting lost. I was always haunted with this particular terror, and once, when separated for one second from my family in the midst of a seething firework crush at the Crystal Palace, started such appalling yells of 'I shall never see my dear Papa and Mama again!' that the crowd instantly divided to enable my father's hand once more to grasp mine.

Fringed with disreputable-looking willows was a duck pond, on which we used to put forth in wine boxes and tubs; and hard by an old elm tree, in which Alice, Johnny and a friend of his built one of the many descendants of the Tree House in *The Swiss Family Robinson*. It had a floor, and heaps of shelves and hooks, and we were allowed to have tea up there when we had been very good. As milk warm from the cow figured among our treats I pretended to love it, but really was rather nauseated, and privately thought milking an improper sight. It seemed cruel, too, to maul the poor cows like that, and when the gruff cowman said they liked it, he was not believed.

I have two special farmyard recollections, one being the occasion on which young Maunsell B. – a schoolfriend of Johnny's who spent most of his holidays with us and considered himself engaged to Mary – promised me sixpence if I would ride a slim black pig called Fairylight round the yard. For some reason or other we were dressed in clean, open-work, starched frocks, and when, after being shot off on to the manure heap, I was dragged into my father's study by our infuriated nurse, it was easy to see he could hardly keep his countenance. The other incident was my bribing the cowman (again with sixpence) to let me see a pig killed – conduct which deeply shocked and horrified Johnny who considered such sights a male privilege. The terrific scolding that followed was unnecessary, since for months afterwards I turned green whenever I heard a pig squealing. At last even the nurse pitied me and would say, 'Bless your heart he's only squealing for his dinner,' which I hope was true. Otherwise I am quite sure I was not a cruel little girl, except perhaps later on in the donkey days, when dreadful things were done with the butt end of a whip; but anyone who has had to do with donkeys will make allowances.

I think on the whole we were a naughty and very quarrelsome crew. My father once wrote and pinned on the wall: 'If you have nothing pleasant to say *hold your tongue*'; an adage which, though excellent as receipt for getting on in society, was unpopular in a nursery such as ours, for words lead to blows and we happened to love fighting. There was one terrific battle between Mary and myself in the course of which I threw a knife that wounded her chin, to which she responded with a fork that hung for a moment just below my eye, Johnny having in the meantime crawled under the table.

Of course we merited and came in for a good deal of punishment, including having our ears boxed, which in those days was not considered dangerous, and my mother's dramatic instinct came out strongly in her technique as ear-boxer. With lips tightly shut she would whip out her hand, hold it close to one's nose, palm upwards, for quite a long time, as much as to say, 'Look at this! You'll feel it presently' – and then . . . smack!

I think I am the only one of the six Miss Smyths who has ever been really thrashed; the crime was stealing some barley sugar, and though caught in the very act, persistently denying the theft. Thereupon my father beat me with one of grandmama's knitting needles, a thing about two and a half feet long with an ivory knob at one end. He was the least cruel of men, and opponents of corporal punishment will say its brutalizing effect is proved by the fact that when I howled he merely said, 'The more noise you make the harder I'll hit you.' Hit hard he did, for a fortnight later, when I joined Alice, who had been away all this time at an aunt's, she noticed strange marks on my person while bathing me, and was informed by me that it came from sitting on my crinoline.

Even in after years my mother could not bear to think about that thrashing. All I can say is it left no wound in my memory as did snubs, and was the only punishment that ever had any effect – for I dreaded being hurt. Indeed to run the risk of ordinary pains and penalties, and make the best of it when overtaken by them, was quite part of our scheme, and I am glad to know that some of our happy thoughts when under punishment extorted unwilling admiration even from our chastisers.

For instance one day, when Mary and I knew that incarceration in an empty room at the top of the house would surely be our lot, we seized as many books as we could lay hold of, and stuffed them into our drawers, which buttoned up at the sides. I remember the agony of feeling them slip lower and lower as we were herded upstairs, and how finally, just as the key was turned on us, down they came in an avalanche. On another occasion we were locked up in Papa's dressing-room and the shutters were barred; but there was light enough to ransack his wardrobe and construct, with the aid of pillows and bolster, a complete effigy of him lying on his back on the floor in full hunting costume. And as finishing touch, the pincushion, with an inscription pricked out in pins, 'For dear Papa', was laid on the effigy's breast. If that didn't melt them I really don't know what would, but as a matter of fact an indiscreet word let drop now and again by visitors made us suspect that a more lenient view of our crimes obtained than might have been supposed. Anyhow I know we were considered very quaint and amusing children, and, as happens in most families, were alternately encouraged by guests to chatter, and snubbed by our parents for being forward.

Like all children we of course 'acted' our parents' friends, and one of Johnny's and my most admired productions was a visit from our neighbours the Sydneys. Lord Sydney, then Lord Chamberlain, was the most pompous old gentleman I have ever seen, exactly like 'the Earl' in melodrama, with his curled grey whiskers and gold pince-nez. He had a way of holding out two fingers to Johnny and saying 'how do boy' which was done justice to by his personator. Lady Sydney was rather a dear, I used to think, and by crinkling up my nose, looking down it, and complaining of the east wind, I was considered not only to resemble her as much as a child of seven can resemble a woman of forty-five or fifty, but to give a satisfactory rendering of what we were told was the Paget manner. I particularly remember the Sydneys, of course, because they were our local grandees – also because their extreme friendliness to my parents caused some heart-burning to other less favoured neighbours.

At this stage of my existence I stood in great awe of my father, but adored my mother, and remember her dazzling apparitions at our bedside when she would come to kiss us good-night before starting for an evening party. I often lay sleepless and weeping at the thought of her one day growing old and less beautiful. Besides this, wild passions for girls and women a great deal older than myself made up a large part of my emotional life, and it was my habit to increase the anguish of love by fancying its object was prey to some terrible disease that would shortly snatch her from me. Whether this was simply morbidity, or a precocious intuition of a truth insisted on by poets all down literature – from Jonathan and David to Tristan and Isolde – that Love and Death are twins, I do not know, but anyhow I was not to be put off by glaring evidence of robust health. I loved for instance Ellinor B., a stout young lady who rode to hounds, was a great toxophilite as they were called in those days, led the singing in church in a stentorian voice, and was altogether as bouncing a specimen of healthy young womanhood as could be met with. Persuaded nevertheless that this strong-growing flower was doomed to fade shortly, I one day asked Maunsell if he did not think she was dying of consumption, and shall never forget my distress when he answered with a loud guffaw, 'Consumption? Yes, I should think she *may* die of consumption, but not the kind you mean!'

At Sidcup too I learned that the accents of tragic passion have as poor a chance of being understood in the nursery as elsewhere. I worshipped my lovely cousin Louie, and one day when she took me on her lap and cuddled me, I murmured, burying my face in her ample bosom, 'I wish I could die!' – whereupon the nurse exclaimed, 'Why, Miss Ethel, whatever makes you say such a thing? *I thought you were so fond of your cousin!'* People's love-affairs, in as far as I could get to hear about them, always arrested my attention, and at a time when I was too young to know either the artist's passion or personal ambition, love seemed to me the only thing that mattered; but nothing less than Keats's unquenchable flame of course. One day a letter from an admirer of Louie's was indiscreetly read out in my presence (she was then a young widow) and I was much puzzled by the phrase, 'O for one hour of your love!' Of what use, I said to myself, could one hour be to anyone? But for once asked no questions.

I think we were fairly well off in the early Sidcup days, especially after the death of my maternal grandmother, whose only surviving child mother was. 'Bonnemaman', as she was known to us in contradistinction to our very English 'Grandmama', and whose name I sometimes remember with a start was once Mrs Struth, lived in Paris and was a mysterious personality. I never saw her myself, but there were legends of her having taken to her bed soon after she was forty,

27

partly because of rheumatism, partly from 'foreign' indolence, and chiefly in order to receive innumerable doctors in becoming caps and bed-jackets. We gathered that she was considered worldly and gifted, also that like all Straceys she had great musical talent, and years afterwards it thrilled me to learn she had known Chopin intimately. They said she had been extremely handsome – as we could judge for ourselves when her portrait by Jonquière came into my mother's possession – and one realized vaguely that an unfortunate second marriage had taken place, it being understood that the initials on the mother-of-pearl counters we played round games with must not be alluded to because they were those of Mr Reece, the second husband. Louie once told us that when a child she had been taken to see her in Paris, and was sent out on to the balcony with a small French boy, who at once began spitting on the heads of passers-by; when suddenly beautiful 'Aunt Emma' shot out and boxed his ears as Louie never saw ears boxed before or since. Later she remembers an awe-inspiring peep of her ill in bed, all white lace and cherry-coloured ribbons; the room was darkened and one went on tiptoe. I recollected these details, because anything like a mystery rouse a child's interest.

One morning, some time in the sixties, a telegram was handed to my mother under the acacia tree; she fainted, and we learned that Bonnemaman was dead. After that I forgot all about her, till, during a genealogical craze, I came upon some rather curious correspondence.

If she, as is evident, was imprudent in money matters, Mr Reece was nothing better than an adventurer, but she adored him and quarrelled with her relations on his account. These must have been odious to a degree, for in one rather piteous letter she says it really was *not* kind of Aunt So-and-so to put about in England that she had large cupboards built in her bedroom in order to conceal lovers; an inspection of the apartment, she adds, would show that the only cupboard large enough 'for such a wicked purpose' is in the dining-room. Finally the stepfather became so impossible that there was a judicial separation, but much to her relations' disgust Bonnemaman declined to come home and face 'I told you so', and lived and died in France. She was considered to have lost caste by her second marriage, and as separations were looked upon as disgraceful in those days, no matter where the fault lay, her situation amply accounts for her having been thus shrouded in mystery. Indeed Alice remembers that some time after her death, my mother, ever unconventional, having casually remarked, 'I wonder if my stepfather is alive?', Papa looked greatly annoyed at such a subject being mentioned before the child.

Such was the woman who was hushed up before her grandchildren as a sort of family disgrace! After reading these letters, especially hers to my mother, I have come to the conclusion that poor Bonnemaman, gifted, warm-hearted, impulsive and thoroughly 'injudicious', would have been my favourite relation.

Not long after her death came the tragedy of all old Indians, the failure of the Agra Bank, and my father lost most of his savings; thus in early days I knew the chill cast on a cheerful household by financial worries. Either then or earlier he made heavy sacrifices to ensure each daughter that should remain single £40 a year. As five out of the six married I am the only one to profit by the arrangement, and the title under which I claim this pension is . . . 'Bengal Military Orphan'.

My Father

My father, a fine example of what is fortunately a not uncommon type, was one of fourteen children, six of whom were alive when I was young. Tall, upright, strongly built, with the pleasant, open, very English countenance we see exaggerated in the portraits of Mr Punch, his bearing was equally suggestive of kindliness and authority. Having to wear spectacles slightly interfered, to my mind, with his military appearance, but in his Horse Artillery uniform with its masses of gold braid and shaggy busby, he was a fine, soldierly-looking man – and in all costumes the picture of a gentleman.

To give an idea how the England of those days flung her youth into the world to find their level, he went out to India at the age of fifteen, he and his brother having been presented with commissions in the Bengal Army by their uncle Sir Theophilus Metcalfe, and a year later was responsible for roads, transport, communications, law and order, life and death, in a district as big as Yorkshire. There is an anecdote connected with his later Indian period which exactly characterizes him – one for whom duty and obedience were paramount, but who was capable of transcending the letter of the law on occasion. During the Mutiny certain men of his battery who had joined the mutineers were caught and condemned to be hanged in their officer's presence. Their senior, a sergeant, the best native soldier he ever had under him, advanced, saluted, and said, 'Sahib, you often told me I did my duty to your satisfaction; grant me one last favour, let me die by your own hand.' . . . 'And by Jove,' said my father, 'though our orders were to humiliate the mutineers in every way, I did as he asked and hanged him myself.'

When quite a young man he became what is well called a martyr to gout; not even a busy life and limitless sport, including boar-hunting (which he hated to hear called 'pig-sticking'), could work off the floods of champagne that flowed in India, so to speak, on the top of my grandfather's hogsheads of port. But between the attacks, right up to the end of his life, his vitality and cheerfulness, and what he chiefly laid store by, his usefulness, were unimpaired.

No man was ever more loved and respected. Single-hearted, shrewd, with great knowledge of the world, partly innate, partly acquired, the watchword of his life was duty, which he pronounced 'dooty', and after leaving the army he threw himself into country work and made his character felt. He often remarked, 'If I had nothing to keep me busy outside the house what a nuisance I should be in it,' and was generally determined to wear out, not rust out. They always said he was first rate on the Bench, but once he astonished his brother magistrates by sharply reprimanding a young policeman, who was boasting how he had hidden behind a hedge and caught a man riding a bicycle on the footpath: 'Then you did very wrong,' said my father, 'to go sneaking about laying traps. You're there to prevent people breaking the law, not to hide and tempt them to break it!'

He combined with his idea of service a simple piety he did not speak of but which his whole life was founded on, and he never went to sleep without reading in one of the little books at his bedside.

He was a keen politician – Conservative of course – and chairman of the County Conservative Union, but advanced in his ideas. Long before the days of Tariff Reform he was in favour of a tax on raw material, and even advocated the enfranchisement of women, a theory no one else in our world took seriously. I remember his pointing out that three-quarters of the land in the parish was owned by women, and that it was monstrous these should be denied the suffrage. True, I think he was convinced that propertied females would vote his own way, but the injustice and unwisdom of their being voteless was what preoccupied him; no one believed more firmly that fair play is the only thing that pays in the long run.

I remember once when I was a schoolgirl telling him I had asked Mr Pursey, the cobbler, why all shoemakers are radicals, and had found his reply, 'Well you see, Miss, we has time to *think*,' rather interesting. But Papa was not at all impressed and said he had never heard such infernal nonsense in his life. He was very tolerant by nature and disposed to hear both sides of a question; still convictions are convictions, and one day, when he was well over seventy, he remarked confidentially, 'I am getting an old man, but upon my word it is very difficult for me even now to believe a radical can be an honest man.' He always took the chair at political meetings in the neighbourhood and nine out of ten of his speeches used to end with an exordium to his hearers to 'do your duty by your Queen, your country, and your God'. We children, and I dare say our neighbours, used to look forward to this peroration with some amusement, yet it was uttered so simply and earnestly that it always ended by impressing even me afresh. Towards the end of his life modern ideas were beginning to undermine the respect automatically paid to the gentry, but no one protested at his habit, when chairman, of silencing objections or awkward questions by rattling his stick furiously on the table and declaring the motion carried unanimously. People just laughed and let 'the General's' high-handed methods pass unchallenged, such was his overflowing geniality.

He was an unqualified admirer of the British Constitution, and though freer than anyone it is possible to conceive from snobbishness, had a delightful old-fashioned respect for Royalty; if in our haste we stuck a postage-stamp upside down he was seriously annoyed: 'It is disrespectful to your Sovereign,' he would say. For distinguished personalities he had the same quality of reverence. I remember an incident that amused me even then, when my sense of humour was immature. To his thinking Gladstone was the Devil, and hearing that great man was coming to speak at Aldershot he remarked, 'If I see the beast I shan't take any notice of him.' We afterwards discovered he was by chance on the platform when Gladstone stepped out of the train. 'And what did you do?' asked my mother. 'Well,' was the reply, 'as a matter of fact I believe I raised my hat.' All the same he was delighted when I evaded a suggestion from a daughter of Gladstone's, a neighbour, to come over one day and sing to him. Alas! young people are terribly earnest, and I never had another chance of seeing the G.O.M. at close quarters.

Between my father and me there was never strong sympathy; perhaps he recognized from the first a stubborn will that was eventually to triumph over his. I think too the artistic temperament was distasteful to him, though it was that of my mother, to whom he was deeply attached. Once when Bob was a child Papa found him busy painting, and flew into such a rage at a boy's indulging in such a pursuit, that he swept the whole paraphernalia on to the floor, and Bob thought he was going to be cuffed.

Yet the odd thing was that in some ways he himself had artistic instincts; Byron, Scott, Wordsworth and other poets of his youth he read aloud admirably, and I was always struck with the musical cadence in his voice when he came to certain sonorous phrases in Family Prayers. Again no one had a keener enjoyment of the beauties of nature, but none of this helped him to see in me anything but the rebel I certainly was.

His excellent delivery of stately English prose came in well reading the Lessons in church, but he was not a reader gifted with presence of mind, and arriving at certain strong unvarnished statements in the Old Testament, usually bowdlerized or omitted, would cough and stumble and get into terrible trouble, much to the delight of the congregation. My mother often entreated him to look at the chapter quietly at home first, but this his pride forbade. His versions, too, of some of the crack-jaw biblical names were sometimes remarkable, but there was a simplicity about him which carried off anything and everything.

He certainly was choleric in the old-fashioned military 'damn-your-eyes' style, and if a footman dropped anything would call out angrily, even at our grandest dinner-parties, 'God gave you two hands, you fool, and why the devil don't you use them?' – strange reproof, for surely dishes cannot be handed round on that principle, but I liked the phrase and hope the footman did.

When his own family fell under his displeasure, betrayed by the verbal unreadiness I referred to, and which excitement and anger greatly increased, he would mix up his parts of speech in the most fantastic manner. Once when Bob, then a child of five or six, was teasing the dog Kitty, Papa exclaimed in violent irritation, 'Now Kitty, if you make Bobby bark I'll brain the poker.' Or again when a chance cab, after leaving someone at our house, agreed to take someone else to the station if not kept waiting, he bellowed up the stairs, 'Come along: no last words: the cab may fly any moment.' In my youth the wine was always locked up by the family after meals, and one of his best '*coq-à-l'âne*', as my mother, whose delight they were, called them, was, 'Now then Bob, lick up the locker . . . well, I mean lick up the shutter.' But it was in the tightly packed Sunday landau, a situation calculated to rasp nerves all round, that this mood would most often overtake him. I remember his saying to Nelly and Bob, who were grumbling at being squeezed to death, 'Well if you two infernally thin people can't sit five in a carriage I don't know who can,' and as we drew up at the church door he added, 'Now Mama, you come first, so just get out of the window.'

Some of the things he said in his public capacity used to leak out: how he advised the Bench to kill two stones with one bird, and informed a Committee that the pollution of the Blackwater, a filthy little local river, was mainly caused by the 'vast quantity of vegetable marrows flowing down from the hills'. But in private life he never beat his advice to the mama of a rheumatic daughter: 'You ought to put her under a masher.' Once started on the wrong path, his conversation would be on these lines for the rest of the day, and my mother would laugh till she cried.

In spite of his insinuating on occasion, as most elderly men do, that he had been anything but a milksop in his youth, I cannot think he was ever wild, but he certainly had a weakness for what he called 'a bit of a scamp', and always maintained his best subalterns were in that category. We noticed, too, that he was more than indulgent to members of the other sex suspected of frailty; so much so that Mary, a particularly favourite married daughter, once said in fun, 'I wonder what you'd do if *I* went off with some other man?' Thereupon he became angrier than she had ever seen him, got up, stamped about the room, and finally went out into the garden in a fury, to reappear five minutes later, poke his head in at the door, and say with terrific emphasis, 'I'd *curse* ye!' Then the door was slammed and he was not seen again for several hours. Such is the logic of the British paterfamilias.

As time went on expenses increased, income diminished, and his children used to think he was rather optimistic and happy-go-lucky about his affairs. I now question if this was so, anyhow I remember being very much impressed – I was about twenty-one at the time – by the quiet good humour with which he said one day, 'I'm not such an old fool as you all think.'

My Mother

To produce anything that gave a real idea of my mother's physiognomy was beyond the art of any known photographer; in the same way I half despair of describing, or rather making live again, her strange, difficult, but most lovable personality.

It was a case of baffled genius and injudicious bringing up combined. Whether Bonnemaman settled in Paris before, or only after, her second marriage I cannot say, but in spite of all the family said and did to prevent it my mother was educated in France, and at that time French was more her language than English. Children are always incurious about their parents' early days, and I never knew much about hers, but when a child myself I was deeply struck by her account of a vanished feature in the Champs Elysées, typical of a gay simplicity no longer met with in this grave world.

It appears there was a path leading under a creeper-covered wire archway to a wooden hut in a shrubbery; from the archway swung a picture of a gentleman in green peg-top trousers, who was raising his hat to a lady in a pink skirt and a hat with drooping ostrich feathers, and remarking, according to the legend below,

> Madame, il faut que je vous dise adieu,
> Un devoir pressant m'appelle en certain lieu.

I also recall her telling us that in the Revolution of '48 her mother's windows were barricaded with mattresses, and that on the wall of the house opposite there was a great splash of blood. Some years previously, owing to the unsatisfactory stepfather and other reasons, it had been settled that she should live at Rackheath, near Norwich, the home of her childless uncle, Sir Edward Stracey, and I gather this very handsome 'frenchified' girl, who sang exquisitely, was looked upon as a dangerous interloper by less brilliant relations.

At that time my grandfather Smyth was director of the Norwich branch of the Bank of England, and thus it came that she met my father, who was home on leave. The wedding took place from Rackheath in 1848, and in acknowledgement of her offices as mistress of his house her uncle presented her with some very fine diamonds, which, when travelling, she persisted in carrying about on her person for safety; sometimes in a brown paper parcel, mysteriously tied on somewhere, sometimes sewn into a garment, but never in a dressing-case. These diamonds were not entailed, but the family had concluded they would go with the place, and one gathers that feeling ran high on the subject. This cannot have mattered much to her, for my father carried her off directly after their wedding to India, where she stayed, as I said, till shortly before the outbreak of the Mutiny.

Indian society was a small affair in those days, and what with her wit and gaiety, her almost Southern beauty, and her music, she appears to have been a sort of queen out there. And judging by later years, when we wished he would put his foot down oftener, my father may possibly have been an over-indulgent husband.

She really was extraordinarily un-English, whether because she was educated in France, or because her grandmother was a certain Mademoiselle de Lagarde – according to her portrait a wooden-faced young lady, with a huge miniature of a Protestant clergyman, her father no doubt, plastered on to her flat chest. The quick vivid gestures, for instance, were foreign, and I always thought were eyed by my father's sisters with some disfavour on that account; but above all her way of looking at things was utterly the reverse of what is called insular. I remember a little conversation between us, the finale of which caused one of my aunts to 'bridle'.

MOTHER (*heaping her plate with fried parsley*): I *do* love parsley!
ETHEL: Yes, fried, but not stuck raw in the middle of one's eggs and bacon.
MOTHER: O, I like it even as an ornament; it makes a dish look appetizing.
ETHEL (*sententiously*): Do you know I have come to the conclusion I don't like anything that isn't founded on common sense.
MOTHER (*impulsively*): And I infinitely prefer things that are *not* founded on common sense!'

If ever anyone was meant for social life it was she; I used to wonder at the change that came over her in society, more especially at her gracious hospitality, the perfection of good manners, in her own house. She adored entertaining, and though I used to reproach her in times of financial crisis for her 'love of dress', I was obliged to admit that, to use the charming French phrase, *elle portait bien la toilette*.

This even in later life; but how I wish I had known her when she was young! One day after her death, Lady Sydney, whom we seldom saw in post-Sidcup days, met Alice in a shop and began talking of mother, saying that when first they knew her, she and Lord Sydney had agreed that never had they come across such a brilliant being. When she dined with them, all other guests, whether English or foreign, became colourless; not because of her beauty and charm, her wit and vivacity, said Lady Sydney – these things one had met with in others to an equal degree – it was the unique personality. 'Had your mother married a diplomat,' she added, 'she would have been known and acclaimed all over Europe.' And having passed a good deal of my life abroad, I feel sure this is true.

She had a great gift for languages, and besides French and Hindustani knew German, Italian and Spanish. Though she had visited none of the countries in which these languages are spoken except France and India, nor had any practice since her schoolroom days, when occasion demanded off she would start with fluency and idiomatic correctness, not to speak of an accent she owed to her musical ears.

For her strongest gift was undoubtedly music; she was in fact one of the most naturally musical people I have ever known; how deeply so I found out in after years when she came to Leipzig to see me, and I watched her listening for the first time to a Beethoven symphony – watched her face softening, tightening, relaxing again as each beauty I specially counted on went home. Old friends maintained that when she was young her singing would have melted a stone, which I can well believe; all the warm, living qualities that made her so lovable must have got into it. When I knew her she had almost lost her voice, but enough remained to judge of its strangely moving timbre. Later on she loved to hear me sing, and it saddens me to think how seldom I gratified her when we were by ourselves; but I always was lazy about singing.

She read at sight very well and her playing of dance music was gorgeously rhythmic. I can see her now, pince-nez on nose, rapping out the beloved old Lancers, leading up to the curtsey, gluing us for ever so long to the floor, and sending us flying back to our places with incredible accent and go. One used to wonder if the children she played for noticed how different it was to the performance of their own mamas, but I greatly doubt it.

The same dramatic instinct made her cross-question us in what we thought the oddest way about incidents of our walks: 'Tell me exactly what happened when you met; did you bow first or did he take off his hat first?' It all had to be visualized.

In those days, Heaven help me! I believed, as men told us, that feminine quickness of intelligence was a sign of superficiality, that it was far cleverer to painfully count up the fingers of each hand than to see at a glance that five and five make ten. I was therefore not as much impressed as I should be now by the extreme rapidity of her mental operations; but I soon noticed that though her judgement on imper-sonal matters was markedly sound, it was quite another thing when she herself was in question. Many of her children have inherited this very common weakness.

As I said, she had the warmest of hearts, and if violent in temper, was a generous forgiver and forgetter. But alas! capacity for affection and for suffering go hand in hand, especially if you have a vivid imagination and neither instincts nor habits to control it with, which was her case; indeed, whenever I think of her, David Copperfield's phrase about his 'undisciplined heart' comes into my mind. No mother ever tormented herself more strangely. After saying good-night to us, apparently in a happy frame of mind, perhaps she would not fall asleep at once; and then, as only too often happens with the hypersen-sitive, the passèd day would shine upon her pillow, breeding many woes. Molehills transformed themselves into mountains of pain and despair, and at cock-crow, as it seemed to us, a piteous Odyssey would begin from one bedroom to another – we used to call it 'Morning Calls' – and in each was recited a list of wrongs and cruelties suffered by her at our hands, slights, veiled rudenesses, or ridicule, the whole thing as often as not wholly imaginary. Explanations were seldom of any use, for even in peaceful moments her own point of view tended to obscure that of the other person – so much so that we often chaffed her about her style of relating a conversation: 'So he said something or other, and I said "*not at all*, that's where you're quite wrong . . ." '

O! those morning calls, and O! the pitilessness of youth! . . . Speak-ing for myself, I fully realized the intense misery of her heart and sometimes met it sympathetically, but more often with impatience and anger. The whole thing was so unreasonable, besides which one wanted to go to sleep again.

For these and other reasons she was always to me a tragic figure. Alice, the favourite daughter, who knew her ten years before I did, in younger, brighter days, thinks her nature was at bottom a happy one, but the self-tormenting strain must always have been there, waiting to assert itself when youth should wane. She certainly had a great sense of humour and her laugh was wonderfully merry to the last; indeed there were touches of lightness in her that sometimes astonished me. In the midst of a scene of despair, for instance, the arrival of a new bonnet from Paris, or a bunch of roses handed in at the window by the gardener, would transform her at once into the most cheerful of beings. Children are generally little prigs, and this trait, which I now find wholly charming and touching, used to affect me not quite agreeably.

When she was well and happy her talk sparkled with subtle turns and comments – *l'esprit français* in English garb – and nothing used to infuriate me more than the stolid faces of the rural swine for whose benefit these pearls were lavished, but she herself took it with smiling indifference. To see things wittily and express them felicitously came naturally to her, and she no more looked for applause than would a swallow circling and darting about over a meadow. All the same this lack of response must have depressed her unconsciously, for I know that my everlasting delight in the point of her conversation gave her immense pleasure.

In 1875 came the great sorrow of her life, the death of Johnny. This eldest son, of whom his masters predicted great things, had a slight hunting accident; his horse swerved jumping a fence and his knee caught in a bough. That was all; neither of them fell, but he went back to Westminster with a slight limp. Perhaps it was only a tiny displacement that with the help of X-rays might have been located and easily put right; as it was he was pulled about and tortured by surgeons, and taken to Wildbad with no result. Then came the slow agony of realizing that all schemes for his future must be abandoned; at last he took to a wheeled chair and died two and a half years after his accident.

Never in all this time did I hear my mother say an angry word to Johnny or even before him; he disliked scenes of all kinds and however close on the brink of the tempest mood she might be, the slightest sign of distress from him would calm her in an instant. I used to wonder at this and might have guessed from it how she loved him and what his death meant to her. But as he had always been inclined to snub me

I had no particular devotion for him myself, moreover was wrapped up as always in my own affairs. Thus it came that I never realized till after her own death, that with him most of the sunshine went out of her life.

Musical Stirrings

In 1867, my father having been given command of the Artillery at Aldershot, we left Sidcup, and took up our abode at Frimhurst in the village of Frimley, a couple of miles from Farnborough, where I lived till his death in 1894.

It must be borne in mind that Frimley was even then not a real country neighbourhood. The proximity of the biggest camp in England, the Staff College, and Sandhurst, brought a great deal of amusement in its train, and also that rarest element in the country, an unfailing supply of men – a consideration when you have six daughters to marry. This factor no doubt weighed with my father when, on the expiration of his Aldershot command, he decided to buy Frimhurst; besides which, as the heads of big units were automatically called on by the county families, we already knew what was dreadfully styled 'the nice people'. On reflection I think the presence of a large floating population brought rather an unstable element into life. At first there was an attempt to interest us in household duties, and we took it in turns to solemnly unlock the store-room door and watch the cook weighing out 10 lb. of rice and 12 lb. of sugar; but by degrees this ideal lapsed, and ended, much to the relief of the younger members of the family, in a sort of budget system, checked on Saturdays by Papa.

About one thing there was no slackness: neighbourliness and entertaining were looked on as duties; everyone who had a garden gave garden-parties, and those who had the means dinner-parties, on which latter occasions terrible things went on after dinner in the way of music. One of our neighbours belonging to the 'nice people' class never dined out without his cornet-à-piston, on which instrument he would blast forth *Ah che la morte ognora*, accompanied by his gentle smiling wife, who said the cornet box was so nice in the brougham, keeping one's feet out of the draught. As for calling, that duty ranked immediately after going to church on Sunday, but it was an axiom that the more exalted the old resident's social position, the less would be the alacrity shown in swallowing fresh bait. Thus from lips of persons trembling on the verge of friendliness you often heard the remark, 'So-and-so hasn't called yet.' I suppose this is human nature but it seems very snobbish and ridiculous.

Then there were the county balls to which of course residents subscribed, and at which the humbler country families had the privilege of mingling with the magnates and trying to identify the brilliant units of their house-parties. At Guildford the ball was not supposed to have really started till the contingents from East Horseley Towers, Peper Harow and Clandon had arrived; and quantities of people only began to enjoy themselves when the grandees, who seldom stayed long, had departed, taking with them the deadly hypnotic power they exercised over the smaller fry.

Of course these great ones gave balls, also humbler people like ourselves, but we called them dances. To step for a moment out of our neighbourhood: staying in Yorkshire, when I was about sixteen, with the mother of a schoolfriend, I was taken to Wentworth, where once a week, all the time they were in residence, Lord and Lady Fitzwilliam received any friends and acquaintances who chose to come. Lord Fitzwilliam, who was then Lord-Lieutenant, wore breeches, silk stockings and his Garter ribbon, and everything, including the stand-up supper, was most gorgeous, yet somehow or other homely. There might be forty guests, there might be 150, according to the weather, and these entertainments must have cost a great deal, but thus did Lord Fitzwilliam conceive his duty towards his neighbour. I remember that my hostess, a cousin of Lady Fitzwilliam's and herself a woman of very good family, made a little curtsey when she greeted the lady of the house – a survival of respect for office which struck me curiously and agreeably. The whole thing was a glimpse of an epoch even then belonging to the past.

To return to Frimhurst. Of our relations with the villagers I have few recollections, nor were they typical, because there was little feudal tradition in such a neighbourhood, and that little in course of extinction. Partly from egotism, but mainly, I honestly think, because it always struck me as indiscreet, I myself did little visiting among our poorer neighbours. I remember that extremely poor old women used to come up on Saturdays for soup, and when a doctor's order could be produced, for a bottle of port. There also were presents at Christmas, and one old woman once wrote to my mother, 'If there are any flannel petticoats or other Xmas gifts going I shall be found very acceptable.'

I have been trying to recall whether up to the time of our migration to Frimhurst I had shown a special bent for music. I don't think I composed in the Sidcup days, but Mary and I sang little duets, simple tunes to which I put 'seconds' as it was called, and in the quality of those seconds and my accompaniments, I myself, had I been listening, should certainly have detected a natural gift. But to judge these things takes an expert, and my mother had had no real musical training. Transposing and playing by ear came naturally to me, but so it did to her, so she would not have been much impressed by that; or perhaps she thought I was conceited enough without special encouragement as regards my music; anyhow I cannot remember hearing or thinking much about it.

In the year following our arrival at Frimhurst, Bob, the boy who was to console my mother for the coming loss of Johnny, was born. He was a very quiet, delicate child, and according to a family legend never spoke till the day he was sitting under the table, clipping the cat's fur with a pair of scissors, and told to desist; whereupon he suddenly burst into speech with the remark, 'All the cats in the *wairld* aren't yours!' and never ceased talking afterwards.

Johnny was now a Westminster boy. My father's youngest sister had married Dr Charles Scott who at this time was headmaster of Westminster, and Mary and I sometimes spent the night at their house in Dean's Yard. From our window we had a grand view of the boys playing racquets against the schoolhouse wall, or flying into school in their trenchers; and occasionally we caught sight of my uncle, in cap and gown, sweeping across the school yard, always in a violent hurry. It was understood that if we met Johnny in the cloisters or any other part of the dear old buildings we must make no sign of recognition and expect to be cut. We were.

Life at Frimhurst up to the time I came out falls into two periods, the governess and the school epochs. Our governesses never stayed long; they pass before my mind's eye in dreary procession; some English, others German; some with dyspepsia, others with unfortunate natures – perhaps the same thing under different names; nearly always ugly, and quite invariably without the faintest notion of making lessons either pleasant or profitable. Certainly we were difficult pupils, naughty and refractory to discipline, still we were quite intelligent children, and later on Mary and I learned something at school; but excepting one, who without intending it determined my course in life, our governesses might have been lay-figures for all we got out of them. I think the whole governess system monstrous and unworkable; even as a child I vaguely understood how impossible is the position of these poor unwilling intruders into the family circle, and hope time will evolve some more civilized scheme of education for 'the daughters of the nobility and gentry'. On the other hand our governesses were specimens of humanity few families, however kind-hearted, could assimilate.

I have said I was subject to 'passions' as I called them, and about this time drew up a list of over a hundred girls and women to whom, had I been a man, I should have proposed; it is therefore no great tribute to the charms of Miss Hammond, the first governess I remember, that her name figured on the list of passions. She was young, rather pretty, and wore a chignon which she told us was her own hair. Perhaps she meant in the sense that she had paid for it, for alas! one day she slipped up on the ice and away rolled the chignon like the heart in Richepin's terrifying ballad, but without asking its owner if she had hurt herself. I said nothing; one is too paralysed by dreadful emotion to speak at such moments, but then and there my passion expired.

And now comes the recital of one of the ugliest things I ever did. A few months later Miss Hammond departed for good in the same low pony-chaise with which these records begin . . . and as it sped down the drive I clung on to the back, hissed in her ear, 'I know your chignon is false!' and dropped off. I was quite aware that my action was hateful, but it is not till old age is in sight that sincerity-mad people can quietly let a deceiver think his deception has been a success.

One of Miss Hammond's successors presented my mother with the most astonishing specimen of German ingenuity I have ever seen, except perhaps similar souvenirs fabricated by the Grand Dukes and Duchesses who clustered round Goethe in his country retreat, and deigned to live the simple life there. This treasure is made of thin wire, small black beads, and eight locks cut from the eight heads of the Smyth children, and represents a bunch of blackberries, the berries being made of beads, and the leaves – how she did it I cannot think – of hair. There were all shades in our family, from black to flaxen, but though the leaves are still shapely and tidy, age and dust have wrought them all to the same dull hue. By immemorial custom this strange object has lived under a glass shade, stuck into one of Prince Charlie's goblets, and there it is, confronting me at this moment.

During the Franco-Prussian war, when we had a rather feeble-minded German governess, we used to rush in to her first thing in the morning announcing imaginary German defeats – and the poor governesses never saw the papers till evening! We were too young to have any bias one way or the other, though my mother of course was all for the French; it was just the ferocious playfulness of youth. The sanctimonious tone of the Hohenzollern telegrams, to which the world is now accustomed, was then a novelty, and caused much astonishment. There was a paraphrase by Mr Punch of one of the King of Prussia's effusions to his Queen which delighted Papa:

> By Heaven's will, my dear Augusta
> We've had another awful buster,
> Ten thousand Frenchmen gone below!
> Praise God from Whom all blessings flow!

By such trivial incidents do great contemporary events hook themselves into the memory of a child. Except the fact that we all picked lint, these are my only recollections connected with a war of which the whole world has not yet finished reaping the harvest! . . .

Not long after our arrival at Frimhurst, Alice was presented and came out. There were five years between her and Mary, and since, as I said, there were four between Nina and me, Mary and I were in a schoolroom group by ourselves. For this reason I can remember nothing about Alice's proceedings with one momentous exception – her first proposal, or anyhow the first at which we, so to speak, assisted. There was a certain young soldier with very pink cheeks and a strange habit of wearing velveteen coats – an assiduous visitor whose attentions became marked. One day we saw him leaving the house in evident agitation, and when, with the tact of younger sisters, we instantly rushed into the drawing-room, lo! there was Alice, supported by mother, being plied with smelling-salts! In Jane Austen's day this was the correct attitude for a girl of sensibility on tender occasions, and to that epoch Alice belonged by education and temperament; but Mary and I were early samples of the coming generation and poor Alice never heard the last of that touching tableau. She declares to this day it was a figment of our imaginations, but it was not, and I am glad to have seen this sort of thing with my own eyes, for we shall never see it again.

Whether forerunners or not, Mary and I were still considered very quaint children. Neither of us was in the least shy, but when in the presence of one of my 'passions', I was liable, under the stress of emotion, to extraordinary contortions; such as standing on the outside of my feet, swaying to and fro, brushing the palm of one hand violently against the other in mid air, as if one were flint and the other steel – antics that Mary, who knew the cause, eyed with scornful astonishment.

Like all healthy-minded children we had our little rivalries and ambitions, a large stock of cocksureness as to who was in the right . . . and both of us had tempers. Hence, though our differences were no longer settled with knives and forks, there were plenty of rows, but as a matter of fact we were devoted to each other, and so closely identified in people's minds that, much to our annoyance, our parents would sometimes say, 'Mary and Ethel, shut the door.'

It had always been an axiom in the family, that from earliest years Mary had been drawn by me into tomboyish ways that really were foreign to her nature. I think this is probably true; anyhow, as time went on, boys who began by being attracted by my independence and proficiency in games, always ended by forsaking me in order to minister to Mary's more feminine helplessness – buckling on her skates for her, or in response to a piteous 'Help me! I'm giddy!' flying to her rescue among the higher branches of the old cherry tree. I remember various incidents connected with faithless boy lovers of mine, but think that in all this I was playing a part, doing what I knew was the correct thing. Now and again a very real feeling of mortification may have swept over me as I saw my admirers succumbing to the charms of Mary, but from the first my most ardent sentiments were bestowed on members of my own sex, and the love-affairs with boys were but imitative and trashy, I fear.

By this time I had taken to composing chants and hymns, music being connected in my mind mainly with religion – a well-known English malady. And to each of these productions the name of a 'passion' was given. Our duets had now become a feature at home dinnerparties, Mary having a very pretty voice and a great idea of delivery. One thing I well remember – wondering how I knew by instinct exactly where she, or other singers I accompanied, would be likely to 'go flat' (for of course one interval was as easy to me as another) and what note, emphasized in time, would correct the tendency. In later years this mystery of critical intervals became clear to me.

There was one musical torture of my youth, however, from which no relief could be obtained. Maddened by a reiterated wrong note I would cry, 'I can't do this sum if you go on playing G natural; it's G sharp!' And Mary would calmly reply, 'I *prefer* playing G natural,' and go on doing it. I consider both parties in this matter blameless and no apologies need be offered for either, but I do blame the wretched governesses, who, themselves incapable of distinguishing wrong from right notes, would tell me to mind my own business and get on with my sum.

Now in extreme cases my mother knew very well when wrong notes were being played, but having survived many years of English drawing-room music she bore it with relative equanimity, and the rest of my world were in the same position as our governesses. Realizing which I became more and more certain that I was in a different class, musically, to my surroundings, and that knowledge did its slow work in my heart, as subsequent events were to prove.

I have said that the whole course of my life was determined, little as she realized it, by one of these governesses. When I was twelve a new victim arrived who had studied music at the Leipzig Conservatorium, then in the heyday of its reputation in England; for the first time I heard classical music and a new world opened up before me. Shortly after, a friend having given me Beethoven's Sonatas, I began studying the easier of these and walked into the new world on my own feet. Thus was my true bent suddenly revealed to me, and I then and there conceived the plan, carried out seven years later, of studying at Leipzig and giving up my life to music. This intention was announced to everyone and of course no one took it seriously, but that troubled me not at all. It seemed to me a dream that I knew would come true in the fullness of time, but I was in no hurry as to the when. Alas, all my life I have paid for those seven wasted years! I want to make it clear, that this was no mere passing idea such as children entertain and let go again; when I came out I was not exactly faithless but slack about it during a few months, for reasons I will explain by and by, but the decision was taken and cast in iron once and for all.

My father's Aldershot command came to an end in 1872. At that time, owing to a block in the promotion list, several old Indian officers

45

of his seniority were given the option of retiring on a handsome pension with the rank of General; and as his family was large, and his next command probably in India, he closed with the offer and bought Frimhurst.

It was a sagacious choice of an abiding-place for an old soldier, well within reach of contemporaries still in the army – and what I think he appreciated still more, old subalterns of his, now some way up the ladder, who simply adored him. On the stretch of heath-land outside our very gates, where most sham fights began, passed, or ended, his own branch of the service could be watched, dashing up and down the heather hills – the guns at any angle you please – over banks, ditches and gravel pits; and not being one of those who think everything is going to the dogs since their own time, nothing interested him more than mechanical and other improvements.

The house was enlarged, the cost exceeding the estimate by a good deal – we were never allowed to know exactly how much – and a gravel lawn-tennis court was added, all too near a certain unpleasant overflow, so that when the wind was in a certain quarter there was no forgetting his celebrated theory about 'a good open stink'.

Being better off now we kept more horses; fences were set up in 'the little field', and over these we were allowed, nay, urged by my father, to lark to our heart's content. Mary was not particularly keen on this amusement, but I remember after she had twice fallen off his insisting on a third attempt, and amid shouted injunctions to 'sit back and give him his head', she sailed over in safety and was much praised, as indeed she deserved. A more ideal parent as regards encouraging his children to take risks cannot be imagined, and throughout the unending series of carriage accidents for which we gradually became notorious, his first, I had almost written his only, question was, 'Is the horse damaged?'

Meanwhile the governess question had become a complicated one, owing to the fact that the younger members of the family were growing up and had to be educated too. A supplementary instructress was tried but it was not a success, for No. 1 considered it beneath her dignity to associate with nursery governesses, and No. 2 spent more time in weeping and retailing her grievances to her pupils than in teaching them the three Rs. In despair my parents began to wonder whether Mary and I had not better be sent to school.

The idea was not readily entertained, for at that time it was not considered the thing to let your girls associate with Heaven knows whom under a strange roof. As usual, when in difficulties, my mother consulted her neighbour Mrs Longman, whose husband, head of the great publishing firm, built and lived at Farnborough Hill, and whose family consisted, like ours, of six girls and two boys. This friend warmly recommended a school at Putney, kept by an old governess of theirs, which put quite a different complexion on the matter. Also, when approached by my mother, Miss D. thought well to intimate casually that among her pupils were the daughter of a Baronet and the daughters of two Honourables. Thus it came to pass – as we were told because we were so unmanageable, but really because there was nothing else to be done – that we were packed off to school.

On the day of our departure Bob, who was then about five, remembers us sitting side by side on a sofa in the bow window, very erect and serious, in long black coats with broad braid, and mauve scarfs tightly tied in a huge bow under our chins, the long ends floating. It was all very solemn, and he felt sorry for us without knowing why.

My school life is a sort of block-memory; I see few details, but of course 'passions' raged all the time. There were walks in long procession of two and two; once we were led, my heart beating furiously, past the house where I knew Jenny Lind lived. From allusions to her triumphs in old volumes of *Punch*, and my mother's descriptions of her supreme art, she had long been one of my heroines, and if anyone had told me that one day I should become fairly intimate with this striking and terrifying personality I should have gone off my head on the spot. The more usual thing was vague rambles across Putney and Roehampton Commons, and I remember the pang of joy and longing that always shot through me at one particular spot, then unspoiled by villas. It was a plateau-edge where we always turned off to the left homeward – a dip in the road, the yellow of the gravel where it cut through the hill, and a blue distant expanse of happy lands where people walked at their own pace and went home when they felt inclined. Masters ('extras') came from London to teach us music, drawing, astronomy and chemistry. I remember the chemistry classes best, because of the breathless excitement as to whether the experiments would come off; sometimes they did and sometimes they didn't, but there never was any doubt as to why schoolboys call this branch of science 'stinks'.

The music master was a black-bearded, spectacled little German Jew, Herr A. S., and all the busts of Pericles and other great men in my *Smaller History of Greece* were furnished with spectacles, had their

47

beards inked, and thus became Herr A. S. By this time I undertook the music in our afternoon home services on Sundays as a matter of course, composed, and made the girls learn, chants and hymns, which bore the names of adored units in the choir – my old system – and generally imposed myself musically. Hence poor Herr A. S. thought he saw a unique opportunity for spreading his reputation as composer, and *L'Alouette*, *Le Rêve* and all the rest of them, French names being in favour because of the success of *La Prière d'une Vierge*, were hopefully unpacked. I rather fancy it was part of his contract that parents should have a certain number of these works booked to them at face value. But I wouldn't even look at them – a fact he recalled to me with infinite good humour in after years, when, an old asthmatic wreck in retirement, he used to struggle up from the country to hear my work performed. And indeed is it likely that one already deep in Schumann, Schubert and Beethoven would add Herr A. S. to the list?

The whole school, except those whose parents struck at the expense, were taken up to Mr Kuhe's yearly Grand Benefit Concert; there for the only time in my life I heard Patti, and, strange incomprensible fact, what struck me most was her coquettish way of trotting onto the platform, followed by a display of ecstatic surprise at the plaudits that lifted the roof – an experience as common to her as the sun rising. The other day, genuinely overwhelmed by her incomparable rendering of *Voi che sapete* on the gramophone, it was bitter to reflect I had once heard the real woman and cannot recall the ghost of a thrill. Was it my childish contempt for florid music – she sang something by Donizetti, I think – combined with insane dislike of affectation even as innocent and ritualistic as hers, or does some spiteful god amuse himself by turning us deaf and stupid for a while? . . . We were also taken to the Royal Academy Exhibition, and again a blank in my memory occurs, to account for which no occult agency need be sought. To the National Gallery we were *not* taken, which sufficiently characterizes girls' schools of that period.

It was in the summer of 1875 – a summer that in any case was to rob her of her favourite daughter – that the great sorrow of my mother's life happened. Alice had been engaged for some time to a young Scotsman, Harry Davidson, and the couple were waiting for an impending improvement in his prospects, when Mary, who had been out but a short time, also became engaged – not to Maunsell B. but to Charlie Hunter, brother of a schoolfriend of hers. There was to be a joint wedding in July, and the invitations, of which I had mercifully kept a list, had been sent out, when it became evident that Johnny's slow martyrdom endured by him with marvellous fortitude and sweetness, was coming to an end. For a fortnight he had suffered from terrible headaches, as usual making no complaint, and one night at dessert, taking up a biscuit, he said, 'How queer, I can't read the letters on this biscuit.' He then sank back, as we thought fainting, but a tumour on the brain had burst, and he became unconscious by slow degrees, his last conscious words being, 'Don't let this illness of mine stop the girls' weddings.'

We used to take it in turn to watch nightly beside his bed, and when relieved spent the rest of the night on a sofa in the hall close by, so as to be ready if needed. One night, after my watch was over, I stumbled and fell, and there I was found when the housemaid came in the morning to open the shutters, asleep on the floor . . . as I had fallen. Such is the sleep hunger of youth. There had just been time to cancel the invitations, but as it seemed that he might linger for some time yet, the marriages took place one morning at Frimley Church, none of the family but myself being present. The bridegrooms went back to London from the church door, and a few days afterwards Johnny died. That afternoon the children had been sent to a kind neighbour, and Nelly says that on their return mother met them at the front door to tell them he was dead, tears streaming down her face yet trying to smile – a picture of grief that has remained with them ever since.

This was my first acquaintance with death, and the sight of that strange unfamiliar face impressed me terribly and painfully. The day after the funeral the married couples departed, and I became the eldest at home.

All this time, whether at home or at school, the main determination of my life, though sometimes obscured, had never wavered; it was like a *basso ostinato*, which, as subsequent counterpoint studies showed me, will sometimes be shifted to a less obvious position in the midst of other voices and seem to the eye of ignorance to have vanished. My father would never let me go abroad willingly, if only for reasons of economy, and I quite grasped that making an allowance to a married daughter, whose future is no longer your business, is quite another thing to financing a maiden's sterile whims. In his mind's eye he would see me, no doubt, returned on his hands a failure and knocking too late at doors in the marriage market; meanwhile his income was none too large to keep the home going.

The arrival of that governess who played classical music to me when I was twelve was the first milestone on my road; suddenly, when I was least looking for anything dramatic, the second milestone loomed into vision – to my great excitement we learned that the composer of 'Jerusalem the Golden', a Mr Ewing, in the Army Service Corps, was stationed at Aldershot! Even my father, who hadn't an ounce of music in his composition, may have been moved by the news, for that hymn tune, in which there is a sort of groping ecstasy confined in *Ancient and Modern* fetters, was considered almost as integral a part of the Church Service as one of the Collects. For my part I took it on trust that at last I was to meet, not a poor musical hack like Herr A. S., but a real musician. And I was right, besides which Mr Ewing turned out to be one of the most delightful, original and whimsical personalities in the world.

Mrs Ewing and my mother were attracted to each other at once and eventually became great friends. Meanwhile she took the whole adoring family to her heart, bade us call her 'Aunt Judy' and wrote us all the most delightful letters. Her lustre was slightly dimmed by a tendency to enjoy bad health; I think she really was not strong, but as her father once exclaimed, according to his son-in-law, 'Dear Juliana is always *better, thank you*, but never *quite well.*' I found a packet of charming letters of hers to mother, written in the most beautiful hand imaginable, which are half spoiled by constant references to her poor back, her wretched head, the air-cushions people lent her, the number of hours spent on the sofa after each journey, and so on.

She was devoted to the other sex, more especially to officers in the Royal Engineers, then supposed to have the monopoly of brains in the British Army, and had discreet, semi-intellectual and wholly blameless flirtations with two or three of these at a time. I did not quite approve of this – possibly from jealousy, for needless to say she at once became the ruling 'passion'. As for her husband, he of course demanded to hear me play and be shown my compositions, after which he proclaimed to our little world that I was a born musician and must at once be educated.

My father was furious; he personally disliked my new friend, as he did all people not true to the English type, and foresaw that the Leipzig idea would now be endorsed warmly by one who knew. The last straw was when Mr Ewing proposed that he himself should begin by teaching me harmony; but on this point my mother, urged on by Aunt Judy, who had great respect for her husband's judgement, came over definitely into my camp. So it was settled that twice a week I was to drive myself over to Aldershot and submit my exercises to his inspection.

These expeditions were the delight of my life. The Ewings lived in one of the wooden huts of which in those days the whole camp, with the exception of the barracks, was constituted. They were stifling in summer and bitterly cold in winter, but full of charm. Some had gardens, and luckily the Ewings' was one of these, for both were gardeners and dog-lovers. I always brought her flowers from Frimhurst, picking with my own hand those she loved best, and generally laid siege to her heart.

I used to arrive at eleven and have harmony instruction till luncheon; besides this my teacher analysed my compositions, and I felt how capital his criticism was, and how pithily expressed. His real instrument was the organ, but with fingers ill-adapted to piano-playing, aided by a very harsh cracked voice, he banged and bellowed his way through the scores of *Lohengrin* and *The Flying Dutchman*, and otherwise introduced me to Wagner. And very definitely I remember that Beethoven appealed to me more than Wagner or anyone else; nevertheless I was bitten by the operatic form of Art – a taste that was to be squashed for the time in Leipzig later on – and decided that my 'greatest desire' was to have an opera of mine played in Germany before I was forty – an ambition fated to be realized. I still have, and really educated myself on, a copy of Berlioz orchestration Mr Ewing gave me; it is full of characteristic marginal notes and ejaculations by the giver, and is a book I often look into from sheer delight in its style.

After luncheon Mrs Ewing would good-naturedly correct and comment on the English of little articles I wrote for some obscure parish magazine, declaring she could turn me into a writer by and by; but I much preferred playing with the dogs and talking to their owners while they gardened.

Meanwhile my father's dislike of 'that fellow', as he called him, became fanatical. With all his geniality he could be extremely forbidding in manner to people he disapproved of, and had a way of looking at them without seeing them, his moustache raised in a slight snarl, that was worse than deliberate rudeness. The sight of even a civilian untidy about the hair, necktie and feet, irritated him, and . . . Mr Ewing was an officer! Fortunately he never saw him in uniform, for difficult as it is to achieve, my friend managed to look even more slovenly in uniform than in plain clothes.

But the worst was Papa's persistent misreading of his moral character. He must have known that bad digestions often cause red noses, but in this case it was ascribed to Scotch whisky; and, most infuriating of all, artists being in his opinion 'loose fish', he put his own construction on my mentor's sentiment for me, which, though very warm and keen, was devoid of the slightest trace of love-making. Nor were matters improved by his learning from innocent Aunt Judy herself that her husband was a successful mesmerist – a talent cultivated exclusively, I fancy, in the interest of his wife's ailments, but one can imagine how its possession endeared him to the father of an impressionable daughter! Knowing nothing whatever about what goes on in an artist's soul, he had no satisfactory clue to the ardour of our alliance, besides which, as I noticed once or twice in after life, unable to sway me himself, he resented my being under the influence of any other man. In short nothing but his reverence for Aunt Judy and her own unfailing tact and charm staved off disaster for the time being.

But it came at last! I have always had a bad habit of strewing my room with correspondence, and one of Papa's amiable weaknesses was a tendency, as my mother put it, to 'go poking about one's writing-table'. On one of these occasions he found a certain letter from Mr Ewing – a charming one, but hardly pleasant reading for parents and guardians! The result was such a terrific storm that the harmony lessons, which in any case were running to a close, the Ewings being under orders to leave Aldershot shortly, came to an abrupt end.

It was during the Ewing epoch that, invited to stay with a cousin of my father's, I paid a first, and certainly memorable visit to Ireland. On the way out I had been chaperoned across the water by a delightful, exceedingly Irish friend of ours, wife of the great soldier who afterwards became Field Marshal Sir Evelyn Wood, and was to rejoin her at the house of her brother-in-law, Lord Fitzgerald, at Bray. There I met a young barrister, Mr William Wilde, with whom I played tennis, and also discussed poetry, the arts, and more particularly philosophy, in remoter parts of the garden. I saw at once he was very clever, and after dinner found he was so musical as actually to put ends of his own to Chopin's *Études*, for which, later on, I might have chopped off his fingers with the lid of the piano; but I then thought it quite wonderful and was glad to find this young man, of whom that great lawyer my host thought highly, was going to England next day in our boat.

We boarded her after dinner, and Willie Wilde, as they all called him, pointed out to me a tall figure clad in dark blue, leaning over the bulwarks and gazing seaward, as 'my brother the poet'. It was the great Oscar, who was at once introduced, and on whom it afterwards appeared, according to his brother, I had the good fortune to make a favourable impression. But as he was as yet unknown outside Oxford the fact left me unthrilled.

The night was glorious, a full moon and no wind, and I was surprised that Mrs Wood at once retired to her cabin, for on the outward journey the sea had been like a mill-pond and I thought the Irish Channel a much maligned piece of water. Willie Wilde produced rugs and he and I sat on deck discussing . . . Auguste Comte! Presently I began to dislike the way the mast moved slowly to and fro across the face of the moon, and must have made some remark to that effect, for my companion flew off to fetch some brandy which he said would put everything right. The next moment I was staggering on his arm to the ladies' cabin, and before the stewardess could intervene, to quote our old friend the enamoured priest, 'the Fate did come and the Curse did fall'. Willie Wilde retired hurriedly, but I was past caring who had seen what.

The next thing I remember is the train at Holyhead and a long carriage with berths for men at one end and for women at the other, between the two a sort of loose box with one seat in it like a small guard's van. Mrs Wood, the most easygoing chaperon I ever met, and who herself had been very seasick all night, vanished into the ladies' territory, while Willie Wilde and I ensconced ourselves in the loose box, he sitting on a Huntley and Palmer's biscuit tin at my feet. And there, in spite of what had happened on the boat, he seized my hand and began an impassioned declaration, in the middle of which the biscuit tin collapsed. This mishap, which surely would have thrown an Englishman out of his stride, he passed over with some remark I have forgotten, though not its Irish gaiety, and resumed his tale of passion; and before the train steamed into Euston I was engaged to a man I was no more in love with than I was with the engine driver!

At Euston we were met by Major Wood and were hustled across to the Hotel, my lover being of course of the party. Trains were few and far between in those days, so we decided to tidy up and stay there for some hours before proceeding to Waterloo, it being understood that

the Woods had letters to look through and momentous matters concerning a new appointment to discuss. They breakfasted in their own
room and we two in the Coffee Room, and when I ran upstairs to ask
if I might go off with Willie Wilde to see some old houses (really to
buy a ring) impatient voices from behind the locked door answered in
duet, 'Yes, yes, go by all means.' Finally I arrived at Frimhurst with a
gold band ending in two clasped hands on whichever was the correct
finger, and for once wearing gloves, my fiancé having requested that
the affair be kept secret for the present.

On reflection I found this did not meet my views; averse to secrecy
at all times, where was the fun of pulling off an engagement before
you are out if no one is to be any the wiser? And then . . . the love
letters began to arrive! Now although to propose to a girl five hours
after you have seen her being seasick is a proof, as I said to myself, of
true love, and though to go on proposing after your seat has given
way beneath you argues not only passion but sense of humour, unde-
featedness and other admirable qualities, the fact remains that I had
accepted this young man from flattered vanity, light-heartedness,
adventurousness, anything you please except love. Consequently the
letters, which I have since re-read, and which are really very like the
genuine thing, rapidly put me off; nor did I like his gentle but continued insistence on the article of silence. In short before three weeks
were over, probably to his secret relief, I had broken off the engagement, adding that I would like to keep the ring as a souvenir! And
keep it I did, until a year or two afterwards, when I lost it while separating two dogs who were fighting in deep snow in the heather. Thus
ended my first and last engagement, the hero of which I never saw
again – a pity, for they say he became even a better talker than his
brother.

Soon after this adventure, the Ewings having meanwhile left Aldershot, I came out, but cannot remember what my then frame of mind
was. I had never dreamed of putting through my musical plans till I
should be really grown up – that would have been too unreasonable
– nor did there seem any need for special hurry. So I suppose I thought
it well to take a look at the world of real balls and other festivities for
which I was now qualified.

On the whole it did not come up to expectations. I loved, and still
love, that soundest form of entertainment, dining out; not only from
greediness and pleasant curiosity as to what you are about to receive,
but because of the mingling of old and young, the talk and laughter,

and the gradual warming up of the atmosphere under the influence of good cheer. After dinner I was always asked to sing at once, and as I took care that no one else should get at the piano the musical torture was eliminated.

But the balls! . . . O, the long drives in a tight white satin bodice, and the entreaties to sit still and not crumple your skirt! But the dancing itself was the greatest trial. I loved dancing with a delirious 'I wish I could die' passion, especially when the music appealed to me, but alas! only one in ten partners had any notion of time, and what made it worse, the nine were always behind, never before the beat. Then it was that I would hear a pretentious, fraudulent, utterly idiotic phrase which I hope is no longer current in ballrooms: 'I generally dance half-time' (!) Sometimes I would firmly seize smaller, lighter partners by the scruff of the neck, so to speak, and whirl them along in the way they should go, but I saw they were not enjoying themselves, and oddly enough I wanted these wretches to like dancing with me.

Nor were these the only drawbacks; if I went to a ball it was to dance, and for no other reason, but I soon found out this is a very incomplete theory of balls. Being a self-sufficing person, who didn't want to cling or be clung to except in the way of dancing, what was I doing in this antechamber of matrimony, the ballroom? It was the old trouble cropping up again of knowing that between my world and me a gulf was fixed, that I was a wolf in sheep's clothing, in fact a fraud. Talent for flirtation I had none – that wants another temperament, not passionate but either light or sensual – and my attempts were amateurish and half-hearted, like the childish love-affairs with schoolboys. Then too there was the humiliating, infuriating idea that if I was 'nice' to a man he would think I wanted to marry him! Notwithstanding these disabilities, being young and not ugly I did pull off one or two little flirtations, or rather had an admirer here and there whom I fear I encouraged with a view to starting a 'proposal list'. But nothing much resulted.

In spite of these social perturbations, for I won't quite call them pleasures, music ran her course more or less fitfully. One day I went with the Ewings to a Wagner concert, and was introduced to her brother, Alfred Scott-Gatty, the successful song-writer, who, knowing his brother-in-law's soaring spirit, entreated me above all things *not to aim high*; 'it's not the slightest use,' he added, and I rather think he was speaking seriously. Wagner, who was almost unknown in England, had rashly contracted for a series of concerts conducted by himself, which I afterwards heard were a failure financially. My party were all hard up, and we sat so far away from the platform that all I saw was an undersized man with a huge head, apparently in a towering rage from start to finish of the concert; I thought he could hardly refrain from whacking heads right and left instead of merely the desk. No doubt the performance was insufficiently rehearsed and execrable, anyhow I was not as much carried away as I expected.

Occasionally, though very rarely, I went to a concert in London, being met at Waterloo and convoyed to St James's Hall by some approved friend, or perhaps by Aunt Susan's maid, and on one occasion was actually presented to Frau Schumann and her daughters. This great event was engineered by a friend of mine, Mrs George Schwabe, of whom more will be related presently, whose mother-in-law – another personality who will reappear in these pages – was an old friend of Frau Schumann's. The extraordinary thing is that in the wealth of impressions I was to gain in after life of that wonderful woman, all recollections of our first meeting have faded, but I gather from a remark in one of Mr Ewing's letters that she gave my musical aspirations her blessing. She could do no less!

Soon after I struck what may rank as a half-milestone in my journey; for the first time I heard Brahms. The occasion was a Saturday Popular Concert at which the *Liebeslieder Walzer* were sung by four persons, three of whom (the Germans) knew the composer personally and afterwards became factors in my life. They were Fräuleins Friedländer and Redeker, Mr Shakespere and George Henschel. That day I saw the whole Brahms; other bigger, and, to use the language of pedants, more important works of his were to kindle fresh fires later on, but his genius possessed me then and there in a flash. I went home with a definite resolution in my heart . . .

That night there was a discussion at dinner as to which Drawing Room I had better be presented at. Suddenly I announced it was useless to present me at all, since I intended to go to Leipzig, even if I had to run away from home, and starve when I got there . . .

I almost despair of anyone believing today, so quickly has the world moved since then, what such a step stood for in my father's mind. We knew no artists, and to him the word simply meant people who are out to break the Ten Commandments. It is no exaggeration to say that the life I proposed to lead seemed to him equivalent to going on the streets; hence the strange phrase he hurled at me, harking back in his fury to the language of Webster's or Congreve's outraged fathers: 'I would sooner see you under the sod.'

After a period of vain efforts to overcome his resistance, which became so terrific that it was no longer possible to broach the subject at all, I quite deliberately adopted the methods used years afterwards in political warfare by other women, who, having plumbed the depths of masculine prejudice, came to see this was the only road to victory. I not only unfurled the red flag, but determined to make life at home so intolerable that they would have to let me go for their own sakes. (I say 'they', but here again I felt that, whatever my mother might say in public, she was secretly with me.) In those days no decent girls travelled alone, third class and omnibuses were things unheard of in our world, and I had no money; but I would slip away across the fields to Farnborough Station, travel third to London, and proceed by omnibus to any concert I fancied. The money difficulty was met by borrowing five shillings from tradesmen we dealt with on the Green, or the postman, 'to be put down to the General'. In order to be close to Joachim and his companions I would stand for hours in the queue at St James's Hall, and ah! the revelation of hearing Schubert's A minor Quartet! . . . All my life his music has been perhaps nearer my heart than any other – that crystal stream welling and welling for ever . . .

From my place I used to watch George Eliot and her husband sitting together in the stalls like two elderly love-birds, and was irritated by Lewes's habit of beating time on her arm with his pince-nez. There is a well-known syncopated passage in Beethoven's Quartet Op. 132, and I noted with scornful amusement how the eyeglass, after a moment of hesitation, would begin marking the wrong beat, again hover uncertainly, and presently resume the right one with triumphant emphasis as if nothing had happened. All this George Eliot took as calmly as if she were the Sphinx, and Lewes an Arab brushing flies off her massive flanks.

The greatest excitement was one day when with beating heart I forced my way past Mr Chappell's Cerberus into the Artists' Room – a place more sacredly awful to me than the Holy of Holies can ever have been to young Levite – and made the acquaintance of Fräuleins Friedländer and Redeker, expressed to them my admiration of their singing, and fell madly in love with Redeker, whose rendering of that divine love-song, *Wie bist du meine Königin*, had all but torn the heart out of my body. They were good-naturedly touched by such enthusiasm and begged me to come and see them some morning, which I did, climbing up stairs upon stairs to the room they shared. It was at 11 a.m., they were in *déshabillé*, the beds unmade, and they were sipping port out of an egg-cup. This unaccustomed sight gave me rather a shock, and for a moment I thought of my father, but supposed it was just part of the artist life; and indeed a few months later such a spectacle would have made no more impression on me than did Mr Lewes's eyeglass on George Eliot.

My financial arrangements with the tradesmen came out of course, as they were meant to, and to my father's ragings I stubbornly replied, 'You won't let me go to Leipzig so of course I have to go to London to hear music.' From this moment he became convinced that, freed from control, I should squander money right and left, and one of the stock phrases was, 'We shall have to sell your mother's diamonds' – a calamity that ranked in our minds with expedients such as debasing the coinage. But in this phrase I thought I saw a weakening of will; he was actually considering possible consequences of surrender! . . .

I had a few friends who backed me up more or less openly and were consequently looked on with disfavour at home. To this rule Barbara Hamley, now Lady Ernle, proved an exception, contriving in a miraculous manner to be my friend and yet keep on excellent terms with the parents, who delighted in her. She effected this miracle by a blend of tact, reasonableness, and sense of humour that must have oiled many locks in her course through life; moreover, but for her sympathy with the Frimhurst rebel, she was a perfectly normal, model young lady, who kept house with great success for her adored and adoring uncle Sir Edward Hamley, then Commandant of the Staff College (one of whose sympathetic traits was a great admiration for my mother). Thus she was in a favourable situation for operations, and her championship of me included a useful element – full comprehension of my father's point of view.

Not so that of Mrs George Schwabe, daughter of Lord Justice James, a clever, hard-riding, whist-playing, particularly cherished friend of mine, who as radical, and one justly suspected of unorthodox views on religion, naturally considered this opposition to my German plans ridiculous and out of date. So too did Mrs Napier, wife of her first cousin General William Napier (the historian's son), who was then in command – or rather Mrs Napier was in command – at Sandhurst. This delightful champion of mine had rebel blood in her own veins, her father, fierce eagle-eyed Sir Charles Napier, whom his daughter was as like as two peas, having eloped with her mother, a Greek. It goes without saying that these two friends of mine were constant subjects of strife, and if my mother, jealous by nature, was specially so in these cases, who can wonder? It was all very well for Mrs Napier to say right and left, 'Of course dear little Ethel must go to Leipzig' – to say it even to my parents themselves, which she did, for she came of a fearless stock. *She* was not my mother, *she* had not to endure daily scenes with my father – scenes which became more frequent and furious as time went on. For towards the end I struck altogether, refused to go to church, refused to sing at our dinner-parties, refused to go out riding, refused to speak to anyone, and one day my father's boot all but penetrated a panel of my locked bedroom door! . . .

There was nothing for it but to capitulate! Fräulein Friedländer was able, by some miracle, to produce adequate testimony to the respectability of her aunt, Frau Professor Heimbach, who lived at Leipzig, and would certainly be willing to take me under her wing till her very own mother had a room at my disposal; the terms suggested confirmed Mary Schwabe's reports as to the cheapness of life in Germany; my father named the maximum of allowance he could make me; it was pronounced to be sufficient, with care; and finally, on 26 July 1877, under the charge of Harry Davidson who knew Germany well, I was packed off, on trial and in deep disgrace, but too madly happy to mind about that, to the haven of my seven years' longing.[1]

TWO

1877–9

MUSIC AT LEIPZIG
LISL VON HERZOGENBERG
BRAHMS

Music at Leipzig

Of the journey I remember little, except that soon after crossing the Dutch frontier the train made straight for a distant range of mountains, and suddenly there was an opening in the chain, through which we passed with the river that had cloven it. This spot, one of the great gates into Germany, and which is like the Guildford gap in the Hog's Back on a huge scale, I have often seen again and never without a thrill. And then came a still more poignant moment, the slowing down through hideous suburbs, and the indescribable emotion with which I read the word 'LEIPZIG' on the platform board. We had breakfast at the little old Hôtel de Rom hard by, and sallied forth to find Frau Professor Heimbach's dwelling, the romantic name of which was Place de Repos, *Treppe G.*

Reposeful it certainly was, being a large block of a building well off the road, jammed in between two other equally hideous blocks; romantic no one could call it, but what of that? Between me and it hung a veil woven of youth and hope – the strongest web of romance; and as we stepped under a dingy archway into a courtyard leading to 'Staircase G', I was passing through the Gate named Beautiful into the Chosen City. We clambered up three pairs of rotten wooden stairs, my brother-in-law curiously sniffing the odours that lingered about them – odours which I really believe are the monopoly of the two or three sluggish streams Leipzig is built on, one of which, the Pleisse at its worst, crawled by close to our house. A stout, shy, motherly person, clad in what I afterwards knew was her best gown, greeted us very pleasantly, and informed us (or rather Harry Davidson, for her Leipzig accent utterly defeated the little German I had) that I should not be cut off from England, in that she harboured another lodger – a *'charmanter Junge'*, Mr B., nephew of a well-known potentate connected with *Punch* and a protégé of Frau Schumann's.

We deposited my luggage, inspected my room and the short wooden bedstead with a mountainous feather bed on it, and started off to view the town, which Harry had known in the past.

Even then it was full of charm; the walls and fortifications were gone, all except the Pleissenburg which, placed in an angle, pulled the whole inner circle of the old town together, and though really unbeautiful in itself, managed to look imposing, with its squat tower and sturdy bulk. The 'ditch', as the Germans call it, had been filled in and planted as a promenade ages ago, and above it, on our side at least – for we were just without the Altstadt – the tall, narrow, tile-roofed houses of Dürer's pictures towered in a curve above the rise they were built on, and beautifully caught the evening light. Close to us, on the fringe of the old town, was the Thomas Kirche, where Bach played the organ, and the Thomas Schule, of which he was Cantor; this is the only dwelling place of the Great Dead that ever moved me, hideous though it was. They have pulled down the Pleissenburg and the picturesque old mill beyond it, but I trust the Rathhaus is still standing. Not very superb late Renaissance, it is nevertheless a fascinating building, with its copper-clad pinnacles greened by verdigris, and the warm, sombre colour of the brick. In my time there were periodical agitations to clear it away, as also to widen three or four narrow streets close by, in which were still some fine old houses, but the Philistines were always over-borne.

We lunched at the best restaurant in the town, Harry remarking it would reassure my father to hear what we had eaten for about ten-pence each, and then walked out into the Rosenthal, a sort of park and wood combined – quite pretty in a stiff style, but reputed to smell of in the spring to a degree that disconcerted even the most ardent lovers. Here I made my first amazed acquaintance with the well-known sign-boards 'Verboten' on which the German Empire is run, and which met us at every turn; I had thought grass was meant to walk on, but evidently this was a mistake.

A peculiarity of Leipzig was that the space between the vanished walls and the promenade was carved up into minuscule gardens about size of a largish chapel in Westminster Abbey, which were let to any-one who chose to apply. We had a rendezvous at 4 p.m. to drink afternoon coffee with Frau Professor in her garden, the approximate spot being described beforehand, and a promise given that Mr B., whom we had not yet seen, would be on the look-out for us. A very untidy youth of the artistic type, with a shock of fair hair hanging into his eyes, whose appearance would have disgusted my father, duly met us and conducted us to our garden, where Frau Professor and her niece Fräulein Friedländer had everything in readiness. In each of the gardens were a tiny summer-house and three or four trees; ours boasted no flowers, but, to our amazement, embedded crazily in the lawn were five croquet hoops; and here after coffee did we start the most fantastic game of croquet I ever played, Fräulein Friedländer and Harry against B. and me. If you could not get through your hoop because of a tree, you simply shifted the hoop, manipulating the angle a little to your advantage. B. was a player of the violent type whose great object was to cannon off the trees, as if by accident, right into the summer-house where Frau Professor and her cat were ensconced with their knitting. I say their knitting, because we were told if the needles stopped one moment the cat became restless and wandered off into neighbouring gardens. When the balls began flying about, Frau Professor calmly piled up the crockery for safety behind the summer-house, and resumed her place, well tucking up her feet on the bars of another chair; and I said to myself, an old lady with such sound nerves must surely be easy to live with.

After that there was a gala supper in our flat; I remember we had partridges stuffed with sauerkraut, which were pressed on us as being *'fein und begannt'*. This phrase I meditated for a year or so, and eventually found out *begannt* was the Saxon for *pikant*. My brother-in-law, fortunately a smoker, was finally conducted downstairs by B., aided by the light of his own matches, leaving me to my first night under a German roof. Next day I saw him off from the station, and began life in a state of wild enthusiasm that transformed the little round rolls into manna, the thin coffee dear to Leipzigers into nectar, and even invested the sanitary arrangements with a sort of local-colour appropriateness. The only water the Town Council supplied in Place de Repos was a thin trickle from a tap in the kitchen, but as I was equal to cold tubs in those days this was of no consequence.

My diagnosis of my landlady's character proved correct; an easier, more philosophic temperament would be hard to find, and with B. to interpret, the accent difficulty was soon got over. But it was not till later days that one wrong impression was put right. When Fräulein Friedländer had spoken of her aunt, widow of Professor Heimbach, we imagined the title implied high university honours, as in cases like Darwin and Huxley; face to face with the lady, one could only suppose her eminent husband had risen from the ranks and married in earliest youth. Later I discovered that he was wholly unknown to fame, and indeed I was never able to learn which university had conferred his title on the late Herr Professor Heimbach.

Young B. turned out to be a harum-scarum, harmless sort of youth, whose parents had evidently dispensed with his presence during the summer holidays, for, as I now learned, the long vacation was in full swing. In my zeal to leave England I had omitted to make inquiries as to when the Conservatorium term began, and the place would be shut for a month yet; so as Fräulein Friedländer, her mother and Fräulein Redeker of the *Liebeslieder Walzer* – also a Leipzig young lady – were to spend a fortnight in the Thüringer Forest, it was suggested I should accompany them. Fräulein Redeker, as I said before, was one of my 'passions', and when informed that George Henschel was to join the party later, I had some notion of the unutterable happiness that was in store for me.

But only a vague notion, for what that first sojourn with real musicians in a little wooden house on the verge of the forest turned out to be, what words can tell? Let it be remembered that never in my life had I met anyone capable of judging whether or not I was the born musician Mr Ewing proclaimed me, and after all he himself was but a gifted amateur. Here I found my compositions listened to by a man who himself was a composer, who as regards musical equipment was on a level with Brahms or anyone else in the great music world, and on his and other faces I read the desired verdict. But the chief bliss was less personal than that. Henschel is one of the superbly cultivated musical temperaments you find only in Germany and Austria; I have listened to many at work, but have never heard anything to compare with his singing – to his own accompaniment of course – of Brahms, Schubert, Beethoven – in fact any and every composer. He would sit down at the rickety old piano in our lodgings, and all the things in musical literature I had ever wanted to hear, not to speak of others I had never even heard of (including his own 'first fine careless rapture', *Trompeter Lieder*), were poured out before me. As some people rejoice in having seen Venice for the first time by moonlight, so I am thankful the *Gruppe aus dem Tartarus* was first made known to me by Henschel, and in my eyes this dear old friend, whom in after years even my father came to be fond of, was like a god.

We used to take long walks, making for one of the beer-houses dotted about the forest, which superior people laugh at, but which I delight in, on our way singing *Volkslieder* in parts, the nearest thing to the improvisations of Slav gypsy orchestras I ever took part in. One day we got lost; it was stiflingly hot, the woods smelt like a great bath of pine-extract, and we felt we should die if we did not soon find our beer-house. Suddenly we came on it round a corner, and to my last hour I shall remember the first glass of beer drunk that day! Henschel had just been somewhere with Brahms; and after telling us the great man's new symphony was to be produced at the Gewandhaus Concerts, conducted by the composer, in the coming season, I remember his presently pointing to me and saying laughingly to the others, 'Look at that face!' . . .

While in Thuringia I found out, to my horror, from two lodgers of Frau Friedländer's who were of the party, that in that house the piano was going all day, and that composing would have to be done, if at all, at night. I was in despair, but eventually a peaceful reshuffling of *pensionnaire* livestock took place between the sisters-in-law, and when we returned to Leipzig I settled down with Frau Professor for good and all. Somehow or other the fact that the only other lodger was a young man must have escaped the lynx eyes at Frimhurst, for I cannot remember any fuss being made about it.

There was yet a week or so of idleness before the beginning of the term. I had been given a letter of introduction to one Leipzig bigwig, head of the great publishing firm Brockhaus, but had no idea of mortgaging my freedom yet awhile, so merely explored the town, inquired into prices, found out what music it was possible to hear in the slack season, and generally looked about me. My first discovery was that the place was full of French names like Place de Repos – relics of the Napoleonic era which a monarch with more historical sense and less *Kultur* than his grandson had not thought it necessary to germanize. If our old block still exists, which is not likely, no doubt it is now called 'Ruheplatz'. There were many other links with the French past, and I came to know an old lady, last survivor of one of the great burgher families, who stood with me in the window whence she had watched Napoleon ride out of the gates to the battle of Leipzig; she told me he looked 'cross and insignificant'!

One day I saw that Hoffmann's Serenade in D, a piece of music I particularly wanted to hear, was to be played next evening at an open-air concert in the Rosenthal Restaurant, and announced that I meant to be present. Frau Professor said this was impossible, that no young girl could go to a place like that by herself and she unfortunately could not take me as the next day was '*Grosse Wäsche*'. This was the great washing festival held once a month in households such as ours, and which, judging by an unsavoury mountain of dirty linen in a certain cupboard, was overdue. The idea of going with B. was ruled out of the question, so I hit upon a plan which this capital old lady somewhat reluctantly fell in with. I hired grey corkscrew curls and a large pair of horn spectacles, borrowed her thickest veil and her gown, which, after I had swathed myself in newspapers tightly tied on with string, and added other contrivances, was a perfect fit. Having finally painted in appropriate wrinkles, I sallied forth to the Rosenthal, sat down with a piece of knitting (for show only) at a small table, and asked for a beer and a '*Schinken Brödchen*' – that is, buttered roll with ham in the middle.

It was a warm September night and the garden was full of burgher families, seated like me at little tables with beer and ham, and listening religiously to the really excellent music – in short it was the Germany of my dreams. The only illumination was Chinese lanterns, but even by daylight, I , my stoop and my hobble would probably have passed muster. I looked about and saw B. sitting with two stout German youths, and presently I went up and asked him some question in a quavering old voice, explaining that I knew no German. The Serenade, a charming piece of music by the by, and everything else I heard that night, enchanted me, and by 11 p.m. I was unlocking our house door, and picking my way by the light of the usual match, among horrible islands of assorted *Wäsche*, to my room. Frau Professor was so well broken to English eccentricity, and so convinced that sons and daughters of our race can look after themselves, that she never even sat up for me – a fact which raised her immensely in my estimation.

Next day at lunch I suddenly repeated my question of the night before in the same quavering voice, and for a moment B. looked as if he were going mad, but he promised to keep the secret. When I became a Conservatorist I found I was already famous, this young man, who was always cadging for invitations, having supped out on that story ever since. But it never got to Frimhurst, which was the main point.

A few days before she left for London, Fräulein Friedländer took me to pay an eagerly awaited visit, for this was to be my introduction to the Leipzig music world. Again a climb up three pairs of rotten stairs, in one of the hideous buildings which flanked Place de Repos; and an hour later, sitting at tea – real tea – with my new friends, Herr Concert-Meister Röntgen, leader of the Gewandhaus Orchestra, and his family, I had found an answer to the question, 'What went ye out for to seek?' In those walls was the concentrated essence of old German musical life, and without a moment's hesitation the whole dear family took me to their bosom.

It all began with a little sonata I had written, a certain B flat in which proved to be the key to their hearts. He was Dutch by extraction, distant cousin of the X-ray discoverer – as great a gentleman and as true a musician as I have known. She was of the old Leipzig musical stock Klengel, a family that could raise a piano quintet among themselves, and together with their Röntgen cousins a small orchestra. Every violin sonata, every piano trio or quartet printed, would Frau Röntgen or her daughter tackle – the mother's performance unplaned perhaps, but of a fire and musicality that carried all before it. Their one servant was seldom a cooking genius and always needed supervision, and between two movements of a trio Frau Röntgen would cry, 'Line, thou canst take the Scherzo,' and fly off to the kitchen, Line replacing her on the music stool till eagerly swept off it again. I remember one occasion when dear old Papa Röntgen, as we used privately to call him, who had a delicate digestion, complained of the Egg-Dish (I do not know how else to translate that basis of German existence, *die Eier-Speise*), and his wife said with simple contrition, 'Yes, I know, it is my fault, I ought to have waited to see her brown it . . . but thou knowest how I love that Andante!'

Their son Julius, composer, viola-player, pianist and all the rest of it, became a conductor and head of a Music Academy at Amsterdam, but Line took to marriage and babies and rather dropped her music. To see Julius and his mother playing pianoforte duets was a sight that would nearly overwhelm strangers, the motions of their spirits being reproduced by their bodies in dramatic and absolutely identical gesture. This is what made the spectacle so curious; you could not believe but that some unseen power was manipulating a duplicate set of invisible wires. At the tender parts of the music they would smile the same ecstatic smile to themselves, or in extreme cases at each other; in stately passages their backs would become rigid, their elbows move slightly away from their sides, and their necks stiffen; at passionate moments they would hurl themselves backwards and forwards on their chairs (never sideways, for they respected each other's field of action) and the fervour or ferocity of their countenances was something I have only once seen equalled – by Sada Yacco's rejected admirer on the Japanese stage. It was all so natural and sincere, that though one could not help smiling sometimes, it never interfered with your enjoyment, once you knew them well enough.

Johanna, the eldest daughter, a particular friend of mine, was a character, and one of the most musical of people, though she played no instrument – already a sign of originality in that family. She was one of the few critics I listened to with respect, and had a phenomenally fine ear. Once I made her sit down sharply on the keyboard and tell me what notes were sounding; she began with the lower and upper ones, a trifle of course to such as her, but with the rest she was equally successful, as far as her bulk would let me check them. She would say, beginning from the bass, 'd, d sharp – *no e* – f, f sharp – *then nothing till b flat'*, and so on, till the echoes died into silence. Let any musician, choosing a slim collaborator if possible, try this and see how difficult it is. Johanna had little or no voice, and what there was of it was poor in quality, but no sheep-dog ever kept his flock in better order than she the altos in choral singing.

She was religious and of a Lutheran turn of mind altogether – a slightly different thing to the Nonconformist conscience but of the same family – in spite of which, finding out that she did not know Maupassant, I rashly lent her a carefully selected volume of his stories. But next day she gave it back with a wonderful snort of which she had the secret, conveying remonstrance with me, pride in her own incorruptibility, and confidence in Germany's power to finally crush creatures like Maupassant. In moments of excitement she spoke almost as broad Saxon as Frau Professor herself, and I cannot refrain, for the benefit of those who know the dialect, from giving her immortal words on that occasion: '*Ne, ich danke dir, so 'nen Dreck les' ich nich! da geniegt mer schon mei Shakespeare und mei Geede!*' ('No, I thank thee, such filth will I not read. My Shakespeare and my Goethe suffice unto me.') Later I was to find out that this is the usual opinion in Germany of modern French literature, though seldom so forcibly expressed.

There was one more belonging to that household, a dear Swedish girl called Amanda Meyer, violinist and composer, who afterwards married Julius; and then for the first time I saw a charming blend of art and courtship very common in those days. Thus it must have been in Bach's time, thus with the old Röntgens, but I don't see how it can come off quite in the same way under modern conditions.

Thinking of the differences between then and now, what most strikes me is the fact that very often of an evening these families would combine to make music among themselves. Not only that, but on every other Sunday members of the quartet Papa Röntgen led, the cellist of which was his nephew Julius Klengel, would come to his flat and play all afternoon. Sometimes of course they rehearsed one of their repertory numbers, but these meetings were mainly for the pleasure of making music. Then there was leisure in the world to love and practise art for its own sake, and that, that, is the tender grace of those dead days! . . .

At the time I signed on as pupil of the Conservatorium, that institution was merely trading on its Mendelssohnian reputation, though of course we in England did not know that. The first person the neophyte would come into contact with was a horrible old doorkeeper, Castellan A., relic of the Golden Age, who refused to do even the smallest of his duties, such as deliver a letter, without a tip. Life was then on a scale that made a halfpenny a matter of long disputes between Frau Professor and her tradesmen, hence one penny was considered by our tyrant a satisfactory gratuity, but I never grudged a penny more bitterly. The real fountain of the universal slackness was of course the then director, an old friend (?) of Mendelssohn's, who had reached the age when, in some natures, thoughts of duty cease from troubling, scruples are at rest, and nothing but emoluments and pleasures – and his were not well spoken of – are taken seriously.

The three masters I had to do with were Reinecke, conductor of the Gewandhaus Concerts, for composition; Jadassohn, a well-known writer of canons, for counterpoint and theory generally; and Maas for piano. The lessons with Reinecke were rather a farce; he was one of those composers who turn out music by the yard without effort or inspiration, the only emotion connected with them being the ever-boiling fury of his third wife – a tall, thin woman with a mop of frizzy black hair – at the world's preferring Brahms's music to that of her adored husband. There were always crowds of children prowling about the corridor of his flat, and he was unable to conceal his polite indifference to our masterpieces, taking up his pen to resume his own before we had got to the door. Jadassohn's classes, held in the Conservatorium, were at least amusing, but equally farcical as instruction; their official length was forty minutes, and when he arrived, always a quarter of an hour late, it was to stand with his back to the stove for another ten minutes telling us exceedingly funny stories with the Jewish lisp I came to know so well in Germany. He diligently set us canons and other exercises, but there was seldom time even to look at the work we brought, much less correct our mistakes. Maas was a conscientious but dull teacher, and if Frau Schumann, when I came to know her later, used to say she didn't mind *hearing*, but couldn't bear to *look* at me playing, owing to the way I managed my hands, it was probably more my fault than his.

At first I was astonished at the lack of musical enthusiasm among my fellow students; gradually I came to realize these girls and boys had come there merely to qualify for teachers' certificates, and certainly whatever flame may have been in their bosoms to start with was bound to burn low in the atmosphere of superficiality and indifference our masters distilled. The glorious part was the rest of the music life, the concerts and the Opera. In modern Germany, and everywhere else except Austria, some special conductor, or the performance of some crack orchestra, is what attracts the public; people who will throng to hear Mr A.'s quartet play anything and everything would not cross the street to hear the same works performed by any other four, all of which is the result of boom of course. But at Leipzig in those days you went simply to hear the music.

The twenty Gewandhaus Concerts were conducted one and all by Reinecke, and though in other towns the custom of playing excerpts from Wagner had been started, such a thing was taboo in those sacred walls. Not even the overtures of his operas were tolerated, and I remember an all but successful attempt to bar the *Siegfried Idyll*. This quite orthodox concert-piece was so ill-received, several of the permanent subscribers staying away to mark their indignation, that the experiment was not repeated. You could not call Reinecke an inspiring conductor, but at all events he let the music do its own business; there were no carefully thought out effects, no rushings and dawdlings, no 'Reinecke touches'; in short there was nothing between you and the thing itself, which is just the quality that moves one to the depths listening to Patti on the gramophone.

What a curious place that old Gewandhaus was! Built, as its name 'Cloth Hall' indicates, for anything but music, and in defiance of all known laws of acoustics, its sonority was nevertheless perfect. Acoustics are queer things – so queer that, pondering them, imaginations run riot. An old gentleman from Magdeburg once told us how a door had been opened in the wall of some concert-room, to the complete destruction of its sonority. Horrified, the Town Council blocked up the door again *with the very same bricks – 'aber es nützte nichts – hin war die Akustik!'* (it was of no use – the sonority was gone). In spite of the delicate touch about the bricks it had walked off in disgust to return no more.

The Gewandhaus tickets were almost all subscribed for, and only by intrigue or charity could you get one. But the rehearsals the day before were supposed to be the real thing, especially as they only cost two shillings and to us Conservatorists nothing at all. Old ladies used to bring their knitting to the concerts in those days, an enchanting practice, as stimulating, I am sure, to aesthetic enjoyment as a ciga-rette; but it was put down as 'bourgeois' in the smart new Concert Hall built three or four years later . . . alas! alas! . . .

The chamber music, in the beautiful 'Little Saal' behind the other, was on the same lines, simple, sincere, and run by local men; and as the director of the Stadt Theater was that go-ahead old genius Angelo Neumann – a man who scented out talent as a pointer marks down game – and the orchestra practically the same as played in the Gewandhaus, the Opera was probably at its best then.

One chapter in an old-fashioned tale for children called *The Story without an End* begins: 'As for the child, he was lost in a dream of delight;' so it was with me during my first season in Leipzig. Great art joys may come to you in later life, but nothing can ever equal a first hearing of Beethoven's A major Symphony, or Schubert's C major Quintet, in the company of kindred spirits like the Röntgens and others then unknown to me – for my greatest musical friendship was yet to be. When the orchestra was tuning for my first Beethoven Sym-phony I remember trembling all over like a horse at covert side, and being far too agitated to note the themes.

In October Frau Schumann played at a chamber music concert, and B. walked Place de Repos with a halo, for his was to be the privilege of turning over for her, she and his father being very old friends. Before a concert, being the most nervous of women, she habitually wept in the artist's room, declaring to the last moment she could not possibly go on to the platform; surely then a greater sacrifice to old friendship could not be imagined than associating herself in public with this near-sighted, abnormally clumsy youth. Of course the worst happened; at one moment the music was on Frau Schumann's knees, thence violently shot by her on to the floor, but mercifully there was no break in the performance. A very few months later I got to know her intimately; she was subject to rather lovable attacks of fury, just like a child, and was very funny on the subject of B. I thought of her years afterwards when attending one of Madame Lind-Goldschmidt's singing classes, in the course of which two pupils left the room in tears. The old school had no patience with stupidity.

By this time I had separated the wheat of instruction from the chaff, and evolved a reasonable Plan of Hours. My only friends were still the Röntgens, a state of things that suited me exactly, for I knew well the condition of perfect liberty is being absolutely unknown. Nevertheless one day shortly before Christmas I at last put on a pair of tidy gloves, and getting myself up to look as English and conventional as possible, went to call upon Frau Dr Brockhaus, the only person I had a letter of introduction to. Doubts had been cast on the value of this introduction by my parents, inasmuch as it had been given me by Mary Schwabe's mother-in-law, the celebrated philanthropist Madame Schwabe, who held Queens and Empresses in the hollow of her hand, who swept everyone she met into the whirlpool of her activities, and who had hypnotized me into giving a concert at Camberley, shortly before my departure for Germany, in aid of some Institution of hers at Naples. And as I have said, the family of Schwabe was not in favour at Frimhurst just then. It turned out, however, that Frau Dr Brockhaus was one of the great ladies of Leipzig, and I was most cordially welcomed there, this delightful house eventually becoming my home during my first winter abroad. Oddly enough, on the occasion of a second visit I met a Neapolitan scoffer, who declared that the main object of Madame Schwabe's Institution at Naples was to persuade the boys who dive for pennies in the Bay of Naples to wear swimming drawers; but this, Frau Doctor explained, was not to be taken seriously.

Herr Dr Brockhaus, head of the firm, was a melancholy, stiffly Saxon, orthodox personality, whose one adventure must have been the selection of a fiery Hungarian Jewess years younger than himself for his life's partner. Torn between worldly and artistico-intellectual instincts, Frau Doctor had, I think, never quite decided what her true bent was, but at that time, two of her sons being of marriageable age, the line was Society mitigated with a sprinkling of the Serious. Her first kind action as far as I was concerned was inviting me to assist at a German Christmas under her roof. I confess that to this day I have not made up my mind as to the merits of that great institution. People began to look pale and careworn about it early in December, and spent half January recovering from exhaustion. Where there are crowds of very young children it may be worth all this fuss, but on the whole I prefer other manifestations of German thoroughness.

Immediately after the festival, Frau Doctor went off to their country place near Dresden – ostensibly on business but probably to recoup – and declared it was her intention to institute herself my mentor on her return, and introduce me into the World. The next great festival, seeing the Old Year out, was celebrated by me at the Röntgens'. We had a grand feast, with sweet champagne in very long, narrow glasses that held nothing, pâté de foie gras and hot punch – a red essence of some unknown alcoholic derivation, mixed to one's taste with boiling water. I noticed as on many subsequent occasions that Frau Röntgen, whose digestion was magnificent, picked all the truffles out of her helping of foie gras and put them on her husband's plate – a proceeding that dear man took quite as a matter of course. After supper we all sang part-songs in which I was tenor, when not bass, and it was remarked by Papa Röntgen that the more punch was drunk the more I pushed up the pitch – an interesting effect of alcohol which makes one think that to hand it round before certain *a cappella* pieces at concerts would be a good plan. On that day Julius and Amanda became officially engaged, and I had my first wondering view of untrammelled German demonstrativeness.

During these months, as most of my associates knew not one word of English, I had been making good progress with German. I have always found that understanding a foreign language as spoken is far more difficult than learning to speak it myself – a common experience, I dare say, of talkative and forthcoming people; and by way of practice, as well as from love of the theatre, had at once started a custom of going continually to the play, especially on Saturdays and Sundays, when there were performances in the Old Theatre, at reduced prices, of the classics, and also of certain well-known box-office trumps such as *La Dame aux camélias* and *Adrienne Lecouvreur*. I used to buy the text in a twopenny edition, get it up thoroughly beforehand, and install myself in the first row of stalls where I drank in every word. Shakespeare was always in the repertory, including plays seldom performed, such as *Coriolanus*, *Cymbeline*, etc.; and once I saw the three parts of *Henry VI* squeezed into two, and *Richard III* played on successive nights. Gradually I came to know all the possible and some of the impossible plays of Goethe, Lessing, Schiller, Racine and even one or two of Calderón, and these Sunday performances were always crammed.

There are one or two incidents in one's past to think of which fills one with self-loathing. Earlier I spoke of such an incident connected with a governess's false chignon; but then I was a child of ten and had been deceived, whereas when the story I am about to relate happened, I was a grown-up maiden whom no one had deceived; it was merely that ignorance had led me where ignorance does lead the young. When the small crash came, the proper course would have been to do nothing and just let the matter drop; but this policy comes hard to some people at all ages, and though in the Protestant upbringing of youth truthfulness is so strongly inculcated, we are never taught that *'toute vérité n'est pas bonne à dire'*! This is the only excuse I can offer for this regrettable occurrence, which is as follows.

In all these plays the actress who took the tragic sympathetic parts was one Marie Geistinger, whose career appealed to me to start with. She had been a very celebrated operetta singer, and if not actual creator of the role, was a specially brilliant 'Belle Hélène'; also, though of course I did not know this, her success in a sister career had been phenomenal, Archdukes, Grand Dukes and great nobles of all nationalities competing for her favours. She must have been a plucky and energetic woman, for when her voice began to go, and with it her celebrated slimness, she vanished for two or three years, to reappear on the stage as tragic actress. She was at that time over fifty, had a very fine stage presence, and was a tremendous favourite with the public. I have no idea how the really knowledgeable classed her, but to me, young, inexperienced and stage-struck, she was the ideal embodiment of all the heroines I loved and pitied, and who were more real to me than most living people, such as Maria Stuart, Adrienne, Phèdre, Hermione (in *The Winter's Tale*) and others. In short I was quite mad about the Geistinger, and after the performances used to stand for long half hours in snow or slush to see her muffled form shoot out of the stage door into her fly. At last I took to buying little bunches of violets or roses and bribing the stage door-keeper to put them in her dressing-room, with my name and a few words of impassioned admiration on a card.

This went on for quite a long time, and at last one happy day I was given a note from 'the gracious lady' saying she was much touched by my attentions, and would like to thank me in person, naming a day and hour at which I should find her at such and such an address. The last was an unnecessary detail, for countless times, with skates in my hand – she lived on the way to the Johannisthal – had I walked up her stairs and past her door to leave fictitious notes on imaginary persons on the floor above, but alas! without ever having had the luck to meet her. When the great day came, as I rang her bell it seemed my trembling knees must surely betray my agitation to the servant.

I don't think I have said that except in the very smartest set, the

family always occupied a room called 'the living room' in contradistinction to the real drawing-room, kept for grand occasions and familiarly
known as *'die gute Stube'* (the good room). This was always a cold and
forbidding apartment, the stove being seldom lit, with highly polished
floor and chairs arranged geometrically round the walls. Opposite the
door, on a smart bit of carpet, would be a table with plush cover, a
square of crochet work and a flower-pot in the centre, behind which,
jammed up against the wall, was the state sofa; and the hostess's first
words invariably were *'Bitte setzen Sie sich auf's Sofa!'* ('Please to seat
yourself upon the sofa.') I was ushered into the *gute Stube*, and without
any delay the object of my adoration appeared, followed by a shy
young man whom she introduced as her husband; and down we two
women sat on the sofa.

Then began the most banal of all banal conversations I have ever
taken part in. The Geistinger had needlework of some kind – a paralys-
ing fact to start with – and no doubt was at her wit's end, poor thing,
what to say to this adoring English girl, whose German at that time
was far from fluent. As for me, the shock of seeing Maria Stuart at
close quarters, in a tight-fitting dark blue satin bodice covered with
spangles, rouged up to the eyes, and wearing a fluffy light wig, produced a commotion in my breast as when the tide turns against a
strong wind. The husband hovered uneasily in the background, till
told somewhat sharply to sit down, which he did, still very far off; but
through it all I clung to the memory of the passionate emotions of the
theatre, and when asked to admire a little white dog of some odious,
fluffy, yapping breed, it was painful to have to say I only liked big
dogs.

This however was a blessing in disguise, for a quite animated discussion about the disadvantages of big dogs in towns ensued, whereas
up to that moment we really and truly had talked about the weather
like embarrassed people in books. When it was time to go I was graciously invited to come again, and any slight feeling of disappointment
was put down to knowing that in my overpowering shyness I had cut
rather a poor figure. True, on reflection, this greatest of great ladies
on the stage seemed, in real life, strangely unlike any lady I had ever
met, but to dwell on this thought was distasteful; indeed the great
difficulty to people of a certain temperament is to admit the evidence
of their senses, once the imagination has been thoroughly stirred. One
won't see, won't hear, won't believe . . .

After a decent interval I went to see her again, and yet again. As I now perceive, she belonged to the large class of actresses who literally have not an idea in their heads beyond the theatre, and O! how distinctly I remember noticing, in spite of my infatuation, that even in the plays she took part in, nothing interested her except her own role – a trait common to most *prime donne* I was to meet with later on. But I got over this somehow, and though a determination to believe in her hair and complexion had to be abandoned, I got over that too, and our friendship, begun in the autumn, went on well into the New Year, though rather haltingly. Strange to say Frau Doctor, who in some ways was very innocent, and whose conventionality was pleasantly inconsistent, did not remonstrate. But remonstrance was to come!

Among the grandees she introduced me to after Christmas were the Tauchnitz family, inventors of the Tauchnitz Edition, he – a German of course – being English Consul. Here also I was more than kindly received, and when it turned out that his friend Lor-r-rd Napier of Magdala was a connection and beloved old friend of my parents there was great enthusiasm, and Frau Doctor must have sighed a sigh of relief. I at once succumbed to the charms of his very pretty and intensely kind daughter-in-law, who like all Tauchnitzes had a fair knowledge of English manners and customs. She had heard, and been greatly amused about, my passion for the Geistinger, but was wholly unprepared for the news that we were on visiting terms. I remember her horrified face as she said, '*Aber Kind, ganz gewiss würde so eine Freundschaft Ihrer lieben Frau Mama sehr unlieb sein!*' ('But child, I am sure your dear Frau Mama would greatly disapprove of such a friendship.') And then, with infinite discretion, she proceeded to lift the veil, Grand Dukes and all. It appeared that the young man really was a husband of sorts, only in that world you married, divorced and married again as often as you pleased. In this particular case two or three husbands had been tried and found wanting, the poor lady's instinct being evidently to settle down, but not, not with an elderly admirer. In the end I quite allowed the acquaintance must be dropped, but unfortunately the only course which commended itself to me was to write and say so; which I did, adding that *if she reflected on her past life she would understand why*! I am thankful to say I got no reply to this odious letter, indeed I had begged there might be none – a cowardly touch added to the rest.

It is to be feared that in those days I admitted no line of conduct, no principles, except those in which I had been brought up, and unrepentant sinners filled me with pharisaical indignation. Thinking over this incident I have often wished one could be certain the Geistinger felt not the slightest pang about it, only amusement. It is more than likely . . . but I regret that letter even more than the chignon business.

Early in January 1878 came the event to which, ever since its advance announcement by Henschel in Friedrichsroda, everything else had seemed but a prelude, the arrival of Brahms in Leipzig to conduct his new Symphony in D major. Henschel turned up from Berlin at the same time, and from him I gathered that at the extra rehearsal, to which we outsiders were not admitted, there had been a good deal of friction. Brahms, as I found out later, for Henschel would have been far too loyal to admit it, was not only an indifferent conductor, but had the knack of rubbing orchestras up the wrong way. Moreover with one or two exceptions – notably Röntgen, once an opponent but now an enthusiastic admirer – the Gewandhaus musicians were inclined to be antagonistic to his music, and indeed considered the performance of any new work whatsoever an act of condescension. As for Brahms, accustomed to the brilliant quality of Viennese orchestras, which was to entrance me equally when I came to know them, he found his own race, the North Germans, cold and sticky, and let them feel it.

Henschel also informed me the great man was staying, as usual, with Heinrich von Herzogenberg, director of the Bach Verein, whose beautiful wife, about whom the Röntgens were for ever raving, was said to be the most gifted musician and fascinating being ever met or heard of. To my mingled delight and horror I learned, too, that Henschel had actually spoken to him about my work, telling him I had never studied, that he really ought to look at it and so on; and after the general rehearsal this good friend clutched and presented me all unawares. At that time Brahms was clean shaven, and in the whirl of emotion I only remember a strong alarming face, very penetrating bright blue eyes, and my own desire to sink through the floor when he said, as I then thought by way of a compliment, but as I now know in a spirit of scathing irony, 'So this is the young lady who writes sonatas and doesn't know counterpoint!' I afterwards learned that Henschel had left a MS of mine (two songs) with him, that he subsequently looked at them, and remarked to Frau Röntgen that evidently Henschel had written them himself!

I saw him again during that week, but as all my reliable impressions of him belong to a later period, when I came to know him well, it is safer to speak here of the Symphony, which, though it deeply impressed me, left me a little bewildered. I had yet to learn that only a conductor of genius – for preference not the composer, except in very rare cases – can produce a new orchestral work intelligibly; at that time too the idiom of Brahms was unfamiliar, and doubtless the rendering lacked conviction. One thing I well remember, that on this occasion I first realized exactly how much critics grasp of a new work not yet available in print. The great *Leipzig Extinguisher*, after making the usual complaints as to lack of melody, excess of learning, and general unsatisfactoriness, remarked, 'About half way through the very tedious first movement there is one transient gleam of light, a fairly tuneful passage for horns.' He had not noticed this was the recurring first theme, which had already appeared for those self-same horns in the second bar!! . . .

The Röntgens, Klengels, etc., who were full of enthusiasm for the Symphony, had been asked to meet Brahms at the Herzogenbergs, and I heard more and more about the wonderful 'Frau Lisl' whom I wondered if I should ever meet, for they said she detested society and saw no one but a handful of intimates.

Meanwhile I had discovered that living *en pension* was unnecessary extravagance, and determined to go into rooms – a plan Frau Professor took in excellent part. This time luck was emphatically on my side. Next door to Frau Dr Brockhaus, who lived in the Salomonstrasse – one of the new residential streets on the other side of the town, all big houses with wooded gardens – I had often noticed a picturesque, French-looking old house, two storeyed, with tiled roof and dormer windows, standing well back in its ramshackle grounds. One day, lo and behold! I saw hanging on the paling a little board with the device 'MÖBLIRTE ZIMMER' (furnished rooms), and the end of it was that I took up my abode there on 1 February.

My new landlady, Frau Brandt, was a nice but very untidy woman with a howling mob of children. There was only one room at my disposal, and that with the wrong aspect too – a point I had learned to take interest in; but as I had fallen head over ears in love with the house and knew it was to pass into other hands in the summer, I decided to put up with everything, provided satisfactory arrangements could be made for the future.

 I don't think I have yet said what perhaps goes without saying, that it was always understood that I should pass the long vacation – in other words the summer – at home; also that Papa and certain relations had been confident that the desire to live abroad, being merely a whim, would not survive my first winter. By this time, however, they were disillusioned on that point and not surprised to hear I was deep in domiciliary plans for the autumn. The incoming people were interviewed, and finding we suited each other perfectly, I secured the promise of two rooms I had set my heart on and settled down contentedly for the time being in Pandemonium.

As I only spent two months in the single room with the wrong aspect, I will describe my lodgings and my manner of life generally as they were in the following autumn, and during the rest of the time I lived in that fascinating eighteenth-century house.

An ingenious system was arranged between my landlady and myself, under which I ate my midday meal either with the family or at a restaurant, according to the way my day was planned; but I invariably had supper in my own room. I would buy a quarter of a pound of cold ham and some butter (a store of beer was always in the corner of my sitting-room), and there, when I came home after a concert or the theatre, I found the table ready laid with a hunk of black bread on it. The outside wall sloped about half way up, and my larder was a new birdcage, resting, among wild vine leaves, on the rain-gutter below the dormer windows, and leaning crazily against the roof. There were adventures with cats, but the birdcage defeated them. On the other side of the house, separating the front garden from the road, was a seven-foot wooden paling, made of uprights and cross bars, the gate in which was locked by law at 11 p.m., but it was of the sort an agile person who has forgotten the huge rusty latchkey could climb, in spite of the spikes. Sometimes there would be belated passers-by or a policeman; if so one walked on up a side street and returned when the coast was clear. When I came to know the smart people, nothing astonished them more than that this feat was performed on an average two or three times a month.

It was of course quite unusual for girls of my class either to go to restaurants or walk about the streets alone at night, and at first friends used to implore me to let a servant see me home; but neither that, nor any other curtailment of my liberty, would I permit. Only once was I spoken to by a strange man in Germany, and remember insisting on the fact to Charlie Hunter, who remarked that was surely nothing to boast about.

Reflecting on it all I am astonished to think how calmly, on the whole, my mentor, now my neighbour, took my proceedings. In the depths of her southern soul was a secret strain of Bohemianism which the rigours of bourgeois life in a particularly conventional North German town had not wholly eradicated; probably she felt too that though I really did my best to please her on side issues, there was nothing to be done with the ground plan. I know that often when I asked her advice she would say in a tragi-comic voice, *'Was nützt's dass ich dir einen Rath gebe? folgen wirst du doch dich!'* ('What's the use of giving you advice? I know you won't follow it!') Moreover she was clever enough to see that though the 'nice people', by way of explaining their indulgence to her protégée, were for ever reminding each other feverishly that I was English (a card I played, alas, poor England! for all it was worth), as a matter of fact I met with more than tolerance, and but for the circumstance that nothing really counted for me but my work, should have been a fair way to become terribly spoiled.

By this time I was beginning to get some idea of social conditions in Leipzig and noticed there was a fairly sharp division between three main classes – the Burgher Aristocracy (or worldly), the Professorial set, and the Artists. To begin with the first; its kernel was the *Gewandhaus Gesellschaft*, a group of about forty leading families, not necessarily wealthy, who had intermarried for generations and owned most of the woodland villages round Leipzig. It was governed by intricate laws like the ancient guilds, and nobles were excluded from membership. Among these burgher patricians patriarchal customs prevailed; in the town married sons and their families generally occupied upper floors of the paternal dwelling, which as often as not was in the same building as their business. In the summer the whole party migrated to the country house (always within easy reach of the town), and while *'der Bappa'* and *'die Mamma'* inhabited the *'Schloss'* – generally a pleasant, homely erection no more like a castle than is many a French château – the young people were dotted about the grounds in not very tasteful villas. This world had the defects and virtues of all provincial society, and although they made kindly allowances for strangers, among themselves their manners were stiff and their ideas rather narrow, always excepting a certain leading family I shall introduce by and by.

The rural aristocracy (*Land Adel*) played no great part in Leipzig society, but later on I saw some of them in their own preserves and found them more like ourselves than the burgher patricians. In fact one realized, as that fierce rule of the *Gewandhaus Gesellschaft* I quoted indicates, that the two classes had kept strictly aloof till quite recent times, with no such medium as our English gentry – blessed result of the open-aristocracy system – to bridge the gulf. The Gewandhaus set was frequented by the military – Generals of 1870, for instance, in slightly patronizing mood and smothered with orders, whose wives gave themselves amazing airs; also by stray members of the *Land Adel* dotted about the country round Leipzig, who occasionally deigned to mix with the rich bourgeois and drink their champagne. You even met sprigs of Royalty in course of being laboriously coached for their degrees by obsequious professors . . . between whiles seeing life under the guidance of our young swells. Despite the pride of class that I so much admired in the old Leipzig families, much fuss was made over these visitors from a higher sphere.

As for the Professors and their belongings – a group stiff with intellectual pretension, whose exaggerated display of mutual respect masked mutual hatred and jealousy I have never seen equalled – these I detested at first sight and after one or two essays kept out of their way for ever more. My initiation into this world – a *'Professoren-Ball'* to which Frau Doctor got me an invitation – is one of the fantastic experiences of my life. Imagine the guests of a Lambeth Palace garden-party of thirty years ago suddenly ordered at a moment's notice to appear for the first time in their lives in a ballroom . . . There were stuff gowns turned in at the neck in a V with a bit of lace sewn in; there were black trousers worn beneath grey waistcoats; there were gaudy students' jackets besmeared with stains from the restaurant; and, worst of all, tubs were evidently unknown in the intellectual world. Maidens writhed with archness and never ceased giggling, young men bowed, scraped, and declaimed, flourishing their arms about, and at one moment I found myself dancing the Lancers opposite a youth whose hair was half way down his back, who wore someone else's swallow-tailed coat, and who was cutting elaborate capers such as a gorgeous Highlander might have envied, in a pair of double-soled boots covered with mud! . . . The elegance of the really great world is incontestable everywhere; once, when I had a fugitive glimpse of a peasants' ball in the Bavarian Highlands, with its beautiful national costumes, long pipes and unaffected jollity, I asked myself, as I do now, why, between Paul Veronese and Jan Steen, must there be this vast tract of senseless, hybrid commonness? . . .

And yet the professor tribe frisking in ballrooms is more sympathetic than pontificating at dinner-tables and in drawing-rooms. Needless to say there were remarkable men among them, people of European reputation whom it was interesting to watch, but not one single remarkable woman. There is a phrase for ever on German female lips

that used to irritate me: '*Mein Mann sagt . . .*' ('my husband says . . .'),
but as uttered by the ignorant, arrogant wives of these infallible ones
it is the least attractive side of German life in a nutshell. In fact the
general atmosphere of the *Professoren-Kreise** (I am speaking figura-
tively – not alluding to their ballrooms) was unbreathable.

The Artists who, as goes without saying, were my chief associates,
were sometimes to be found wandering about forlorn in the circles
of Professordom, but they professed and sincerely felt unmitigated
contempt for the worldlings, and were seldom if ever met in their
haunts. As stranger and *Engländerinn* – and in those days Germans
had a sneaking respect for English freedom of spirit, and above all for
English table manners – I was admitted to all these various groups,
and confess it was delightful to meet again among the rich burghers
certain habits of life one was accustomed to, but might vainly hope to
find elsewhere in Leipzig – things like tubs, horses and tennis, for
instance. Even to have the door opened by a smart footman was not
without its appeal; and when some of my artist friends wondered how
anyone could care to frequent such frivolous society I would stolidly
reply, 'In my father's house are many mansions' – a phrase which, in
the German equivalent, *'in meines Vater's Haus sind viele Wohnungen'*,
lends itself with very comic effect to a strong English accent and for
that reason had a great success. It is almost impossible for a young
artist to avoid being narrowed in matters artistic by his own set, but
socially I have always held firmly to a profound, hereditary conviction
that it takes all sorts to make a world.

Later on I found that the snobbism of rank and wealth is of course
the same in Dresden and Berlin as in London or other capitals, but the
one type you never met at Leipzig was the International Smart. I could
name twenty such, labelled English, French, German or Italian, as the
case may be, who wear the same clothes, think the same thoughts and
are practically identical; such of course never dreamed of coming to
Leipzig, hence you could there study German burgher life in a state
of comparative purity.

In all the different groups mentioned the particularist feeling was
sure to crop up sooner or later. Stray Prussians were perpetually having digs at the Saxons whom they considered servile, false and rather
stupid. The Saxons, for their part, cordially hated the Prussians, but
also feared them; for which reason, being a race not distinguished for
moral courage, their sentiments were only revealed in an outburst or

* Professorial Circles; thus they describe themselves. (E.S.)

in confidence. Some of the Saxon turns of speech certainly tend to give their own case away; for instance an adjective I have never heard elsewhere is '*hinterrücksch*', used to qualify people who take malevolent action behind your back; and a real good old Leipzig joke is to say, if someone disappears without apparent reason from the circle, 'He must have taken offence at something!' But their most characteristic phrase is one that prefaces any remark whatsoever which, if repeated, might have unpleasant consequences: '*ich will nichts gesagt haben!*' – whereby you are warned that if necessary the remark will be disavowed. Farther than this caution cannot go! Still, as soon as I became capable of distinguishing, I infinitely preferred the kindly, humane, homely Saxons to the overbearing Prussians, particularly after a winter spent in Berlin.

From the very first, dialect interested me – a matter which can be only studied to a very limited extent among the educated in our islands; thus I soon mastered the varieties and found out what a soul-revealing medium it is. To speak of only a few blatant instances, the Prussian dialect is harsh, clean cut and uncompromising; the Bavarian, though easygoing and good-natured on the surface, suggests fathomless depths of brutality below; whereas through the Austrian turn of speech – careless, fascinating, and slightly nasal – there gleams at its worst a cold, smiling, rather Oriental cruelty as unlike brutality as the East is unlike the West. But in the peculiar language spoken in Leipzig, including diction, intonation and every imaginable harmonic, there is a deliberate wallowing in the inaesthetic, a cult of the ungraceful, of which Leipzigers themselves are quite conscious though few emancipate themselves wholly from its thraldom. And no one reviles the Saxon dialect more mercilessly than travelled Saxons.

Meanwhile, in whatever set I might happen to find myself, three names were constantly on all lips, uttered with respect, admiration or devotion, as the case might be. Hitherto for various reasons I had met none of these evidently remarkable personalities; then suddenly Fate made good, and in the course of a single week Livia Frege, Lili Wach and Elisabeth von Herzogenberg swam into my orbit.

When you whisper certain names to yourself a cathedral lights up in the dark recesses of memory, and all who knew her would agree that the name Livia Frege is one of these. In her youth she had been a very celebrated concert singer, and some of Mendelssohn's and Schumann's finest songs are dedicated to 'Livia Gerhardt'; now, on the threshold of old age, she was a great lady, but also the simplest-hearted, warmest friend of every true artist in the place. One of those women born to the purple, with the prestige of a glorious artistic past thrown in, there was a sheer lovableness about her that I partly ascribe to the bluest, most eternally youthful eyes ever seen. She had married when very young a Leipzig banker and left the concert-room for ever; some say nothing short of this renunciation would satisfy the burgher-patrician parents-in-law, but to separate Livia Frege from music was beyond anyone's power.

I first met her in the sort of State Box over the orchestra in the old Gewandhaus, which, though other mortals in part owned it, was always called the '*Frege Loge*'. She had heard of me from the Röntgens, and when someone told this Queen that in the little basket I hung on a peg in that sacred box was a parcel of cold ham, she replied, according to legend, 'And pray why not?', in a manner that rolled the would-be mischief-maker out flat. Livia had once been a very poor young artist herself, but perhaps her interlocutor had forgotten the fact. Though stately to a degree, and prejudiced in an old-fashioned, pleasant way, she took me at once into her good graces, told me to call her '*Du*' and 'Frau Livia', and I am certain had pleasure in the adoration it was impossible even for the old and cold, let alone the young and hot, to help lavishing on her.

She was very religious, not in the alternately blatant and gushing style affected by many pious Germans and hallmarked by the Hohenzollerns, but with absolute simplicity. On the subject of evil communications corrupting good manners she was particularly strong, and once told me she had never listened to a Wagner opera because she wished to keep herself 'musically pure'. Said as she said it, and given her past, this was not in the least unsympathetic; it fitted in somehow with her gentle, serious idealism, which again was saved from sentimentality by a gift of pealing laughter that made heavy-minded admirers stare. So beautiful, so dignified, almost an old woman, and yet able to nearly die of laughing like the very young! I used to note the beauty in her face and voice when she spoke of Mendelssohn, who, with his wife, had been of her most intimate friends. A world that since then had begotten Brahms, not to speak of Wagner, was growing contemptuous of its former idol, and she was aware of the fact, but did not consider it necessary even to discuss the matter. No insistence on his merit, no apology – just the old love and faith. I thought this attitude wonderful, but to carry it through you had to be Livia of the light-holding sapphire eyes.

Many a young musician used to be given a preliminary canter at Frau Livia's house before a select audience, and it was on the first of these occasions attended by me that I met the two other bright jewels in Leipzig's crown.

Lili Wach was the only absolutely normal and satisfactory specimen I have ever met of a much-to-be-pitied genus, the children of celebrated personalities; she was Mendelssohn's youngest daughter, and judging by their portraits must have been more like her Christian mother than her Jewish father. Yet both the delicately cut profile and soul to match had a touch of Israel at its best, and she used to say, 'Make allowance for Jewish caution!' when a certain shrinking from positive statements held back the emphatic 'Yes' or 'No' demanded. She was very musical, but being her father's daughter and extremely reserved by nature she kept the fact so dark that few people knew it.

My friendship with Lili Wach was destined to become only second to the still closer relation I am about to speak of. As for Wach, who had a great reputation as mountaineer, his wife always maintained it was natural that we should have taken to each other at first sight, being chips of the same block. His theories on large families, which I confess to sharing, were ultimately her death, she being far too frail for child-bearing on the scale he insisted on. But I loved these too numerous children, in whose eyes, because of clambering over the paling (and later on because of a big dog of mine), I became a sort of legendary figure, and with whom I kept up a warm friendship that only the war interrupted.

Lisl von Herzogenberg

And now, if these memoirs were a Masque, I should bid the musicians and electricians conspire with me to usher on becomingly the last and best beloved of my trio of Ls – Lisl, otherwise Elisabeth von Herzogenberg.

The published correspondence between her and Brahms has given the world some idea of the personality of this remarkable woman, in whose house I became what he always called me, 'the child', till Fate violently and irrevocably parted us. At the time I first met her she was twenty-nine, not really beautiful but better than beautiful, at once dazzling and bewitching; the fairest of skins, fine-spun, wavy golden hair, curious arresting greenish-brown eyes, and a very noble, rather low forehead, behind which you knew there must be an exceptional brain. I never saw a more beautiful neck and shoulders; so marvellously white were they, that on the very rare occasions on which the world had a chance of viewing them it was apt to stare – thereby greatly disconcerting their owner, whose modesty was of the type that used to be called maidenly. In fact the great problem was to prevent her swathing them in chiffon.

About middle height, the figure was not good; she stooped slightly, yet the effect was graceful and ingratiating, rather as though she were bending forward to look at you through the haze of her own golden atmosphere. In spite of this ethereal quality there was a touch of homeliness about her – to use the word in its best sense – a combination I have never met with in anyone else. Of great natural capacity rather than well informed, a brilliant, most original talker, very amusing, and an inimitable mimic, she managed in spite of all her gifts to retain the childlike spirit which is one of the sympathetic traits in the German character – and what is more, to blend it with the strong-pinioned fascination of one who could but know, like Phyllis in the song, that she never failed to please. And this is surely a remarkable achievement! It really was true that with her sunshine came in at the door, and both sexes succumbed equally to her charm. As her marriage was notoriously happy, possibly too because her brilliant talents inspired a certain awe, men did not dare make love to her, not at least the sort of men she met at Leipzig. But I fancy that in other circumstances a small flirtation would not have been disdained; I used to tell her that when talking to men she became a different woman – a difference which though slight was perceptible – but this mild accusation didn't fit in with her scheme of things and was eagerly repudiated.

In a burgher world it certainly went for something that this siren was an aristocrat. Sincerely as everyone in the artist set despised worldliness, I think her exploits in the kitchen (for among other things she was a Heaven-inspired cook) gained in picturesqueness when you reflected that had the Court of Hanover not come crumbling about their ears in early youth, she and her sister Julia Brewster would have been Maids of Honour. Logic has made great strides in Germany, but at that time there were still a few illogical people about.

The essential point was of course her musical genius. Almost by instinct she read and played from score as do routined conductors, and in judgement, critical faculty and all round knowledge was the perfect musician. And yet, though if ever I worshipped a being on earth it was Lisl, her singing and playing left me cold. This critical attitude on the part of a novice might well have vexed one accustomed to unqualified admiration on all sides, from Brahms downwards; but being quite unspoiled she was only puzzled, and used sometimes to ask, 'How comes it that thou alone dost not love my music-making?' to which I would reply, as I believed, that thinking too much about voice-production and fingering interfered with her spontaneity, never guessing that what was lacking was the one thing needful, passion. At the bottom of all that tender warmth and enthusiasm – *Gemüth*, as the Germans call it – was a curious hardness of which in all the years of our friendship I saw but one passing sign, and which perhaps nothing short of one of those catastrophes that shake human nature to its foundations would have laid bare. Her music betrayed it, but here again she was so richly equipped, and the spell her musicality cast was so potent, that as far as I know others were not conscious of fundamental coldness. Years afterwards her brother-in-law, Henry Brewster, told me that he had guessed it, and once in the early days of our acquaintanceship in Florence (in 1883) I remember his saying that to drive a spear too deeply into that soil might be to break its point. But as I was the only outsider on spear-driving terms of intimacy with her, no one had put it to the proof, and at the time that remark was made it was indignantly brushed aside by me.

I noticed early in the day, however, in connection with a third person, that she had not much psychological instinct, not in deep places at least. Complex natures baffled her, and I would sometimes charge her with lacking the sort of poetic imagination that saves you from cracking your brain over odd twists and turns of character. 'Surely if you do this or that, *it is natural* that the other person should react thus and thus?' she would say in cases where it was obvious that the person would react in quite another manner; and once she astonished me by writing, 'To understand a person's action means, surely, that you yourself would act thus in this place?', which I thought a fantastic interpretation of understanding.

Again I had always assumed that harmony was the crown, the final polish, the ultimate subjection of possibly dissonant elements, not the avoiding of dissonance for the sake of consonance. 'Take all that comes along, all at least that matters, and work it into your scheme somehow'

– such was my unformulated creed . . . but it was not Lisl's. In the light of what happened afterwards – the eternal small crises all down the years as well as the final breach – I see in her not only a temperamental worship of harmony at any cost, but recognize how almost unconsciously, and with infinite skill, she avoided conflicts; also that those who associated with her, from her husband downwards, took care that no tempest should ruffle her sunny serenity. This dislike of stress and storm was never connected in my mind, nor I think in the minds of those who conformed to it, with the valvular heart disease which was a perpetual source of secret terror and distress to me, and of which she was to die when relatively a young woman. But nowadays, having noticed how an obscure instinct of self-preservation determines the course of persons thus afflicted, I think her malady was probably as great a factor in our story as any other.

Herzogenberg, or, to give him his full title, Heinrich Freiherr von Herzogenberg, was a few years older than his wife, and had been brought up by the Jesuits for the priesthood, as are many younger sons of noble Austrian families; but on reaching adolescence he rebelled in order to devote himself to music – as unheard of a thing in his walk of life as in mine. The family was originally French, his grandfather, Vicomte Picot de Peccaduc, having emigrated to Bohemia at the time of the French Revolution and taken the name and title of Freiherr von Herzogenberg – a correct but inadequate rendering of his own fine patronymic. A slight Jesuitical strain in the grandson, which he was quite aware of but which never affected him in the larger issues of life, worked in delightfully with his humanness, culture and abounding sense of humour. Though without her glamour – and who would wish to find two such shining ones under the same roof? – he was quite as much beloved by those who knew them well as his wife. Of course he adored her, and in one of her early letters, she, the least vain of women, told me how delighted she had been, when finding himself near her at some smart party (and of an evening she was positively dazzling) he remarked in the dry, comic way his friends knew so well, *'Abgesehen von aller Verwandschaft muss ich gestehen dass du hübsch bist.'* ('Apart from relationship I must confess that thou art pretty.')

A more learned musician can never have existed; without trouble he turned out fugues, canons, etc., etc., that could be read backwards, upside down, or in a looking-glass – a gift that has as little to do with music, perhaps, as tying yourself into knots or playing twelve games of chess at once, but which is certainly rare and remarkable. He used to compose for a given number of hours daily, and as may be guessed the result was often dry. I know not with what ambition he started his career, but remember his once remarking rather touchingly that he made no claim to having anything new to say – merely hoped to hand on the good tradition. As was inevitable with such a wife, he arranged all his works for piano duet, which was one of the very few trials connected with this ideal couple, for he had a touch like a paving stone. She was as devoted to him as he to her, and in sympathetic company a very discreet little mutual demonstration would sometimes take place; this their adoring world found delightful, and eventually I learned to accept it as part of the German civilization.

The Wachs and Herzogenbergs, who at once became the kernel of my Leipzig existence, associated but superficially and in a slight spirit of superiority with various other friends of mine to whom I was deeply attached – worldlings in whose company certain aspects of home life were found again. Chief among these was a family whose name heads the list when I am meditating unpayable debts for kindnesses received. The master of the house, Consul Limburger, was a wealthy wool merchant and the only real man of the world in Leipzig, gay, handsome, well turned out, and without a touch of German heaviness. Serious persons considered him frivolous but were none the less obliged to follow his lead, for he was the moving spirit of the whole place. As president of the Gewandhaus Concert Committee he fought hard against the intense conservatism of that body and it was mainly his work that the *Siegfried Idyll* was forced on to the programme – a crime to forgive him which took all Frau Livia's Christian charity, and needless to say she was among the absentees at that concert. He further managed the Gewandhaus Balls, the big suppers given to passing celebrities, and started various innovations in sport, such as paperchases on horseback and I think polo. Finally he had the best cook in Leipzig, and once told me his luxury was to expect whatever wine he ordered to appear on his table and . . . never to check his cellar-book.

His wife had, in certain subtle ways, more affinity with the people one knew at home than anyone else in the town. I cannot quite sum it up by saying she was a gentlewoman – there were other Leipzig ladies who could claim to be that of course – but these had a touch of provincialism, whereas behind her quality was a larger civilization, something which I really believe none of her intimates noticed except myself. She was of an old patrician Frankfurt family and her conversation was interlarded with French phrases like the letters of Goethe's mother, another Frankfurt woman. Now here is a curious fact. I had no enthusiastic soul-to-soul alliance with her as with Frau Livia and others – it was just the friendly relation between a woman of the world and a girl she is kind to; and yet, at the most difficult moment of my life, merely by taking it for granted that certain people don't do certain things, however strongly circumstances seem to point that way, she in great measure saved the situation for me – as will be told when the time comes. Expressed gratitude, expressed anything, would have embarrassed her beyond words but . . . she knew that I knew; and afterwards, when terrible sorrow came to her, I think it was some comfort to talk to me by the hour, that silent bond being between us.

In my experience with her I first learned what subsequent knowledge of life has confirmed, that when you are in a tight place worldlings are often better Christians than the elect. And another thing; this old friend had peculiarities that most people found rather ridiculous and beyond which they never got. But such eccentricities often argue an absence of all preoccupation with self, a purity of spirit that seems to me beyond all else rare and lovable – and this was her case.

The Limburgers were typically German in that, with the exception of the mother and the one daughter, every member of the family was as much at home in music as ducks in water. They danced, shot, rode, skated, besides being assiduous young men of business, but all played the piano or some other instrument, and a new work performed at the Gewandhaus was as much an event for them as for the Herzogen-bergs. Their criticisms may have been less technical but I discussed music as gladly with them as with many an expert; and this is the supreme charm of a musical civilization – that amateurs are in it and of it as well as professionals.

Having given some idea of the people who made up my new world, I will go back to the moment when I first met the Herzogenbergs, that is the end of February 1878. I knew at once for certain that we belonged in the same group, as the ensuing years were to prove, and though aware of her notorious aversion to new relations, trusted to music to build a bridge between us, which it did. Both of them told me they had heard great reports of my musicality and I was at once asked to show off. I well remember that Herzogenberg was far more forth-coming than his wife; and though she upbraided me in a friendly, semi-jocular manner for not having joined the Bach Verein and urged me to do so without delay, it was he who, after cross-questioning me about my studies, suggested I should bring him my exercise books to look at.

Of course I turned up with them next day, and was overwhelmed by his raillery of Conservatorium teaching, as he pointed out one gross uncorrected error after another. Both were genuinely interested by my compositions, but again I noticed she was the more reserved of the two, and understood this reserve had nothing to do with the music. Finally Herzogenberg proposed undertaking my tuition himself. 'It will be great fun,' he said, 'for I have never given a lesson in my life; and what is more,' he added, turning to his wife, 'thou, who hast so often bewailed thy contrapuntal ignorance, shalt also be my pupil . . . and I shall meanwhile learn how to teach.'

Needless to say I fell in rapturously with this proposal, insisted on his accepting some nominal fee, for honour's sake, ceased attending my Conservatorium classes (ostensibly on the score of health) and it was understood that before leaving for the summer holidays I was to give formal notice. I at once joined the Bach Verein and began, with my lessons, an initiation into Bach. Strange to say he did not reveal himself to me at once, not even in the *St Matthew Passion*, which I heard on the ensuing Good Friday for the first time. Yet is it so strange after all? Between Bach and Beethoven there is at least as wide a gulf as between Giotto and Giorgione, and at that time my musical intelligence was only cultivated in patches. Before six months had elapsed Bach occupied the place he has ever since held in my heart as the beginning and end of all music; meanwhile the Herzogenbergs were doing their best to speed up matters.

Shortly after joining Bach Verein an incident occurred which opened my eyes to the fact that Germans harboured feelings about the English of which we had no suspicion and which certainly were not reciprocated. My enlightener, a stately black-bearded man with extra-polite Leipzig manners and rather a friend of mine I had imagined, was a certain Herr Flinsch – treasurer of the Bach Verein, one of our leading basses, and also, although I did not know it, a wholesale stationer. One day I went into a smart-looking shop and asked for some English writing-paper. An article was produced which did not meet my wishes, and I began describing exactly what was wanted, repeatedly saying, 'it must be *English* paper'. Suddenly from a back room in the shop, my black-bearded friend darted out in a violent passion, and without one word of greeting launched into a diatribe about the paper trade – informing me that as a matter of fact all the best so-called

English paper was made in Germany, and merely sent to England and stamped 'English' to satisfy (alas!) the snobbishness of his own countrymen, who still believed in the supremacy of English wares. A day was at hand however when German industry would no longer suffer these humiliations – when all the world would know where the best of everything comes from, namely Germany. After which outburst the speaker bounced back into his den, again omitting any sort of greeting, and banged the door. When next we met at rehearsal, and ever after, our relations were distant and dignified.

During the few weeks of opportunity that remained to me for the time being, I applied myself busily to two tasks: the first orders of counterpoint, and the stealthy undermining of my fellow pupil's delicate but unmistakable aloofness. Meanwhile, it might be asked, what did Frau Dr Brockhaus, hitherto my great friend and confidante, say to these new developments? It had been arranged ages ago, long before the dawning of Lisl, that I was to go to the Berg, their country place near Dresden, for a few days after Easter; and though the idea of leaving Leipzig was now intolerable, especially since the Herzogenbergs were departing in the second half of April, I shrank from hurting kind Frau Doctor's feelings by breaking my engagement. But I was not a good hand at keeping things to myself and she soon found out she had a rival. Yet such was Lisl's reputation for charm, genius and so forth, that my older friend no more blamed me than Calypso and Circe would have blamed Ulysses for falling in love with Minerva, had the goddess seen fit to give that complexion to their alliance. I duly went to the Berg, but despite warm feelings of gratitude and affection towards my hostess, blessed the grand final Bach Verein concert that brought me back to Leipzig on duty after four days' absence.

Then suddenly Fate did me a good turn. Immoderate work, combined with too much excitement generally, was telling on me. I had among other things become subject to violent fits of palpitation, and there were yet more drastic warnings, that health was giving way under the strain. At last one day, at a birthday party at the Klengels, I collapsed altogether. Lisl who was present, and who, though I was unaware of the fact, had gradually become attached to me in spite of herself, insisted on taking me straight back to my attic, and during the rather severe illness that followed, really a nervous breakdown, nursed me as I had never been nursed before, putting off her departure from Leipzig a fortnight in order to see me through the worst.

And there, amid the homely surroundings of sloping roof and ramshackle furniture, began the tenderest, surely the very tenderest
relation that can ever have sprung up between a woman and one who,
in spite of her years, was little better than a child. I had heard, but
almost forgotten, that the one sorrow of her strangely happy life was
that she was childless; now I came to know that this grief, though
seldom alluded to, was abiding and passionate – (as a matter of fact
this was the only spot of passion in her). Shortly before I met her hope
had finally been abandoned, and though one or two attempts to coax
unwilling nature were made later on, it was without much hope as far
as she was concerned. Thus I became heir to a fund of pent-up
maternal love.

Every day during that happy fortnight as the clock struck eight I
heard her slowly climbing the stairs, pausing for breath methodically
at every fourth step; then the door curtain was pushed aside and the
dear face, framed in a haze of golden hair, peeped in cautiously lest I
should still be asleep. Asleep! . . . when I knew Lisl was coming . . . !
Except for two hours at midday, when her maid was sent to mount
guard, she stayed with me the whole livelong day, washing me herself, performing all the sick-room offices for me, cooking on her own
little cooker the most tempting dishes her culinary genius could
devise, reading to me, alternately petting and keeping me in order.
And as I got better she used to play Bach and Brahms, including her
own wonderful arrangement of the new symphony, knocked together
in a few hours from the full score lent her by him before she had ever
heard a note of it – the sort of thing she did with no trouble, and made
as light of as she did of her heart complaint. It was settled that though
my mother must never hear of it I was really her child, that, as she put
it, she must have 'had' me without knowing it when she was eleven;
all this with a characteristic blend of fun and tenderness that saved it
from anything approaching morbidity, of which she had the greatest
horror. At that time our conversation was carried on in both languages,
later always in German. She was one of the very few foreigners I have
met to talk English with whom was not distressing; her accent was
admirable, not indiscreetly so as is sometimes the case, but, like her
vocabulary and handling of the language, easy, original, funny, and
somehow or other just right – as indeed was everything about her.

At the beginning of my illness the doctor had feared permanent
heart damage; not till this danger was finally ruled out and my con-
valescence in full swing did she consent to leave me and depart for

95

Austria with her husband, appointing Johanna Röntgen chargée d'affaires. At every stage of the journey postcards were sent, and during the two weeks that elapsed before I was fit to start for England the daily letter was the only event that counted, though mysterious boxes of chocolate, flowers and books were continually being left at my door 'by command of the gracious lady von Herzogenberg'.

I missed her so dreadfully that most nights my pillow was wet with tears – a babyish weakness which, when she heard of it, touched but still more distressed her. Never was anyone more enamoured of gaiety and serenity than she. After her departure I was allowed to see a few friends, and learned that in the early stages of my illness, Anna, the servant, had remarked to one very stiff Leipzig grandee who had asked what was wrong, *'Vielleicht ist das Fräulein zu lustig gewesen'* ('Perhaps the Fräulein has been too gay') – the sort of thing you would say of a student recovering after an orgy.

For a moment I had feared this illness might furnish my father with an excuse for opposing my return to Leipzig later on, but that dread was dispelled by a sentence in a dear letter from mother. 'Of course, darling,' she wrote, 'you shall go back; I told Papa it would kill you not to.' This was the sort of thing that made me adore her so. Eventually I started for home about the middle of June in the charge of a girl I had made friends with, Nancy Crawfurd by name (now Mrs Gould Ross), whom Lisl once referred to as 'that nice girl with the kind nose', and who actually put off her own journey home till I was fit to travel, having promised my new mother to deliver me safely into the hands of the real one.

What a wonderful return home it was! Invalid and incipient 'Phoenix', as mother persisted in calling me sometimes, I was spoiled to my heart's content, the children, whom I called my white slaves, fetching and carrying for me, and even lacing up my boots. The glamour of home, which even at Leipzig had never paled, seemed positively dazzling; how well I remember the flavour of it all – the incredible youth and jollity of the young ones, the lovingness of mother, the beloved dogs and horses! I had not expected much cordiality from my father towards an unrepentant and apparently justified rebel, but the fact that my allowance had not been exceeded by one penny, together with the less important one of countless testimonials to my seriousness of purpose, went a long way, and I found the life I had chosen was an accepted fact.

But presently, when the novelty wore off, I began to review the situation with dismay. My Leipzig doctor had drawn up a document which might have been headed by the word dear among all others to the German heart, *'Verboten'*, for it was a list of forbidden joys that included, with the exception of work (which was permitted in moderation), all the things I loved best, namely tennis, riding and dancing. I had shed what seemed to Lisl inconceivably childish tears over this document, but solemnly signed it, as did she and Dr Langbein. Hardly had I been ten days at home, however, when all the worst symptoms disappeared by magic, and I began to kick against the pricks. The matter was complicated by a rather comic infusion of jealousy. No one ever rejoiced at heart more unselfishly than my mother at any kindness shown to her children, and for Lisl's love and care of me she was deeply and touchingly grateful. Nevertheless when it came to my life at home being regulated by far-off strangers, when her wondering ears heard me refusing even to handle a racquet for fear of temptation, although it was plain to sensible English judgement that there was no longer any reason why I should not play, this was more than her philosophy could bear.

As the summer went on, the old feeling of the staleness and pointlessness of home life came back, and with it a furious longing for Leipzig and my new friends. About this time, too, my father announced that we had for some time been exceeding our income, but it seemed impossible to work up zeal for a whole-hearted scheme of retrenchment. This theme was the source of constant and fruitless sparring, and of friction between me and my mother, with the very natural element of soreness as to foreign influence thrown in.

Again, though I was no longer exactly a black sheep in my father's eyes, he seemed to me wilfully antagonistic, and I wrote miserably to Lisl that I was becoming wicked at home – hard and rebellious; that I never should learn self-control and that there was 'a perfect devil in my heart that sleeps only at Leipzig'. In fact I could hardly await the end of the holidays, particularly as I had finished a bit of work that I felt certain would please Heinrich better than my counterpoint, namely *Variations on an Original Theme*, one of the variations being inspired by, and named after, a filly I had broken. Mercifully the friction between me and my mother was presently forgotten in her perfect appreciation of this early effort and my consequent delight in the depth of her musical instinct! I remember flinging my arms round her and saying, 'You are more musical than all my friends put together,' which in a sense was perfectly true. Thus, at the end of September, in a glow of restored affection and harmony, I left for Germany, this time being allowed without remonstrance to travel under my own wing.

From now onwards I became, and remained for seven years, a semi-detached member of the Herzogenberg family; wherever they were bidden I was bidden too; not a day passed but that one or other of my meals was taken with them; and though like horses I have always preferred getting back for the night to my own stable, the little spare room, stocked for my needs, was always ready when required. And after I was in bed Lisl would come in, comb and brush in hand, her hair streaming over a white dressing-gown – 'all in white and gold', as I put it in my youthful enthusiasm – to make sure I had everything I needed. Daily I became more conscious of the fineness and strength of her personality, but on one point I want to lay special stress because in the years to come, when it militated so terribly against me, I tried to remember it had once been my chief delight; I mean a certain strong simplicity of soul that reminded me of the Elgin marbles, something at once womanly and incorruptible that suggested possible limitations but had a subtle majesty of which not even the greatest degree of intimacy dulled my perception. Witchery, an un-Greek element perhaps, was supposed to be her chief characteristic, and certainly her dear lovely person carried out that idea more than the other. Nevertheless, had the Venus of Milo been a mortal, I think the large, quiet motions of her spirit would have been like Lisl's except for two traits that may have been lacking in the goddess: a curious, most touching humility, lurking, unnoticed by most people, at the bottom of her soul, and a lovingness that had the sweetness of ripe, perfect fruit, and which no one but her husband and I knew in its fullness. When I add that Herzogenberg was on far too big lines to begrudge her a semblance of what nature had withheld – or me the blessing of her tender mothering love – it will be allowed that the foundation of our friendship seemed well and truly laid.

In musical matters Lisl and I saw absolutely eye to eye, and it was a strange intoxicating thing to realize that in moments of musical ecstasy the heart of the being on the earth you loved best was so absolutely at one with yours that it might have been the same heart. I think I was always more critical than either of them as regards weak spots in Brahms, or even the older classics, and was never able, as they were, to admire every single page Bach ever wrote; but on the summits we met. No doubt, too, the catholicity of taste I acquired in after life would have shocked them, but that day had not yet dawned. Meanwhile Lisl and I plodded away at our counterpoint in friendly rivalry, and used sometimes to wonder whether Brahms, given a *cantus firmus* to work in four parts, would turn out anything so very much better than our productions. Herzogenberg was a splendid teacher, but though my industry and zeal left nothing to be desired, quite the reverse, he told me I wasn't really a good pupil – which I suppose any master would say of a beginner who always claims to know best!

Of course I spent Christmas with the Herzogenbergs, and the table round my little tree was paved with miniature scores of Beethoven quartets. By and by, borne along by Papa Röntgen's teaching enthusiasm, and despite hands ill adapted to the instrument, I began learning the violin and eventually became equal to taking second violin in easy quartets. The lessons were arranged to include the excellent sit-down Röntgen tea – blessed cry of his Dutch blood – and after tea he taught me chess. I got so passionately attached to the game, though a very poor player, that eventually it had to be given up, otherwise I should have spent my life doing nothing else.[2]

Brahms

Not long after the Franco-Prussian war there emerged in German literature a figure that dominated every one's consciousness for a couple or so of decades. Her name was Frau Buchholz, and I believe she had a husband and children. But the massive personality of the *Hausfrau* dwarfed her domestic setting, as well it might; for in her was summed up the entire soul of the more or less cultured German *bourgeoise* of the last quarter of the nineteenth century – an epoch at which every shopkeeper, every lodging-house keeper had an *abonnement* ticket for the best local concerts, listened with intelligence and rapt attention, and, if a woman, only ceased to knit at the very *piano* passages.

What brings Frau Buchholz into one's head at the present juncture is the fact that Brahms cherished a special affection for one of her classic utterances; and being far too big a lion to mind repeating himself, you might hear him once or twice in the same evening therewith cutting short the effusiveness of an admirer, more especially if elderly and of the female sex. 'O, Herr Brahms,' such a one would say, 'how exquisite is the modulation in the third movement, where the second theme reappears in the tonic!' Whereupon, transfixing his victim with that terrifying bright blue stare of his, Brahms would reply, 'Yes dear lady; and as Frau Buchholz says, the great point about music is, that not only is it such a delightful thing in itself, but it also provides such a handy subject for conversation at the weekly coffee-parties of excellent ladies like yourself!' Such was the master's style in the matter of defensive repartee.

To me these impassioned talks about music, which resounded all down the street as concert-goers were wending their homeward way, used to be one of the delights of swimming in the dear old sea of German music that surged about the feet of Brahms; feet clad in the good, stout boots of a man who loves walking. Hence I saw nothing ridiculous in Frau Buchholz's remark; and later on when I went to concerts in England, the hasty brushing aside, whether on the part of executants or audience, of the preoccupation that after all had brought us to that concert-hall, affected me painfully. With what a wave of longing and regret would I recall how, after a chamber concert abroad, the four quartet players would go off together with a few intimates to some cheap restaurant and talk ceaselessly – not about golf, or football, but about the works they had just been playing, including the Haydn quartet! Eventually, one got accustomed to the reserve at home, labelled it 'English', and put it aside as irrelevant, though often – for instance while watching the faces of the Berlin Philharmonic orchestral players – one asked oneself, 'Is it so irrelevant after all?'

When I became practically the adopted child of the Herzogenbergs, I got to know Brahms very well, and owing, no doubt, to his profound affection and admiration for 'Frau Lisl', as he called her, he was extraordinarily kind and fatherly to me; yet I cannot say I really liked or felt happy with him, though if ever he was to be seen at his best it was in that house. A salient trait of his was the greediness I consider one of the hallmarks of the true artist, and the Herzogenbergs not being at all well off, all they could manage in the way of a cook was a series of moderately gifted practitioners, with the then North German ideas as to plenty of grease in the soup, very few beans in the coffee mill, meat baked in the oven, with all its juice extracted to make up something else, and so on. This, however, was of no consequence, for Lisl was not only a superb cook but practised the art with exactly the same sort of passion she brought to bear on disentangling the parts of a Bach motet. And, upon my word, I think that if Brahms had honestly examined his heart, he would have hesitated as to which ranked first for him among the attributes of this wonderful woman – her musical or her culinary genius.

As time went on he came oftener to Leipzig, the while declaring that but for the Herzogenbergs nothing would induce him to set foot in the horrible place – a remark he particularly enjoyed serving up to a crowd of Leipzigers invited in his honour to one of the big burgher houses. At the Herzogenbergs' things went better, for there it was less a case of meeting the aborigines, distinguished or obscure, than of hobnobbing with musical celebrities who came flocking from various towns within reasonable distance of Leipzig to prostrate themselves – some with, some without dignity – at the master's feet; men like Theodor Kirchner, Philipp Spitta, Volkland, Eduard Grieg, Dvořák and many others. And when artists like Frau Schumann or Joachim were involved in whatever Brahms work was being produced, appeared also their respective families, the 'Schumann girls', as they were called, and that wonderful singer poor Frau Joachim, whom later the world decided to cold-shoulder.

Of course it was child's play for Lisl to guide into safe channels a conversation that looked like taking a wrong turn, or extricate victims from the lion's claws before they had been too badly mauled – a proceeding often called for in the course of a *Brahms Abend*. He really was unbelievably deficient in the quality that Italians, even among the peasantry, call *educazione*, particularly when some innocent person who had been genuinely stirred to the marrow by his music tried to say so and thank him. Now we all know how difficult it is to express to a genius our gratitude for the raptures he has given us, though, after all, it is partly for our sakes that the creative act has been consummated. Moreover, in the realm of music, until the crotchets and quavers are actually displacing the ether a score cannot be said to have come to life. When, therefore, is a wretched admirer to speak, unless while the blood in his veins is still tingling with that rapture? And surely it betokens a certain lack of simplicity – let us put it at that – in the soul of a great man if all he can do, in response to some stammered outpouring, is to stroke his grey moustache, stare at you fixedly, and say, 'And did indeed the gracious lady have all those beautiful feelings thanks to my poor quartet? . . . and where did they lodge? Beneath the little blue shawl? Or perhaps under the cockyolly bird on her hat?' (a fragment of conversation I overheard at a Herzogenberg party).

One didn't so much resent the maltreatment of worldlings like my kind friend Consul Limburger, a great social force with plenty of go and money, who happened also to be very musical, and as chairman of the Gewandhaus Committee exercised a most beneficent influence on that hidebound body. But it was really unpleasant to see the defenceless trampled on, and had anyone pointed out to the trampler what pain he was giving, perhaps he might have mended his ways. But except Lisl – and that only very occasionally – no one did. So the thing became a habit, and towards the close of an entertainment in his honour at the Hotel de Prusse or some such place (entertainments which went on till the small hours, Brahms the while devouring ham rolls washed down with glass upon glass of beer and cup upon cup of strong black coffee), a sort of 'after the battle' atmosphere would occasionally hang over the scene. Some of the injured had been removed in stretchers; others were licking their wounds, brooding over a sortie that had gone awry, and hoping for a chance of making good before the lights were turned down. How well I remember a very dear and deeply musical old maid standing sadly near the door of the ladies' cloakroom and murmuring half to herself, 'If only I could just explain to him that I was alluding to the Andante! . . . how *could* he think I should make such an inappropriate remark about the Scherzo!'[3]

I think what chiefly angered me was his views on women, which after all were the views prevalent in Germany, only I had not realized the fact, having imagined '*mein Mann sagt*' was a local peculiarity. Relics of this form of barbarism still linger in England, but as voiced by people gone mad on logic, worshippers of brute force, and who visualize certain facts with the hard stare of eyes devoid of eyelashes, these theories would, I fancy, repel even our own reactionaries. George III, himself a German, might have subscribed to William II's famous axiom about women being out of place anywhere except in the kitchen, nursery and church, but you often heard it quoted with complete assent by German women themselves in my day.

Brahms, as artist and bachelor, was free to adopt what may be called the poetical variant of the '*Kinder, Kirche, Küche*' axiom, namely that women are playthings. He made one or two exceptions, as such men will, and chief among these was Lisl, to whom his attitude was perfect . . . reverential, admiring and affectionate, without a tinge of amorousness. It specially melted him that she was such a splendid

Hausfrau, and during his visits she was never happier than when concocting some exquisite dish to set before the king; like a glorified Frau Röntgen she would come in, flushed with stooping over the range, her golden hair wavier than ever from the heat, and cry, 'Begin that movement again; that much you owe me!' and Brahms's worship would flame up in unison with the blaze in the kitchen. In short he was adorable with Lisl.

In his relations with her husband, who completely effaced himself as musician in the master's presence, he took pains to be appreciative, but could not disguise the fact that Herzogenberg's compositions did not greatly interest him. Once when he had been in a bad temper and rather cruel about them, Lisl rated him and wept, and Brahms kissed her hand and nearly wept too, and it appears there was a most touching scene; but the thing rankled in her bosom for a long time.

To see him with Lili Wach, Frau Schumann and her daughters, or other links with his great predecessors was to see him at his best, so gentle and respectful was his bearing; in fact to Frau Schumann he behaved as might a particularly delightful old-world son.[4] Though she loved him and thought all the world of his music, she was not in the least afraid of criticizing it, and would sometimes fall foul of points that stirred my special admiration; witness what she called 'the extra bar tacked on' to the exquisite melody of his *Variations on an Original Theme* in D major. 'You've made a *nine*-bar phrase of it,' she would cry, 'and out of pure perversity, too! for anyone can see that *by nature* it would be an *eight*-bar melody!' Brahms's patience and good humour during these onslaughts never failed him, and it was pleasant to see him reining in, for once, the sarcastic spirit his less august friends had to put up with as best they could.[5]

His ways with other womenfolk – or to use the detestable word for ever on his lips, *'Weibsbilder'* – were less admirable. If they did not appeal to him he was incredibly awkward and ungracious; if they were pretty he had an unpleasant way of leaning back in his chair, pouting out his lips, stroking his moustache, and staring at them as a greedy boy stares at jam tartlets. People used to think this rather delightful, specially hailing it, too, as a sign that the great man was in high good humour, but it angered me, as did also his jokes about women, and his everlasting gibes at any, excepting Lisl of course, who possessed brains or indeed ideas of any kind. I used to complain fiercely to her about this, but her secret feeling was, I expect, that of many anti-Suffragist women I have known, who, for some reason or other on the pinnacle of man's favour themselves, had no objection to the rest of womenkind being held in contempt – the attitude of Fatima the Pride of the Harem. To be fair to Lisl I never heard her express definite sentiments on the subject, about which I had never thought myself, but as she was of her epoch and intensely German, her instinct was probably that of Fatima.[6]

With Lili Wach, Brahms desired to be specially charming. But Lili was ultra-sensitive, and though she did her best to be friendly and forthcoming, contact with those incredibly awkward manners of his shrivelled her up; so the Brahms evenings at that house were seldom a success. Special qualities, among them animal spirits, self-confidence and courage, were necessary to carry one over the frequently recurring moments when the stream of conversation between him and his inter-locutor suddenly dried up, and whole rooms-full of people, embar-rassed witnesses of the silence in Heaven, were similarly stricken dumb. For, of course, a Leipzig party had none of the ease of the great world; it was just an agglomerate of socially rather helpless pro-fessional and industrial units whom the presence of a far less alarming celebrity than Brahms was apt to disconcert.

Young and enthusiastic though I was, it was impossible to me to join in the chorus of unmitigated admiration that prevailed in that world. For one thing, I never fathomed wherein lay the intellectual supremacy Brahms was credited with, and suspected it was a case of subscribing to a gradually built-up legend. Sayings of his were quoted, and handed around with exclamation points, in which I failed to see anything so very wonderful. Professor Wach often let fly splinters of wisdom, of shrewd criticism, of humorous reflection on life, that seemed to me far more striking than anything one ever heard Brahms say. Or again many a remark of Eduard Grieg – as modest, golden-hearted and natural a creature as ever breathed – had exactly the fresh, fascinating quality of his music. As for volcanic Frau Schumann, if certain subjects were mentioned, incandescent fragments of scorn shot upwards from the depths of her artist soul, and, descending, burnt holes in Lisl's parquet floor. Sometimes the name of Wagner sufficed to cause an eruption, and of course she failed to do him justice. But who cared? What mattered was the quality of the phrase forged in the molten lava of her wrath.[7]

I like best to think of Brahms at the piano, playing his own compo-sitions or Bach's mighty organ fugues, sometimes accompanying him-self with a sort of muffled roar, as of Titans stirred to sympathy in the bowels of the earth. The veins in his forehead stood out, his wonderful bright blue eyes became veiled, and he seemed the incarnation of the restrained power in which his own work is forged. For his playing was never noisy, and when lifting a submerged theme out of a tangle of music he used jokingly to ask us to admire the gentle sonority of his 'tenor thumb'.

One of his finest characteristics was his attitude towards the great dead in his own art. He knew his own worth – what great creator does not? – but in his heart he was one of the most profoundly modest men I ever met, and to hear himself classed with such as Beethoven and Bach, to hear his C minor Symphony called 'the Tenth Symphony',* jarred and outraged him. Once, when he turned up to rehearse some work of his, Reinecke had not yet finished rehearsing one of Mozart's symphonies – I forget which – and after the slow movement he murmured something to Lisl that I did not catch. She afterwards told me he had said, 'I'd give all my stuff (*Kram*) to have written that one Andante!'

When Brahms came to Leipzig, as I have said, many other composers – unenvious admirers of the greater master such as Dvořák, Kirchner, Grieg, etc. – used to turn up by magic to do him honour; and of course they all flocked to the Humboldtstrasse. My first meeting with Grieg, whom I afterwards came to know so well, I remember chiefly because of a well-deserved smack in the face it brought me. Grieg, whose tastes were catholic, greatly admired the works of Liszt. Now it was the fashion in my world to despise Liszt as composer. But what had to be borne as coming from mature musicians may well have been intolerable in a student, and some remark of mine causing Grieg's fury to boil over, he suddenly inquired what the devil a twopenny-halfpenny whippersnapper like me meant by talking thus of my betters? Next day at cock-crow the dear man came stumping up my stairs to apologize, and this incident laid the foundation of a very warm feeling between me and the Griegs which came to fruition later on.

My musical education was possibly being narrowed in the severely classical atmosphere of the Brahms group, but I suppose every scheme of education is either too narrow or too diffuse. Certainly the impulse towards opera, of which I had been conscious in the days of Mr Ewing, was checked for the moment. Though exception was made of course

* The implication was that it equalled, or surpassed, Beethoven's Ninth Symphony. (E.S.)

in favour of Mozart and *Fidelio*, my group considered opera a negligible form of art, probably because Brahms had wisely avoided a field in which he would not have shone, and of which the enemy, Wagner, was in possession. Besides this, the Golden Age of Leipzig had been orchestral and oratorial, and both musicians and concert public were suspicious of music-drama. The old families, who had been rooted in their Gewandhaus seats from time immemorial, seldom hired boxes at the Opera – partly, perhaps, because under the system of *abonnement* it was played alternately with drama; anyhow it was not the fashion among our Leipzig grandees. I used to go and hear *Carmen*, still my favourite opera, whenever I had a chance, and was indignant at Herzogenberg's patronizing remark that Bizet was no doubt *'ein Geniechen'* (a *little* genius). But in that school Bizet, Chopin and all the great who talk tragedy with a smile on their lips, who dart into the depths and come up again instantly like divers – who, in fact, decline to wallow in the Immensities – all these were habitually spoken of as small people.

Another curious thing about the Brahms group was that orchestration apparently failed to interest them, consequently it played no part in my instruction. No one holds more strongly than the writer that content comes first; before you speak it is well to have something definite to say. But in that circle, what you may call the *external*, the merely pleasing element in music, was so little insisted on, that its motto really might have been the famous 'take care of the sense and the sounds will take care of themselves' – hardly an adequate outfit for a musician even if the sounds did take care of themselves, which they do not. Once some orchestral variations of Herzogenberg's were performed which I scarcely recognized for the same I had admired as one of the inevitable piano duets, so bad was the instrumentation.

But whatever the defects of my environment may have been, in it I learned the necessity, and acquired the love, of hard work, as well as becoming imbued with a deep passion for Bach, which I think is in itself an education. Herzogenberg and his Berlin collaborators were constantly discovering and editing new wonders, and though the Leipzig branch of the Bach Verein was not a very grand affair the arrangement and production of these 300-year-old novelties was enthralling to him and us.

By the time Good Friday (1879) came round, Papa Röntgen considered me fit to take my place among the second violins in the annual *Passion* performance – no great compliment as will presently be seen – imploring me passionately to keep my eye on the leader and not cut in at wrong moments in my excitement. These performances – held in the very Thomas Kirche for which the work was originally written, and of which Mendelssohn, who rediscovered the *Passion*, had made a great tradition – are among the most unforgettable experiences of my life. The proceeds were devoted to the Widows and Orphans Fund of the Gewandhaus Orchestra, but according to a curious by-law, only those who had taken an active part in the performance had a claim on that year's balance. Now many modern instruments have no place in the orchestra of Bach's time; consequently trombones, bass clarinets, and other outsiders vamped up in spare hours enough violin to scrape their way through Bach's very easy string parts, sitting generally in the ranks of the second violins. And so vilely did they play that I quite understood why I had been allowed to join them. This was the only time I ever performed in an orchestra, and, as may be imagined under the circumstances, I was astonished at the hideous noises produced round about me – and still more astonished the following year, when I sat below, to notice how little it matters in a big choral work what goes on at some of the second desks!

I count it as one of the great privileges vouchsafed me that I learned to love the *Passion* in that place of places, the prestige and acoustic properties of which make up for the dreariness of its architecture. In one of the side galleries, close up to the orchestra, which was grouped aloft in front of the organ, sat the Thomaner Schoolboys, representatives of the very choir of which Bach was Cantor. I suppose realizing these things has something to do with it, but never, so it seems to me, is the Chorale in the opening chorus so overwhelming as when trumpeted forth with the pride of lawful heirs by the *Thomaner Chor*.

I despair of giving an idea of the devoutness of the audience. Generally speaking, most of the inhabitants of Leipzig, including nearly everyone I knew, were either exceedingly conventional church-goers or unbelievers, but on this occasion the dull mist of religious indifference appeared to lift for the time being. It was not only that the church seemed flooded with the living presence of Bach, but you felt as if the *Passion* itself, in that heart-rending, consoling portrayal, was being lived through as at no other moment of their lives by every soul in the vast congregation.

The Good Friday solemnity is the supreme flower and conclusion of the Leipzig musical season, and shortly afterwards Lisl's father and mother appeared on the scene, but at different moments, for they did not get on and seldom met. I had been requested when in England to send some fairy-book 'for my mother, who is herself a regular old fairy-tale'. When I saw Baroness von Stockhausen, née Gräfin Baudissin, I said to myself, 'The Wicked Godmother!', and looking the other day at a superb bust of her by Hildebrand belonging to one of her grand-children, there is no denying that this portrait of the Evil Genius of my life bears out that idea. Handsome, gifted, violent as ten devils rolled into one, I found this old woman, who looked like a Louis XV Mar-quise, very attractive, and hoped she would like me; but unfortunately I was hated at first sight with the vitriolic jealousy of one who had never permitted her children to have friends, or even playmates. Herzogenberg, who was rather fond of his mother-in-law, once said that but for his Jesuit training he could never have achieved the win-ning of his bride, and I noticed that his jocular reference to that agitat-ing time rather distressed Lisl.

The father was an icy-cold Hanoverian nobleman for whom the world had ceased revolving round the sun on the day when the Court of Hanover, to which he had been Minister, was liquidated. After a first brief meeting with these two august personages I was implored to shun the house during the remainder of their respective visits. Lisl was deeply pained and humiliated by her mother's outrageous unfriendliness towards one in whom she had professed the most charming interest, but there was nothing to be done. As well reason with Vesuvius. Then, for the first time, I noticed my friend's abject terror of conflicts . . . and also her inability to cope with them.[8]

THREE
1879–91

HENRY AND JULIA BREWSTER

THE BREAK WITH LISL

IN THE DESERT

Henry and Julia Brewster

The Christmas of 1879 I spent in Berlin. There had been much lamen-
tation on my part because the Herzogenbergs were suddenly summoned to spend the Festival with her mother at the Austrian aunt's
Schloss, but shortly before their departure I made the acquaintance of
a couple, the Conrad Fiedlers, who were destined to play a great part
in my life. He was the younger son of a grand old *Leipzigerinn* who
lived with her eldest son's family in the town house in winter, and at
her beautiful country place a few miles off in the summer. All the
Fiedlers were very rich, and why the Conrads had settled at Berlin I
never could make out, for they both detested it and were on the point
of migrating to her native town, Munich.

Conrad was of a type you seldom meet in Germany, a fairly well-
known writer on philosophical subjects, an acknowledged authority
on painting and sculpture, a generous patron of struggling talent, and
yet . . . O wonder! attached to no Institution . . . merely a gentleman
at large. More than usually encased in a certain Saxon frigidity that
contrasts strangely with the geniality of the other brand of Saxon, I
noticed that everyone secretly coveted his esteem and that his word
always carried weight. His wife was one of those people whom all
portrait painters pursue, more especially if the husband is a wealthy
art patron. At that time she was quite young, tall and striking looking,
with daring, gloriously blue eyes, yellow-gold hair, and incomparable
colouring. We were very fond of each other for years, and later on,
after her first husband's death, when she and Frau Wagner became
great friends, we gradually drifted apart. A gulf was bound to open
up sooner or later between intimates of Wahnfried and people refractory to the Wagner *cultus*. Meanwhile, whether at Munich, at Crostewitz (his mother's country house, where an ideal summer retreat had
been contrived for them at one end of the homely farm quadrangle
attached to the *Schloss*) or at their Florentine *villino*, their kindness to
me was inexhaustible.

I first met these new friends, as I said, before what promised to be a desolate Christmas bereft of Lisl, and with the warm impulsiveness which was her chief charm, Mary Fiedler bore me off to Berlin then and there.

Curiously enough I cannot remember anything about my first impressions of the town itself but plenty about the people I met there. Of the Joachims I saw a good deal. She was the finest contralto I ever heard, and until she got too fat, the Orpheus of one's dreams. Joachim according to all English people was of course perfection, but I saw him in another setting and never wholly liked him – perhaps among other reasons because trouble was brewing in his house and all my sympathies were with the wife, who, though socially far less satisfactory than her husband, was a warm, living, human being. I wished she would not crawl under the supper table in a fit of New Year jollity, armed with a hat pin, but why did Joachim allow it, I asked myself? Why did he sit serenely at the head of the table looking like a planed-down Jupiter and utter no remonstrance? In a certain letter Rubinstein's answer to this riddle may be found, and though obviously grotesque, it proves that I was not the only Joachim-heretic in the world.* That evening he told me he had just heard Melba, and raved about her: 'How can one speak of coldness,' he asked, 'in connection with such phrasing?' Perhaps he knew that the same accusation was often levelled against himself, and in both cases it is obvious what people meant – the 'coldness', compared to Renaissance work, of the Delphic Charioteer, which is not to everyone's taste.

It was in Berlin that Christmas that I first met Rubinstein, and in unexpected mood too. A totally talentless maiden, relying I suppose on her great beauty – for his weaknesses were notorious – had insisted on playing to him with a view to being advised as to whether she should make music her career. When she had done he remarked quite simply, 'How should *you* ever become an artist?' and then, taking up her hand, he pointed in succession to her fingers, her forehead and her heart, slowly saying *'hier nix, hier nix, und hier nix!'* – a terrible sequence of nothingness that needs no translation. There was one thing only that roused the mild-mannered Conrad Fiedler to frenzy – half talents, and when I reported this incident he was delighted.

I also saw a good deal of two paladins of Brahms's, Philipp Spitta, the chief excavator and editor of lost Bach treasures, and Chrysander,

* Rubinstein suggested to Lisl that Joachim was encouraging the break-up of his own marriage in order to be free to marry 'an English Lady Somebody'. When Joachim subsequently divorced his wife, Brahms, chivalrous but clumsy, took her side. There was an estrangement between the two men for some years.

the biographer of Handel, who told me there were masses of yet unde-
ciphered early English music in the British Museum compared to
which the work of Palestrina and Co. was the groping of children, or
words to that effect. After Brahms's death two letters of mine were
returned to me (one being written at Sir George Grove's request to beg
the loan of the *Tragic Overture* for the Crystal Palace Concerts) and I
find I well rubbed in the learned Chrysander's tribute to despised
England. When next we met Brahms asked me to play him some
Scotch music, and after listening to one of those archaic reels the first
phrase of which is, for instance, in D major and the second in C major,
the remark was, 'And this people claims to be musical' ! . . .[9]

The moment has come to express regret that unlike other women
writers of memoirs, such as Sophie Kowalewski, George Sand and
Marie Bashkirtseff – if for a moment I may class myself with such as
these – I have so far no orthodox love-affairs to relate, neither soulful
sentiment for musician of genius, nor perilous passion conceived
among the reeds of the Crostewitz lake for proud Prussian guardsman.
In my letters to Lisl, where all the secrets of my heart stand revealed,
I again and again express a conviction it is foolish to insist upon, so
obvious is it, that the most perfect relation of all must be the love
between man and woman, but this seemed to me, given my life and
outlook, probably an unachievable thing. Where should be found the
man whose existence could blend with mine without loss of quality
on either side? My work must and would always be the first consideration, and the idea that men might think one wanted to catch them
checked incipient romance. For a space I had imagined myself in love
with the husband of one of my friends – a ridiculous fancy at once
confessed to his wife, who was rather gratified and not at all alarmed.
This fleeting sentiment was mastered and consigned to limbo without
its object being any the wiser; and all the time I was more or less aware
that had this individual been eligible such an idea would never have
entered my head. As in the case of my own admirers, immunity from
consequences favoured the tender illusion of a hopeless attachment.
What Fate had in reserve for me as regards the supremest relation
of all who could say? Meanwhile the desire to be looked after,
helped and loved was as imperative as the instinct of independence
that seemed predominant. And as, in order to receive you must
give . . . give I did!

Let me say here, that all my life, even when after years had brought me the seemingly unattainable, I have found in women's affection a peculiar understanding, mothering quality that is a thing apart. Perhaps too I had a foreknowledge of the difficulties that in a world arranged by man for man's convenience beset the woman who leaves the traditional path to compete for bread and butter, honours and emoluments – difficulties honest men are more aware of, perhaps, than she of the sheltered life. I had no theories about it then but I think I guessed it. Even among the conformists I saw good, brave women obliged because of their sex to give way before dullness, foolishness or brutality; and in natures inclined to side with the handicapped these things kindle sympathy and admiration. And further it is a fact that the people who have helped me most at difficult moments of my musical career, beginning with my own sister, Mary, have been members of my own sex. Thus it comes to pass that my relations with certain women, all exceptional personalities I think, are shining threads in my life.

In one of her letters Jane Austen remarks that so-and-so is 'too apt to like people' – a tendency which is possibly a sign of a generous temperament, as one would like to believe, but which also implies lack of self-control, and sometimes a wilful drugging of one's critical faculties. Owing to this weakness I often made mistakes, yet only one bad one – a misfortune mentioned from honesty, as it happened long after the date at which these Memoirs close. And I may add that if the world is inclined to scoff or speak ill of women's friendships, this is one of those cheap generalities which will pass muster only as long as women let men do their thinking for them, and which moreover are given the lie to by the experience of many who hand them round, did they but choose to testify. Having said this I will now pass on to the next on my list of great friendships.

Barbara Hamley had often spoken to me of Agnes and Rhoda Garrett, who were among the first women in England to start business on their own account and by that time were well-known house decorators of the Morris school. Agnes was sister to Mrs Fawcett and Dr Elizabeth Garrett Anderson – Rhoda, their cousin, rather older than Agnes, daughter of a clergyman whose second wife had practically turned her predecessor's children out of the house to fend for themselves. Late in the autumn of 1880 Barbara introduced me to these great friends of hers, and during the next two years their house became the focus of my English life owing to the friendship that sprang up between Rhoda and me.

Both women were a good deal older than I, how much I never knew – nor wished to know, for Rhoda and I agreed that age and income are relative things concerning which statistics are tiresome and misleading. How shall one describe that magic personality of hers, at once elusive and clear cut, shy and audacious? – a dark cloud with a burning heart – something that smoulders in repose and bursts into flame at a touch. . . . Though the most alive, amusing, and amused of people, to me at least the sombre background was always there – perhaps because the shell was so obviously too frail for the spirit. One knew of the terrible struggle in the past to support herself and the young brothers and sisters; that she had been dogged by ill-health as well as poverty – heroic, unflinching through all. Agnes once said to me, 'Rhoda has had more pain in her life than was good for her,' but no one guessed that like her brother Edmund – champion of Rhodes, youthful collaborator with Lord Milner, cut off at the zenith of his powers – she carried in her the seeds of tubercular disease. And yet when the end came there was little of surprise in one's grief; thus again and again had one seen falling stars burn out.

I spoke of her humour; on the whole I think she was more amusing than anyone I have ever met – a wit half scornful, always surprising, as unlike everyone else's as was her person . . . a slim, lithe being, very dark, with deep-set burning eyes that I once made her laugh by saying reminded me of a cat in a coal scuttle. Yet cat's eyes are never tender, and hers could be the tenderest in the world.

I always think the feel of a hand as it grasps yours is a determining factor in human relationships, and all her friends must well remember Rhoda's – the soft, soft skin that only dark people have, the firm, wiry, delicate fingers. My reason tells me she was almost plain, but one looked at no one else when she was in a room. There was an enigmatic quality in her witchery behind which the grand lines, the purity and nobility of her soul, stood out like the bone in some enchanted landscape. No one had a more subtle hold on the imagination of her friends, and when she died it was as if laughter, astonishment, warmth, light, mystery, had been cut off at the source. The beauty of the relation between the cousins, and of that home life in Gower Street, remains with us who knew them as certain musical phrases haunt the melomaniac, and but for Agnes, who stood as far as was possible between her and the slings and arrows which are the reward of pioneers, no doubt Rhoda's life would have spent itself earlier. Her every burden, human and otherwise, was shouldered by Agnes, and both had a way of discovering waifs and strays of art more or less worsted by life whose sanctuary their house henceforth became.

I think I have never been happier in my life than at the old thatched cottage they rented at Rustington. An exhausting fight against the stream of prejudice, such as the Garretts had waged for many years, was not to be my portion till later. Of course both cousins and all their friends were ardent Suffragists, and I wonder now at the patience with which they supported my total indifference on the subject – an indifference I was to make up for thirty years later.

Their great friends the Parrys had a house close by, and besides helping me with invaluable musical criticism and advice Hubert Parry lent me a canoe, in which on very calm days, cautiously dressed in bathing costume, I put out to sea. There too I got to know the Fawcetts, and saw how that living monument of courage, the blind Postmaster General, impressed the country people as he strode up and down the hills in the company of his wife. I thought Mrs Fawcett rather cold, but an incident that happened the summer after the death of Rhoda, to whom she was devoted, taught me otherwise. One day when I was singing an Irish melody I had often sung at Rustington – 'At the mid hour of night' – I suddenly noticed that tears were rolling down her cheeks, and presently she got up and quietly left the room. After that for many years I never saw her. Then came the acute Suffrage struggle, during which the gulf that separated Militants from National Unionists belched forth flames, but through all those years, remembering that incident, I always thought of Mrs Fawcett with affection.

The deep, swift friendship with Rhoda Garrett was abruptly broken two years later, when Ethel received a telegram in Italy bearing the news of Rhoda's death.

The years 1880–81 were uneventful. The summer of 1881 was spent in England with the Garretts. Much to Lisl's disappointment, Ethel went home for Christmas. She further pained Lisl by announcing her intention of spending the following winter in Florence. After the customary summer visit to England, she wanted to travel to Italy via Switzerland, joining Lisl in Venice if dates permitted. In Switzerland she would stay with the Wachs, in the chalet at Interlaken, where the Professor would initiate her in mountaineering.

The Wach chalet in the commune of Wilderswyl was about 1,000 feet above Interlaken, and though its owners were a thing apart, in no way differed from all chalets. There I got to know Wach in quite a new aspect and the one I loved best – a big boy in knickerbockers, madder than any adolescent about mountaineering. So impatient was he to initiate his guest that he would have arranged our first climb for the day after my arrival, but for the gentle icy opposition of Lili, who guessed the fatigues of a long journey third class, and insisted on twenty-four hours of rest.

And now let me ask anyone who from youth upwards has greatly loved two things, scenery and adventure, if memory holds anything to compare with such a first experience? The Schildhorn is of course a beginner's mountain but it gives one a taste of the whole thing – an unequalled view of the 'three Bernese giants', as it is almost impossible to help calling them, and above all the sonority of perpetual avalanches – one of the most beautiful noises under Heaven. The boys were then about twelve and fourteen, and there was a moment when it seemed the younger was about to receive a thrashing from his father for collapsing in the snow and declaring, while tears ran down his blue little nose, that he could go no farther; but who could stand up, or rather lie down, against Wach? On the top of that mountain I noticed what was so often to strike me afterwards, that in the joy of difficulties vanquished the mind of Fainthearts is miraculously cleansed from all memory of these passing weaknesses.

I began my career as mountain climber with a bit of bad luck. At a dance in England, saving a fall of the usual kind, I had strained one of my knees slightly, but felt it for only a day or two. Needless to say it was this very knee that was struck bullet-fashion by a bounding bit of rock on the up journey, about 4,000 feet from the top. In all I walked eleven hours with that damaged knee, including leaping down the mountain with the leg held stiff which of course jarred the hip, and the result was for the time an end to mountaineering. The disappointment only ceased to rankle when for the first time I saw the Gotthard and was well on the way to Venice, little knowing what awaited me there.

To my amazement I was met on the platform by Heinrich only, and horror-stricken I learned that Lisl was once more in family fetters. Not only had her mother suddenly turned up, but also the one being who in their youth had slipped through the meshes of Frau von Stockhausen's anti-friend net, and been tolerated as high-born distant cousin – a young lady of a certain age, called Mathilde, hitherto on mere cousinly terms with Lisl, but who now at once made common cause with my enemy in cold-shouldering the foreign intruder.

Never had anyone a more disastrous first sight of Venice. I had cut short my stay at home on purpose to see everything with the Herzogenbergs; what happened was the most humiliating and unsuccessful game of hide-and-seek ever played, it being understood that the sight of me drove Frau von Stockhausen into convulsions. Four days were spent lurking in corridors, slinking into side chapels, jamming down my parasol over my face in gondolas and so forth; till at last, given Lisl's dislike of conflicts and utter helplessness as regards the whole situation, I departed prematurely – in sorrow but still more in anger – for Florence. I had thought my mother difficult to deal with, but she was sweet reasonableness itself compared to that beautiful old termagant.

Not being Pater or the terrible Ruskin, I will not launch forth into ravings about Florence; besides which, my leg being evidently in a bad way, enterprise was checked for the moment. Lest the dreaded fate of immobility should overtake me, which it soon did, I determined to lay in a stock of human companionship, and at once went to call on the Hildebrands. They lived outside the Porta Romana in a convent at S. Francesco di Paola, the immense ground floor of which had been turned into studios. From the floor above, decorated with frescos by Hildebrand and his friends, and full of beautiful things, you got what is perhaps the most famous view of Florence, and behind the house was a neglected garden. The family consisted of several children, mostly girls – all of them budding sculptors, painters or poetesses – and Frau Hildebrand, once a celebrated man-enslaver and still gracious and desirable though no longer in her first youth. One almost regretted that so much receptivity to the touch of life had been finally tamed to domestic uses, for nowadays she was rather by way of being fattish and motherly on principle. Yet I remember one evening of reminiscent youthful grace, when after some little domestic festival they all accompanied their guests as far as the Porta Romana; then suddenly she danced a step or two down hill among the fireflies, and I saw a graceful Bacchante hanging aslant between me and the moon. She was a great dear, radiating warmth, kindness and hospitality, but I got on best with him.

There was a queer mixture of simplicity and shrewdness about Hildebrand – a lawyer's shrewdness I mean, not the peasant cunning of a Rodin, aware of the market and for all his genius never forgetting it. The public only existed for Hildebrand as a corrective. He used to ask what one thought of his statues, and once when I said a certain arm looked to me too long, he explained that though as a matter of fact it was too short, the remark put him on the track of the real error, which was elsewhere; a thing I have often felt myself about the judgement of the man in the street – the only criticism of real value, as a rule, to the artist. He was a tremendous arguer and theorizer, and would discourse till all hours of the night on a subject like '*Raumvorstellung*' for instance ('concept of cubic content' is the nearest English I can find) and its connection with plastic art. His talk was so free from pedantry, so luminous, that any artist, or indeed any cultivated being, could listen to it with pleasure, and watch his clear laughing eyes become like pinpoints, as, with raised forefinger, he drove his argument home.

Of the other couple of prospective friends, the Brewsters, I had learned a great deal from Lisl, her deep admiration for her extraordinary sister having been the main theme of many letters. It appeared that these relations of hers were superhumans and that they lived in an Ivory Tower, knowing not a soul in Florence except the Hildebrands. This solitary frequentation was born of the fact that once, in pre-S. Francesco days, Hildebrand found the mysterious lady who lived on the floor below them sitting patiently on the stairs with a sprained ankle, whereupon he carried her into her apartment. Nothing short of that would have done it. I knew that Julia Brewster was eleven years older than her husband (who at that time was thirty-one) and had heard about their extraordinary views on marriage which did not commend themselves to Lisl, though, as she often insisted, they lived in a world of their own and could not be judged by ordinary standards. It appeared that they had only gone through the marriage ceremony in church in order to avoid wounding the feelings of Julia's family and had found it very 'comic' at the time – especially some incident about hassocks which I have forgotten – but it was not looked upon as a binding engagement. If either of the couple should weary of married life, or care for someone else, it was understood that the bond was dissoluble, and there was a firm belief on both sides that no such event could possibly destroy, or even essentially interrupt, their 'friendship' as they called it, founded as it was on more stable elements than mere marriage ties. 'Do not be afraid,' they said, 'of anything life may bring; face it, assimilate it, and the gods will see you through.' (I may add that such was H.B.'s gospel to the end, though as the years passed he came to realize there is a thing called human nature, and didn't quarrel with it for sometimes playing havoc with theories.)

This much I had gleaned from hearsay concerning Lisl's relations; face to face with them I soon found out that the real hermit was Julia, her husband being rather an embryonic lover of humanity, hitherto accustomed, owing to circumstances, to pay exclusive attention to abstractions. As I learned many years afterwards Julia was just then beginning to notice in him a new and strange impulse to extend a furtive hand to his fellow creatures and thought it wisest to offer no opposition. Thus it came to pass that instead of being politely warned off the premises as I had half expected, I was warmly welcomed in Via de' Bardi.

My acquaintance with the man destined to become my greatest friend began, it is amusing to reflect, with 'a little aversion' on my part, although his personality was delightful. Having for years had no real intercourse with anyone save his wife, he was very shy – a shyness like that of a well-brought-up child, and which took the form of extreme simplicity, as though he were falling back on first principles to see him through. In one who was obviously what is called an *âme d'élite* this trait was of charming effect and in spite of it he managed to be witty, amusing, and when he felt one liked him, companionable. He seemed to have read all books, to have thought all thoughts; and last but not least was extremely good looking, clean shaven but for a moustache, a perfect nose and brow, brown eyes set curiously far apart, and fair fluffy hair. It was the face of a dreamer and yet of an acute observer, and his manner was the gentlest, kindest, most courteous manner imaginable. But alas! . . . as thinker I found him detestable! Half American, half English, brought up in France, he was a passionate Latin, and the presence of an Anglomaniac, loud in praise of the sportsman type of male, and what was worse, in love with Germany, goaded him into parodoxes and *boutades* it was impossible to listen to with equanimity: such as that Shakespeare was an agglomerate of bombast and bad writing; that Goethe's gush about Nature was positively indecent; that a work written without *de l'affectation* is coarse; that spontaneity is the death of inspiration, and so on.

His inveterate dislike of everything German was shared, oddly enough, by his wife who, half German, half Austrian, had a Polish strain on the mother's side. Julia was the strangest human being, if human she was, that I or anyone else ever came across, fascinating, enigmatic, unapproachable, with a Schiller-like profile and pale yellow hair; and though completely under the spell, I knew far less of her at the end of my two Italian winters than at the beginning. The home medium of this extraordinary couple was French – a fact that deeply impressed Lisl and me; they addressed each other in the second person plural, and though evidently the greatest of friends never uttered a word in presence of others that could suggest anything as bourgeois as affection. Given their turn of mind it may be imagined that the matrimonial angle of the Herzogenbergs seemed to them comic, parochial, and slightly redolent of sauerkraut; moreover Julia spoke of Lisl as one might of some charming, very musical woman one had met somewhere and would be quite pleased to meet again if not pressed to fix the date. I was jealous for my friend, thinking of her uncritical worship of this gently critical sister, but the Brewsters were more amused at my enthusiasm than convinced that anyone who patted her husband's hand in public could be a really civilized human being. In fact the domestic aspect of life was deemed negligible, and my first impression of that household was two dear little fair-haired children, beautifully dressed, to whom, as they slunk out of the drawing-room, no one said good-night. I believe this attitude was modified later; certainly when after many years, during which we never met, their father and I came together again, he had become to his children what he was, I think, to everyone who knew him intimately – the one person who counted.

To sum up, the Brewsters came under no known category; both of them were stimulating, original talkers and quite ready to discuss their ethical scheme, including its application to domestic life, but of course only as a general thesis. On the other hand their friend Frau Hildebrand, human and natural to a fault, and who claimed for herself the wisdom of Sancho Panza, would privately maintain that all these fine theories must inevitably crumble at the first touch of the realities against which they so carefully fenced themselves in – a proposition I vehemently disputed, being quite carried off my feet by the impersonal magnificence and daring of their outlook. This readiness to cope with any and every turn of the wheel on your own terms went well with my views as to how life should be lived – but I had never dreamed of courage and love of adventure on such a scale as this.

My initial dislike of H. B.'s mentality began to yield to interest as he proceeded to open up a mind hitherto hermetically sealed to the Latin race. In spite of my mother's leanings the only countries that counted for me were England and Germany, and no John Bull ever held more foolish notions as to French superficiality and moral instability . . . a confession it costs me something to make even now, years after conversion. It was H. B. who first persuaded me to study Flaubert, Baudelaire and Verlaine seriously, introduced me to Anatole France, and kindled a flame of enthusiasm for French literature generally that was an endless subject of dispute between me and Lisl – both by letter and otherwise. On that rock, however, I beat in vain; there is no bridging the gulf between Latin and Teutonic civilization, and her aversion to French poetry is common to all Germans, though few of them express it as frankly and forcibly as she did.

Just before I left Florence news came that the Brewsters' château near Grenoble, a grand old pile made habitable by them at great expense, had been burned to the ground. Julia, the superwoman, was overwhelmed, and remained invisible for two or three days, but the bearing of H.B. was a revelation to me; he took it as one might take the loss of an old cigarette-holder. It was understood, my Italy having been a failure owing to my lameness, that I was to come back in the autumn, and early in July (1883) I left for Berchtesgaden, where the Herzogenbergs were building a little house, and which lay on the road to my real destination – a Bavarian village called Aibling, where there was a primitive but well-spoken-of mud-bath cure.

At Berchtesgaden I had a *Wiedersehen* with my friends that effaced all memories of the Venice fiasco, he being delighted with my musical output, and she, whose letters had given me a foretaste of the old tender comradeship, apparently bent on bringing its enduringness home to me.

In connection with my adoring reverence for Julia an amusing little psychological study awaited me; now for the first time a slight tinge of criticism crept into Lisl's appreciation of her wonderful sister. On one point we saw eye to eye. My home life at Frimhurst had always been warm and human, and though I was not fond of small children, I did not like to see them excluded from the general scheme as they were in Via de' Bardi. As for other aspects of life in the Ivory Tower, I discovered that Lisl had but vague notions as to the exact tenets of her strange relations, and above all seemed wholly unacquainted with the Julia I knew, my account of whose opinions and points of view seemed to produce a bewildering effect on her mind. This was not surprising. The Brewsters were not apostles of their own creed, least of all among the Gentiles, and apart from her dislike of conflicts Lisl would shrink from discussions that might chill the warm temperature she longed for in that quarter. But in face of my admiring trumpeting forth of their gospel it was difficult to shirk comment, particularly on the burning subject of the marriage bond. She realized, and slightly resented, their gentle ridicule of her own simple, instinctive views, would stoutly defend them, and like Frau Hildebrand maintained that when it comes to the point, everybody, no matter what their theories may be, feels exactly like the concierge and his wife. Still there was no denying the fact that neither of her relations could be called instinctive and simple, and she had nothing to oppose to my amused and rather scornful refrain: 'But . . . you don't *know* them!' In short our conversations on the Brewster mentality, as regards this particular point at least, led to nothing, and as they evidently rather distressed her were not persisted in. After all, as she said, there was little likelihood of these fantastic theories of theirs ever being put to the test, so we left it at that.

Meanwhile I pottered about, my leg being still leaden, and incidentally got through a good deal of sketching; but the great event of that sojourn in Berchtesgaden was that now for the first time I made real friends with Madame Schumann.

With all her sixty-odd years Frau Schumann was more a child than any of us, and up to that time, as she afterwards confessed, the new element in the life of her beloved Lisl had rather upset her. But once Frau Schumann accepted you it was generously done. I had written a little *Prelude and Fugue for the Thin People*, thus styled because the hands crossed rapidly and continually, deeply invading each other's territory. This piece she was determined to study, and when I gently demurred, from modesty of course, she flared up in her own peculiar fashion with, '*Aber* so *stark bin ich doch nicht!*' ('I'm not as fat as all that!') – a phrase that gave play to that endearing little lisp of hers. Her daughters reported her as completely engrossed in this athletic problem, murmuring to herself amidst her struggles, '*Gehen* muss *es aber!*' ('It *must* be managed!') and in the end it was dedicated to her, title and all, by special request. She had visited England regularly for nearly half a century, but all the English she knew was 'Alright!' spoken as one word and thrown into her German haphazard, as often as not inappropriately. One day, fancying I had offended her, I sent over an apologetic note to her lodging, and presently back came a card with 'ALRIGHT!' written on it, for once applied as intended. Another time I found her examining a sketch I had made of the fine old cloisters at Berchtesgaden, the colour effect of which I was rather pleased with; after a painful silence she remarked, 'But surely those cloisters are not all blue and yellow like an Austrian bank note?' She then hastily

added, 'But what do I know about painting? Nothing at all!' and I had
to assure and reassure her that I was not at all hurt.

I always think with amusement of one of Frau Schumann's unexpected little rages, because one so often suffers under the cause oneself.
Two or three of her humble satellites had followed her to Berchtesgaden, much encouraged thereto by her daughters, who found their
mother's holiday passion for cards excessive; and one day, just as they
had started a game of Skat, one of the satellites observed that if they
had thought of it they might have played dummy Whist instead.
'There!' cried Frau Schumann, 'if there is one thing I abominate it is
people who as soon as you have settled down to one game suggest
another, or when you are going to play one piece ask for some other
piece . . . *Ach! diese ungeregelten Geister!*' ('these undisciplined spirits!'), and so on, till her wrath died down in Lisl's peals of laughter.
It wasn't everyone however who had Lisl's courage and could carry it
off; in other company the air was often thunderous for quite a long
time after one of these outbursts, till suddenly the thunderer herself
came forth with her indescribably beautiful smile from behind the
clouds, and all was well. These are the faults that endear people to
you almost more than their virtues.

I only stayed a short time at Berchtesgaden, the pressing matter
being to get my leg cured, and departed for Aibling with a half-promise
from the Herzogenbergs to join me there later. Aibling, like all places
where you have finally got rid of a haunting terror – for Johnny's fate
had been much in my mind, as in my mother's – is a loved recollection.
But for a diminutive *Kur Haus* it was an enchanting, absolutely primitive village, cut in two by a couple of clear brown streams running
parallel to each other, and spanned every hundred yards or so by
wooden bridges – and at the back of beyond was a most rugged,
threatening-looking section of the Alps. I spent an exquisite August
there, learning quantities of Rossetti by heart while under treatment;
and one evening, following one of the little rivers up a rocky valley,
laughing young voices rang out, and round the corner I came upon
some twenty naked youths, bathing, skylarking, and chasing each
other among the trees. Here at last was a bit of old Greece . . . and it
was my miserable duty to walk on hurriedly looking the other
way! . . .

By a wonderful bit of luck I came in for one of the village ceremonies
that still survive in Catholic Alpine districts, the consecration of the
Aibling Veteran Society's new banner. No fewer than fifty-seven

societies attended this festival with thirteen bands. At their head marched a magnificent peasant girl dressed like a *vivandière* (I wish I had asked why) followed by twenty Aibling virgins in white muslin and blue ribbons, whose twenty self-conscious, stuck-up-looking countenances shone blowsily beneath flowery wreaths. All the women and most of the men wore gorgeous old peasant costumes, and as the procession wound among the little bridges, crossing and re-crossing the rivulets to the sound of *Volkslieder* beautifully played, I could have wept that, knowing nothing of the festival, I had not urged the Herzogenbergs to come one day sooner. When they did arrive they fell head over ears in love with the place, as I had promised them they would, and a week later I started for England, happier than I had been for months.

The Frimhurst situation I came home to this time was, if anything, more fantastic than ever. I recently lit upon a tragi-comic letter to Lisl describing it in full: the unutterable jollity of the young ones; the chatter at the breakfast table which always fascinated me afresh; the ever-recurring financial crises; Papa's announcement that in *two or three years* (!) we must let Frimhurst; mother's tears at this prospect; her countless new and gorgeous gowns; my estimate of their cost; and finally the abstention of us younger ones from butter and sugar – an attempt at bringing moral weight to bear on our parents which entirely missed fire. We children thought they must love our home less than we did, otherwise surely they would take action, but of course it was the common shrinking of minds no longer young and elastic from drastic resolutions.

In the autumn I met for the first time the Empress Eugénie, who after the death of the Prince Imperial had settled at Farnborough, and who became the most wonderful friend to me and mine. I remember saying to a mutual friend that it was hard to believe that she could ever have been more beautiful than now, and the reply was, 'I think in some ways she is more beautiful now than when she was young, because years and sorrow have done away with the accidents of beauty – youth itself for instance, and colouring – and revealed the exquisiteness of design.' And as first impression another incident may be recorded – a very characteristic one. A fat middle-aged Jewess of vast possessions, whose elaborate red-gold wig indicated what the colour of her hair may have been in her youth, and who possibly had resembled the Empress in other respects some twenty-five or thirty years ago (which she proclaimed to the world was the case), informed her hostess over the tea-table at Farnborough Hill that she was constantly being taken for her in London. A thrill of secret horror and amusement ran through the assembled company, but the Empress's rejoinder, innocent of the faintest tinge of secret irony, was, '*Mais c'est très flatteur pour moi, Madame, puisque je suis bien plus âgée que vous*' – the first of innumerable lessons in good manners one was to learn in that school.

The following spring (1884) in Italy more than made up for the previous year's failure. I worked as never before and contrived between whiles, alone and happy, to see most of the principal Umbrian towns; also Rome, where, the lodging of my desires being owned by a hairdresser who declared he never let rooms, inspiration prompted me to let down my hair, whereupon he gave in at once. In Hildebrand vein I ask, where except in Italy could you find a landlord like that?

An exquisite trait in the Italians, the only race I am uncritically in love with, is this easy response to a human touch, a certain closeness to nature which welds all ranks together at the base. Their heads may be in different social strata but the feet of all are on that rock. In spite of imperious authority on the one side and unbounded reverence on the other, my old friend of later years, that greatest of great ladies Donna Laura Minghetti, treated her butler and was treated by him as an equal at bottom, and it is the same throughout Italian society. That very spring I am writing about, thanks to my one aristocratic friend, the Dowager Duchess of Sermoneta, who took me to all sorts of otherwise invisible villas, I was privileged to see a certain fat Marchesa, bearer of an historic name, rating her gardener so furiously that apoplexy seemed imminent, when the old man gently put his hand on her arm and said, 'But, *figlia mia*, peas won't grow in the open in February.' My very first essay in shopping the year before had given me a taste of the quality I mean, to which I owe as many twinges of delight, walking the country, as to the scenery itself. They had told me that people who have a soul above haggling are looked upon by Italian shopkeepers as dull and unsportsmanlike, in fact that to buy anything without bargaining is equivalent to shooting a sitting pheasant. I bargained therefore over a certain teapot as keenly as my knowledge of the language allowed; suddenly it was put into my hands at my own price, with the remark, 'Do me at least the pleasure to break it soon!' . . . And then the politeness of them, the serene disregard of red tape in Post Offices and other solemn places! At that time attempts were being made to bring home to the people the dangers of spitting, and noticing that this national custom was nevertheless in full swing, I once asked casually in an up-to-date hospital whether spitting was forbidden in the corridors? The answer was: '*Sissignora, ma faccia pure il suo commodo.*' ('Yes, Madam, but don't let that inconvenience you.') How I loved, how I love the Italians! . . .

I had known for some time that Salomonstrasse 19 was among the many monuments of dead and gone burgher ideals doomed to demolishment; that summer the blow fell, so that when I went back to Leipzig in October new quarters, with the indispensable outlook over green, had to be found. The loss of the dear attic suite would have been heart-breaking but for the fact that my days in Leipzig were numbered; for it was now an open secret that Herzogenberg had accepted a post offered him by Joachim (Professor of Composition at the Hochschule) and of course I was to follow them to Berlin. Having to say goodbye to certain friends in Leipzig would be very sad, but on the other hand I looked forward to studying the Prussians – after all the hub of the German Empire – at close quarters.

I remember vividly two incidents in that winter season. When I think of one of them my blood boils even now; the other is among the most delightful memories of my life.

The first was connected with the Egyptian Campaign of 1884–5, throughout the course of which I had been lectured right and left by the Germans. The culminating point was the death of Gordon, a hideous tragedy that made me ashamed to look anyone in the face and was the beginning of a life-long horror of the Liberal Party. A day or two after the news came I was sitting in the Limburgers' box at a Gewandhaus concert, and so was the Commandant of the Leipzig garrison, a well-known 1870 General of the thin, snappy type. Suddenly, during the interval, he turned on me, and in loud rasping tones expressed his opinion of a nation that left its best servants in the lurch. The offensiveness of his manner was indescribable, but being only too conscious of deep national humiliation I let the waves meet over my head. At last Frau Limburger, in spite of the absurd awe in which these military bigwigs are held, took up the cudgels and asked why they should arraign poor me for the sins of the English Government? To this the Commandant solemnly replied that on the contrary it was the duty of right-thinking people to seize every opportunity of bringing home 'our German feeling in this matter' to all and any members of the offending race. I am quoting verbatim from a contemporary record the words of a distinguished General Officer to a young stranger dwelling in their midst! . . . This time, and no mistake, I realized that as regards our country Germany was a huge cistern full to the brim of hatred – military hatred anyhow – and that I was sitting under the escape pipe.

It is a relief to turn to the other incident, the realization of a long cherished hope – namely my mother's visit to Leipzig, which fell in April 1885. Naturally I wanted her to be a success in every way, and as it turned out her triumphal progress among my friends flattered my fondest desires. I never saw her more entirely at her best, more radiant. Of the effect of the music on her I have already spoken, and knowing how it would increase her pleasure I used to play beforehand the themes and chief beauties of everything she was going to hear. My dear kind friends competed with each other for her presence in their *Logen*, lent her their carriages and generally showered hospitality upon her. But what made me happiest was her adoration of Lisl, who was so perfect with her that even now, thinking of it, my eyes fill with tears. They saw each other daily and mother's room was always stocked with flowers sent by her: 'I have always loved you for loving them,' she said. After Lisl, I think Frau Limburger was nearest to her heart; she saw at once how the jolly home life, more reminiscent of Frimhurst than anything I found elsewhere in Leipzig, must appeal to me, and knew how generously I had been allowed to share it. Of course too she at once detected the breeding hidden beneath eccentricities of manner that endeared that old friend to one rather than otherwise – in a word saw eye to eye with me in everything.

The finale was a grand dinner party given by her to many whose kindness to me had been unwearying for the last seven years. She looked amazingly handsome, wearing all her diamonds, and insisted on Herzogenberg taking her in to dinner – a touch everyone appreciated – Lisl being on the other side of her left-hand neighbour. Dr Philipp Fiedler wrote a really charming poem in her honour, full of course of kindly references to her daughter. Limburger's speech, for there were several, was brilliant, funny, and in English, and she took Wach's, the polished diction of which was a little beyond her, for granted, asking me afterwards if his German wasn't rather *difficult*. The next day she went back to England, and I am certain was not exaggerating when she said many and many a time afterwards that she had never been happier in her life than during that fortnight.

Soon afterwards the Herzogenbergs left Leipzig, and I, who was going next day to Crostewitz (where I usually spent ten days or so before returning to Frimhurst), went to the station to see the last of them, as the phrase runs . . . to see the last of them, as one says hundreds of times in a lifetime with an unforeboding heart. I remember few dates, but that date, 7 May, will be remembered to my dying day. As the train moved off and slowly rounded the curve, I saw Lisl still waving at the window . . . never to see her again in this world, except in dreams.

The Break with Lisl

I have now reached a difficult part of my Memoirs, in that it is not possible for me to relate the inner history of an event that shaped my whole existence. The merest indications must suffice, such as will render the rest of my story intelligible, and above all throw light on what was for me the apex of the tragedy and the dominating fact of the years yet to be dealt with in these pages – my severance from the Herzogenbergs.

It is a question whether a sorrow such as a broken friendship can be allowed to assume in the written page the proportions it did in real life. Personally the dissolution of anything that once had strong vitality, from a civilization to a human bond, has always interested me even more than origins. I remember, for instance, how the gradual turning into hatred of Saul's love for David – still to my mind one of the burning incidents in literature – preoccupied me as a child, and it was the same with the disappearance of the Aztec civilization. Perhaps others feel as I do about this particular form of death in life. I hope so, for if the only claim to interest put forth by a writer is that his tale is faithfully told in every detail, how can one treat what went deepest as a side issue? It must be remembered that this friendship was the cornerstone of the keenly lived, complex sort of existence I have been trying to describe, and that when it gave way life had to be begun afresh – which, as a wise woman I know once said, is a thing we must be prepared to do an indefinite number of times to the very end. But apart from other considerations the case in question seems to me unusual, puzzling, indeed almost inexplicable as psychological study. I spoke of a way of looking at moral problems, as with eyes devoid of eye-lashes, which even in the days of youthful enthusiasm struck me as characteristically German; it may be that in this experience with my friend I struck a primal strain of nationality. Be that as it may, after all these years I think I can undertake to tell the story fairly and without bitterness; almost as impersonally, too, as if it had happened – which sometimes seems to be the case – to someone else. But first I must go back a little.

It may be remembered that the Brewsters held unusual views concerning the bond between man and wife, views which up to the time of my arrival on the scene had not been put to the proof by the touch of reality. My second visit to Florence was fated to supply the test. Harry Brewster and I, two natures to all appearance diametrically opposed, had gradually come to realize that our roots were in the same soil – and this I think is the real meaning of the phrase to complete one another – that there was between us one of those links that are part of the Eternity which lies behind and before Time. A chance wind having fanned and revealed at the last moment, as so often happens, what had long been smouldering in either heart, unsuspected by the other, the situation had been frankly faced and discussed by all three of us; and I then learned, to my astonishment, that his feeling for me was of long standing, and that the present eventuality had not only been foreseen by Julia from the first, but frequently discussed between them. To sum up the position as baldly as possible, Julia, who believed the whole thing to be imaginary on both sides, maintained it was incumbent on us to establish, in the course of further intercourse, whether realities or illusions were in question. After that – and surely there was no hurry – the next step could be decided on. This view H. B. allowed was reasonable. My position, however, was that there could be no next step, inasmuch as it was my obvious duty to break off intercourse with him at once and for ever. And when I left Italy that chapter was closed as far as I was concerned.

I then went, as has been related, to Berchtesgaden, and there, accustomed as I was to lay bare my life before her, Lisl had learned all there was to know. Blame neither attached to me nor was laid at my door; we saw eye to eye in all points, and parted, as may be imagined, more closely if more tragically knit than ever.

But before I had been many weeks in England it became manifest that the chapter was not closed after all, and a correspondence began between my two Florentine friends and myself which continued throughout the following winter – the winter which culminated in my mother's visit to Leipzig. The point under discussion was whether my policy of cutting the cable was appropriate to this particular case, whether it would not be to the advantage of all three of us (which was H. B.'s contention) that he and I should continue friends – not necessarily meeting, but at least corresponding.

If the people concerned in a drama such as this are respectively cruel, treacherous, faithless or hypocritical, any and every development is conceivable; but in this case, insane as we may all seem, neither were H. B. and I bent on pursuing a selfish end regardless of giving pain, nor was Julia consciously playing a part. The story of those months – a fantastic chapter in psychology – will never be told by me, if only for the reason that it is not my story alone; what has been said must suffice – and I think it will suffice – more or less to explain Lisl's subsequent action. And if asked how I came to swerve from my decision not even to discuss the 'friendship' theory, I can only say that the case was not as simple as it seems, and that a very genuine doubt existed in my mind as to how I ought to act – a doubt shared at times, though I think against her better judgement, by Lisl herself.

That winter was not a happy time for either her or me. Every turn in the situation, every action, every thought of my heart was known to her, and if those who were presently to hound the Furies in my direction had counted on having revelations to contribute they were disappointed. But the fact of my having gone back on my first decision not to discuss the matter disquieted her profoundly. She knew and allowed that I was not playing for my own hand, but her simple instinctive nature, distrustful of subtleties and superhuman points of view, clung to the proven ways of tradition rather than the road I was travelling. On the other hand, to admit her contention that all wives feel the same in certain cases, human nature being always bound to have the last word, would to my mind have implied scepticism where I felt profound faith, as also to drag a proud banner – and it was not my banner only – in the mud. Thus there were interminable and sometimes distressing arguments – distressing especially for her since she was not sure of her ground. But I was, or thought I was, sure enough of mine; borne along by the strongest, most intoxicating wind that drives human souls before it, being moreover the only person among those concerned who had taken her into confidence, as often as not I ended by bringing her round to my point of view – in other words I dragged her out of her orbit.

It is easy afterwards to say, as some of her critics did, that she ought to have stood up to me better. Later on she ascribed her quasi-acquiescence in the situation to affection for me; but a greater reason was her own uncertainty, and the greatest, perhaps, the moral and physical shrinking of a diseased heart from perpetual warfare. And all this time she was suffering . . . suffering; but her self-control and power of making the moment suffice were such that not till years afterwards did I realize it fully.

Thus the winter wore on. Shortly before we parted that May morning, one of her relations, I think her brother, had written to her insinuating things so unjust and cruel about me, that every other feeling had been overborne by the old faithful protecting love which, in spite of some difficult moments, had never really failed me. Let one trivial incident show how impossible it was for me to foresee what was to happen, how far she herself was from foreseeing it. That evening I took her some roses; she was out, and the next day the following little note arrived, written in her quaint English (which signified, in later years, a harking back to the tender springtime days of our friendship) – signed, for the last time, with the name she had given herself:

Your roses touched me deeply, my darling. I am quite warmed up by their scent and colour, and soothed by their nice cool touch. It was something so new and old at the same time to get flowers from you, and you don't know the pleasure you made me. What pleasure little things can sometimes make! Darling, have faith in my faith. I have a heavy heart and still I enjoy somehow the idea of having to fight for you, for my true loyal child. Don't distrust me when a word seems sometimes to contradict me! *Credo, credo in te!*

Your old, old Mother.

From Leipzig she went straight to Dresden where she was to encounter the brother, but before they had met she wrote me a long letter to Crostewitz, in which the differences between us are once more threshed out; full of tenderness and pain it ends thus:

Ethel! child of my sorrow! . . . I was too tired and miserable, after all, to write in the train, so waited till I got here, but I doubt if the result will give you much pleasure! Farewell! . . . if I loved you less how little I should suffer!

Your faithful Lisl.

Meanwhile, as various wild reports had reached my host and hostess, who knew that whole Florentine group, I told them the real story in confidence, informed Lisl I had done so, and waited day by day in great agitation for news of what was happening in Dresden. It was our custom to write to each other once a week, sometimes oftener, and now, at the most critical moment of our lives, dead silence! . . . Not till I was back in England did the longed-for letter, dated 15 June 1885, arrive, and if in comparison with others I was to receive later it is still almost loving, there was a new tone in it – the work of disintegration had begun. Its gist was that our common life could not continue for the present, and that if it gave me as much pain to read these words as her to write them, she thought I would nevertheless see, on reflection, that it was inevitable. Of breach not a word; on the contrary entreaties for 'good' letters that should show her I understood and accepted the situation. This was not all however; reproaches were levelled against others, demands made, past incidents raked up, and my replies were as may be imagined; in fact it was a correspondence between two worn-out people, disputing as to which particular wave had cast the vessel on the rocks, and whether shipbuilder, chartmaker or captain was to blame.

Suddenly her letters ceased altogether. As I afterwards learned a new figure had now come on the scene, a woman whose chronic jealousy was a legend, and who during my long spell of delightful intercourse with her and her husband had had cause, in early days – perhaps during a week – for jealousy.* It had happened long ago, the whole thing was utterly harmless, born of high spirits and vanity, indeed more jocular on both sides than anything else; still no doubt I deserved the drubbing administered by Lisl after confession. Since this peccadillo jealousy had died down – as well it might – and all three of us had been the best of friends and comrades ever afterwards.

It is only fair to say that this lady was much attached to Julia Brewster, and rather late in the day had developed into a strong upholder of the domestic hearth – as beseems a convert, a jealous woman, and a mother; all the same I sometimes wonder whether in that summer of 1885 some real cause of complaint against her husband accounted for the zeal with which they both joined in the hue and cry led by my old enemy. Men and women are mean on different lines, and there is a particular sort of male meanness inherent in the relations of the sexes which permits erring husbands to go to great lengths in the way of propitiation; otherwise I cannot account for this belated

* References in later pages make it clear that the woman was Frau Hildebrand.

doublebarrelled zeal against me. But its effect was deadly, for it appears to have been a necessity of Lisl's nature to harden her heart against me before she could summon up courage to break our bond; and just because these two were by way of being my friends, their influence told where ancient animosity such as that of her relations would probably have achieved nothing.

At length in August came a letter in which only the exquisite hand-writing – she used German characters and made them strong, flowing and decorative – reminded me of Lisl. There were no fresh accusations to bring, but everything I was and ever had been was drawn by the hand of a stranger – almost of an enemy. It appeared I was a Juggernaut car driven by a *Lebensteufel*, or rather a wild horsewoman blinded by self-love, galloping rough-shod over all I met. It was conceded that I was innocent of desire to wreck any fellow mortal's happiness, least of all that of a woman I dearly loved, but of what avail, asks the writer, are innocence and excellent intentions if none the less devastation marks your path? . . . And harshly as she judged me, the rest of the situation she gauged correctly; reading what she had to relate, as one divorced from theories and at last in contact with the realities of a situation, it became evident to me that human nature had indeed pre-vailed over superhumanity. The scales fell from my eyes and I sud-denly saw myself, not as co-adjutator in a noble reading of Destiny, but simply as thief of someone else's goods . . .

Lisl had spoken of devastation; but if for a passing moment there was a phase that seemed to come under that heading, the chief agent was the evil genius of that group, my old enemy. Where tact, wisdom, moderation, fairness were needed, bitter, reckless violence held the field – but that too I only learned long afterwards; meanwhile what more obvious than that I, and I alone, was responsible for every-thing? . . . To return to the letter, I was upbraided for venturing to reproach the writer for her long silence, for mentioning my own pain at all in this connection seeing what others were suffering, for speaking as if I had any claim on her as compared to the claims of others. Then came bitter self-reproaches for having played her part so ill during the past winter, and I guessed she felt that from the first her line should have been: 'Act thus and thus, or our friendship must come to an end.' Would it have changed anything? Possibly . . . for the time being . . . for life was inconceivable to me without Lisl; but no such ultimatum had been presented – an omission for which she was never to forgive herself. Finally she wrote that her expiation must be to give me up –

that the only reparation I could make was to accept the fact . . . and disappear. Hardly believing my eyes I read that, given my faculty of getting all there was to be got out of life, I should no doubt find consolation; and last of all, what cut me to the heart most, came the words: 'the foundering of our little boat is but an episode in the general shipwreck' . . .

Reliving this shock, as I did the other day, it seems to me strange that I did not go mad. For seven years my life had been as inextricably mixed up with the Herzogenbergs' lives, whether musically or humanly, as if I really had been their own child; so much so that when owing to her parents' jealousy I had to keep away from the house even for a day or two, it seemed to us a small tragedy. And such was my bottomless faith in Lisl, that though her letters abound in protestations of undying fidelity – a thing that strikes me curiously now – in none of mine is to be found the slightest word to call them forth. As soon would I have asked a promise from the sun to rise daily. If therefore the idea of even a temporary separation seemed to me, at first, monstrous, the core of the anguish was suddenly finding myself confronted with a total stranger. Had she written words such as these: 'However long our parting may last, if for ever and ever, believe in my faith and love as I do in yours; keep my picture bright and untarnished before your eyes, as I will yours before mine,' then I think – or so it seems to me now – that I could have achieved resignation. Of course her 'distress' is spoken of, but every word which could suggest that our past was a living, aching memory in her heart seemed to have been carefully eliminated.

I wrote to her, bewildered, appealingly, in despair, and received one or two more letters in reply, each colder than the last; finally, on 3 September, in the very words I should use today, I bade her farewell till better days should dawn, and silence fell between us – a silence to be broken by her, for one brief moment only, two years later.

As epilogue to this part of my story let me say that I am now old enough to realize how great a role our own hopes and desires play, without our knowing it, in the shaping of our course. This conceded, I can only say my mistaken reading of Julia's soul was honest, and that if that time were to be lived through again, I believe, given the lights I then possessed, that I should act as I did then; to do otherwise would have been to use a measure unfit for the standard of that case as I saw it. This I know; into that mistake of mine I put better stuff than into many a blameless enterprise of later years; and after all, if, as I said, the word 'success' does not mean for me all it implies, still less does the word 'failure'; how will our wisdom and our foolishness look to us in another world? Nevertheless I had been faithless to my own instincts – and for that the penalty had to be paid. The strands of what was to become the fundamental friendship of my life were severed, not to be re-joined for many years. I burned my boats and went into the desert.

And now the question was, how my future life should be shaped. Lili Wach, who had suspected nothing, was now told all – as far as such things can be told in letters. She never admitted for a moment that the breach could be anything but a passing necessity, and urged that for more reasons than one it was my obvious course to vanish for a while from the German scene. If I effaced myself in every way the waters would surely subside, whereas my presence among people who knew us both could only increase the gossip, turmoil and bitterness. Eventually I came to be of this opinion, and the fact that Herzogenberg was to enter on his duties in Berlin, not in 1886 but that very autumn, simplified matters. So I took the hardest resolution of my life – to remain quietly in England instead of going back to face the situation, which was my passionate desire. It was never easy to work at home – but I then believed I should never again work anywhere.

My mother, now fully informed, was perfect; the Leipzig visit had shown her my normal life abroad, and having learned to love Lisl she knew exactly what the breach signified in every sense. Being at bottom a very reasonable woman, she maintained that for the time being Lisl had probably no choice but to break off relations; but she too felt certain that inasmuch as no one accused me of anything but blindness and lack of judgement, all would come right in the end.

Meanwhile Lili Wach hoped much, and so did I, from a meeting between her and Lisl (hitherto successfully evaded by the latter) which was to come off in the early winter. But this last and best card was played in vain. It was impossible, wrote Lili, to elicit any satisfactory explanation of her attitude towards me. She had begun by saying it was forced upon her by others, then retracted and passionately declared it was herself who willed it so. The separation . . .yes, Lili Wach had answered – that I too accepted now as inevitable; but how should I or anyone who had watched our relation all these years understand the accompanying circumstances? How came Lili, for instance, to forward to her the letter of a third person who knew me but superficially, and who held that at bottom I was of a light nature, one incapable of deep feeling, who played with human material as a sculptor plays with clay? I can imagine the gentle, mordant irony with which Lisl would ask how the judgement of an outsider could possibly affect that of people who had known me for years and years? . . . and perhaps poor Lisl regretted that piteous attempt at self-justification. Then Lili had tried by every means in her power to hold up before unwilling eyes the picture of their common friend, feeling the while that she was achieving nothing. At last, after repeated entreaties not to pursue the subject, it had been dropped as hopeless, and therewith a painful interview had come to an end.

There is a wonderful poem by Goethe about the way the gods lead you into mischief and pass on, leaving you to bear the consequences as best you may. Often and often I thought of that poem in connection with the activities of the couple I spoke of; for this letter, the stone that brought down the avalanche, was from the husband! Surely there was something fantastic and impersonal about such a Nemesis for a harmless little flirtation . . .? For that reason I bore these blind instruments of Fate no grudge and met them with pleasure in after years.

I will not dwell upon other incidents of those nightmare months, on the campaign of defamation embarked on by my old enemy, at Florence and elsewhere, reports of which reached my mother and must have cut her to the heart. At last Conrad Fiedler wrote to Lisl urging her to break her damning silence – a silence the world could but interpret in one way, namely, that I had committed some heinous crime, and that my best friend, having now found me out, had repudiated me. Her reply was that those whose feelings it was her first duty to consult asked but one thing of her, to discuss the matter with no one, and that she was bound to respect that wish! . . . Finally I made up my mind to return to Leipzig in about a year's time, come what may – a decision approved by the Fiedlers who insisted that I should begin by staying at Crostewitz.

I left England in September 1886, going direct to where the Fiedlers were staying. More than a year had passed and Lisl had steadily refused to discuss the reasons of our now notorious breach with any of our mutual acquaintances. This being so, Conrad decided to constitute himself my champion in Leipzig, more especially since I now felt free to show him certain letters proving that Lisl had been told everything from the first, and that I was guiltless of deception, treachery or anything that could alienate anyone's sympathies, let alone merit social ostracism; also that if it was a question of apportioning blame for what had happened, others were at least as culpable as I. He thereupon wrote once more to Lisl, demanding as an act of *bare justice* that she should corroborate certain statements he proposed to make in certain quarters; and this time he gained his point.

The return to my old haunts taught me one thing, that human nature is kindlier than pessimists would have one believe. The Fiedlers told me that many of my old friends, notably Frau Limburger, had refused from the first to believe ill of me; that others had dimly suspected a situation unsuitable to the convenient black-and-white methods of melodrama; and that even those who had cheerfully believed the worst were not sorry to know they were wrong. Perhaps no one likes being taken in too grossly.

But one bitter disappointment awaited me; I ought to have foreseen it perhaps, but . . . I didn't. Soon after my return the Fiedlers left for Munich via Berlin, and Mary was full of the representations she meant to make to Lisl, which, she believed, must surely change the whole situation. Alas! the result merely showed what, when she chose to put them forth, Lisl's powers of persuasion and fascination could achieve. Up to now the two had been on rather distant terms; there was lack of affinity to start with, moreover when, as was the case with the Fiedlers, a husband interested Lisl more than the wife, she took no pains to conceal the fact – and Mary was accustomed to adulation. But on this occasion, as I read between the lines, she laid herself out to capture the whole position . . . and succeeded. In the pages upon pages I got from Berlin there is not the faintest allusion to the real point at issue, the harshness and brutality with which the breach had been effected, the early attempt to make the Fiedlers drop me, and all the rest of it, nor is my everlasting question, 'does she speak kindly of me?', as much as referred to. Feeling that after all I had been left in the lurch in a matter at least as vital to me as my good name, I wrote bitterly, and presently the interchange of letters ceased.

From February 1887 onwards I was no longer alone in my lodgings. Ella Limburger had met in the streets of Vienna, fallen in love with, purchased, and brought home, a huge sprawling yellow-and-white puppy of the long-haired kind generally seen dragging washerwomen's carts. Half St Bernard, and the rest what you please, Marco was an entrancing animal, but as there were already three sporting dogs of Julius's about the house, Ella yielded to my passionate entreaties and gave him to me.

For twelve years that dog was the joy of my life, and latterly the terror of my friends. Like many other geniuses Marco became nerve-rasped and ferocious in his old age, but in his youth, though always a desperate character, he was wholly amiable, and took to life on the third floor, his head reposing on the pedals of a seldom silent piano, as if washerwomen had never been heard of.

A greater philosopher, a more perfect comrade for a busy woman can never have existed; if, in the stress of work, I put off his dinner too long, all he did was to shut his eyes and moan very, very softly, like a baby. I gave him a toy, a thing called 'Marco's purse' – really a little netted blue bag with long strings, which eventually became a repulsive object but nevertheless travelled with us everywhere, wrapped in fold upon fold of the *Weekly Times*. Sometimes when bored, after many yawns and sighs he would get up and lay his head on my lap; but at the words 'Don't bother, Marco', he would stand still, reflecting, then suddenly pounce on his purse, roll over on to his back, hold it up between his paws, and making it sway backwards and forwards, alternately catch it in his mouth and let it go again. Having worked off his energy this way, he would get up, lie down very carefully on the exact centre of the purse, and go heavily to sleep – an object-lesson to many human beings.

I never knew a more hilarious temperament than his – so much so that, invited to attend a rehearsal Brahms was holding of his Piano Quintet at the flat of Brodsky the violinist, it seemed advisable for once to leave him in the street. I was seated at the piano turning over, when suddenly the door burst open and with a bound Marco was beside me, while the cellist's desk, taken in his stride, went crash. Having spoken disparagingly of the great man's sense of humour, it is only fair to say he rose to this occasion and declared the whole thing took him back to the Harlequinades of his youth.

Early in the music season I met the great violinist Sarasate in private life, and was amazed to find this sad, tragic, romantic looking man literally bubbling over with fun. That evening he had stepped for a moment into a *Carmen* performance and went into peals of laughter at the idea of any public accepting our admirable but hideous prima donna, Moran-Olden, as Carmen; although he greatly disliked Germans, it was well worth coming to Germany, he said, to see such a *'trait de mœurs'*. Talking to him I realized for the first time that though

139

Spaniards thoroughly endorse Mérimée's story, the treatment of it in the opera infuriates them, as does also the mitigated French handling of their desperate national rhythms. I knew too little of Spanish music to contest the point and as I love *Carmen* hope this is a purity of feeling to which only Spaniards need aspire; but all musically cultivated countrymen of his I have met since are of the same opinion as Sarasate.

I think it was in November that year that Fanny Davies and Brodsky played a Violin Sonata of mine in the Kammermusik, and the critics unanimously said it was devoid of feminine charm and therefore unworthy a woman – the good old remark I was so often to hear again.

In March 1888 I sent Joachim the Violin Sonata, hoping that though it had been mercilessly slated by the Press, he might perhaps be of a different opinion and see his way to performing it in London. I recommend his answer to the attention of any young musician assured by a great authority that he has no talent, for this, according to Joachim, was my case; he added a hope that I would not resent his expressing this conviction (which by the by he solemnly retracted twelve years later when I didn't care two straws what he thought) and comforted himself by reflecting that if my musical bent was genuine it would survive his lack of appreciation.

All this time I had been seeing a great deal of the von Webers, people I had met off and on in Leipzig society for many years, but who, though cultivated and musical, were not in the sacred Herzogenberg set. Weber, a captain in the Leipzig regiment, was either grandson or nephew of the composer, and his wife a Jewess, niece of old Madame Schwabe's; but what gave special point to intercourse with this couple was the constant presence in their house of Weber's great friend, Count Paul Vizthum, a Saxon officer on the Headquarters Staff. But for the fact that I knew he was deeply in love with a young married woman, a friend of mine, I think I should have completely succumbed to the charm of Vizthum, a sort of Bayard nearer forty than thirty, not exactly handsome but of a magnificent presence and a *grand seigneur*.

The poor Webers' subsequent history was tragic. Gustav Mahler, who was then one of the conductors at the Leipzig Opera, fell in love with her and his passion was reciprocated – as well it might be, for in spite of his ugliness he had demoniacal charm. A scandal would mean leaving the Army, and Weber shut his eyes as long as was possible, but Mahler, a tyrannical lover, never hesitated to compromise his mistresses. Things were getting critical, when one day, travelling to Dresden in the company of strangers, Weber suddenly burst out laughing, drew a revolver, and began taking William Tell-like shots at the head-rests between the seats. He was overpowered, the train brought to a standstill, and they took him to the police station raving mad – thence to an asylum. Always considered rather queer in the Army, the Mahler business had broken down his brain. I afterwards heard he had lucid intervals, that his wife in an agony of remorse refused to see her lover again . . . and the rest is silence.*

Mahler was far and away the finest conductor I ever knew, with the most all-embracing musical instinct, and it is one of the small tragedies of my life that just when he was considering the question of producing my opera *The Wreckers* at Vienna they drove him from office. At the time I am speaking of in Leipzig I saw but little of him, and we didn't get on; I was too young and raw then to appreciate this grim personality, intercourse with whom was like handling a bomb cased in razor-edges.

Throughout the greater part of the winter of 1887–8 the Griegs were in Leipzig and it is then that my real friendship with them began. When Grieg appeared on a platform, whether alone or accompanying his wife's superb rendering of his songs, the audience went mad, but there was a simplicity and purity of spirit about them that success could not tarnish. Out of action, these two tiny people looked like wooden figures from a Noah's Ark, the transfiguration which ensued when they got to work being all the more astonishing. Frau Grieg sang in Norwegian of course and one often had only a vague idea as to the meaning of the words, and one wept, laughed, and thrilled with excitement or horror without knowing why. The song over, she again became Noah's wife. Grieg is one of the very few composers I have met from whose lips you might hear as frank a confession as he once made concerning one of his later works. I had been so enthusiastic, and he was always so keen to get at honest impressions, that I ventured to say the coda of one of the movements seemed not quite up to the level of the rest. 'Ah yes!' he said, shrugging his shoulders, 'at that point inspiration gave out and I had to finish without!' I remember too on a certain occasion his being invited for a huge sum to conduct not only his own work but the whole programme, and refusing on the ground that he was too bad a conductor. 'But the public won't mind that,' pleaded the manager; 'they'll come to *see* you conduct: besides which,

* Baron von Weber was the composer's grandson. In his biography of Mahler, Henry Louis de la Grange suggests that these descriptions of Mahler's behaviour as lover and of Weber's madness are exaggerated.

as you conduct your own music you surely can get along with other people's well enough for all purposes?' At this remark Grieg shook his pale yellow mane angrily: 'My own music?' he snapped. 'Any fool can conduct his own music but that's no reason for murdering other people's' – and the manager had to drop the subject.

But of all the composers I have known the most delightful as personality was Tchaikovsky, between whom and myself a relation now sprang up that surely would have ripened into close friendship had circumstances favoured us; so large minded was he, that I think he would have put up unresentingly with all I had to give his work – a very relative admiration. Accustomed to the uncouth, almost brutal manners affected by many German musicians as part of the make up and one of the symptoms of genius, it was a relief to find in this Russian, who even the rough diamonds allowed was a master on his own lines, a polished, cultivated gentleman and man of the world. Even his detestation of Brahms's music failed to check my sympathy – and that I think is strong testimony to his charm! He would argue with me about Brahms by the hour, strum passages on the piano and ask if they were not hideous, declaring I must be under hypnotic influence, since to admire this awkward pedant did not square with what he was kind enough to call the soundness of my instinct on other points. Another thing that puzzled him was my devotion to Marco, of whom he was secretly terrified, but this trait he considered to be a form of English spleen and it puzzled him less than the other madness. For years I have meant to inquire whether dogs play no part in the Russian scheme of life or whether Tchaikovsky's views were peculiar to himself; anyhow it amused me, reading his Memoirs, to find Marco and Brahms bracketed together as eccentricities of his young English friend.

On one point we were quite of one mind, the neglect in my school, to which I have already alluded, of colour. 'Not one of them can instrumentate,' he said, and he earnestly begged me to turn my attention at once to the orchestra and not be prudish about using the medium for all it is worth. 'What happens,' he asked, 'in ordinary conversation? If you have to do with really alive people, listen to the inflections in the voices . . . there's instrumentation for you!' And I followed his advice on the spot, went to concerts with the sole object of studying orchestral effects, filled notebook upon notebook with impressions, and ever since have been at least as much interested in sounds as in sense, considering the two things indivisible.

I must not forget to record a strange manifestation of the German spirit witnessed during the spring of 1888 – an incident of the same order as the scenes with the peppery stationer and the egregious Commandant of the Leipzig garrison, but more astounding even than these, in that the hero was one of my most intimate friends.

It will be remembered that most of the great German doctors had pronounced the German Crown Prince's malady to be cancer, and that Sir Morell Mackenzie, called in by the Crown Princess, was of a different opinion. No one who was not in Germany at that moment can realize the lengths to which an inspired Press will go, the least of the charges brought against this noble woman being that the whole thing was a plot between her and Morell Mackenzie to secure her the pension of a German Empress, inasmuch as an heir stricken with a mortal disease might possibly be excluded from succession!

One day, at the height of this disgraceful business, I was lunching at the Wachs, Lili as it turned out being ill in bed, and naturally I imagined that Wach would share my horror and distress. Not at all! The discussion began fairly temperately, by his asking me how English doctors would have liked it had the Prince Consort been similarly afflicted and a German doctor called in to reverse their decision? I replied that though they would in all probability have hated it, such a scandal as this malignant Press campaign was absolutely unthinkable in England. But my remarks were brushed aside angrily. Wach's voice rose and rose, so did mine, and finally when I said, 'But after all she is an English Princess,' he bounded up, rushed round to my side of the table and vociferated – his clenched fist within three inches of my nose: 'How *dare* you say she is an English Princess? She married our Crown Prince and is a German . . . a GERMAN . . . a GERMAN!! do you understand?'

At this point all the children fled from the table, pelted down the corridor, and as I learned afterwards burst into their mother's room, half in terror, half in wild delight, screaming, '*Mama! Mama! der Papa schlägt die Ethel!*' ('Papa is hitting Ethel!.') . . . Meanwhile I too had jumped up, and declaring I would not stand being spoken to like that by anybody, rushed into the corridor, seized hat and coat, banged the door behind me, and struggling into my garments, rushed down the three flights of stairs into the street. But hardly was I fifty yards from the house when I heard my name being called, and there was the Professor, table-napkin in hand, tearing after me, his longish stiff dark hair standing erect in the wind. Being devoted to him of course I accepted his apologies without difficulty, and was led back in triumph to the deserted luncheon table; the children, a little disappointed that murder had not been done, were collected again and the meal went on in peace. But my amazement at this extraordinary display survives undiminished to the present hour.

In the Desert

In the autumn of 1885 Ethel Smyth had been introduced by Edith Davidson, wife of the Dean of Windsor, to Mrs Benson, wife of the Archbishop of Canterbury. Born Mary Sidgwick, she had married Edward White Benson (1829–96) in 1859. Their sons were Arthur (A. C.), headmaster at Eton and master of Magdalene College, Cambridge; Edward (E. F.), author of Dodo *and* Lucia; *and Robert (R. H.), who took Anglican orders and later became Roman Catholic. There were also two daughters, Nelly and Maggie.*

Throughout all these years, the mainstay of my life had been Mrs Benson, and needless to say no one could have striven harder than she did against the long cold night of the spirit that fell upon me when all hope of a reconciliation with my friend had to be abandoned.

Meanwhile I had come to know the rest of the clan, meeting them occasionally in a fugitive manner at Lambeth, and more satisfactorily at Addington. Everyone knows what an unpermissibly gifted family they were. I say were, thinking of the five who have since passed away, the last to go being the mother – that wonderful woman, whom to call 'Ben', as her intimates did, seemed as fitting when she was over seventy as it did when first I knew her. Be the void she has left what it may, I am thankful that to the last, in spite of failing bodily strength, there was no other change. One could not have borne to see her slower at the uptake, less deadly in repartee, less amused at the infinite comicalities of life.

It is a curious fact, and one that proves the richness of her equipment, that though she was one of the many ladies pronounced by Mr Gladstone to be 'the cleverest woman in England', her master passion was undoubtedly the cure of souls. A great part of her life was consecrated to her patients, as I used to call them, who when bereft of her physical presence were kept going by words of counsel and comfort written on letter-paper so diminutive that it inevitably suggested a prescription. I really think the spiritual or moral dilemmas of Mrs Jones the curate's wife interested her more than what Lord Salisbury said last night at dinner, and fancy the position she occupied, involving automatic and effortless contact with the most distinguished personalities of the day, gave her no great satisfaction. Speaking of her astonishing unworldliness, I once said as much to a very worldly old peeress, who thoughtfully answered, 'Yes, poor thing, you see she has *no precedence*'. I remember once walking with her through the huge dining-hall at Lambeth when the table was laid for some state banquet; appalled at the solemn spectacle I asked whether champagne was served on such occasions, and this amazing hostess's reply was, 'I haven't the faintest idea!'

The one of the family who eventually became my particular friend was Nelly – take her all in all the most remarkable of the younger generation as personality, in my humble opinion; but as she died on what is merely the threshold of life for women of that calibre one cannot be certain. Re-reading her letters, penned in easy profusion, the handwriting so identical with her mother's as to baffle one again and again on the envelope, I realize that in a wonderful collection of correspondence I have nothing to touch this particular blend of humour, profundity and high spirits. There is the same fastidious literary quality as in Arthur Benson's writing, *plus* something indescribable that may be called genius for life. Nelly was the only close friend I ever had to whom games and adventure meant exactly what they do to me; a bond as great as our other link, a twin taste in humour.

Of the Archbishop I stood in deadlier awe than of anyone I ever met in the whole course of my life. To begin with there was the beauty I find so disconcerting in a man; then his office, which deeply impressed me; and lastly and chiefly the fact that like many hypersensitive people he was seldom quite at his ease – a state of things that in my youthful days utterly deprived me of my means, as the French say. Watching the progress of our duologues from her end of the table, with the particular look of devilment one knew so well on her face, Mrs Benson would afterwards declare that the mouse-like voice which replied to the Archbishop's remarks was a very beautiful thing to listen to. The sight of his majestic form approaching the tea-table scattered my wits as an advancing elephant might scatter a flock of sheep. I never did quite such stupid things with other people; nothing but sheer nervousness can have induced me, for instance, to contribute a certain anecdote one day at luncheon, for I could read the domestic storm signals and guessed that the Archbishop was not at his most serene that day.

After a few bad moments the conversation had turned to printer's errors – as well it might in a family, six out of seven members of which were authors – and I had got as far as saying I had recently read about a printer's error, merely the omission of a final *d*, that really was . . . and here I stopped, overcome with misgiving. But there was no disobeying His Grace's acid-affable 'Pray let us hear the case in question,' and with death in my soul I told them how a local newspaper had stated in connection with a recent visit from General Booth, that after his train had left the station a large crow remained on the platform for half an hour singing *Rock of Ages*.

Whether at another moment, or given another narrator than myself, His Grace would have been amused, and let this very innocent specimen of joking on sacred subjects pass, I do not know; what happened then was, first silence all round, then someone tried to laugh, then Mrs Benson said cheerfully, 'A fine athletic performance anyhow!' and instantly asked the Archbishop whether the Dean of Rochester had spoken well at the meeting that morning . . . 'But it really *was* a funny story,' I afterwards pleaded to Nelly who had not been present. 'Funny!' she replied gloomily, 'of course it was funny, but what on earth has that to do with it?' . . . What indeed!

Apart from the fact that as Mrs Benson once put it, 'We all realize that you and the Head of the Church are *not* two dewdrops destined to roll into one,' my relations with the Benson family though enthralling – to me, at least – were rather tempestuous, most of us being more or less aggressive and cocksure. To my mind the women of that family had not an ounce of artistic blood between them, and though I delighted in the reason Maggie gave for not going to hear the *Passion* – 'I don't like Bach because he is so very ugly' – this difference of breed was no doubt the main source of jars. People who only admit one view of moral law – that of the Church – can hardly mix at bottom with those who see life through an artist's eyes; not at least unless artistic kinship is there to bridge the gulf between them. When first I knew the Bensons – the time at which I was closest to them – the artist was in abeyance, and though I was not a believer our outlook was more or less the same; but even then the dissimilarity of grain made itself felt.

Eventually I got so terribly on the Archbishop's nerves that it was found expedient to smuggle me into Lambeth by back entrances and hastily herd me into side rooms; in short the scenes of the memorable sojourn in Venice with Frau von Stockhausen were enacted on sacred English soil. It appeared that even the mere sight of me from a window, strolling with Mrs Benson along 'the Apostolic Succession', would infallibly wreck whatever work the Archbishop might happen to be engaged on at the moment; and though I was assured that some of the boys' friends were in the same case, and though it is rather flattering in a way to inspire so intense an aversion, the situation was more exciting than agreeable. Yet such was my veneration for Dr Benson, my intense appreciation for all he said and wrote and did as priest, that I bore him no ill will, and often think, among other sympathetic memories, of a little scene at Addington that touched and impressed me – the Head of the Church sitting at the feet of his guest, Mr Spurgeon, and humbly soliciting information as to the spiritual needs of the London poor. In short he dwells in my memory as one of the loftiest-souled men I have known.

Mrs Benson once said it was rather hard that any resentment I might feel on the subject of the Archbishop's really outrageous rudeness seemed cherished against her! This was quite true; if the men of the family are insupportable it is generally the fault of the women for not standing up to them – and vice versa . . . as we so often remarked to each other at home!

All this time, though I had been working steadily at orchestral composition as Tchaikovsky had advised, it was becoming more and more clear to me that unless my musician's soul was to be lost I must go back to Germany; back to a country, to mention one point only, where friendly conductors give one a free run-through of one's first orchestral attempts – a thing impossible, of course, in mercenary England. But apart from this I now knew, after giving it a long patient trial, that to live an artist's life at Frimhurst was an impossibility. All brain-workers need peace and quiet, but I am certain the musician's temperament is more easily rasped than any other, perhaps because musical creation involves no soothing contact with outside realities. The painter, the sculptor, depend upon the exterior world; the poet's material, words, is the medium of ordinary intercourse; alone among artists is the composer bereft of this greatest element of sanity, concerned as he is with exteriorizing a world that only exists within. Thus the constant presence of a violent spirit, uncontrolled and uncontrollable, such as my mother's was devastating; all the more so because, loving her, I was harrowed by the spectacle of her moral suffering and maddened by constant scenes in which my violence equalled hers and was the subject of bitter remorse afterwards.

Throughout the autumn of 1888 right on to the summer of 1889 I think she was going through some slow, painful moral crisis – perhaps the final realization that in spite of the youthfulness of her heart she was an old woman; for in January 1889 she had drawn up an informal Will, dividing her lace and jewellery among her children. She shut herself up a great deal in her own room, had a strange aloofness of manner, and when I was staying away there was little or no correspondence between us – all of which was even more distressing than actual scenes. And thus it came that the decision to pass the following winter abroad had to be taken, though now more than ever the thought of her loneliness in the empty house weighed tons on my heart. My brother Bob, who for many years, thanks to the never-failing kindness of the Duke of Connaught, had been on HRH's Rifle Brigade list, had just been up for another examination – his last chance but one – and if he passed might possibly be posted to a battalion on foreign service. My father, whose great idea was to bundle the young ones out of the nest without delay, and who considered it 'right and proper' to disregard maternal feelings in such cases, was strongly in favour of this course; but the prospect hung like a Damocles sword over my mother's head.

On the other hand Nina Hollings, a very favourite daughter, was only three and a half miles off, and the Hollings babies, who were coming along, could be counted on as a great source of interest. Then too there would be visits from the elder batch of grandchildren; but though mother adored and was quite delightful with children, these visits involved collisions with nurses (who resented criticism of their methods) and other not enjoyable incidents. On the whole, therefore, the outlook was not very satisfactory; but mother, whose unerring instinct told her I ought to go back to the musical world, said not a word to make it harder for me – on the contrary protested that she would be perfectly happy, that Bob wasn't off yet awhile, that Alice would come and stay in the spring after he was gone and so on. As I am never tired of saying, at the worst moments her bigness of soul came into play – then she never failed us.

In September 1889 I said goodbye to the dear family and turned my face Munich-wards with a feeling I had never known before, dread of the future. As a rule any new departure rouses a spirit of adventure; but it is not easy to make a fresh start when your heart is aching, your health indifferent, and your conscience ill at ease – for the thought of my mother gave me no rest. Moreover the prospect of meeting the Fiedlers was agitating. A certain revival of correspondence between me and Mary had taken place, but since I believed that her once keen realization of my wrongs was blurred, there had been no reopening of that question between us . . . a question of which my intimate friends had heard more than enough! To pass through Munich without making a sign would have been unnatural and churlish, but I rather wondered whether the news of my coming would give her unqualified satisfaction.

On the contrary her reply, written in the old warm-hearted vein, informed me that this meeting had long been ardently desired by her. I further gathered that during the Herzogenbergs' long sojourn at Munich in the winter of 1887–8 yet another revulsion of feeling had set in. Closer acquaintance with Lisl, further reflections on her action towards me had dimmed the charm – in short Lisl was dethroned. I am certain that sympathy with my hard case had a great deal to do with it, but I also knew that Mary, always an ardent Wagnerite, had meanwhile fallen under a stronger sway than Lisl's, having in spite of Conrad's aloofness from Wagnerism become an intimate of Wahnfried. In various little digs at the Herzogenbergs and the limit- ation of their outlook both in Art and Life, in remarks about coteries of manacled spirits congratulating each other on the purity of their little ideals, and carefully keeping out every breath of fresh air, I at once recognized the voice of Cosima.

This wonderful woman was far too clever, far too much a woman of the world, not to appreciate the decorative value of an occasional and carefully selected heretic in her inner circle; hence she had no objection to a man of distinction, such as Conrad Fiedler, declining to fall flat on his face before 'Our Art', or even questioning, as he did, its fundamental principles. Besides which Conrad was wealthy – in her eyes a supreme merit. Similar heterodox views on the part of Hilde- brand, a still more famous man, were put up with for analogous reasons, and meanwhile both men did ardent homage – as well they might – to her genius. But what she could not tolerate was that eminent personalities in the musical world such as the Herzogenbergs should recognize Wagner as one recognized Anarchy or any other destructive force, the while worshipping Brahms as the true god. In after years two staunch satellites of Cosima's told me she was never more magnificent than when denouncing the Herzogenberg crew; thus I was rather surprised, when I met her for the first time in my life at Berlin, to learn from her own lips that the premature death of Elisabeth von Herzogenberg, one of the glories and graces of Germany, had caused her heart to bleed. Suddenly I recollected that our hostess, who was standing close by and had adored Lisl, was a power – in fact, one of the greatest ladies in the German Empire!* Whatever her faults may have been Cosima did nothing by halves.

I have often noticed that when Fate has a phenomenal run of ill luck in store for you, she begins by dropping a rare piece of good fortune into your lap, thereby enhancing the artistic effect of the sequel. Later events will show the bearing of this remark on the fact that when my short visit to the Fiedlers was over I instantly lit upon charming lodgings – a great point just then, for a spell of hard and hurried work was before me. That summer I had made friends with August Manns, the conductor of the celebrated Crystal Palace Concerts, and after seeing a String Quartet of mine he had held out hopes of producing one of my orchestral pieces in the spring of 1890, provided I could let him have the score and parts by 1 January. Now I had never yet written for orchestra, and foresaw that after hearing my work there would be various improvements to be made – and what that involves only composers know! Unfortunately the hearing could not take place yet awhile, for a sort of minor Wagner Festival was coming on, and given the endless rehearsals the Festival conductor Hermann Levi insisted on, I knew that the sight of a new MS on their desks, to be run through by favour, would be more than even his orchestra could bear. So I just let him know I had arrived, and why, begged him now and again to give me a free pass to the Opera, and proceeded to make my first real acquaintance with Munich.

Because of what was to befall me there, for many years I shrank from the very thought of Munich; scene, as occurs to me while I am writing, of the bitterest disappointment of my life twenty-six years later . . . the ideal production of *The Wreckers* annulled by the war! . . . At first the place put a spell upon me; I even appreciated the strivings after the architecture on the far side of the Alps which some people find so ridiculous. But the chief fascination lay in the Alps themselves – on certain days apparently not more than ten miles off (really forty) – and the fiercely rushing green Isar, which brings you still closer to the glaciers for which the heart of the mountain climber ever yearns.

* A later account, in *As Time Went On . . .*, identifies their hostess as Countess von Bülow.

Marco hurled himself daily into that icy river after sticks he seldom succeeded in timing properly, so violent is the current; realizing this he took to rushing on ahead and plunging in long before I reached the bank, to be swept backwards downstream, his eyes passionately fixed on my right arm . . . O he was a gallant dog! . . . Another sympathetic feature was that town and country seemed far more intermixed than elsewhere; peasants came to market in costume, and not having yet learned that the Bavarians are the least reliable race in the world, I was captivated by what seemed to me their simplicity and bluff good humour. Here too one at last found traces of religion on a German scene. Even in the town the churches were thronged by men as well as women, and in the rural districts there was a certain fantastic element that Roman Catholicism seems to bring with it, which redeems village life from the unutterable flatness of Lutheran and free-thinking communities in North Germany. Finally, to crown all, Munich owned a town witch, or had till four months ago, when owing to irregularities in money matters she had been banished to an outlying village. But her enormous clientele, many of them people of high rank, remained faithful, and were in the habit of going out quite openly by train to have their horoscopes cast.

Early in November I made my first acquaintance with Bavarian slipperiness, my landlady suddenly informing me that the owner of the house – the omnipotent *Hausherr* – had threatened to give her notice unless she turned me out immediately, the flat having been let on the express understanding that there were to be no female lodgers. Learning however that my rent had been prepaid up to 1 December, he had graciously consented to tolerate my presence till that date. I wondered if the *Hausherr* was a woman-hater, a lunatic, or what, but there was no time to take futher action just then for a note arrived from Levi bidding me present myself with my scores next day; namely a Serenade in four movements, and an Overture to *Antony and Cleopatra*. The result was eminently satisfactory – according to Levi – but I saw that many details could be improved and that to get these done by 1 December would take me all my time, so the search for other quarters had to stand over for the present.

In spite of work I managed to go to the Opera occasionally. When it was too late to claim the opulent seats Levi placed at my disposal I used to sit, or more often stand, in the gods, and as there was little time for correspondence at home I once began a letter to Nelly up there, standing and holding the writing block in mid air. Presently a

151

nice ugly young man who was sitting just below me turned round and said, 'May I offer you my back as desk?' and bent forward to put himself into position. In common gratitude the letter had to be a short one, but remembering this sympathetically German incident, which caused no sensation whatever in the gods, I see that life at Munich was not without poetic charm.

On another night I had a stall for a *Lohengrin* performance, and, looking round the house, to my surprise caught sight of some English faces I knew in the Dress Circle – Lady Trevelyan and two of her daughters, friends of my sister Mary Hunter's whose acquaintance I had made in London during the summer.

The Trevelyans were inexplicable people, as absolutely musical, and what is more, as completely at my own standpoint in matters of art, as any of my friends abroad. And though Lady Trevelyan was Irish one cannot say that explains everything, for Sir Alfred was of course English, but as unlike the ordinary Englishman in his views and tastes as the rest of the family, and incidentally one of the most original and delightful of personalities. The girls had studied music in Germany and like their mother not only felt, but knew and judged. Absolutely unworldly, not caring two straws about society, they thought for themselves and belonged to no set in particular, which is perhaps the only receipt for keeping a really fresh mind. Though it is impossible to think of Trevelyans being standardized, it may have helped matters that they were Catholics, devout Catholics, but of the Old English type – in fact I think Sir Alfred was a bit of a Gallican – consequently the main idea of the Manning school, the conversion of Anglicans, played no part in their scheme. This much it had been possible to glean in the one or two meetings achieved in London, also that Pauline, the eldest girl (there were no sons) was probably the most musical of the party, anyhow the chief executant. But little did I dream that when all else had failed, when, with the cheapening of what had been my great treasure, life seemed almost worthless, a miracle would be wrought by what one calls chance . . . and that the agent, humanly speaking, was to be Pauline.

At that moment only Lady Trevelyan and two of the other girls were in Munich, Sir Alfred and Pauline turning up for the *Ring* later on. Although the strange dread of the future never left me, their presence made all the difference for the time being, and we revelled in music together, especially in a wonderful performance of Beethoven's *Missà Solemnis*. Probably because of my then state of mind it seemed to me

I had never heard it before; the terror of a certain veiled, rushing passage for violas and cellos at the thought of sin, death and judgement . . . the wild triumph of the trumpet call flaming out of it . . . how it haunted me in the hours to come! . . .

The morning after the performance I went to see Levi when he was at breakfast, and remember how he rushed to the piano with a piece of black bread and butter in one hand, saying, as he strummed bits of the Mass with the other, '. . . and this passage for instance . . . was there ever anything like it?' And presently the bread and butter was cast aside, and this overworked man, full of cares (as he was just then) and on the brink of a severe illness (as he turned out to be) instead of finishing his breakfast began to play with the fiery enthusiasm of a boy. I told the Trevelyans about it, and we felt we were well met in this land. But I must not forget to record how one illusion of ours, that the English are less hated in Bavaria than in North Germany, was dispelled by Beatrice Trevelyan overhearing one street boy address another in furious *crescendo* as '*Du Kameel* . . . *du* ZULU . . . *du ENGLÄNDER!*'

During these weeks began what, as I have said, was destined to be an eventful relation, my friendship with Pauline. Wondering how to give some idea of her personality I remember a remark Lady Trevelyan once made to me at Nettlecombe, their home in Somersetshire: 'If I were to go into Pauline's room,' she said, 'and find she had suddenly vanished, melted into air leaving no trace, it would hardly surprise me.' There was neither sentiment nor apprehension in her manner, it was merely a characterization that conveys what for lack of a better word one might call the unearthly element about Pauline. Her extreme gentleness and delicate beauty had something to do with it, but these were only the garments of her soul. Full of enjoyment of life, a grand laugher – and this I think stands high on the list of merits – there was yet the abiding suggestion of a visitant from another planet lent to this world for the time being . . . and as it turned out not lent for long.

It was strange to realize that this most serene and contented of beings had been acquainted with physical pain from youth upwards, indeed was seldom free from it; here then was one key to her saintliness. But on another point enlightenment of a less distressing kind awaited me; it appeared that every man she met fell in love with her – generally two men at a time – and the lives of her mother and sisters, so they said, were sometimes made a burden to them by Pauline's disconsolates. Yet nothing in her demeanour would have led you to suspect she was the object of embarrassing homage – surely a rare and exquisite trait.

I often noticed how, quite unconsciously, she imposed her ways on all around her – merely by the penetrative strength of 'a gentle noble temper, a soul as even as a calm'. The quality of her spirit sometimes put her beyond one's reach; I did not always understand her, but was invariably and perfectly understood. There seemed to be no limit to her instinctive grasp of life and its intricacies; essential rays that got broken and dispersed on the rough surface of other minds passed easily and unbroken into hers. You could have been silent with her all your days and yet know you had become part of her mind. Assurances were neither given nor needed . . . her quiet reticence bred a faith that nothing could trouble.

I loved Lady Trevelyan, who worshipped and in many ways resembled Pauline, with the same kind of affection – a feeling from which her intense reserve and shyness would have made her shrink had she realized its existence. A pure-bred Milesian, she found Anglo-Saxon placidity rather a trial, as did my mother, and once remarked, 'So many English people seem to live at such a *low ebb*; they speak so softly you can't hear them, they enjoy so discreetly that you'd never suspect it.' And I also remember her declaring that she didn't want the United Kingdom or any other country to prosper as long as men disregard God's laws and look upon immorality as a thing that goes without saying; as long as tradesmen hold that only by sharp practice can you make a fortune; as long as advertising a performance is considered more important than the performance itself. Gentle, wise, subtle, and yet infinitely simple and single-hearted, it was this underlying passionateness that I loved so in her. I once told Pauline I would rather confess to her mother than to any priest on earth, and pictured to myself with amusement how she would turn white with horror at the thought and flee upstairs, gently muttering prayers for herself and me.

Needless to say Lady Trevelyan had a great sense of humour – as essential a note in the ideal confessor as saintliness or anything else – and musically speaking even a greater critical faculty, perhaps, than Pauline. You had to finesse to get her opinion, but any amount of trouble was worth the deadly hitting on the nail that followed. Pauline had the same dislike of categorical statements, and in her case matters were further complicated by the side I used to call 'Mrs Winslow' – the Irish side. As she was intensely absent-minded (a very delightful quality) the soothing syrup would sometimes be administered hastily in a spirit of propitiation before the matter in hand had been fully grasped, but there was never any doubt as to her ultimate opinion. Another trait the two had in common – a curious one in such gentle people – was a faculty of getting white with anger; I remember first noticing it in Lady Trevelyan when we were talking about people who won't take care of their health – a form of tiresomeness she had no patience with. The whole family were more or less on the same lines, and I have the impression that you might search in vain for their prototype outside the Roman Communion; to be honest I must add that these were among the very few devout Catholics I have met who struck me as full-fledged, responsible human beings.

In the middle of December the Trevelyans left for Cannes, and then came the worst nightmare of my life. I say it deliberately, for when the breach with Lisl had taken place I was well in mind and body and had never yet had to call up my reserves; now I was ill and morally at the end of my tether.

The search for lodgings was begun in appalling sleet and slush, and then, not till then, did I discover what Fate, in permitting me to drop at once into ideal quarters two months ago, had purposely hidden from me till the weather became impossible – namely that furnished rooms for lady students of my type do not exist in Munich. The lunatic landlord had merely been a normal Munich burgher! If you were respectable you lived at a pension (and as lady composers were scarce in those days, pianos on every floor were I suppose considered no deterrent), if you lived in rooms like a man you were disreputable . . . Quite simple.

Hounded from pillar to post, I at last found a room on the ground floor – situation hateful both to rheumatics and lovers of light; but as the landlady assured me there were no pianos, that all her other clients were students – that is lodgers who are never in the house except from 2 a.m. to 10 a.m. – and that the baby crying was her great granddaughter whose Mama was on a two days' visit, I engaged the room. It afterwards turned out that one of the students had a lady with him – a lady who called the filthy maid of all work 'Fräulein', which gives an idea of the class – and that the baby was hers and the student's property. I had to fight for a table to write on, for a vanished armchair I had seen a few days back when engaging the room, for firewood, for briquettes, for everything, and was soon off again, rheumatism all over me, once more facing the same sleet and slush, the same insulting refusals to take in single ladies. Eventually I found another miserable room; again I was told there were no pianos in the place, and asking what the tramplings overhead might mean, learned it was only preparations for the Christmas tree. By this time I believed less and less the accounts given by landladies of their establishments, but how test the matter otherwise than by taking the rooms?

Because the incidents that now follow proved to be a turning-point in my life, because too, strange to say, contemporary words tell a personal story almost impersonally, I shall let one of my letters speak for me. It was written to Nelly Benson on 21 December, the day before I fled from the vicinity of the student, his lady and their ever-squalling infant:

. . . Yes, you are right, I am ill; that is one reason why my letters have flagged. Seeing what the Trevelyans' relation to God and the world is, loving Pauline at once almost as I did (I swear to you chiefly because of that but also because of herself), feeling so broken-hearted when they went away, finding my vaunted strength and calm gone, coming back to this miserable lodging . . . all this brought about a crisis.

And now let me tell you a detail. Pauline had left a little *Imitation de Jésus Christ* at her Hotel here and asked me to claim it for her; not to send it but to give it back when I should see her next. So I went to the Bellevue; nothing had been handed in at the Bureau, but their apartment was still unlet if I would like to take a look round. To my joy I found the book under the sofa cushion, which will give you an idea both of Pauline and Bavarian housemaids, but struggling against the awful wind and snow from the mountains it must have got jerked out of my pocket, and when I got home . . . it was gone! I was in despair. I had thought perhaps in her heart she had wanted me to keep it hoping I might read it, though as you can imagine I didn't ask her if this was so. Anyhow I had meant to . . . and now it was lost! . . . Well, I advertised, and O Nelly, last night it came back, almost like a message from him whom the book is about.

I can't tell you what these days have been. There *is* a piano in the house after all, though a long way off, but the faintest sound of a note makes me tremble all over. I have lain for hours on the sofa, powerless with fear of life, feeling that I am broken and done for. I thank God for two things, that Mary Fiedler is here, and Marco, for I know but for these two I should have killed myself. I felt I was going mad, losing control, yet hated the idea of leaving such a horrible legacy to the dear Fiedlers . . . and still more the thought of poor lonely distracted Marco! Then this book came back and I feel as if I had been purposely driven into my last entrenchments. I give in and am ready and longing to try and learn there is another refuge and strength than human love and my own powers. I know it will take long but I believe it won't be denied in the end.

I cannot tell you how good Mary F. has been. I went to her yesterday to ask the doctor's address and broke down; she has a pitying way with me that does upset my fortitude, but perhaps it does good afterwards. She sees how my nerves are all weak and jarred, and is so unutterably dear to me. I told her all, why life looks so black, etc., and she made me swear if I felt like that again to send to her, which I will do. Of course she urged me to go and stay with them for a bit, but that is not what is wanted; I must, must stand on my own feet and this she understands.

I think she has a perfect horror of Lisl since she realizes things more, I mean how my life was rooted in them, and also that owing to dear old mother it can't take root in England. Ah! how Lisl spoiled me for this sort of thing . . . but what I realize more strongly than anything is that if I were rooted else-where I shouldn't mind it all as I do. O! and I have been so unwilling, so caring for other things . . . But I will stop this account of my troubles. I don't know but what you are too young to write such a letter to at all.

While I have been writing Marco lies slumbering peacefully at my feet, little knowing what a definite part he has played in my career. The thought of him . . . nobody's dog . . . (he is awfully nervous) or even travelling alone to England, moved me . . . ah me, what was it? Marco, for one thing, and other things too. Thank God it is over and done with now.

Finally, to sum up the situation: (1) My life seems smashed up, for I don't think I can stànd Germany without Lisl. (2) You know why England is out of the question. (3) I know the music in me isn't dead, only cowed into silence. (4) I at last believe – with relapses, but still believe – that a way may be found for me.

Farewell. E.

Looking through some 150 letters addressed to her it is a relief to find that on two occasions only, both of this epoch, was poor Nelly harrowed in this way! But it is strange to see how little I seem to have realized what an enormous amount of courage is necessary to the coward's end.

Next day I moved into the new lodgings, of which I had a latchkey and where the tramplings raged overhead as before. I had specially begged that the room be very warm, but the stove was out and not a soul in the place. As I had found elswhere, there was no service, no machinery to meet my case – I was a waif and stray; the sort of ladies who inhabit furnished rooms have maids, and as I said, students are never at home. So I went into the kitchen to look for wood and noticed a letter addressed to me lying on the table; it was from Conrad to say that Mary was ill in bed, with pains all over her and a temperature . . . After seventy-five years of quiescence the influenza epidemic, unrecognized as such for the time being, had again put in an appearance! . . . For the first time in my life I should spend Christmas alone . . . and in this place!

That night in bed I read a few sentences in the *Imitation*, as one might finger a shilling or two of a fortune which may, or may not, turn out to be meant for you, all the while possessed by a not unreasonable presentiment that the worst was yet to be. Next morning I was awakened at 5.30 by what I was told was the sweeps, and as the days of closed shops were approaching went out to buy a few necessaries. I remember coming back at midday and falling with a flop into the armchair; then, crash, bang, as if to welcome me home, with a few violent well-known chords a stentorian voice on the floor above launched into the recitative of a celebrated scene in what we English call 'Grand Opera' . . . I rushed upstairs and was informed that the new tenor of the Hof Oper, Herr So-and-so, had taken the suite over-head for six months! . . . That afternoon, although in this case I had been obliged to prepay a month's rent, the frantic hunt for the non-existent was taken up again under the usual weather conditions, and continued till long after sundown, by which time I was well in the grip of familiar symptoms – burning heat and shivering fits; and when I came home the tenor was still studying his new part.

Next day was Christmas Eve. I lay on the sofa, far too ill to go out room-hunting, and again opened the *Imitation*. The tenor boomed away overhead but presently I ceased to hear him, reading and reading throughout the day . . . reading at the restaurant where I tried to eat a midday meal . . . reading on into the night . . . awaking after an hour or two to light my lamp and begin reading again. If I did not remember that it was Christmas Eve it would seem to me that I read ceaselessly for days and days . . . Now all was clear to me: I had always thought of myself, and of nothing else . . . of what I had to achieve in life, of what my duty to myself was . . . always myself. No wonder I had failed; no wonder all I had touched, no matter with what excellent intentions, had turned to dust and ashes; no wonder that even Lisl was lost to me and that I had gone into the desert in vain . . . Now my path was clear . . . music must be thrown overboard too; there was only one road to happiness, renunciation. I must go home again and take up the burden I had tried to lay down; no one would know more than that I was ill and needed home care, which was true. Of course I would try to go on with music at Frimhurst . . . but as well try to make water run up hill. Well, renunciation meant that . . .

Next day I telegraphed home to say I was ill and coming back, and then dragged myself somehow to the Christmas Morning Service in the little English Church. I stayed there in a dark corner, weeping, weeping . . . stayed on while others were communicating. I remember one or two people glanced at me curiously, and that the officiant paused a moment when all the communicants had returned to their places and looked my way before turning again to the altar. I did not communicate myself, but went home full of a great peace, though so ill that nothing but a long habit of organizing my own journeys can have carried me automatically through the next twenty-four hours.

I have never quite known how I got home. There were no dining-cars on that train, and I knew that as the hours wore on I might become too ill to get out and eat at the Buffet. So I bought, I forget on what principle, a piece of fillet of beef, cut it up raw into small cubes, and filled a soda-water bottle with weak brandy and water – strange fare for one in a raging fever! The only accommodation for dogs was a sort of square tunnel running under the luggage van, and I shall never forget the anguish of shoving that huge frightened dog backwards into the horrible place and seeing the door locked on his poor white nose. Whenever I could during that night and the next day, I staggered through the snow and storm to the torture chamber to have a little reassuring conversation with him through the ventilation holes, bribing the guard to bring water and let me feed him now and again. Throughout that journey I was too ill to read, but held the little red book in my hand all the way, and am as certain as of anything in life, that but for that amulet I could never have reached home. I have no recollection of the arrival except as usual of mother's welcome, but know I was a few days in bed, generally with fever and always in pain somewhere or other . . . and then executed the usual lightning recovery.

Early in 1890 Bob was gazetted to the 21st Lancers and sailed for India in March. Throughout those two months mother's bearing with him, a certain bigness about the way she abstained from giving advice or otherwise tampering with his freedom, impressed me deeply. But magnificently as she played up, his going cut her to the heart, and when a day or two after he had gone she said quietly, 'I shan't see Bob again,' I was more thankful than ever at having come home.[10]

159

In spite of the rumpuses usual in large families we were a very united lot; and neither warfare on a large scale involving the departure of the soldier contingent for the seat of hostilities, nor matrimony, nor any other shattering incidents had so far loosened the bond between us. My two elder sisters were established in the far north. Beloved Alice Davidson lived at Muirhouse, the enchanting home of her husband's parents on the Firth of Forth. Mary Hunter, the beauty of the family, who for many years was financially and otherwise my standby in my musical ventures and who afterwards became a well-known lover of pictures and a lavish hostess, was at that time hibernating in County Durham. And season after season, whenever I was for a brief spell in England, did my generous, hard-riding brother-in-law Charlie Hunter mount me.

Nina, my next sister, married a neighbouring young squire and therefore was an integral part of the Frimhurst scene. She was one of those people who habitually go dead straight for any end that attracts them, no matter how fantastic. And once Nina started no one could stop her, least of all her husband, Herbert, who, as so often happens in these cases, was of an orthodox and methodical turn of mind, averse by nature from improvisations, from wild statements, and from still wilder expenditure. He had done wonders at Winchester both in cricket and football, had played racquets for his college at Oxford, and only just missed taking a double first. Now a JP and pillar of the Conservative Association, he was looked upon as the natural successor of my father in all county matters. But nevertheless he was powerless to deflect Nina by one hair's breadth from her course, and could only periodically breathe a hope that she was 'not going to do anything to make herself conspicuous'.

On one occasion, having been told that all children can swim if thrown into the water young enough, she cast her two small boys into the lake, and finding the experiment looked dubious, stalked in after them and bore them up to the house, one under each arm. It was Sunday morning after church and she was arrayed in black satin and bugles. And the only comment of a placid elderly relation who had been watching these proceedings was, 'Dear me, Nina, what a determined woman you are.' She always succeeded in anything she attempted: at Frimley Fair, after watching the failure of several brawny youths to 'ring the bell at the top', she picked up the hammer and did it without effort. At one moment the craze was making fireworks, and when the eldest boy, recovering from something very like brain fever, had been relegated by the doctor to solitary confinement in the nursery, by way of relieving the tedium of the sickroom his mother laid a train of gunpowder opposite his window and blew up a round flowerbed full of geraniums, calceolarias and lobelia.

But if anyone thinks Nina must have been a lunatic, they are greatly mistaken. A magnificent horsewoman, later an intrepid car driver with a passion for charging up perpendicular Welsh hills – while you had to hop out at intervals and shove boulders behind the wheels – she and her friend Lady Helena Gleichen the painter raised a mobile ambulance outfit during the war and were decorated for valour on the Italian front. She was also far and away the most naturally musical of my family, but as time went on they all thought well to leave that department to me.

After Nina came Violet, married to Dick Hippisley of the Royal Engineers. This is the sister who during their engagement begged her fiancé, a student of both philosophy and mathematics – not an unusual combination – to 'explain to her in two words the system of Zoroaster'. I apologize for adding that this sister, too, was very pretty, but only last week a contemporary of mine remarked, 'You certainly were a very good-looking family,' and if so, why not say so? Violet was altogether a charmer, very kind, exceedingly amusing, and according to her great admirer H. B., the best brain of us all.

Of Nelly, the last of the sisters, I knew less in those days (though we made up for it afterwards) than any of the five. When she came out I was almost always in Germany, and after her marriage in 1888 to Hugh Eastwood of the King's Dragoon Guards, they went straight off to India. Hugh was the delightful person who, some years later, when I asked why one of his girls, then aged six and eight, should not marry one of my 'beastly foreigners' as he called them, replied with his peculiarly sweet smile, 'Why not a gorilla?'[11]

Meanwhile, rather to my surprise, August Manns had at once accepted my Serenade and put it on one of his April programmes. This would be the first public performance of any orchestral work of mine, and indeed of any work at all in England. I was then new to the business of one more desk of violins being required at the last minute – of suddenly discovering that all the percussion was played by one man (or, if you had put it all in one part, by three men) and similar complications. And through it all Pauline burned like a steady light beside me, warm and quiet, helpful and practical.

When the great day came the excitement at home was immense,

even Papa, who had never been at a real concert in his life, insisting on being present. The Serenade was admirably rendered, and being a first work one could more or less count on a good reception; but regardless of how that might be, he had ready in his pocket a short telegram to Bob in India – 'GREAT SUCCESS' – which no doubt would have been dispatched in any case.

No sooner was the first movement over than Papa rose to send off the telegram . . . and get away himself; pulled down by mother, he attempted the same thing after the second, and again after the third movement. But after the fourth and last, having given up all hope, he remained patiently sitting, and thus had the gratification of seeing his daughter warmly called to the platform by that most delightful of audiences. I went home by a later train than the family, and when I met him before dinner he was beaming with delight, and said, 'Well, you had quite a jobation.'

A strange thing had happened at that concert. When summoned to the front I naturally looked towards the seats where the family were installed, and to my amazement, sitting just behind my mother was a man I did not recognize; but there was no mistaking the face I had always known as clean shaven, but for a moustache – a face I had not looked upon for many years . . . it was H. B. He had been passing through London on his way to America, and seeing my name on a poster had run down to the Crystal Palace. I afterwards learned that when Violet was claiming her reserved seat at the ticket office a strange man had said to her, 'I beg your pardon, but surely you must be a sister of Ethel Smyth?' We had imagined no two people were less like than I and Violet, but H. B. recognized the family type instantly. After the concert we met in the corridor, had tea together, and that night he started for Liverpool.

The result of the production of the Serenade was that other works of mine were now accepted for performance without difficulty, and suddenly, to my delight, I found that the power of work had come back. For one thing at last I was at peace; the Munich mood was no passing one, and for the next eighteen months, in spite of arduous work, at the bottom of my soul was one thought only – Christ. Hatred and contempt of Lisl fell away from me never to return, and though her action was as incomprehensible to me as ever, at that time my own failings and shortcomings were enough for me. I never lost the sense of our fate being interlinked, but if I perhaps hoped that some day things might alter, that hope played no part in the scheme. Never again was her peace troubled by useless remonstrances, and I steadily turned my thoughts in another direction, as one who dreads vertigo might force his eyes away from the precipice . . . And I remember, too, another thought that was brushed aside as dangerous, or at least futile; it occurred to me one day that Thomas à Kempis would certainly have disapproved of Shakespeare . . . ! All the same I went on reading the plays, but not the sonnets and other poems that too obviously base on what the author of the *Imitation* would have called the carnal affections.

Meanwhile life at home assumed a different aspect; things in my mother that used to drive me frantic seemed not only bearable but of little consequence. And now a sort of eventual fairness came into play; if an argument could be kept in smooth channels she would presently admit that she had been 'trying', and one day she amused and touched me by recalling that her grandmother used to say of the family she had married into, 'The Straceys are the *Jingle* family, my dear, much brilliancy and no foundation.' But I could assure her, without flattery, that this was not her case!

That spring the invention of ladies' bicycles was to demonstrate her superiority to stupid prejudice. In the *Illustrated London News* were to be seen pictures of wild women of the usual unprepossessing pioneer type riding about Epping Forest, and I at once decided to buy a bicycle. Aunts, cousins and friends were horrified . . . never has the word 'indelicate' been bandied about with more righteous conviction. But my mother said this was perfect nonsense. 'When we are dead,' she would reply to objectors, 'she won't be able to keep horses, and I can think of nothing more sensible than her buying a bicycle.' And buy one I did – with bad paces too, for pneumatic tyres were not yet invented; I also took lessons at a place called Cycledom, and the scene of my first unaided attempts was, O wonder! the gravel sweep in the front of Lambeth Palace, where I even had the honour of giving instruction to the Dean of Windsor. (Needless to say this was during a brief period of favour with the Archbishop.)

Strange to say one then looked upon this very useful and sometimes pleasant way of getting from one place to another as a form of sport, and though for many a long day to come no 'nice' women rode bicycles, I pursued my solitary course with enthusiasm. By degrees, as we know, the thing caught on, and one day, about eighteen months later, when I met Mrs R., the arch-prude of the neighbourhood, wobbling along the high road, and beheld her fall off her machine at my feet to explain that she had taken to it in order to avoid having out the horses on Sunday, it was clear that the indelicacy ghost had been finally laid.

During the spring months I saw a great deal of Mrs Benson, and our relations went through a curious phase. My conversion, as Evangelicals would have called it, could but give her great pleasure (if one may use the word in such a connection) but as regards methods we were not of one mind. When I was young, engrossed as we all were in the story of the Oxford Movement, I had been very High Church, and later, when belief passed, this aspect of Anglicanism had never lost its grip on my imagination; naturally therefore the new religious conviction that now welled up within me poured itself into the old channel. I may add that an aversion to Low Church views and ways, which was instinctive and violent, had been confirmed by many a subsequent experience, the type, the attitude of mind towards sacred things being the same whether met with in England or Germany.

In order to round off the story of this phase of intense belief – belief in the strictest sense of the word – I ought to say that during this and the ensuing year I was composing a Mass, which was eventually produced in London in 1893. Into that work I tried to put all there was in my heart but no sooner was it finished than, strange to say, orthodox belief fell away from me, never to return; and ridiculous as it seems, the fact that Thomas à Kempis would have condemned Shakespeare's sonnets had a great deal to do with it. True, I remembered wise Lady Trevelyan once commenting on the ease with which one brushes aside exaggerations of specialists (such as abound in this book written by a monk for monks) and asking who would take literally the command to hate your father and mother for Christ's sake? Nevertheless I held, and still hold, that it is impossible to reconcile the teaching of the *Imitation* with many of the circumstances of an artist's life . . . or with many of the movements of his soul. Further, it is not given to everyone to accept dogma, and I for one had evidently not the gift. H. B., the most deeply religious spirit and the most inveterate enemy of creeds I ever met, used to infuriate me in after life by attributing this particular development to influenza; but if that be the explanation what matter? Who shall fathom the Divine Plan? Only this will I say, that at no period of my life have I had the feeling of being saner, wiser, nearer truth. Never has this phase, as compared to others that were to succeed it, seemed overwrought, unnatural, or hysterical; it was simply a religious experience that in my case could not be an abiding one.

*

Late in the autumn of 1890 Maggie Benson wrote to say that Nelly was ill in bed. A few posts later I learned it was diphtheria, and almost immediately came the news that all was over . . . I remember walking dazed into my mother's room and saying, 'Nelly is dead.' She put aside her breakfast tray, burst into tears and held out her arms . . . Very fond of Nelly, miserable for me, her first words were, 'O poor, poor Mrs Benson!'

The damp cold of autumn always told upon my mother, and though this year she had tried hard to make the best of her ailments – which were increasing fast – and as usual cheered up between whiles, it was evident that in the depths of her heart she was very unhappy. The worst thing was the deafness, for though by no means marked, it bred a constant idea that people were slighting her. What with one's helpless pity – and the endeavour to combat this illusion (which mercifully she never entertained with regard to me) – life at home became even a greater strain than in the days of perpetual storm. To manage a proud, morbidly sensitive nature like hers, to pilot her through a dinner- or tea-party without her feeling herself neglected or pained, to do all this in such a way that she, the cleverest of women, should not see it – all this told on one's vital force. My father never noticed these efforts of mine; merely saw that some visitors preferred talking to me rather than to her, and resented it bitterly. Yet I think she understood, for a few months previously she had told Alice she felt more *certain* of my affection for her than that of any of us, except of course Alice; but she never fully realized what a grip she had on the hearts and imaginations of most of her children.

In December came the bend in a lane that seemed to promise no turning, and a correspondence, as between two great friends – the only matter that had been under discussion five years previously – now began between H. B. and myself. Why what once had been impossible now became possible, the striking of what exact hour set me free to leave the desert for ever . . . these are things that cannot be told here; the explanation roots in a silent section of the past. I will only add that from now onwards our friendship became the pivot of my life – as it is today though my friend died many years ago.

We had a very jolly Christmas that year, the Henschels to whom my mother was much attached being for the first time our guests; and my father, whose prejudice against artists had long since yielded to the

irresistible 'good fellow' quality of Henschel, instantly took a great
fancy to his wife. On one occasion, Christmas Eve it was, we were
discussing who should drive, who walk, to church next day, and Mrs
Henschel in an access of candour remarked to her neighbour, 'I'm
going to your church tomorrow, General, but I think I ought to let
you know I am a Unitarian.' Whereupon, bending forward with the
geniality that was so characteristic of him, my father replied in a burst
of confidence, 'Well, Mrs Henschel, I've often said, and I dare say they
are all tired of hearing me say it, that some of the best fellows I have
known in my long life were Mohammedans.' And why everybody
laughed, more particularly the lady to whom the remark was
addressed, he was far too simple to understand.

In later years, whether she liked them or no, resident visitors were
seldom a success with my mother, the chief reason being that, owing to
deafness, general conversation escaped her; and as there was always
plenty of it across our dinner-table the attention of the guest engaged
in a tête-à-tête with her would sometimes wander; or perhaps after
dinner he would join the younger group with too much eagerness. In
short she felt out of it, neglected – as she often put it, a cipher in her
own house. On this particular occasion, however, I was thunderstruck
at the way she pulled herself together, at her evident determination
not be be a kill-joy, and in writing to Mrs Benson about it attributed
this wonderful change to the obscure working of her influence. But
nothing is more common than reaction after a great moral effort and
on the following New Year's Day she[12] announced quite suddenly
that, more or less crippled as she was for half the year, she could stand
Frimhurst no longer and must really live in London! . . . It was tragic
– this dream of beginning life afresh at sixty-six, these visions of theatres, concerts, and other distractions for which she no longer had
health and strength! . . . I think she herself felt the hopelessness of
the idea, for a few days later she told me she had abandoned it, and
meant to try and make the best of things as they were . . .[13]

This strange symptom of deep inward distress greatly upset my
father; indeed for some time past, though he said little, we knew he
was as profoundly troubled about her future as we all were. Presently
she got quite cheerful again, and one day in the first week of January
after going to an afternoon party, she told us, evidently much pleased,
that someone had complimented her on looking so well and young.

I have said she had always suffered from an internal weakness; that
night she was suddenly seized with what proved to be her last illness

and died on 12 January 1891.[14] Of her death I cannot speak, except to say that it was piteous, heroic and probably unnecessary. Had the doctor at once recognized what was wrong, had a surgeon been fetched without delay, perhaps her life might have been saved. Of these things, too, it is useless to think; but as time goes on my certainty increases, mercifully for me, that some day we shall have a chance of making good our shortcomings towards those whose memory haunts us most abidingly – the people who really loved us.[15]

After the funeral I told Alice about her wonderful good temper and self-control during Christmas week. From my reports and her own observation she had known that during the whole of the past year there had been a continuous moral effort, which in spite of occasional relapses, had completely changed the aspect of home life; and we agreed it was as though, having at last really tried to accomplish it, she had been released from a task that was perhaps beyond her strength. For my own part I confess that a deep sense of relief was mingled with my sorrow. And I know it was the same with my father at the bottom of his heart . . . just because he loved her so dearly.

Meditating the events that ended in that nightmare return of mine to England at the close of 1889, I count it is the greatest mercy ever vouchsafed me that we thus were together during the last year of her life. And when I summon up the vision of her seated at her writing-table, eagerly cutting out all the favourable criticisms she could collect of those unripe productions of mine to send to Bob in India, it is good to know she believed, without shadow of doubt, that her faith, or rather her unfailing, most loving sympathy and support, had been justified by the event.

After my mother's death, perceiving ever more clearly the unique-ness of my father's personality, my admiration for him increased. Even the fact of not enjoying his unreserved approval was scarcely a subject for regret; one would have hated to see his character and instincts weakening. There was a moment when I feared this was happening, namely when we were allowed to play golf on the home course on Sunday, though lawn tennis had always been forbidden! Later on I came across Dr Johnson's remark that 'relaxation' is permissible on Sunday but not 'levity'; 'people may walk,' he says, 'but not throw stones at birds'. This cleared the matter up satisfactorily. We had plenty of subjects in common, and as a kindlier and less exacting com-panion could not have been imagined we got on excellently, and I had looked forward to our living together at Frimhurst for many years; but he died in 1894.

Those who believe in 'judgements', in the nursery sense of the word, might almost think a certain childish folly had been scored up against me, for of the five friends of my youth whose lives were most closely linked to mine – Lisl, Lili Wach, Rhoda, Nellie Benson and Pauline – two died young, and two on the very threshold of middle life – and of these deaths three were sudden! Even the last to go, Lili Wach, did not live to be an old woman.

Late in 1891 Pauline Trevelyan married a distant cousin of hers, Gilbert Heathcote of the Cameronians. After their marriage they followed the drum, and as I was much abroad and my life very strenuous, Pauline and I did not meet as often as formerly. In 1897, hearing she was ill and that they had taken a house in London so as to be near competent doctors, I went to see her and understood at a glance, though she was perfectly cheerful and full of plans for the future, that there was no hope. A country practitioner had mistaken certain symptoms, galloping consumption set in, and three weeks later she died peacefully.

To pass to my German friends; two of these died in the same year as my mother, Consul Limburger and beloved Frau Livia Frege – the latter after a painful illness borne with heroic fortitude and patience. Like my mother she was her best, and more than her best self at the last.

Of Lili Wach I saw much in after life on various scattered occasions. In 1892 she came to England and I had the delight of showing her Lambeth and introducing her to Mrs Benson, whom she had loved and venerated from afar for many years, knowing what a friend she had been to me. The presence of the daughter of Mendelssohn, composer of *Elijah*, cast a vicarious glamour on Lili's unsympathetic friends, and the Archbishop, who was adorable with her, was more than gracious to me . . . so much so that Mrs Benson and I agreed we had better leave it at that and not risk further experiments. The last time I saw Lili was in 1906, when I went to Leipzig for the first production of *The Wreckers*, and not long afterwards, never even having heard she was ill, they wrote to tell me she was dead . . .

In 1895 the gentle Conrad Fiedler came to a violent and most tragic end. Slightly paralysed in the lower limbs, he was trying to let down the heavy blinds of one of their windows on the second floor, lost his balance, fell, and was killed instantaneously on the pavement below.

Another sudden death, that of dear old Papa Röntgen, is, on the contrary, one of the most perfect stories I know. The great annual event of his life, as leader of the Gewandhaus Orchestra, was playing the violin solo in the Benedictus of the *Missa Solemnis*. He was not a believer, I fancy, but it was even more a religious than a musical event to him, and as he was no longer young – and the music is notoriously very exacting – the nervous strain of the week preceding the performance was always a trial to himself and his family. On the occasion of which I am speaking it appears that he played that unearthly *obbligato* more divinely, with more warmth, nobility and freedom than ever before. Those who heard it were amazed, saying to each other that even in the days of his strong-nerved youth he could not have done better. Johanna told me that he went home like a man in a happy dream, and remarked at supper, 'For the first time in my life after the Benedictus I can say it . . . tonight I satisfied myself!' Uttering which words he leant back gently, smiled . . . and was dead.

And now there remains but one to be spoken of – the friend who for seven years had been my great joy and who for ever after was to be my great sorrow. Not that such griefs maintain their keen edge – who could live if that were so? But a tragedy of which the passing years bring no solution is never lived down.

I have said that during the spiritual crisis spoken of, hatred of Lisl passed away for ever, but I was no nearer understanding what had happened than before. I had to face the fact that my greatest investment in friendship had failed, and banish ghosts as best I could. By tacit consent Lisl's name dropped out of my correspondence with Lili Wach and Mary Fiedler, was only once mentioned, I think, between me and H. B., and never between me and English friends. It was understood that that chapter was closed, and if I thought of a possible reunion some day it was vaguely, as one thinks in youth of one's own death. So at least I believed.

In December 1891 H. B. wrote me that his mother-in-law was evidently not long for this world. I remember thinking of Frau von Stockhausen's celebrated heart complaint – far worse than hers, Lisl had always said – which had caused all doctors to declare she could never live to be an old woman. Calculating her age by her daughter's (Lisl was then forty-one) I came to the conclusion that she must be about eighty, but what of that? Inasmuch as her death would remove the one absolutely unsurmountable barrier between us, she was probably immortal . . . There is, too, a certain letter of Byron's which begins,

'My mother-in-law has been dangerously ill; she is now dangerously well' . . .

Early in January 1892 came further news. My old enemy, having done as much mischief as could reasonably be expected of one individual in a lifetime, had really quitted the earthly scene at last; but before I had even answered the letter which gave me these glad tidings, a telegram was put into my hand. The sender may have fancied that I had heard from others what she herself had shrunk from telling me; but doctors are fallible, and no one had cared to speak. Thus it came that without the faintest preparation, without even knowing that she was in other than perfect health, I read the words, 'LISL IS DEAD - LILI.'

I learned later that on old Leipzig friend of hers, Helene Hauptmann, who had nursed her through her last illness, was going to live with and keep house for poor Herzogenberg; then the curtain fell, and life went on as before . . .

And now I realized that, apart from my work, what I had chiefly been living for all these years was to see my lost friend again. There is a sensation of bleeding to death inwardly that has ever since been associated in my mind with no other form of sorrow, however bitter, but only with the flickering out of a secret and passionately cherished hope . . .

. . . the night at length when thou,
O prayer found vain, didst fall from out my prayers.

Often and often in the years that followed her death I have been at or near St Remo, where she lies under cypress trees, and have sometimes wished my feet would take me to that spot . . . but it seemed impossible. Again at Vienna, in 1914, turning over some photographs of modern sculpture, I suddenly came upon something that I laid aside quickly without examining it; it was a portrait-medallion Hildebrand had carved for the headstone of her grave . . . Thus I thought to feel about her and all that concerns her to the end of my life.

And now comes what is for me the strangest part of our unusual history. Opening that locked door and staring into the darkness behind it, little by little I have come to see light, and as final word of my story can say what I never thought to say in this world – that her death has lost its sting for me . . . at last I understand.

This is how I see our story now. Commanded by her mother to

choose between us, I cannot doubt that, under the psychological necessity I spoke of, she at first threw me overboard not only actually but in a certain sense morally. In one of her early letters is a confession that now seems pregnant: 'I fear I rather lose the feeling of people when they are far away.' Perhaps this helped her to let go of me. Though I do not believe the faithless mood lasted long, it lasted long enough, combined with the frenzied activities of her relations and friends, to precipitate for the time being the catastrophe they all wished to avoid; after that there was no deflecting from the line taken.

Perhaps she had no wish to deflect: 'Action must be simple,' she once said, 'in order to be intelligible'; but supposing it were otherwise, and that she had determined to convey to me some indirect assurance of unchanged faith and affection, her great integrity would have forced her to make confession to those whose will was her law. And if the terrible scenes which would have followed were more than she could face, it is not for people the valves of whose hearts are sound to judge her harshly. Alas! in those days I knew nothing about heart disease and had always found her dread of conflicts rather absurd . . .

I am not trying to force the case in her favour. The instinct to belittle someone you have loved, in order to find strength to uproot that person from your life, is a mean cowardly instinct it is impossible to defend. On the other hand, given Austrian family traditions, it was as natural to her to divest herself of all responsibility towards me at their command, as it seemed – and still seems – monstrous to me. And once she saw her duty, consequences were not her business; the city, given over to fire and brimstone, must perish – the divine command was . . . not to look back.

But where I did her grievous injustice . . . how this was borne in upon me when for the first time since youth was left behind me I re-read her letters! . . . was in believing that because she made no sign our parting caused her little or no suffering. It would be impossible to reproduce those letters as they stand. Even in the language better fitted than any I know to convey multiple shades of emotion without falling into sentimentality, one could neither lay bare nor inflict upon others this tenderness lavished on one whom she looked on as her own child, this constant, touching dread lest essentials should be neglected in what seemed to her a fantastic progress through an eternal transformation scene. But one thing is certain; all this is not mere froth and foam on a picturesque but shallow stream; a deep nature is involved.

It certainly was not an easy one to read. For instance, among her gifts was a rare intellectual imaginativeness, yet imagination of the heart she had none; and as, but for her unsatisfied mother-instinct, she had never known sorrow, many things were hidden from her. In reality it was a stiff nature undeveloped by life, yet bafflingly suppled and disguised on the surface by a voluptuous ease of moods and rhetoric – a combination which accounted for the abrupt, cruel transition from midsummer to winter. When all was well between us it was natural to her to give an almost bewilderingly rich, tender form to affection; but the rock below, the possibility of seeing in one thing – and one only – her duty, the consequent ruthless sacrifice of all the rest, in a word the nameless something that chilled her music for me . . . this was equally Lisl. The one element that fuses all other elements was denied her, and perhaps only passionate temperaments can stand erect in elemental storms. Conrad Fiedler said she was deficient in depth of feeling, and possibly this is what he meant, but I think that with these letters before him he would have put it differently.

I think, too, Lili Wach was right in saying as she once did, that Lisl's was a too 'simple' affection, a mere matter of personal inclination, lacking the subtle, tenacious web of moral issues that is woven unconsciously into all perfect relations. But Lili never wearied in trying to persuade me that, be that as it might, she suffered cruelly. And it was *I* who refused to believe this, I who alone among all her friends knew of her ever-recurring grief at her childlessness, who admired her effort to accept the inevitable cheerfully and hide her pain in the depths of her heart! In one of her letters she once spoke of this attitude towards harsh necessity as part of human dignity; if such was her instinct where no loyalty to others was involved, how much more in this case? . . . It is hard for people who are apt to translate feeling into action to admit any other test of sincerity; but . . . there are other tests, and today it is I who am crying into the void, '*Credo, credo in te!*' . . .

One more thing became clear to me as I retravelled our road. It looks as if those at whose demand she cancelled her past accepted the sacrifice with something very like indifference – perhaps, who knows? with a touch of a still colder feeling. From a letter written after her death by H. B. it is evident that the devoted couple were Julia and her mother, Lisl being relatively of little account . . . if so what pain for her! In this light one phrase in her final letter to me acquires a pathetic significance; 'Heinrich, the only being I possess in this world!' . . .

Meanwhile neither she nor her doctors saw any reason why she should not live to be an old woman. We were both young, and some day, in the natural course of things, the blind, passionate will that stood between us would disappear. And so she made no plans, but lived, as was her wont, in the present, till the day death fell upon her unawares.

Such I believe is the explanation of what has been for the greater part of my life a tragic inexplicable mystery. And as I lay down my pen it is stranger than any dream to find that the ice-bound years have melted, that there is still a debt to be paid – a debt which, across the faint line that divides the living from the dead, I can go on paying to the end.[16]

FOUR
1891–4

LADY PONSONBY
BALMORAL
LAUNCHING THE MASS
ONE OAK

Lady Ponsonby

It must have been in the middle eighties that I first set eyes on Lady Ponsonby. I had accompanied some foreign ladies who were staying with the Empress Eugénie at Farnborough Hill to a minor military function at Aldershot – sports I fancy – and one of the Princesses was giving away the prizes. Madame Arcos, a sort of unofficial lady-in-waiting to the Empress who was shepherding the Farnborough Hill contingent, after presenting her homages to the Princess exchanged a few words with a short striking-looking woman evidently in attendance on Her Royal Highness. So instantly did she arrest my attention that I asked who she was. 'Oh, that's Lady Ponsonby – wife of the Queen's private secretary,' said Madame Arcos; and another woman, reputed to be in the know as to Court gossip, volunteered, 'A very clever woman – said to be the only person the Queen is afraid of;' or it may have been 'the only person she is afraid of is the Queen'. In after years I related this incident to Lady Ponsonby, adding that my informant had a relation who was something or other at the Court. 'Probably one of the footmen,' said Lady Ponsonby.

Then came the years when I was so much at the Deanery at Windsor, and gathering on all sides that Lady Ponsonby was, in truth, a remarkable woman, of course I longed to meet her. One day – I think it must have been in 1890 – her two daughters, Betty and Maggie, came to tea; and shortly afterwards, on the 'cutlet for cutlet' principle, Edith Davidson and I were duly bidden to Norman Tower, the official residence of the Queen's private secretary, and at last I found myself in the presence of the lady of the house.

But not for long. Afternoon tea was a ceremony that bored her, and what she had heard so far of Edith Davidson's friend, Ethel Smyth, had not inspired her with a wish to make my acquaintance. On the contrary! True, Sir Walter Parratt, the beloved organist of St George's Chapel, had specially praised my counterpoint, and as the Ponsonbys were musical this should have told in my favour. But Lady Ponsonby was also aware of my passion for hunting, and declared that a contrapuntist *doublé* with Fred Archer, as she put it, sounded very tiresome. As soon therefore as politeness allowed she pleaded urgent letters and vanished.

In my youth I sang a great deal, and Edith now suggested I should sing my own edition of the beautiful Irish melody 'Come o'er the Sea' to the girls. No sooner was it over than Betty jumped up saying, 'Mama *must* hear that,' ran out of the room, and presently came back leading in her reluctant and deeply sceptical mother. The song was repeated and after that there were no further difficulties; in fact it became my habit to bribe her with music and then settle down to the interminable talks that were to be my joy for the next twenty-six years.

As transformed by Lady Ponsonby nothing could be less suggestive of officialdom than Norman Tower, and the same was true of the London house in St James's Palace. Some people have a knack of converting their dwellings into an outer shell of their own personality, and this miracle was even performed on Gilmuire near Ascot, the essentially modern house she bought after her husband Sir Henry's death and in which the rest of her life was to be spent. But nowhere could a more perfect setting for the unique quality of this greatest of great ladies exist than Norman Tower – a dwelling hacked out of the thickness of the outer wall of the Castle (this is a flight of fancy but gives a good idea of the place) and perched above the old moat, now converted into a hanging garden. Most of this garden circled round the tower at an acute angle, and on a flat portion of it, Lady Ponsonby, who adored anything to do with tools, had erected a shed with carpenter's bench and lathe.

In former times the guard were lodged in Norman Tower, of which two octagonal chambers served as State Prisons, and one of Lady Ponsonby's first preoccupations was to obtain through her great friend among the Princesses, the Empress Frederick, the Queen's permission to tear down the plaster and paint with which some philistine official had thought to brighten up these sad rooms. The two ladies themselves took a hand in this work and presently names and rough graffiti, scratched prisoner-wise with nails, revealed themselves on the walls, which of course were now left bare. The Prisons became Lady Ponsonby's sanctum and the extraordinarily characteristic furniture included a tool-table with a glass of water on it ready for painting. In fact there were facilities for 'occupations', as the family used to call them, all over the house; in her bedroom window an easel at which she often painted, in another little room a table sacred to silver repoussé work, and books, books, books everywhere.

My very first encounter with her brought one of the sharp joys that, so far, the rough file of piled-up years has been powerless to blunt – the strange, half physical pleasure a beautiful speaking voice can still induce in the present writer, and if this looks like extravagance of sensation, it is an extravagance permissible in a musician. In Lady Ponsonby's case the effect was heightened by a clean-cut enunciation slightly tinged with a soft Northumbrian burr – no doubt a feminine edition of the same thing in Harry Hotspur's speech and, as in his case, the charm lay perhaps in the fact that it was so emphatically herself. I never knew what my Christian name could sound like till she came to use it.

The next visit provided another vivid impression. She was seated at her writing-table the appliances of which were as carefully thought out as a conjuror's stock-in-trade, and anything with steel, silver or brass about it had a burnish one came to associate with her mental operations. But what specially struck me was the way her small, extremely strong hands tackled ordinary little tasks, such as sharpening a pencil, sealing a letter, adjusting a lamp, finding her place in a book – rapid, delicate, accurate movements as of a world in which fumbling is unknown. Later on I grasped the fascination these things had for me; it was the suggestion of force combined with restraint – the swift, controlled energy of the violent. Once I said to her, 'There's nothing exciting about picking up a pin with an old pair of scissors. But suppose some huge hammer, capable of squashing a Great Northern engine as flat as a flounder, and furnished with tiny claws at the end, were to descend rapidly, noiselessly, and pick up that pin, wouldn't it thrill you?' And though told not to talk nonsense I think the idea pleased her, for she was rather proud of her muscular strength, and only a couple of years before her death made me feel her biceps, remarking, 'Not bad for eighty-two!'

After that we must have met occasionally, for in a letter to my brother I find mention of a 'wonderful new friend of mine, stepped straight out of the eighteenth century'. But this was true in a limited sense only, for in essential matters, as beseemed the granddaughter of Earl Grey, she was a modern woman. When Girton College was started in the early sixties, Mrs Ponsonby, then a young married woman, was, together with Miss Emily Davies, one of the hardest workers on the original Committee. And ten years later when the first

Trade Union for women came into existence no member of the board was more indefatigable than she. Like other young women she was fond of riding, skating, dancing and society, but she seems always to have gravitated towards people who had serious interests in life. Indeed, such was her respect for intellectual achievement, that when presented to George Eliot, before she realized what was happening she suddenly found herself in the midst of one of the profound curt-seys she reserved exclusively for the Queen.

Never was a woman of more catholic tastes. From the first she had been devoted to music and painting, and like all Bulteels took her own line in all things. She told me that she fancied the Queen had selected her as Maid of Honour not because she was the niece of her private secretary, General Grey, but partly because she had the reputation of being a first-rate actress, and chiefly because she was of a different type from the generality of courtiers. None the less, when Sir Henry, who had been equerry to the Prince Consort, succeeded General Grey, according to Lady Ponsonby it took his Sovereign Lady ten years to understand that the former Maid of Honour had no ambition to pull strings. Shrewd though the Queen was, I suppose no potentate can be expected to assume complete indifference to intrigue in the wife of one so near the throne as the royal private secretary – particularly if that wife is a woman of brilliant intellect and strong personality.

Lady Ponsonby's equipment included many other qualities it is easy to catalogue – culture, sense of humour, courage, inflexible rectitude, sense of duty, and a religious instinct which I once pleased her by defining as a blend of paganism and Christian mysticism. But in no human being I have ever met were hidden such inexhaustible stores of fire as in the heart of this apparently calm, deliberately reserved, rather Sphinx-like being, who possessed among other peculiarities the art of settling down with her book or newspaper in her armchair, or in a railway carriage – quiet as the hills and as though established there for all eternity.

Let me try to describe her person. The mould of the face was mass-ive, the hair wavy and grey. She always wore a cap, but in her dressing-room you could verify what you would have affirmed on oath without knowledge – that what grew beneath it was alive and plentiful. The whole build expressed energy and powers of endurance. Of her hands and feet she herself would have said, 'I hope they are the hands and feet of a lady.' Her eyes, greyish-blue, or rather bluish-grey, had a light-holding quality I have seen in more obviously striking orbs, but eyes more arresting I have never looked into; and when she was angry, furiously angry, they turned so coal-black that one member of the family would say to another when temperatures were rising, 'You needn't have black eyes about it!'

It was always engrossing to watch expression chasing expression across that fraudulently impassive face of hers. Her nephew Maurice Baring, who afterwards became one of my greatest friends, once said to me that he would be content to spend his life watching her face. She was devoted to Maurice, who at that time was studying German at Hildesheim, and had reached a stage of youthful effervescence which those who have only known him since he came relatively to years of discretion may have difficulty in realizing. I remember Lady Ponsonby frigidly remarking, 'I wish Maurice did not think it amusing to shy his spectacles into the fire' . . . Yes! words like 'shy' and 'bag' had crept into the intimate vocabulary of this mother of three sons, and occasionally turned up in the oddest way. For instance, I remember her remarking in connection with a mutual acquaintance who was given to timid deprecating pilferings in the matrimonial or extramatrimonial preserves of her friends, that she hoped I never stooped to that sort of '*mesquinerie*' – 'so like the maids prigging hairpins'.*

As hinted in the above sentence, the chief peculiarity of her diction was a habit that might have been irritating in anyone else of interlarding it with French phrases to such an extent that one never heard her use the English equivalents of *hochements de tête, l'infiniment petit, injures, mesquineries, inepties, à tête reposée* and dozens of similar words. And a thing she never could get over was that the fluent French speaker I think I can claim to have been in those days should be so hopelessly inaccurate in her genders; 'And you a musician too!'

This accuracy expressed itself in the extreme daintiness of her person, a point of coquetry which she considered obligatory in the old. Not that she appeared to take much interest in the actual cut of her clothes, in fact I suspect that many women of her age and epoch whom no one could accuse of over-fussiness in such matters gave them more thought in a month than she did in a year. And though I never saw her 'trying on', I feel convinced that, patient up to a certain point, the moment would come for a decided 'Thank you, that will do,' after which, let the fitter plead as she might, no further pullings and pinchings and pokings would have been submitted to.

But when she sallied forth to dine with the Queen, or to attend some

* 'Prig' – to steal.

function it would not quite do to disregard, I loved to see her for once in a way in a handsome gown, wearing her ribbons and orders and all the rest of it – '*Cela ne gâte rien*,' as the Empress's old *Dame d'Honneur* Madame le Breton used to say when urging me to put my hat on straight, and even the most precious stones (I am alluding not to myself but to Lady Ponsonby) look none the worse for a fine setting.

I spoke of the fire that underlay everything and come now to the quality in her I chiefly delighted in, the extreme violence of her temperament. But let me preface by saying that what must have struck the ordinary observer most strongly of all will have been a serenity it would seem impossible to ruffle. Indeed, to my untold astonishment one of her nieces wrote recently to another member of the family, 'I suppose you know best, but myself I can hardly believe that dear Aunt M'aimée *could* be violent!'; reading which words I said to myself, 'Then she missed the best part!'

In my opinion the two things, violence and serenity, are absolutely compatible. Each has its hour. But violence is not one of the traits that figure in epitaphs or even in obituary notices; and perhaps it is this discretion, this delicacy, this training of an unreal roseate light on the departed that makes all epitaphs and the majority of obituary notices such unsatisfactory reading. No one is more acutely aware of the inadequacy of this little tribute to Lady Ponsonby than its writer, but that particular defect it shall not have; so without further ado I once more turn to what I have always looked upon as one of the most attractive, the most lovable symptoms of intense vitality.

I remember her telling me at Gilmuire of a heated dispute with the old gentleman who owned the property next to theirs, how in the night he had clambered over the fence and staked out a yard or so on her side of the ditch declaring that this was the true boundary; how she had marched down with the manservant, commanding him to pull up the stakes, and how while this was proceeding the old gentleman suddenly appeared on the bank and bade the man stop at once or he would have the law on him. Whereupon Lady Ponsonby not only ordered him to go on, but began pulling up the stakes herself (I have said she was very muscular) and flinging them back over the bank on which the old gentleman was still vociferating. 'You can't do anything to me,' she told him. 'I have no vote and am not a citizen so don't come within the operation of the law. But let me tell you' (here a vigorous pull at a stake) 'I intend to stick to my rights all the same. And as for you' (whizz bang went the stake – but *not* aimed at the enemy!) 'how dare you come skulking over the fence at dead of night, trespassing on my property?' And stake after stake flew over the fence, while W. murmured nervously, 'Oh, my lady, you'll hurt yourself.'

Speaking for myself, though she was dearer to me than any woman in the world, never in my life, except perhaps with my mother, have I had such elemental rows with anyone as with Lady Ponsonby, particularly during the first year or two of our friendship. Accustomed to being considered rather violent myself, it always seemed to me that compared with her I was milder than milk and water, but this may have been a delusion. I will confess that in days gone by owners of shrieking canaries and squawking parrots would declare that except when I was in the room the bird never uttered a sound. Similarly when in third-class carriages horrid little children slithered off laps, wriggled out of restraining arms, lurched over to me and began pawing me about, their mothers never failed to remark that until I entered the compartment the child had been as good as gold – always *was* good in a train.

After the break-up of my old home I took a cottage at Frimley, about seven miles from Gilmuire, and often used to bike over and stay the night, while Maggie, rightly judging that 'two's company and three's none', would dine with their neighbour the Ranee of Sarawak. One night after dinner in the midst of some extra-fierce argument Lady Ponsonby remarked, 'Will you kindly shut that door unless you wish every word you say to be overheard by the servants you are so fond of imitating.' At this I jumped up, ran into the porch, and began lighting my bicycle lamp. It was 9.30, a wild, wet, blustering, King-Lear night, and the long Bagshot Hill and seven miles of pedal work against the wind lay between me and my cottage. The drawing-room door opened and Lady Ponsonby advanced into the hall. 'What on earth are you doing?' she asked, and I flattered myself her voice sounded rather alarmed; 'Don't be absurd – put out that lamp.' I uttered one word only – 'Good-night' – and shot out into the storm. Next day Maggie wrote to Betty, 'When I got back Ethel had been gone half an hour, and the house was still rocking.'[17]

Balmoral

It was about a year after my career as public musician began that I came to know the Empress Eugénie well, and from the very first she followed my proceedings with the greatest sympathy. The fate of the Mass interested her particularly, because most of it had been written during a stay with her at Cap Martin in 1891; and being wholly unmusical herself – a great asset in a musical patron – she readily accepted the composer's estimate of its worth! I do not think that she was less delighted than I myself when, in the autumn of that year, Mr Barnby (later Sir Joseph), director of the Royal Choral Society, provisionally accepted the Mass for production at the Albert Hall. By 'provisionally' I mean that I could not get him to fix a date, but the general idea was that the performance would be in the second half of the ensuing season, that is about March 1892.

Mr Barnby's reluctance to name the day rather troubled me, and the Empress thought it would help matters if she commissioned me to inform him that she herself might possibly be present – a wonderful concession to friendship, for since 1870 she had refused to appear officially in any public place.

This proposal of hers, which I should never have dared to suggest, showed how thoroughly she had grasped the musical situation in England, where, even before the war denuded the country of concert-going Germans, good music does not pay. That being so, composers who have money fight their way with it, and those who have not try to get up a little boom – which comes to the same thing. If you cannot afford to distribute dozens of tickets among friends and supporters, the public must be induced to buy; and Sir Thomas Beecham once said that the safest plan would be to introduce an elephant that can stand on its trunk, or some such spot of relief, into every concert programme.

In this spirit, then, did the Empress tackle my problem. Further, learning that the Duke of Edinburgh was president of the Royal Choral Society, she thought there could be no harm in manifesting her sympathy for me under the eyes of the Royal Family. An excellent opportunity of doing so lay to hand; it had been for many years the Queen's habit to put one of her Scotch houses at the Empress's disposal during the autumn months, and thus it came to pass that in October I was invited to join her at Birkhall.

Birkhall was a laird's house, not big, but comfortable, about eight miles from Balmoral and in the midst of most beautiful scenery. My first amazed impression had nothing to do with the landscape, however, but with the Empress herself. O horror! She, who loathed caps and never wore them, now appeared at the front door with a little erection of black lace on her small, beautifully poised head! What did this portend?

It portended that the Queen did not approve of capless old ladies, and this compromise was the result. I was indignant at such pusillanimity, but she only laughed and said what on earth did it signify? '*Si cela fait plaisir à votre Reine!*'

The day after my arrival the Duke and Duchess of Connaught and Prince Henry of Battenberg came over to see her, and as the Duchess and the Prince were both fond of music I was asked to sing. Following on that, the Queen sent a message to say that when she came to pay her own visit next day I was to be presented.

Next day a storm was raging that, whatever one may say about the fleeting character of Scotch storms, began at breakfast and lasted till nightfall. I could never have believed that any old lady would venture out in such weather, but I was informed, and it proved to be true, that the Queen would infallibly turn up, and probably in an open carriage; also that her ladies would wear the minimum of wraps, as the Queen herself never caught cold and had a great objection to being crowded out by rugs and furs.

Some of her ladies were old and frail, but the rigours of a Scotch 'waiting', including a north-east wind *with rain*, were evidently nullified by the glow of loyalty within their bosoms. On the other hand, dread of displeasing 'the dear Queen', as she was always called (and rightly – for, if dreaded, she was greatly beloved), may have had something to to do with it. Terror often acts as a tonic, and the first rule in the Primer for Courtiers – a fine rule that fashions heroes and heroines – is: 'Never, never be ill.' Anyhow none of her ladies seems to have died of pneumonia, as might have been expected, after these terrific drives that sometimes lasted hours and hours.

The Queen was expected at three o'clock, but long before that time the Empress was scouting in passages and peering into the storm-tossed garden to make sure that the coast was clear, for the Queen had the greatest horror of coming across stray people. Indeed I know of a case where an unlucky Maid of Honour, surprised in the corridor of Windsor Castle by the unexpected appearance of Her Majesty in the far distance, remained concealed and trembling behind a curtain for half an hour, while the Empress of India was supervising the placing of tributes from an Indian Prince. And when, on the stroke of three, the Royal carriage arrived at Birkhall, but for the Empress, Madame Arcos and the footmen it might have been a deserted house.

The Empress and Madame Arcos received the Queen and Princess Christian at the front door, and the red carpet, unrolled in a flash, was sopping wet before the august visitors and time to set foot on it. The three Royal Ladies then disappeared into the drawing-room, while Madame Arcos and Lady Ampthill, who was in waiting on the Queen, came into the room where I in another sense was also in waiting. Presently the Empress herself looked in, beckoned to me, I followed . . . and lo! I was in the Presence.

Seated on one of the ordinary cane chairs, no doubt because easier to get up from, was a wee little old lady with exactly the face of the photographs, though paler than one expected, on her head a close white straw hat, tied under her chin with a black ribbon (the only possible plan, given the storm and an open barouche). It is a well-known fact that in spite of a physique that did not lend itself to effects of majesty the personality of the Queen was dignified and imposing to the last degree. So awe-inspiring was the first impression that I should have been terrified but for the wonderful, blue, child-like eyes, and the sweetest, most entrancing smile I have ever seen on human face.

The Empress had told me that though the Queen had chronic sciatica and walked with a stick she never permitted anyone to help her out of her chair, even when that chair had no arms. Much to my astonishment she now got up to shake hands with me, lifting herself with a sort of one, two, three and away movement, which it took all one's strength of character not to assist with a hand under her elbow.

I cannot remember what passed at that interview except that she was markedly kind, and that Princess Christian, who, as I was to find out later, always knew what the helpful thing to say was and said it, at once remarked that she had heard a great deal about me from the Bishop of Rochester and his wife, the point being that the Bishop had been Dean of Windsor, and besides being the Queen's private chaplain was one of her most valued friends and advisers. A further passport to favour was the fact that I could claim to be connected with him, his brother having married my eldest sister.

It was not the Queen's way, and not according to the tradition she had been brought up in, to put you at your ease, as some Sovereigns do, and bring about anything distantly approaching conversation. But the Empress, who was the most socially competent of beings, talked away cheerfully in her own easy, delightful fashion, all in adopting a manner I had hitherto seen no trace of and which was reserved exclusively for the Queen – something of the manner of an unembarrassed but attentive child talking to its grandmother.

Presently I was asked to sing, and sang several German songs which seemed to please my audience so highly that the Empress was emboldened to say, 'You ought to hear her sing her Mass!' Whereupon I performed the Benedictus and the Sanctus after the manner of composers, which means singing the chorus as well as the solo parts, and trumpeting forth orchestral effects as best you can – a noisy proceeding in a small room. I had warned the Empress that if I did it at all it would be done in that fashion, and being a most courageous woman she took the responsibility – with no dire results, as subsequent events were to prove. Indeed, she remarked afterwards that beyond doubt the Queen was delighted with this novel experience, not merely being polite.

The Queen then expressed a hope that the Empress would bring me to Balmoral, after which I was dismissed and joined the official ladies in the other room. There we had tea, and I listened for the first time, in high edification, to the delicate and guarded style of intercourse that appears to be the right thing between such interlocutors. The storm, which had somewhat abated in honour of the Queen's arrival, was now raging more wildly than ever, the rain descending like one continuous waterfall. It was hardly possible to hear oneself speak, but I managed to ask Lady Ampthill if the Queen would have the carriage shut going home, and to catch her serene reply: 'O dear no, I think not.' Watching their departure from behind a curtain a little later on, I saw that this incredible prediction was fulfilled, and my ideas on the subject of what 'Queen's weather' really amounts to were modified for evermore.

The Empress told us, after she was gone, that from first to last the Queen made not the slightest comment on the tempest, nor any move to depart till a gilly came banging at the drawing-room door, and said, 'Your Majesty must go – the horses can't stand this' – the sort of thing not one of her children would have dared to say, unless, perhaps, the Empress Frederick.

In due time came the promised command, and one evening I found myself struggling to achieve as presentable a toilette as possible, having been bidden, with the Empress, to dine at Balmoral. At the last moment she herself put a few finishing touches, producing and arranging upon my head a grand jet serpent and disposing other jetty splendours about my person, for the Court was, as usual, in mourning.

I, of course, dined with the Household – such an everyday affair to hundreds of people that they would hardly deem it worth talking about. But to me it was a new, interesting and rather alarming experience; nor has custom staled the impression, for it remained solitary of its kind.

I was impressed by the air of distinguished boredom, combined with a well-bred but unmistakable consciousness of occupying an enviable position, that, as I was to find out in after years, people about a Court invariably distil. I cannot claim to be constitutionally shy, which may be a sign of conceit, and may, on the other hand, indicate that the drama itself, and not your own part in it, absorbs most of your attention; but surely, I said to myself, the genius of this place must affect even the most brazen! With what invisible pitfalls is one surrounded, how terrible must be the penalties incurred by one false step, since all are keyed up, as a matter of habit, to this extraordinarily high pitch! No ups and downs of mood here, no enthusiasm, no individual opinions, and for Heaven's sake no originality!

All the same, dinner was very pleasant. I had met one or two of the Equerries and Maids of Honour at the Deanery, and as Tosti, the songwriter, whom I liked extremely, sat on one side of me, I was quite sorry when the doors were flung open by scarlet-liveried footmen, signal that the Queen was ready for our presence.

I must now nerve myself to recount the story of one of the most appalling blunders I ever committed in my life; even today, though I can laugh about it, the thought of it gives me a slight sinking! At the moment, though conscious of having sinned against ritual, I did not realize the full enormity of my crime – you must have been bred to Courts to do that. And though, as time went on, I grasped it exhaustively, somehow or other I shrank from cross-questioning the Empress on the subject. For one thing, so great was her kindness that she would have attenuated my *faux pas*; for another, knowing what her agony must have been as she watched her young friend's proceedings, I fancied she would prefer not to live through it all again! Finally, truth to tell, the whole thing was a humiliation to me to think of! Despicable, no doubt, to take it as hard as all that, but so it was.

Why no one prepared me for the situation I was about to become part of, why no one gave me a hint how to comport myself in it, I cannot imagine. The Empress was always thinking out and guarding against eventualities in what seemed to me an almost feverish fashion, yet this time she said not a word, and I can only suppose she felt certain that my darkness would be enlightened by Madame Arcos or one of the Maids of Honour. But it was not, and when we left the dinner-table, being the only guest of my sex present, I gaily headed the procession drawing-roomwards, my mind innocently set on making myself agreeable when I should get there.

It was a large room with deep bay windows, and the first thing I noticed was that the sofas and chairs were tightly upholstered in the gay Stuart tartan – a proof that to be Queen of Scotland involves painful aesthetic concessions.

On a large hearth-rug – tartan, too, I think – in front of the grate, in which I rather fancy a few logs burned (though given Her Majesty's hardy habits it seems improbable), stood the Queen, conversing with the Empress in a lively manner that contrasted with the somewhat halting intercourse at Birkhall. Evidently, I said to myself, the animating effects of a good dinner may be counted on even at the less frivolous European Courts.

Leading up to the two august ladies was an avenue composed of Royal personages – ranged, as I afterwards found out, in order of precedence, the highest in rank being closest to the hearth-rug – which avenue, broadening towards its base, gradually became mere ladies and gentlemen of the Court, and finally petered out in a group of Maids of Honour huddled ingloriously in the bay window.

What I ought to have done, I believe, was to stand rigid and silent among these last, try discreetly to catch the eye of the Queen and the Princesses, curtsey profoundly when successful, and await events. Will it be believed that what I did do was to advance unconcernedly up the avenue, with a polite intention to say 'How do you do' to the Queen?

If a young dog strays up the aisle during church no one says anything, no one does anything, but, none the less, he soon becomes aware that something is wrong. Even so, as the distance between

myself and the hearth-rug diminished, did I become aware that something was very wrong indeed; my cheerful confidence waned and my
step faltered. I saw the Queen slightly turn her head, look at me for a
second as if I were some strange insect, and resume her conversation
with the Empress. If I had been a Brobdingnagian spider as big as a
Newfoundland she would not have acted differently. Someone would
remove the creature; that was enough. I did not catch the Empress's
eye, but I now know that since she could not shriek, '*Mon Dieu, n'avan-
cez pas!*', she must have wished the earth would open and swallow her
up. At this moment dear, human Princess Christian, who had come
more in contact with low life than the Queen, stepped forward and
shook hands with me – and somehow or other, I know not how,
I backed away into the obscurity from which I should never have
emerged.

Afterwards I heard all about that Hearth-rug, and could gauge the
dimensions of my audacity. It was as sacred a carpet as exists outside
Mohammedanism, and the distance from it at which people were permitted to station themselves – if invited to come near it at all – was the
measure of their rank and importance. Only Crowned Heads trod it
as a right, or occasionally, as supreme honour, some very favourite
Minister, like Lord Beaconsfield. If such as I had set foot upon it, as,
but for the blessed intervention of Princess Christian, I might have
done . . . but, no! A miracle would have been wrought, a thunderbolt
would have fallen upon a tartan sofa and created a diversion, something – anything would have happened rather than such sacrilege
could have been permitted!

When the legitimate moment came for my presence being recognized by the Queen I cannot recall how it was accomplished, whether
she went the round of the company, or whether I was summoned to
her chair. But whichever it was, my scandalous entry was evidently
condoned, for nothing could be more gracious than her manner. And
presently, having received the command to 'let us hear some more of
your Mass', I was seated at a huge, yawning grand piano, with the
Queen and the Empress right and left, in closest proximity. I ventured
to ask whether the music was to be rendered as at Birkhall – a proceeding which seemed unthinkable in these surroundings – but I was
assured that exactly that rendering was 'so very interesting', and
would be welcome.

I looked round the frozen ranks of impending listeners, each one of
them exhaling decorum and self-restraint unutterable. A vault beneath

a church would have been a more kindling *mise en scène* for an inspirational effort on a large scale. Not because of the Royalties, who one and all showed genuine and kindly interest, but because of their inevitable adjunct, 'the Court'! Straight in the line of vision, glued against a distant wall, stood Lord Cross, the Minister in Attendance, looking startlingly like his caricature in *Punch*, 'Very Cross'. I afterwards learned that I had not a more appreciative listener in the room, but how could one guess that? . . . Well, there was nothing for it but to dismiss this Madame Tussaud-like company from my mind and concentrate upon the Mass.

Strange to relate, once I got under way there was something inspiring in the very incongruity of the whole thing, the desperateness of such a venture! Never did I get through one of these performances better or enjoy doing it more. I cannot remember what numbers I chose, but the Sanctus must have been one of them, for in it is a D trumpet which I remember rang out astonishingly in that superbly acoustic drawing-room. I dared not let my eyes wander in the direction of the listeners while the high D was being held, lest what I might see should wreck everything. But I need not have been afraid, as I was to learn presently.

And now, emboldened by the sonority of the place, I did the Gloria – the most tempestuous and, I thought, the best number of all. At a certain drum effect a foot, even, came into play, and I fancy that as regards volume of sound at least, the presence of a real chorus and orchestra was scarcely missed! This time, fortified by the simplicity and genuineness of the Sovereign's appreciation, I thought I would risk a glance at the faces of her terrifying Court. What matter if astonishment and secret scandalization be there depicted? I was well down in the saddle now, not easily to be thrown!

I glanced. They were stupendous. No surprise, no emotion of any kind! – a spectacle so exciting, because so fantastic, that the result was a finale to that Gloria such as I had never before succeeded in wresting out!

Once more the Queen seemed really delighted – whether for the Empress's sake or because she liked it, who shall say? Anyhow, the Hereditary Grand Duke of Hesse who was a cultivated musician seemed really to understand what he had been listening to, and so did Princess Christian, who was constantly in touch with serious music and musicians. And I could see that the beloved Empress, in spite of the incident in the Royal Avenue, did not repent her of the role she had undertaken – according to her the role of a foreigner who introduces a gifted Englishwoman to the Queen of England!

Then Tosti, accompanying himself, sang some favourite songs of his own composition with exquisite blending of voice, phrasing and accompaniment. It was small art, but real art. Most of the people to whom I expressed an ecstasy that even the prevailing discretion could not damp, replied instantaneously, as if uttering one of the responses in church, 'Yes, but what a pity his voice is so small!' And I perceived that this was the accepted formula for Tosti.

When the Queen said good-night to me she added a hope 'that we shall see you at Windsor', and then she and her Imperial guest moved towards a special Royal exit; for though the Empress, the Marquis of Bassano (who was in attendance on her), Madame Arcos and I were all driving home in the same carriage, it would never do for us three to go out by the same door as a Crowned Head.

This was lucky, for I now had the chance of witnessing a wonderful bit of ritual. Arrived on the threshold, the while we mortals stood rigid, the Queen motioned the Empress to pass before her; this the Empress gracefully declined to do. They then curtsied low to each other. The movement of the Queen, crippled though she was, was amazingly easy and dignified; but the Empress, who was then sixty-seven, made such an exquisite sweep down to the floor and up again, all in one gesture, that I can only liken it to a flower bent and released by the wind. They then passed *together* out of the door, practically shoulder to shoulder; but I believe, though far be it from my ignorance to dogmatize, that on such occasions the visiting Sovereign is permitted to permit the home Sovereign to lag about one inch behind.[18]

Next Christmas a Royal incident occurred which amused me a good deal. Great potentates who came to Windsor were apt to offer a memento to Sir Henry and add something for his wife; but these presents were always refused, because, as she put it, he did not wish it to be supposed that the Queen's servants could be tipped like a butler; in accordance with which principle some magnificent turquoises had recently been sent back to the Shah of Persia. Now Lady Ponsonby's sole passion in jewellery was turquoises, and this incident caused her such a pang, that when a beautiful carpet, offered by some other Eastern potentate, arrived, she begged Sir Henry to speak to the Queen before sending it back, pointing out that the drawing-room at Norman Tower was badly in need of a new carpet.

Accordingly Sir Henry did speak to the Queen, explaining his reasons for always returning these presents. The Queen's reply was: 'I think you are perfectly right. *You might send on the carpet to me.*'

Launching the Mass

Christmas 1892 was in some sort a replica of my mother's last Christmas on earth two years ago, when for the first time the Henschels had come to Frimhurst. Now again the Henschels were with us, and little did we dream that when another Christmas should come round my father would be lying stricken to death, so well, so cheery was he. I particularly recall the beauty of his reading of the lessons at Morning Service; also that on the previous Sunday he had introduced an emendation of the text, informing the much astonished congregation that the punishment awarded to the Israelites in the desert for grumbling was a visitation of 'fiery flying pheasants' (serpents). His shooting days were over but evidently they still haunted him.[19]

To complete the story of the Mass, I must first say that the Empress's kindness in bringing about that Balmoral performance was of the greatest possible use, though in the autumn of 1892 it had still been as far off materializing on a Royal Choral Society programme as ever. But by that time my lifelong friendship with Lady Ponsonby had begun, and one day, at her instigation, Sir Henry told the Duke of Edinburgh, whom I did not know, how matters stood.

The Duke had heard all about the Mass, thanks to the Empress, and the result was that it was at once put down for performance.[20] Barnby and I then met, and as the concert of 18 January suited the Empress Eugénie admirably, that date was fixed.[21] Not only had the Empress definitely undertaken to be present, but Princess Christian and Princess Henry of Battenberg did the same. And whereas singers with reputations are not anxious, as a rule, to take part in novelties by practically unknown composers – not, at least, unless they are heavily subsidized by the composer to do so – it now became emphatically worthwhile to sing in the Mass. Thus I was able to command the services of admirable soloists.[22]

During Christmas week Henschel was angelically helpful with the proofs and orchestral parts of the Mass, and it was decided that on the night before the performance we were all to have dinner at his house; that is, my five sisters and their husbands, my father, and also (though we did not think it necessary to spring the fact on the latter just yet) Harry Brewster, who was coming to England for the occasion. On previous visits he had made great friends with the hospitable Henschels, and this seemed as good an opportunity as any other to bang together those two very *disparate* heads, Harry's and my father's. But I was too deeply preoccupied with the musical aspect of the next three weeks to bother much about possible complications, whether sentimental or domestic.

During January the rehearsals became intensive. Never had I hated anything so much. All composers who have not yet arrived know what it is to sit helpless while your explicit instructions as to tempi, volume of sound and everything else, are being brushed aside as irrelevant . . . and O! your timid attempts to modify the conductor's reading without putting his back up . . . terrible! terrible! But worst of all are upsurging floods of hatred for the work itself – result, one hopes, of nerves – followed by an inclination to say to some conscientious soloist, 'O *please* don't take all that trouble! It really isn't worth it!' The soloists and chorus were delightful, and so was Barnby, although he afterwards confessed it was not till the last rehearsal that he discovered what he called 'an iron rod' running through music that hitherto had struck him as disjointed, over-exuberant and unnatural. Anything so different to the Three Choirs' outlook and technique would inevitably seem all that to an English Choral conductor of the early nineties – at least until he got accustomed to it.

The high-water mark of misery was touched at the first orchestral rehearsal, when I realized various mistakes I had made – for instance, scoring the solo parts of the Sanctus for a quartet of soft brass. When the poor contralto, emerging from a welter of choral and orchestral billows, attacked one of her solo passages, I perceived that a brass curtain ring flung to an overboard passenger in mid-Atlantic would be about as adequate a 'support' as my four lonesome instrumentalists, who in that vast empty hall sounded like husky mosquitoes. No sooner was the rehearsal over than armed with music-paper, scissors, stickphast and all the accursed paraphernalia of composers, I ensconced myself in the bowels of the edifice and re-scored the Sanctus, as it were at the cannon's mouth.

This incident deepened the gloom induced by listening to the noises for which I was responsible. The standard of orchestral playing and sight-reading was very different then to what it is now, and whereas a seasoned composer, hearing his music stumbled through for the first time, knows that by and by it will sound very different, I had written too little, and heard what I had written too seldom to be confident as to my scoring, particularly in the case of a first big choral work. Henschel kept on reassuring me, but I put it down to kindness, and went home despair in my heart.

Next morning at the final rehearsal an unforgettable thing happened. Barnby had told me they would begin by putting through its paces that good old Choral Society war-horse, Haydn's *Creation*, two parts of which made up the second half of the programme; so that if I turned up at 11.00 it would be soon enough. By 10.30, however, I was tearing madly round and round those labyrinthine corridors, up and down those countless staircases, vainly trying to find the way to the stalls. Now nearer, now farther, what in my fever seemed to me exquisite orchestral sonorities assailed my ear: 'Ah!' said I to myself, in sick misery, '*that's* how I'd like my music to sound!' . . . Drawing nearer suddenly a phrase seemed strangely familiar . . . ! Merciful heaven! it was my own Mass!

The night before the performance the Henschels' unforgettable dinner-party took place. This was the first meeting between my father and H. B., and though my father's behaviour was impeccable, we who knew him noticed that occasionally as his glance rested on this rather foreign-looking stranger, his upper lip rose slightly in a fashion that always reminded us of a dog who doesn't mean to fight, but now and again can't help showing his teeth – a demonstration less noticeable, luckily, in an old gentleman with a moustache than in a dog.

Papa, who, like Lady Ponsonby, pronounced his *a*'s in North Country fashion, as in the word 'passage', remarked afterwards to one of my sisters that Brewster had 'a nästy face'; and though this remark infuriated me at the time, I now see in it one more proof of perspicacity and extensive knowledge of the world. Harry was a dreamer, but as my readers will have gathered by no means a despiser of the joys of the flesh; and though the face was almost ultra-refined, to the eye of experience these traits could be read on it. In fact his was a type of which an old soldier would instinctively disapprove.

The peaceful outcome of their meeting was therefore rather a relief to me, for, given what a last-century parent would consider a reprehensibly unconventional friendship between his daughter and a married man, I had half expected he might refuse to come to the party. By and by, meditating his accommodatingness, I came to the conclusion it was partly because such of my family as knew Harry liked him so much, partly because Henschel and his wife were perfectly devoted to him, but mainly from a dim sense that this sort of thing was outside his ken and that it was wisest not to make a fuss. After all, Brewster was evidently no pauper . . . perhaps his wife was an invalid and some day our friendship might end in marriage . . . who knows? And seeing that in past disputes I had never got the worst of it, the situation had better be accepted. Few incidents in my life cast a more maturing ray on such knowledge of human nature as I possessed than this strand in the make-up of my old-world, simple-hearted, rigorously brought-up father; an obscure instinct he could not have formulated which occasionally prompts even a martinet of morality to let his blind eye see him through.

Altogether the evening was a brilliant success. In Germany no festive meal is thinkable without at least one speech, and during dinner Henschel proposed the health of General Smyth, 'without whom this party could never have taken place . . . *nor indeed the Mass!*' – a fact which I fancy had escaped the General's attention, as it certainly had mine!

The performance next day was, I believe, a really fine one. The chorus was first rate, compact too of friendliest enthusiasm, and judging by the reception of the work it seemed as if the Mass had come to stay. My sister Mary had secured the box next the Empress's, and in *The Puppet Show of Memory* Maurice Baring, whom that night I met for the first time, has recorded how our hunting friends from the North rallied round us. One of them, Mr Sheldon Cradock, my sister's favourite pilot in the hunting-field, whispered in her ear during the Credo, 'I *say*, Mrs Charlie! . . . this is slashing stuff, what?'

The only other unofficial comment I recall is that of Archbishop Benson, who overhearing bits of it at Addington, remarked afterwards that in this Mass God was not *implored* but *commanded* to have mercy.

The after story, which began next day, was tragic enough. Except as regards the scoring, which got good marks on all sides, the Press went for the Mass almost unanimously – some with scorn, some with aversion, in all cases adopting a tone of patronage it was hardest of all to bear. No one seemed to recognize anything praiseworthy in it, and my sole comfort from outside was a letter from a German named Krall – critic, I think, on some Northern journal – the gist of which was, that though the thing was probably knocked out for the time being, I must not lose heart, because . . . and here followed a judgement, both spiritually and technically motivated, of such warmth that it might have been written by Levi! Talk about life-belts, how I clung to that letter in the months that followed . . . and long after!

I think the slaying of the Mass (for knowing England he must have been aware it amounted to that) not only distressed but honestly surprised Barnby. Yet gazing back into the nineties, with the accumulated experience of forty years to clarify vision, I see that nothing else could have been expected. Year in year out, composers of the Inner Circle, generally University men attached to our musical institutions, produced dull affairs – which, helped along by the impetus of official approval, automatically went the round of our Festivals and Choral Societies, having paid the publisher's expenses and brought in something for the composers before they disappeared for ever. Was it likely, then, that the Faculty would see any merit in a work written on such very different lines – written too by a woman who had actually gone off to Germany to learn her trade?

In the middle twenties, my pre-war musical activities having been staged mainly in Germany, I bethought me, I forget in what connection, of the Mass, which had never achieved a second performance, which none but grey-beards had heard, and the existence of which I had practically forgotten. A couple of limp and dusty piano scores were found on an upper shelf, and after agitated further searchings the full score turned up in my loft. In spite of the judgement of the Faculty the work had evidently been appreciated by the mice, and on sitting down to examine it I shared their opinion, and decided that it really deserved a better fate than thirty-one years of suspended animation. But when I consulted the publishers as to the possibility of a revival, the reply was, 'Much as we regret to say so, we fear your Mass is dead.'

This verdict stung me into activity, and to cut a long story short, in 1924 Adrian Boult produced it brilliantly in Birmingham and the following week in London. This time the Press was excellent.

Harry, who was in the throes of a migration from Florence to Rome, and had merely rushed over for the Mass, returned to Italy next morning, and I went down to Osborne to write my name in the Queen's book – she having sent me through the Empress a wonderfully kind message about the Mass – and incidentally to see Lady Ponsonby who to my distress had not heard it.

Next day Mary bore me off to their house, Selaby, near Darlington, for a spell of hunting. That very night Henschel was conducting one of his Symphony Concerts, and I had had to break to him at the party that I should not be present. This he could hardly believe. I had explained that I was worn out, and possessed by only one idea – to get away from London and music; then had followed (haltingly) a confession that hunting was a master-passion I could but seldom indulge, and that to miss the very best meet of the Zetland hounds (this point took some expounding) was a sacrifice no one who knows what the clutch of sport can be would ask of a friend. At last Henschel had more or less taken it in, but all evening he kept on murmuring at intervals, 'And this is the woman who wrote the Mass!'

The circumstances at Selaby were favourable for me just then, for Mary was rather ill and I was to have the use of her horses, of course the best in the stable, whereas as a rule I rode Charlie's – big powerful animals with mouths and manners formed to his really rather desperate style of riding, he being the sort of man who, if he had taken a wrong turn, would literally cram his horse at anything rather than go round 200 yards.

He was a Northumbrian, son of a coal-owner. He and Mary had made a love-match on about £200 a year, but nowadays he was making a fortune, and more generous with his many hunters than any man I ever heard of – generous to the point of liking to see them ridden for all they were worth.

He did not know what fear meant. Once when he was a young man I saw him make a rush for the Newcastle train which was already moving out of Morpeth station at a good speed, the engine being already under the bridge, and take a header through the window of a smoking compartment, landing on the knees of several businessmen who were already deep in the morning paper. Ten or fifteen years later, when my sister became the friend and model of many painters and sculptors – Rodin, Sickert, Monet, Sargent, Jacques Blanche and the like – few people guessed that the sporting husband in tweeds who settled the bills had perhaps an even greater natural love of fine pictures, and more particularly of fine furniture, than Mary, though I think many would have agreed with me that on almost any subject his opinion was worth listening to; more so than that of some of his wife's brainy friends, with whom he was perhaps not quite at his ease.

A happy couple, they lived even now on a large scale, but occasionally Mary would bewail a certain economical twist in his make-up, which was partly no doubt a reaction against an exactly opposite twist in hers that yearly became more manifest. One day she said to me with solemn emphasis, 'I consider it my *sacred duty* to spend every penny I can of Charlie's money.' Later on, alas! she went beyond the limits of this pious resolution; but whether because he was in love with her to the last, or because no human force could stop her once her will was set, he was powerless to put on the brake.

My idea being to get in as much excitement as possible in the time, he and I suited each other to perfection in the hunting-field. As an amusing sidelight on marital balance I will add that once or twice he said to Mary, 'You're making that mare refuse: I shall put up Ethel on her on Thursday!' – a remark she greatly resented and which was drawn out of him because, by refusing, the horse cast an aspersion on his knowledge of horse-flesh and of horse-dealers. On the other hand he was rather jealous at the appreciation my singing met with, and often said 'Well, my dear, *I* think Mary sings a lot better than you!'[23]

Thinking of those days, it is sad to remember that Mary's kindness to me – a feeling which I think survived in essentials to the end, *but very deep down* – had then the character of a gift to one you love, and was accepted as one can and does accept such gifts. Also I loved her. But life brought out something that was always there, though in early days, when, as she always proclaimed, I was her first consideration, and before her own life took another turn, neither of us perceived it; namely, the fact that if you had run all the human beings in the world through a toothcomb, you could not have found two people more unlike in some of the fundamental instincts and habits of mind; besides which she was almost devoid of sense of humour and emphatically a man's woman. H. B., who liked her very much, always said there were two Marys – one for men and one for women. Many of her friends did not perceive this, obvious as it was to her family circle. She never wavered in her absolutely genuine belief in Ethel the musician; it was the human being that got on her nerves and enraged her, the real trouble being dissimilarity of grain. But to the last I was far fonder of her than she of me.

On another visit to Selaby some years later, the change I spoke of, which eventually sundered me and Mary, had become more marked. Charlie, persuaded by her to fight two successive constituencies (and secretly he yearned for the House of Commons and would have done admirably there) had alas! been defeated on both occasions. The second defeat disappointed him grievously, and one day Mary assured a large house-party that if he expected her to 'settle down', as he called it, and be thrilled because the black bull had put on six pounds in so and so many days, he was much mistaken. It was about this time that she began bewailing his everlasting protests against her extravagance. I couldn't help laughing one day when she informed us that why she had left the room suddenly while Mrs So-and-so was praising the omelette was because she saw in Charlie's eye that he was on the point of asking her what wages she gave the new cook! 'And such disgraceful tendencies must be checked at once,' she added, and there was something in her rather fierce and far from jocular manner that I did not like. In fact, during that visit I became aware that the rapidity with which Charlie was making a fortune, and the fact that Sargent apparently could not stop painting her, had gone to her head. She was just as kind to me as ever, wanting me to let her pay for a copyist to do some tiresome mechanical work I had to get through, and so on. But success was changing her fibre, and the part of her character on which my affection was based seemed less and less to the fore.

She was fond of Charlie, but I had never thought she rated his general intelligence high enough, nor, indeed, an artistic instinct that did not express itself in the language of Tonks, Sickert, Sir William Eden, George Moore and all the artistic friends she was now so intimate with, but which was at least as strong as her own. And I came to feel that he was secretly and angrily struggling against an utterly uncalled-for inferiority complex which she could have conjured away had she chosen to take the trouble. But she did not! Yet he was so fond of her – really in love with her, I suspect to the last – and so exactly did she know how to manage him, that, when, goaded beyond bearing by her unreasonableness and extravagance, he was about to put down his foot, she always won the last round.

In such ways – in other words at getting what she wanted – she was a remarkably clever woman. But when the hour came for going back home, I felt that the dear old comradeship when we saw eye to eye about most things was going . . . going . . . if not gone.[24]

Mary Hunter carried out her 'sacred duty' only too well. Every penny of Charlie's money was spent, and in her last years (he died in 1916; she lived on until 1933), her sisters came to her rescue. Christopher St John quotes the following from Ethel's diary: 'She must have known that I had a good deal to do with this Friends' Fund, but never did she say one word of gratitude. She had been the rich giver, I the poor recipient, for so many years that I suppose the idea that I was helping to finance her was more than she could bear.'

That same spring (1893) I received one of those shocks that for the time being disintegrate the present scene. Two years previously my bachelor outfit had arrived from Germany, including a bundle of Lisl's letters – eight years of them. I re-read one or two, but it hurt too much and I locked them away in an iron box, as in a tomb. Another shock occurred in the following year, when the Empress Eugénie, with whom I was staying at Cap Martin, driving through San Remo suggested I should walk through the cemetery with her and her nephew: '*C'est tellement joli là-bas,*' she said, '*sous les pins.*' But I knew that Lisl lay under those pines and stayed in the carriage. And then a month later, turning the leaves of a 'Hildebrand Album' at Munich, I suddenly came across a reproduction of the medallion he had carved for her gravestone, and quickly turned the page.

Now came the worst pang of all – worst, because with the pain were mingled bitterness and anger. A letter arrived from Mary Fiedler enclosing on behalf of Herzogenberg a photograph of Lisl together with a card on which he had written, in German of course, 'Think of this angel and of me with feelings of old friendship.'

The nature of this Austrian nobleman endowed with an astonishing gift for counterpoint, who had taught me all I knew about that department of music, singularly fitted him to be the husband of Lisl. Of passion there was not an ounce in his composition, nor the faintest desire to peep over the rim of live craters; indeed he instinctively looked the other way. But though masked and corrected by good breeding and sense of humour, sentimentality was his keynote. He had recently made over to Mary Fiedler the hundreds of letters I had written to his wife during the eight years of our friendship (after all then she had not had the heart to destroy them!) and as Mary could be very ruthless at times, perhaps some comment of hers had resulted in this gesture of reconciliation.

But I knew he had been rather relieved – which perhaps was natural – at my disappearance from their scene, and when they had stayed with the Fiedlers on that journey to San Remo from which Lisl never returned, he had specially begged Mary not to mention my name because it agitated her. But now everything was to be bathed in a roseate mist and the era of all-round forgetting and embracing ushered in! On the same lines, soon after Lisl's death, the Hildebrands, who had worked our doom both with Julia and the Herzogenbergs, began sending olive-branch messages to Harry, expressing the kindliest feelings towards him (also to me!) evidently counting on a proximate reconciliation. In all these advances I saw a desire to compound with a bad conscience; and if Herzogenberg or any of them thought the slate could be wiped clean whenever it suited their convenience, they were mistaken. I was glad to know Harry had merely replied that they were leaving Florence because he disliked being in the same town as 'friends of his wife whom he declined to meet'.

I got an interesting letter from him on the subject of forgiveness. 'There is something in your attitude towards Herzogenberg,' he wrote, 'that reminds me of my own towards the Hildebrands. I can reason all resentment away and say to myself, "let bygones be bygones". Then comes a feeling of impoverishment, a sort of obscure warning that there is in our nature a necessity for feud that must be expressed somewhere. Perhaps a lot of bad temper comes from not having enemies. And we cannot invent them; there must be some good reason. If we have got one it may be well to think twice before throwing it away. We can quite well forgive them in eternity and while we are subject to the mechanism of time keep them as buffers for the exercise of our extensor pushing-away muscles. People who are very tolerant intellectually like you and me perhaps need this more than anybody; at least it is only in this roundabout way that I can forgive myself for not forgiving everything and everybody, since *"tout comprendre c'est tout pardonner"*.'

Later on, after Julia's death, when I used to spend part of most winters in Rome, my implacability relaxed. But at the present moment Herzogenberg's step merely roused scorn and indignation. I made no response, and when the letters came into my possession put them together with Lisl's in the iron box – not to open it again till fifteen years later.

During the summer – a period of intensive work and boiling heat – came rather an upsetting letter from Harry. It appeared that, during a visit to the Wagner Festival that year, when he and I had been together at Munich, the Hildebrand children had caught sight of us and had reported the fact to his daughter, Clotilde; that Frau Hildebrand now laughed at herself for the attack of jealousy in which she had smashed a bust her husband had made of me; and that they were brimming over with love for both of us, having apparently forgotten their responsibility for half the trouble. I seem now to have asked Harry if he were prepared for the facts of our association coming to Julia's ears, and whether it would not be better to tell her we met occasionally, though merely as friends? And let me here remark that there had been nothing resembling love-making – in the law courts engagingly described as 'familiarities' – except during that fatal winter of 1884–5, when he twice turned up at Leipzig, convinced that Julia was coming round, and when we were as good – or as bad – as an engaged couple.

To this suggestion Harry replied, 'Of course I have contemplated the possibility as one does that of slipping from the Matterhorn, but I don't know if that constitutes a preparation. You risk it, but if it happens it is a catastrophe all the same. Julia has not the mental equilibrium necessary to stand the blow. I have the feeling that I must protect her from solitude of the worst kind, and have not the abnegation or the strength to sacrifice my life entirely to this task. I should fall into the same solitude myself. Therefore I stake upon my skill – also partly upon chance. A gambler's life! . . . So much the worse if he breaks his neck.'

Being interpreted this meant that if he told her about our occasional meetings, implacable, heroically uncompromising as she was (for she loved him all this time), Julia might say, 'Very well; but if this goes on I refuse to see you again.' And he felt he could not take the responsibility of condemning her to an isolation that might well have ended, as he hints, in something like a mental overthrow. True, his only crime against her had been faithfulness to the ethical scheme on which their union had based, but the fact remained that when the test came she repudiated that scheme, and wished him to live on with her for ever in the bleak world of metaphysical abstractions they inhabited when I had appeared upon the Florentine scene. This death in life he could not face. And since, for her, reality was the head of Medusa, could he bring himself to hold it up before her, force her to face it, and watch her turn into stone? No! I knew Julia, and knew it was as he said. Well then, '*à bon entendeur salut*'! Evidently there was nothing for it but to go on as we were and trust to luck.

In my opinion, however, Julia was not a diplomatist's daughter for nothing. After Lisl's death she had been coldly warned by me that I should henceforth take my own path in life regardless of her existence

on the same planet, and I believe she knew more than Harry suspected. Anyhow to the day of her death there was never any allusion
between them to the subject.

In the autumn I spent two rapturous days at North Berwick staying
with the Willie Mures, and there realized what cruel heartless brutes
a devouring passion makes of us. Harry was to be in England for a
week, and when he wrote proposing a meeting, I had the effrontery
to suggest that he should come for those two days to an hotel at North
Berwick – he who loathed the very name of golf! I knew exactly what
would happen, but couldn't, *couldn't* give up North Berwick! One
night I dined with him at his hotel, the next he dined with the Mures.
Mr Mure was a typical steady-going Scotsman (also a very fine golfer)
and to my amazement he was absolutely bowled over by Harry. 'What
a clever amusing fellow your friend is,' he volunteered next day. I
said, 'I half expected you to be put off by his fluffy hair and foreign
ways.' But Mr Mure sailed over that remark and added, 'I never saw
such a clever man with such a quiet unassuming manner,' and I
thought more highly than ever of the Scots.

Otherwise poor Harry had a detestable time, and all I can plead in
defence of my outrageous conduct is that I knew he would be over for
a longish time about Christmas. I golfed all day, lunched rapidly with
him at his hotel, and not till darkness fell did I rejoin him there, study
the draft of a new book he was writing, *The Statuette and the Background*,
and act more or less like a friend. One day he sallied forth to watch
me having a lesson, and coming too close got a crack from me on the
head. But my heart had turned into a golf ball and I didn't pretend
that it hurt me more than it hurt him. We did a little strolling on safe
parts of the links, but it was blowing an equinoctial gale – or, if not,
some other kind of gale – and whatever we talked about half my mind
was on my golf instructor's 'last remark but one'.

After he was gone I evidently suffered from remorse and conveyed
the fact to him in suitable words; for he wrote me that he was studying
theology, and that this experience, demonstrating 'the freakiness of
the Holy Ghost', convinced him that the Holy Ghost is a woman built
on the pattern of a revolving light of uncertain periods. 'You run after
her to Scotland and bang your head against darkness and a golf club;
you turn back, and she sends gentle beams after you across the sea' (I
was glad about the gentle beams). 'Such,' he adds, 'are the mysteries
and beauties of theology.'

Rather by good fortune, while he was at North Berwick, a letter had arrived from Lady Ponsonby raising an old, old point: wondering how he could put up with my megrims – in other words accept the regime of austerity which I imposed upon our relation. 'You say she is more accessible to French than to English modes of thought,' he remarked when I told him about it. Then, taking up a volume of Montaigne's *Essays* – he rarely travelled without one – and pointing to a certain passage, 'refer her to that,' he said; 'perhaps she'll understand then.'

Here is the passage:

Un galant homme n'abandonne pas sa poursuite pour être refusé, pourvu que se soit un refus de chasteté, non de choix. Nous avons beau jurer, et menacer, et nous plaindre; nous mentons, nous les en aimons mieux. C'est stupidité et lâcheté de s'opiniâtrer contre la haine et le mépris; mais contre une résolution vertueuse et constante, meleé d'une volonté reconnaissante, c'est l'exercice d'une âme noble et généreuse. Elles peuvent reconnaître nos services jusques à certaine mesure, et nous faire sentir honnêtement qu'elles ne nous dédaignent pas. (Livre III, v.)

Most people understand French, but for those who don't here is the gist of the above passage. If a woman turns you down as lover from moral scruples (he says) that is no reason for abandoning the pursuit; the man may curse and swear but he respects and loves her the more for her resistance. To persist in the face of *hatred* or *contempt* is stupid and cowardly, but to combat a *virtuous* and *constant resolution* is an exercise worthy of a noble and generous soul, and will excite no woman's contempt. And he further suggests that at the bottom of her heart the adored one is perhaps grateful for the homage.

Exactly. Harry knew, and I knew, that when the right hour struck, the '*résolution vertueuse et constante*' would take unto itself wings. And above all he knew that, recognizing what type of man he was, I loved him all the more for his patience.[25]

One Oak

When, in the year 1894, my father died, our old home was broken up. Frimhurst was put up for sale, and among the things I bought in with the lump sum left me by my father for that purpose were a beloved revolving dumb waiter, the handiest shelf of which was, and is, very groggy, and the old schoolroom table beneath which our brother Johnny had taken refuge when Mary and I, aged nine and seven, threw knives at each other, and which is still garnished with the tin-tacks a younger sister drove into its sides and limbs.

I determined to start life on my own, and soon found an ideal eight-roomed cottage in our old neighbourhood, surrounded by fields and woods. What its real name was I never knew; but as there was one special oak tree standing up on a mound just in front of the house, and as what counts is the only thing that ever need be counted, I called my cottage 'One Oak', regardless of the fact that there were other obscure oak trees all along the fifty yards or so of frontage.[26]

My life at Frimhurst alone with my father, who was the easiest of men to live with – always occupied with his county business, interested in all questions of the day, and equable in temper (except when in for a violent attack of gout) – had been very happy; but life in a house of my own was a perpetual intoxication. The last occupants of the two front rooms had been a pony and a donkey; the sanitary arrangements – practically non-existent – were now supplemented by a tank perilously balanced on rafters in the roof, and occasionally fed by the asthmatic pumpings of a series of 'handy' boys. H.B. had established himself in rooms in London for the summer, and often came down to One Oak for the day. Not cut out by nature for agricultural pursuits, he was none the less roped into the job of turning a rough half acre of long-neglected field into a future flower garden, and requested as first step to dig a hole 'large enough to hold a cow', into which were bundled various unsavoury objects left behind by the owners of the pony and the donkey.

One fantastic incident in his career as gravedigger shapes in my memory like a scene in a strip of tapestry. One day when he was hard at work stamping down old saucepans, fireguards and what not in the grave, a stag, followed by the Queen's staghounds, burst out of the wood, taking hole and man in its stride. It was a piteous sight to see Marco barking as if seized with madness, while not a single hound paid the slightest heed to him. When the pageant, dashing over my fence and the road beyond, had disappeared across the fields as by magic, poor Marco stood like a dog in a dream; would not come when called, would not eat his dinner, and was utterly broken in spirit for two or three days. Such an humiliation had never befallen him at Frimhurst – unless, perhaps, when the cat kittened in his bed in the loose box.[27]

The servant problem seemed likely to present difficulties. It must be someone who did not get on with other servants and therefore preferred solitary service; on the other hand her spirits must be equal to life in a small house where little 'company' was seen, and where the mistress played her own operas from morning till night. But even before One Oak was found the problem had resolved itself.[28]

We had had at Frimhurst a young cook who adored my mother but departed shortly before her death owing to a dangerous addiction to evening walks on the pretty towing-path of the Basingstoke Canal in the company of boating officers from Aldershot or cadets from Sandhurst. We found her a splendid place, but three years later, when the news of the break-up of Frimhurst reached her, she wrote that for love of my mother, myself and dear Marco she wished to come and 'do for me' for whatever wages I could afford – or, if necessary, for none at all.[29] She was an exceedingly pretty Devonshire girl named Ford, with wonderful grey eyes, rippling black hair, an exquisite complexion, the smallest and roundest of waists, and both physically and mentally of a suppleness and grace that suggested better breeding than her pedigree would have shown. Her manners, though not those of her class, were perfect; in fact she was neither a servant nor a lady – she was Ford.

She instantly revealed herself as the ideal general servant, and if the place had been her own could not have taken greater pride in it. Except my mother I have known few people so devoted to flowers, and the house was always full of them, though where they came from I thought best not to inquire. For my garden was never very grand, a row of stocks under the windows, a crimson rambler over the porch, a few creepers, and two round beds dedicated to the mid-Victorian combination of geraniums, calceolarias and lobelias (from which I emancipated myself later on) being the extent of my floral achievements. In the winter she would scour the lanes for belated bramble sprays or anything else decorative, and never came home empty handed.

Her relations with Marco, which at Frimhurst had been tender but fugitive, now became continuous and passionate. Everything about him enchanted her, his fierce reception of the tradesmen, his marked friendliness towards tramps, and other points that one would not select for admiration. Sometimes, especially when another dog was barking in the neighbourhood, he would wolf his food, after which a kind of stately, subterranean hiccough would afflict him. On one such occasion I remember her putting her head on one side and exclaiming sentimentally, 'Hark at him breaking wind like an old man!'

As for her cooking, whether from the point of view of economy or greediness, how shall words describe it? We know what Schubert has done with three notes on a posthorn, or a nasal little fragment of a phrase ground out on a barrel organ. Ford's genius was of the same quality. She would make superb soup out of two claws of a grouse, or an old mutton-chop bone, in short out of anything or nothing, flavouring as only genius knows how. As for the simpler achievements that defeat the incompetent – boiled potatoes, for instance, or pancakes – everything her hands touched became a work of art, whether it was food in a dish or flowers in a vase.

She bore the loneliness of our life heroically for the first year, although now and again there were symptoms of low spirits, particularly when one of my periodical absences was imminent, or just concluded. She was one of those people predestined to unfortunate attachments, and I often fancied that my return coincided with the funeral of a cherished dream. But as time went on, the fits of depression becoming deeper and more frequent, I began to suggest that having seen me well into my career as householder she ought to give some less lonely place a trial. The answer was always the same . . . tears, and an assurance that she could not bear to leave me and dear Marco. About a fortnight later, after a period of ceaseless tears, she herself agreed that a change of scene was advisable. I found her a splendid place, engaged a caretaker, and in mutual love and sadness we parted.

Ford died in the latter half of the One Oak period. Coming home one day from abroad I found a letter from the matron of a Bath hospital, dated three days previously, telling me that a former servant of mine had been brought in, suffering apparently from tumour on the brain, and that just before she became unconscious she had begged that I might be written to. 'I know she'd like you to tell her I am here,' were her words. I telegraphed to say I would come at once, but almost immediately a second letter arrived saying she had died without recovering consciousness.

'If only I had been there!' is a refrain that accompanies most people through life. But in the case of that strange, gifted creature, so lovable and so lonely, it has always had for me a peculiar sadness.[30]

Ford's successor was a Highlander, six feet one inch in her stockings, whom, in a fit of recklessness and adoration of the Scotch, I had engaged without asking for references. Towards the end of her short sojourn at One Oak she declined to scrub the kitchen floor ('I won't go down on my knees for anyone,' was the way she put it), or to give Marco his meals ('I'm not paid to wait on the beasts of the field,' was the way she put *that*). Eventually she was dealt with by H. B., who was in England just then. One knows the fabulous strength and devastating violence of the mild when possessed by Berserker rage; he suddenly seized her bodily and threw her into the fly I had ordered for her, and which at the last minute she absolutely refused to enter.[31]

FIVE
1894–1903

FANTASIO

DER WALD

'Fantasio'

From 1894 to 1898 my chief aim of existence was the completion and launching at some German opera house (for of course there was none in England) of my first operatic attempt – a comic opera called *Fantasio*, founded on Musset's play of that name. It was Hermann Levi, the great Wagner conductor, who, after getting to know my Mass, urged me along the operatic road he maintained I was by nature meant to travel. His estimate of *Fantasio* was such that innocents like H.B. and myself believed the future of this work was as safe as the Bank of England. All the same, he realized that a woman composer – and a foreigner too – would have little or no chance with an average German Kapellmeister; and his advice was that I should enter *Fantasio* for a certain operatic competition at which he was to be one of the five or six judges. The operas had to be sent in by 1 April 1895, and the sealed envelopes containing name and address of each composer were not to be opened till the title of the successful work had been publicly proclaimed. As far as I remember, the prize was a lump sum of money, the printing and publishing of the work, and a guarantee of its first performance at one of the first opera houses in Germany, and at a certain number of others afterwards.

In the course of these pages the fate of *Fantasio* will be revealed; here I will only say that from first to last Levi had not the faintest doubt of its sweeping the board. 'I know all that is doing in this line in Europe,' he said, 'and there is not a soul you need be afraid of.' And as Levi was universally looked upon as supreme authority, one had some right to count this particular unhatched chicken.

Thanks to a six-month postponement decided on by the Opera Competition Committee, I was able to fall in gratefully with the Empress Eugénie's suggestion that I should take a month of repose at Cap Martin. When I arrived there however, in May 1895, the atmosphere was anything but reposeful. Her villa (Cyrnos) was not quite, quite finished, and unaware of this Queen Victoria had proposed herself for a visit next day. A *Demoiselle d'Honneur*, who always got sadly on the

Empress's nerves, partly because she was so strangely unhandy with her arms and legs, took the opportunity of slipping up on the terrace and breaking her leg in two places – the sort of thing not calculated to excite sentimental pity in the hearts of Royal employers. Hearing of this mishap the Queen seems to have concluded the Cyrnos terraces were built of block-ice, and begged that they might be liberally carpeted with rugs. And there was a dearth of rugs at Cyrnos! In short, everyone's temper was rather on the jump; and when the late Prince Imperial's doctor – rather a nice old thing between fifty and sixty, I imagine – asked Madame le Breton to find a wife for him, *'mais une jeune'*, she rapped out, *'pour qu'elle vous rende cocu, je suppose!'*; and when he asked what *cocu* meant she replied, *'Inutile de vous l'expliquer; vous le saurez par expérience.'* Whether men are as fatuous today as they were in those days I do not know; one of the Empress's pet gibes was, *'Ah oui! les hommes ne vieillissent jamais!'* but this one said at last, 'Well, what about Mademoiselle Rose d'Elchingen?' (the charming daughter of the Duchesse de Rivoli – rich, pretty and about thirty). 'Perhaps *she'll* do?' Madame le Breton only snorted, as well she might, whereupon he said, *'Eh bien . . . Mademoiselle Smyth?'* on which she walked away saying, *'Mon cher Scott, vous êtes idiot.'* I did adore that old woman!

Madame le Breton did not know that even had I wished to marry an elderly Indian doctor, according to my own ideas I was no longer in the running. H.B. was in Paris, and on my way to Cap Martin I had stopped there with a fixed purpose in my mind and had carried it out.

When I was settling in at One Oak, M., a very amusing friend of mine, whose husband was stationed at Aldershot and who had met Harry at the Hippisleys', remarked one day, 'But you can't ask H.B. to *stay* here, can you?' I replied, 'Certainly I shall! I shall ask him, or Sargent, or Riaño or Maurice Baring or anyone I choose, to come for weekends, and intend to establish the fact that I am Caesar's wife.' 'O Elly,' she exclaimed (that being her name for me), 'what *does* that mean? I suppose *past fructification.'* (I was then thirty-six.) In fact, but for a vague wish not to end my life as what she called a 'Stonehenge Virgin', I had no immediate intention of changing my estate.

But now the time to change it had come. 'Why now?' is an unanswerable question. On Tuesday you look at a certain corner of the lawn . . . nothing! On Wednesday you look again; still nothing. But by Thursday evening the crocuses have 'crept alight'. For one thing this jaunt would be the first deliberate break in my life of work for two years, and perhaps I now had leisure to reflect how generously and patiently he had borne with me for ten; how his time and thoughts had been devoted to my affairs, without ever an attempt to overcome my reluctance to cross the boundary between friendship and love – a matter that means so much more to men, I think, than to women. Anyhow it seemed to me negligible compared to what I already possessed in him and set chief store by.

I knew too that Julia must have fully taken in the significance of what I had written to her three years before: that from henceforth, as she had let Lisl die without permitting her to send me one loving word, I should henceforth shape my life as though she, Julia, did not exist. Probably she imagined this new shaping had begun then and there. Harry said it might or might not be so, but that he fancied she no longer gave a thought to the actualities of our relation, and was only concerned with the metaphysics of the story as seen by her, and indicated in a little volume he published after her death called *Via Lucis* – a series of abstractions too subtle for ordinary minds to follow, but containing passages of strange sombre beauty.

This view of the case is probably correct; if anyone on earth knew Julia it was Harry. But on the whole I felt he was still as unable to see clearly into large tracts of her mind as he had been eleven years ago when our adventure began.

After I got back to England I told Lady Ponsonby about the Paris episode, and, as I knew would be the case, she was not best pleased; partly because her own proclivities were on usual lines in such matters,[32] partly I think because not informed till two or three months afterwards, and then in quite a casual manner. Hence perhaps her very unexpected remark: 'One can understand a *surprise des sens*,' she said, 'but I don't like that sort of *cold-blooded schemin'*.'

(And here is a general comment on my friendship with Harry, made to Lady Ponsonby by a rather venomous but extremely amusing connection of hers who habitually left out unnecessary parts of speech: 'Ethel not like idea old maid so trumped up little affair.')[33]

Since those days the world's views have become less rigid – whether for good or evil I neither know nor care – and after what has already been said on such topics, present-day readers (if any) would probably 'understand' my action better than Lady Ponsonby did – whether on the point of what Rossetti called 'supreme surrender' without blessing of priest or registrar, or on the closely allied one of marriage, which was to become a burning question sooner than any of us thought.

And now came a bolt from the blue that changed the colour of my future life. Harry, who had been in England, making arrangements for the education of his children, both of whom were bent on English University life, left England in July to join his family at Fribourg, where they then lived. Julia's heart had always been a weak point, and towards the end of the month came an attack which even she, a constitutional Spartan, could not disregard. The specialist's verdict was that these crises were now certain to recur, and might at any time prove fatal.

'She knows her state perfectly,' wrote Harry, 'is fantastic, obstinate beyond words, cheerful, affectionate, witty, quite unmanageable, and to me very touching. I am not at all muddled morally. The gist of my meditations is simply that our monogamic system is not suited to all natures. If we were Mohammedans, nobody and none of us, the concerned ones, would find it at all strange that I should take tender care of one wife and sit soothingly at her bedside all night as I have just done, and at the same time love another one. Yet because of our marriage laws and the artificial psychology in vogue, I must be supposed to wish evil to one woman and forget a past for which I am deeply grateful, because I wish well to another woman, and the present is richer with her. All I can say is that the lie is not in me but in the system. And it does not trouble me much. Nor am I afraid of your not understanding me: you have not the feeling that the affection you give to others robs me. Of course there remains the practical privation and the limitations that the system imposes on us, and I cannot wish you not to dislike these even as I dislike them; but is is a comfort to me to know that you have a great many drawers in your brain, and that you don't jumble up their contents.'

In September came the next crisis, and it proved to be the last. She was buried in the pretty graveyard at Fribourg, 'the mountains and the forest looking on in gentle silence'. I have said that by mutual consent we never discussed Julia; this time, for a moment, he broke that silence. 'I want to tell you this once,' he wrote, 'how I feel towards her now that she is gone. Think of a beautiful villa with a garden of unsurpassed dignity in a malarious, desolate country. It is ague and almost death to linger there, and yet almost impossible to tear oneself away. I have loved her and hated her deeply; not successively but simultaneously. I told Herzogenberg so, who was here and by the way *very* nice and genuine; he has gained much in my esteem – a brave struggle for light in a narrow brain.'

'Fantasio'

The death of Julia Brewster 'grievously disturbed the smooth flow' of Ethel's relations with H.B. by raising the spectre of marriage – to her an 'odious idea'. She travelled to Rome in order 'to have it out in peace and quiet' and persuaded him to drop the notion. Lady Ponsonby, 'completely captivated' by H.B., nevertheless was convinced of the rightness of their decision. She was fortified by the opinion of the Empress Eugénie that Ethel and marriage 'were not made for one another'.

Shortly after Ethel left Rome, Julia and Frau von Stockhausen being now dead, Harry at last decided to make it up with the Hildebrands.

Frau Hildebrand desired to make a clean breast of it; said that she deeply repented a lying letter she wrote in former years, goaded on by Frau von Stockhausen and her own jealousy, to Lisl, but believed that with that exception she had always spoken well of me ('of whom,' Harry added, 'she seems to have a really warm appreciation as soon as her husband is out of her mind'). She confessed that she demanded to rank first in the sympathies of any friends they had in common; wondered whether, if life should throw us together again, she would again be jealous of me – half hoped such a meeting might one day take place, half dreaded the idea, and was 'sorely perplexed'.

Reading this letter I was struck by the fact that I had always believed some special act of perfidy in that quarter had broken the back of Lisl's loyalty, and facilitated the defection exacted by her relatives. A year or two later Frau Hildebrand and I did meet again. But apparently she had forgotten all about her confession and took the line of having always been my friend. I left it at that, for at the bottom of her heart it was true; but jealousy, 'cruel as the grave', brings about landslides in which truth is buried – and perhaps someone's life lost.

Late in September 1896 a postcard from Levi informed me that he had now read fifty out of the hundred and ten operas handed in, and that none of them could touch mine. Then suddenly dead silence, and I wondered whether he had discovered among the sixty remaining operas a masterpiece that would put *Fantasio* out of court? Not at all! One day came a postcard saying that Levi and Mary Fiedler had determined to marry, though the date was not yet fixed. For years Levi and Mary had been supposed (I think wrongly) to be *en liaison*; she was very rich, and he the last man in the world to have feathered his nest during his quarter century of faithful service to his god, Wagner. He was poor, too, in health, and when at the end of November I went to Germany, I was horrified to find some people believed that Conrad

Fiedler had killed himself . . . he, a philosopher, a man incapable of giving Mary, let alone his old mother, such a shock! He was obviously suffering from creeping paralysis, and should never have attempted to manipulate those heavy Munich outside shutters.

Now that the thing was settled, after a characteristic description of her happiness, Mary wrote, 'What a glorious wedding present for us if *Fantasio* is crowned victor!' And next day Clotilde Brewster, who was with the Hildebrands, told her father that Levi had now read the whole hundred and ten operas and was still convinced that mine must surely win.

At length a telegram from Munich arrived, and if I have dwelt on the above particulars, it is because the feelings may be imagined with which I read the following message: 'NO OPERA HAS RECEIVED THE FIRST PRIZE. FANTASIO HIGHLY COMMENDED. LETTER FOL-LOWS. LEVI.'

I never was able to ascertain how many jurors there had been, nor what their names were; but this, I gathered, is what had happened.

Of the hundred and ten works, ten had been selected as 'in the running', one of which was *Fantasio*. From these three were chosen between which the prize was divided; *Fantasio* was *not* one of these three, but was among the seven 'highly commended' ones! Of the original ten set aside, one, *Fantasio*, had been deemed worthy of the Crown and received *one* vote to that effect! But one vote was not considered enough, and when Levi announced in secret session that he was that solitary voter, the others were surprised, and two of them – Schuch of Dresden (one of the most brilliant opera conductors in Germany) and Hofmann of Cologne (a deeply musical man who greatly admired Levi) promised to examine *Fantasio* once again (and evidently did so, as subsequent events proved).

Some thought that what Henschel and others feared might happen in a case of such a very 'open secret' had happened – that the identity of the composer had leaked out. Another thing; I wrote German as well, perhaps, as is possible for a foreigner, but I dare say a turn of two of phrase may have suggested a foreign librettist. And the jurors would certainly have hated the idea of a foreigner carrying off the prize.

And now, if instead of a verbal diagram of one hundred words which could easily give the essential facts, I am about to go relatively into detail as I trace the zigzag Flying-Dutchman course I pursued during the rest of 1896 and 1897 – a course absolutely commended by

Levi, though by the time his blessing arrived I had already started – it is because that sort of thing went on all my life.

Towards the end of November this was the situation. Dear Levi had written a flaming account of *Fantasio* to Mottl, the great Carlsruhe conductor; and the Empress Frederick, who knew all about the inaccessibility of Count Seebach, the grim and very successful intendant at Dresden, had written to him, begging that if Schuch's report of my opera should be favourable, he would receive me and listen to it himself.

Accordingly, I now started on a 'Round Journey', as the Germans call it, including Carlsruhe, Dresden, Leipzig (where I had hopes of getting the Mass done) and Cologne. My pathetic belief at each of these places that 'all was now settled' was due to the ignorance of a tyro who did not realize that an intendant and his first conductor are Spenlow and Jorkins. A conductor, if he really likes your work, is probably only too ready to produce it, and not afraid to say so because in the background is the person who has the decision, and who is generally 'away at that moment but returning shortly'.

This occurred first of all at Carlsruhe. Mottl really was 'mad keen', as my postcards informed well-wishers like H.B., Lady Ponsonby, and my poor family. He assured me again and again that his intendant was certain to make no difficulties; that he was *definitely expected in three days*; that I must sing him Danila's air, 'which is irresistible', and so on. In fact, Mottl was a charmer. Naturally I decided to stay on, and it was only quite by chance that I saw in a two-days'-old newspaper that the intendant had put off his return for *some weeks*! That is the maddening part of theatre life; no one ever tells you anything; too busy, I suppose!

I then wrote to Schuch, who by now knew the opera and had informed a friend of his that it was 'quite charming', entreating him to persuade Seebach to give me an appointment, and departed for Leipzig where I should be in clover at the Limburgers' fine town house, there to await the return of Seebach to Dresden, for of course I had got a wire from Schuch to say the great man was out of town just now, 'but expected back shortly'.

While I was in Leipzig it gradually leaked out in the papers that there was to be a Wagner Festival at Carlsruhe in January, Frau Cosima to be present, and that on 1 March the theatre was to be closed for repairs till the autumn, all of which must have been settled long before I arrived there, but no one breathed a word of it! A nice lookout for me! Yet strange to say, I did eventually get a letter from the intendant, saying Mottl was enchanted with the opera, but I would understand that given the circumstances it was impossible to undertake fresh commitments now; would I apply again in *nine months' time* (!).

The Opera at Cologne, where Ethel paused en route *for England, accepted* Fantasio *for the following spring, but then withdrew after the managing director, Hofmann, decided he could not cast the title role.*

Exhaustion set in but did not prevent another round of journeys in February 1897 – to Hamburg (no good), Wiesbaden (polite procrastination) and finally Rome, to join Brewster and with him explore the Abruzzi on bicycles. Then by stages northwards to the Italian Alps, solitude and mountain air having been prescribed. Here Ethel received news of the death of Pauline Trevelyan.

Harry and his daughter, Clotilde, joined her for some climbing – her farewell to mountaineering. She then set off on foot for Bayreuth to join her sister Mary. From Bayreuth they went together to Munich.

While I was at Munich a certain Baroness B., whom I had met in Rome at Donna Laura Minghetti's turned up, and put an entirely new idea into my head. She was on her way back to Weimar where she lived, and being a friend of the Grand Duke's, and also of the intendant and his wife, she knew the ropes in both worlds and I gathered was a power. Hearing that I and *Fantasio* were rather at a loose end, she said, 'What about Weimar?' I consulted Levi, who thought it an excellent plan to have a second string to my bow. Mottl, he said, was an absolutely sincere enthusiast, but unfortunately forgot all about it ten minutes afterwards! Of Stavenhagen, the young conductor at Weimar, he had heard excellent reports, as also of the musical forces there, and he gave me a blazing introduction to him. Frau von B. did the same as regards the intendant, and certain letters were to be sent off from Carlsruhe if Mottl should prove shifty.

Levi's instructions had been: 'You go to Mottl and bang on the table and say you must have a straight answer as to *whether he can or cannot bring out* Fantasio *next season*' (i.e., the season 1898–9). But there was no occasion for table-banging. Mottl disarmed me by saying, 'Look here; give me eight weeks and then I swear you shall have the answer. And if you don't get it, go on bombarding me till you *make* me answer.' Upon that, I thought I had better tell this best of good fellows my Weimar plan; to which he not only gave his blessing, but wrote to Stavenhagen, saying that but for this unforeseen (?!) decision to close down the theatre at Carlsruhe on 1 March he himself would have been conducting the première of *Fantasio* this very season, etc., etc. (O, how I hoped that Stavenhagen had not as penetrating an acquaintance with dear Mottl's 'charm' as I had!)

Without knowing anything about the musical conditions there, I had always cherished a hankering for Weimar. Chiefly, of course, because of Goethe, but also because I knew that the present ruler did all he could to maintain a tradition of liberalism and culture diametrically opposed to the Prussian spirit against which the Emperor Frederick and his wife had striven in vain. It was said that he was no great admirer of the present German Emperor, and even the exceedingly bourgeois and conceited group of 'art-loving' Leipzigers were forced to concede, though unwillingly, that he really was an 'art-patron'. And now that I knew what my two big friends thought of the musical outlook there, it was satisfactory to recall that the Duchess of Connaught had once said, 'If you ever think of Weimar perhaps I could help, for the Grand Duke, who is an old dear, is my uncle.'

I shall have so much to say about what were really unique experiences, that I am tempted to throw the tale of my personal campaign into the mould of a *dramatis personae* list. And the pith of my story is that though I held all the cards, and brilliant ones too, the game would have been lost again and again but for the masterly activities of one of the most remarkable women I ever met, Baroness Olga von Meyendorff.

I will begin with the two powers, the Grand Duke and this lady, in whose hands my fate lay.

The Grand Duke, when a child, had frequently sat on Goethe's knee, and I confess that this fact so deeply impressed me that only with difficulty could I refrain from asking him whether it was a comfortable seat. He was then seventy-nine, tall and active, and his intelligence and readiness to listen to and discuss new ideas were those of a man of fifty. A *grand seigneur* if ever there was one – simple, kindly, genuine, with just the right kind of dignity – the thought that anyone should presume to consider him and his old-fashioned ways 'ridiculous' filled me with scornful indignation. He was a good scholar as princes go, romantic and chivalrous to a fault, and reported to avoid as much as possible interfering with his functionaries.

I confess to having worshipped at many shrines in my life, but never I think with more wholesale devotion than at Baroness Meyendorff's. If she liked you, if you interested her, it was like associating with a powerful magnet. She was daughter of the Russian Minister Gortchak-off, widow of a Russian diplomat, and one of the closest friends of Liszt to the end of his life. Indeed, she was one of the many ladies in whose arms Liszt is said to have died; with what scorn would she have demolished that silly lie had anyone dared to allude to it in her presence! But it is undoubtedly true that she was at one time the rival of Princess Wittgenstein in the great man's capacious heart.

It was said that the Grand Duke, whose veneration for her was unbounded, took no step without consulting her, but one could not imagine anyone less desirous of pulling strings, or emerging without necessity from her fortress. All the same, from the moment I had the certainty that in her view *Fantasio ought* to be produced at Weimar, I felt it would be done. One day, after about the seventh trumped-up difficulty had been got round, she said in her deep quiet voice, '*Je ne suis pas une lâcheuse*,' which in a backer of *Fantasio* was a priceless quality.

The intendant was a gentleman, and if left to himself would have been all right . . . but his wife was of another class. Madly ambitious, at first she was fire and flame for me and *Fantasio*. Then, she discovered that I knew Baroness Meyendorff, whom she detested and of whom she was furiously jealous, because of her supreme influence over the Grand Duke. From that moment she tried by hook or by crook to prevent the performance of *Fantasio*. Stavenhagen, the conductor, was a young fellow on the make – worthless as character, gifted as musician, but without a spark of interest for anything but his own advantage. Lazy, vain and ambitious, the idea that he might be called to London to produce *Fantasio* was the only thing that inclined him if anything to be on my side.

Lassen, Stavenhagen's predecessor in Weimar, composer of a ter-rible song, *Es war ein Traum*, which is the German equivalent of 'The Lost Chord', was honest, very likeable, and both liked and trusted by the Grand Duke. Decidedly my friend, he had a tired old man's predilection for a quiet life.

The fact that Baroness Meyendorff would doubtless have a finger in my pie did not ooze out till after a grand party given by kind Baroness B., in order that I might play the opera to her great friends, the intend-ant and his wife, who expressed the greatest delight with it, as did the other guests, most of whom were influential people, who had already taken up their winter residence in Weimar. At that time I did not know how the land lay, but meeting the intendant's lady a day or two after the party, I detected a slight coolness in the air when she told me it would be many days yet before her husband could announce his decision.

Meanwhile there came suddenly a summons from Baroness Meyendorff, who had been away for a few days and had purposely held aloof from these proceedings. It appeared that she had seen the Grand Duke (who would not be back in his capital till November); that he was delighted with the idea of *Fantasio* being produced at Weimar, and said there was not the *slightest doubt* that it could be done this season! She told him about the verdict of Levi, and Mottl, and Schuch, but what moved his chivalrous soul most deeply was finding out that my career was a matter of interest to the Empress Eugénie.

It emerged that one reason why Fantasio was not taken up at Dresden and Wiesbaden was that the libretto was felt to be 'lacking in literary dignity'. Ethel resolved to avoid the possibility of a further refusal by having the text rewritten. She arranged this in Leipzig on her way home to England. In November 1897, while she was at home, she heard that the Grand Duke was 'all impatience' to meet her, and hurried back to Weimar.

Then came a minor tragedy that again and again befalls solitary travellers whose heads are full of engrossing matters. Knowing that Baroness Meyendorff had fixed up a big party at which the Grand Duke would be present to hear me play and sing my opera, and that nowhere do clothes play a more important part than at these little Courts, I had packed up my best *grandeurs* with special care, and . . . forgotten to see them examined at the frontier! – and there, of course, they had remained! And as I had never had time to put even my workaday clothes in order, I felt shy of arrriving at Weimar with nothing but what I stood up in! However, by getting the whole of Consular Weimar on the job, the luggage arrived in time (but only just).

Throughout the party, which was an amazing success, the intendant's wife was a study. Baroness Meyendorff had to invite the couple, of course, and we thought that the intendant had feared to tell his wife that *Fantasio* would have to be done, preferring to let her learn it in presence of the Grand Duke. I did not see all the fun, being engaged in doing the opera – O, how badly! for Nature had afflicted me with every ill on her list; but it did not really matter. 'Madame Intendant' tried hard to sit next to the Grand Duke, but was circumvented by our hostess, who calmly took a chair, placed it where he could not even see her, and invited him to sit thereon. And Baroness Meyendorff's invitations were commands.

After the music was over, Frau Intendantin said to Baroness Meyendorff, 'This opera may be very charming, but of course there can be no question of a performance *this* season.' 'Oh, but it's all settled,' said the other. Then for the first time the mask was dropped. 'Nothing of the sort!' snapped out Frau Intendantin. 'Why, it would upset our whole repertory!' 'Nevertheless,' said Baroness Meyendorff, 'it is so; listen to what the Grand Duke is saying to Miss Smyth, who moreover has been settling dates with your husband.'

I hardly looked at Frau Intendantin, whose face was now crimson with rage, feeling, as Marco does in such cases, 'Better not! if I look at her I shall growl . . . and perhaps bite.' But the whole room was watching her, predicting a bad attack of jaundice.

And now at last the contract was signed, and it was curious to reflect that twenty years ago when starting – a successful rebel – for Leipzig, I had said to my mother, who kept a record of the remark and passed it round to all and sundry, that if I could get an opera accepted at a first-class opera house by the time I was forty, I should be satisfied. As it was I saved my bacon – but only just, for my fortieth birthday would be on 23 April 1898!

Though I intend to say not another word about further alarms and excursions, let no one think that the battle was now won and all plain sailing. The date having been fixed for 20 January, in the end, thanks to every sort of malevolent action on the part of the intendant's wife, whose reasons I never quite understood though I believe the sole idea was to spite Baroness Meyendorff, the opera was not produced till 24 May! Of course I knew that my absent protectress was probably in touch with the Grand Duke, and if necessary could (and would) take steps; but as may be imagined, I was loath to break in on her among her Greek statues and studies; and though I could not prevent the enemy putting spoke upon spoke between the wheels and holding everything up for *four long months,* she could not quite stop the machine; that would have been too dangerous for her husband!

I think it was Saint-Saëns who said, 'It's bad if they don't perform your operas – but when they do, it's far worse.' No truer word was ever spoken, yet my recollections of my time in Weimar are full of charm. The Grand Duke liked those attached to the Court to make a great display of elegance, and I entreated friends and relations who meant to attend the performance to bring their most *décolleté* gowns, for in this Grand Duchy nudity stood for respect. In fact, despite great correctness, the atmosphere was the reverse of puritanic, not at all akin to that of Windsor, which in my ignorance I had imagined was characteristic of all Courts. But dreading to be a rock of offence, I forgot all this, and inasmuch as I was hoping that H. B. would turn up at least a week before the rest of my party, I had thought well before she departed to ask her whether it would shock the Grand Duke if I took a room for a very great friend of mine, Mr Brewster, at my hotel, the Elephant. The half-amused, half-contemptuous look I got in reply sufficiently answered this very provincial question!

In spite of the elegant nudity, and an implied tradition of intellectual distinction as opposed to Prussian brutality and militarism, there was an immense simplicity in the habits of these Weimar courtiers. The old *abonnement* system obtained in the theatre, and on their day these high-born ladies, many of whom were as poor as church mice, would be trudging through the snow, smart liveried footmen holding umbrellas over them; and in the *garderobe* they would kick off their galoshes, remove their wraps, and reveal an evening toilette that often was simply a summer day-gown pinned back in a V; Thackeray's Court of Pumpernickel, if you will, but as ruler, a cultivated and conscientious *grand seigneur*, and on all sides the legacy of Weimar's great past – a genuine and intelligent love of the arts. I found the place delightful in every way and hoped once more to feel, as one does or did there, the close, close presence of Goethe; above all on the little hill where he wrote his most perfect lyric, *Uber allen Gipfeln ist Rüh'*, in a woodman's hut and pinned it on the wall.

Harry joined me about 10 May, and a contingent of family and friends duly arrived about four days before the date fixed for the première. They consisted of three of my sisters, Alice with her eldest girl, Nina, Mary Hunter with two of her girls (Kitty and Sylvia), Violet Hippisley and her husband, Henschel and his daughter Helen, and last but not least, Clotilde Brewster. All took rooms at the Hotel zum Elefant, and Henschel entreated the company not to criticize Germany in public. 'All the waiters,' he said 'speak English, and all are more or less spies; and though in the end, if they reported you, your Consul would of course make it all right, it would be tiresome and not worth it.' That, he added, was why he had been naturalized English. So much for freedom of speech in Germany, even in those days! Mary, dissatisfied with the food, took charge of the commissariat, and said there must be *beef and chicken at every meal*. The waiter feared there were not enough chickens in all Weimar for such a demand. 'Then get some from Dresden, or Berlin, or anywhere you like,' commanded Mary in her usual lordly way, and probably the waiter thought she was mad, as he fled from the room.

The other incident I shall never forget concerns Violet, and is all the more remarkable in that she was more emphatically *feminine*, I think, than any of my sisters. On the other hand she was passionately devoted to animals and had a very pitiful heart. Here is the story.

A deputy for a minor role had to cut in at the third performance, and as usual there was a little rehearsal for him in the morning. My sister, Harry and I were proceeding theatre-wards in rather a hurry, when suddenly a huge bulldog appeared from nowhere and fastened on to the throat of one of those mongrels that draw washerwomen's barrows in Germany – in fact the race of my Marco. The poor beast was not only elderly and harnessed to its little cart, but muzzled, and consequently utterly helpless. The laundress shrieked; vainly we tried to pull off the bulldog, and things were looking black for his victim when my sister cried out to Harry, 'Take the brute by the collar and I'll bite his tail.' This was done. The bulldog promptly let go, and seizing his profusely bleeding tail Harry swung him round and round in the air till the laundress and her outfit had been safely hustled through a *porte-cochère* and the door banged behind them.

It was Sunday morning and no one was about. Harry now launched the bulldog in a parabola across the street and it made off as fast as it could lay legs to the ground, while Violet, whose face was one smear of blood, was conducted half-swooning into a *conditorei* and plied with cognac. The odd thing is that you could not have found in the whole world anyone apparently less likely to hit upon and execute such a desperate expedient than she!

In the course of the day two equerries were sent by the Grand Duke, the first to inquire after the heroine's nerves, the second to convey to her His Royal Highness's appreciation of her courage and humanity.

When I think of the first performance of my maiden effort in opera, I regret more than ever that nearly all the dear relations and friends who were present are dead and cannot touch up my vague memories. Judging by the enthusiasm and plaudits it was a 'great success', but the Press had not a good word to say for it except as regards the scoring. Before I left Weimar I had a long talk with Lassen – an absolutely honest man and an expert. No one saw more clearly than I what cuts would be advisable, also the desirability of some of those little changes that in all arts (and indeed not only in the arts!) make all the difference. 'Do you think,' I asked him 'that given these adjustments the thing would be *lebensfähig?*' (i.e., capable of life). And Lassen, like all the other experts asked later, said, 'Most certainly.'

I think they were wrong, though perhaps it was not till I had heard an almost perfect performance of *Fantasio*, conducted a year or two later by Mottl, that I came to that conclusion.

However, even the critics had allowed what Levi had found out years ago when he used to run through my early attempts with his band, that I had a natural feeling for colour. This is equivalent to the same thing in painters, but the worst of it is that the more sensitive your ears, the more impossible it is to keep your hands off improvable spots. As Delius once remarked, 'There is simply no end to it,' and Fauré declared the only way to exorcize the demon was to print, *'car alors il faut se résigner!'* So far this bromide had unfortunately been out of my reach, but after Weimar, Schott of Mainz had promised that if I could get a definite promise out of Mottl they would help me with the printing of *Fantasio*.

As I was now quite certain that Mottl would produce it sooner or later (it turned out to be later – early in 1901!) obviously I must (1) execute the cuts and polishings I had felt the need of at Weimar; (2) do some table-banging at Carlsruhe; and (3) square up matters with Schott.

I had not too much time, for action must be taken in Germany in October at the latest; but the first condition of good work is keeping fit – i.e., for me, plenty of tennis – and that I could count on between the Watchetts (the Hollings's), Farnborough Hill, and at one or two other houses where you were not expected to sit about and chat, but just to play tennis, drink a cup of tea, *and go*.

In October I was ready to return to Germany, this time under particularly delightful circumstances. Lady Lewis (wife of Sir George Lewis, the great solicitor), who was a great friend of my sister, Mary Hunter, had introduced me to her sister, Frau Bertha Hirsch of Mannheim, who was then on a visit to England. Two of her daughters were settled in London; one was the wife of Lady Lewis's son, the other – beautiful Ella – had married her cousin, young Mr Joshua, a golf enthusiast; and Sargent, who was a great friend of theirs, had painted the whole clan.

I and Bertha Hirsch, the straightest, kindest and most uncompromising of characters, made friends at first sight. A musician easily
gauges the quality of another person's musicality, and as a matter of
fact, also in other ways we two 'belonged in the same cage', as a friend
of mine, who looks upon the world as a sort of Zoo, is fond of putting
it. Hearing that I was off to Mainz in the autumn, and on what quest,
this kind woman invited me to make her house my headquarters, for
Mannheim and the other two places are close together; and in October,
heartened by the thought that this time hotels would play but a negligible part in my career, I started for Germany.

Never had my pursuit of musical aims landed me in such ideal quarters as at Mannheim. What I found there could never be found in
England; a family of well-to-do burghers to whom, though the head
was a keen businessman, music was the chief thing in life, and who,
when they now and then associated with professionals of high standing, would do so on terms of musical equality, aware that they had as
much right to an opinion about the pace of the Scherzo in a Brahms
symphony as men like Mottl and Nikisch.

When the summons from Mottl came, I found that at last a real crisis
had occurred. Sick of insulting letters from indignant composers to
whom the amiable and rather weak Mottl had promised more than he
could perform, the intendant had left Carlsruhe in a passion! Some
said Mottl could always put through what he chose; others said (and
I expect this was true) that he had rather taken advantage of the loose
rein on which he was ridden. Anyhow, I found him remorseful and
rather subdued, and perceived that he had sent for me, firstly to apologize for previous wobblings, secondly to repeat that he really *wanted*
and *intended* to produce *Fantasio*, and thirdly not to ask him *now* for a
definite date. 'It *may* be possible this season after all,' he said. 'All I
beg of you is not to lose faith in me.'

Now the day before this interview I had arrived in time to witness,
as he had begged me to do, his performance of Gluck's *Orpheus*, an
opera I had never seen and which Frau Hirsch said it was worth crawling on all fours from Mannheim to Carlsruhe to hear!

That performance was a milestone in my musical life. What that
opera became under the hands of a genius like Mottl, whose soul was
as sensitive to the beauty of all things Greek as to the divine music in
which Gluck has clothed the Orpheus legend, I shall never forget; the
Elysian fields, the ballet (O, that cold, distant, passionate flute!), the
indifferent, dazed Eurydice – not a human being but half-conscious

immortal – led across the stage and vanishing . . . Then Orpheus enters, plunged in hopeless grief, never even seeing the women who are dancing round him. But someone whispers to him that all can yet be well . . . Eurydice comes back again; with averted face, for he may not look at her, he holds out his hand and leads her silently up the rocky hill-path, back to the world . . . I do not think I ever sobbed so unmanageably in public as then, and could I see (and hear) Mottl's *Orpheus* tonight, I believe that even now it would be the same!

After that I felt – and I think I told him so – that though I had been inclined, supposing he could give me no definite promise, to try my luck elsewhere, *Orpheus* had killed that idea, for the notion of a performance anywhere else now seemed vanity and vexation of spirit. I said I would trust him to do his best for me after Christmas, but that in any case *Fantasio* should wait till he was ready for it; and once more I felt that though aware, thoroughly aware, of the weakness of his character, I did well to trust him! The kind Dr Strecker, who was the head of Messrs Schott's firm, had come to the same conclusion, and said I need not fear Messrs Schott coming down on me for the expenses of printing *Fantasio* should the performance again be postponed.

Ethel returned to Carlsruhe to see Mottl in the late summer of 1899, when he informed her that Fantasio *was booked for the following March. She was suffering at the time from 'composers' complaints' – nervous exhaustion and liver trouble – for which a Mannheim specialist recommended three weeks' cure at Carlsbad. While there, having been a heavy smoker for many years, she suddenly gave up the habit.*

On my return from Carlsbad I spent the night of my arrival with the Hunters, who generally took a flat, or rooms in an hotel, in London for the season. That night Sargent was dining with Mary. Though highly appreciative of the good things of this life, he had remained simple and fairly unspoiled, and was quite ready to put up with primitive conditions. In the early days of One Oak he used often to spend the night there, though obliged to sleep crosswise – as it were NE by SW – in the double bed of my spare room in order to extend his limbs. But the one thing he could not bear was any person giving up any pleasant habit, and when Mary had informed him that I had given up smoking he had said he did not believe it and that I probably made good privately in my bedroom (which all assured him was certainly not the case). On my arrival that night I sat next him at dinner and thought he was rather cross; at last he blurted out, 'What's this nonsense about your having given up smoking?' I said it was true – and that the reason was my inability to observe moderation. There ensued quite a hot argument, and at last he said with manifest disgust, 'Well, I never should have thought you were so weak-minded!' – an unexpected rebuke for one who, as Harry would have put it, was if anything 'feeling for her halo'.

That autumn (1899) the Boer War broke out, and Bob had the luck to get attached to the 13th Hussars, who were going to South Africa. This departure, recalling that of the Prince Imperial, brought out the adorable human side of the Empress. She went through what remained of her son's kit, and finding nothing suitable to give him, she asked Violet to make Bob choose a present from her that was to cost not less than £20. (Eventually he got a belt, a sword, a revolver, and a clasp-knife for the money.)

One day a postcard arrived from Mottl saying that on 19 February the rehearsals of *Fantasio* would begin. By then I was absolutely intoxicated with work on my second opera, *Der Wald* – in fact, as I am told happens to impending Mamas on another field, I was far more interested in the coming event than in its predecessor. Soon after this Mottl wired that it would now be impossible to give *Fantasio* till *the end of April*, which is unfavourably late in the season. Would I prefer that to a *fixed promise* (which he advised me to choose) for the following October?

Instantly I decided on October. By then I should have finished *Der Wald*, and while in Germany could be orchestrating it. My chief object that spring was to get it finished up to a point where I felt a four weeks' divorce from it would do it no harm, and also give me a chance of showing it to Levi, who I knew would be in Florence in early May. On 1 April I was able to beg Maurice Baring, who was *en poste* in Paris then, to buy me a ticket for the *Aiglon* performance on 7 April. The only other fixed Parisian point in this hasty flight via Cap Martin to Rome, was a visit I intended to pay to Augusta Holmès, the nearest approach to a large-scale woman composer that the world had yet seen.

George Moore gives us in *Memoirs of My Dead Life* a charming glimpse of this brilliant Irish girl, who, in hatred of England, Frenchified her name with an *accent grave*; with whom, in the eighties, all artistic Frenchmen seem to have been in love and whose opera, *La Montagne noire*, had at last, after fourteen weary years of waiting, been performed at the Opéra Comique. One knew that her famous lover,

Catulle Mendès, having failed, as everyone predicted he would, to marry her, she had fallen on evil days; and though her melodious, extremely voluptuous settings of her own words (for she was also a poet) were still occasionally sung, she was looked upon now as old-fashioned. Years ago I had guessed what a woman has to go through before she can get an operatic work performed, and had contrived to see the opera. And now, wrongly thinking that I might put my own exploits to some account and get up at least a Holmès concert in London (an idea that delighted Harry, who, as a youth, had been rather in love with her himself) I went to see her.

The first sight of her – a convalescent arrayed in a red flannel dressing-gown – was rather a shock. I had always thought of her as tall – on the contrary she was short and fat, her red hair powdered white – who shall say why? – and her white face, helped out with black, red and white, vigorously and wildly applied, as by one who could not be bothered to use a looking-glass and preferred doing her face 'by heart'. In fact, the general appearance was that of a barmaid of sixty, of whom you would say, 'What a curiously well-cut profile – evidently of gentle origin!' Speaking voice charming, manner very natural and frank.

Any hints I may have given in my letter to her as to my own trade, and which I dare say my tailor-made costume seemed to her eyes to belie, were obviously forgotten. I saw in two minutes a *ci-devant* accustomed to *des hommages*. She began the conversation with the usual banalities, but I dropped on to these like a ton of bricks, and after that we got on splendidly. She was evidently a real good sort, lovable and full of natural intelligence.

I spoke of Harry and asked if she remembered him. 'Remember him!' she cried. 'Why, he was as beautiful as a Greek god, that boy – the style I have always liked.' (I thought to myself, '*You will have!*') But she said he had the reputation of sitting alone in silence drinking champagne; so I was glad to tell her that nowadays the latter habit had survived, but that he now loved company and talked glibly. I also told her what was the case, that one day, after a drive back from Versailles, when she sat on the folded-back hood of the *sapin* and sang and sang, and the branches of the cherry trees brushed her head and smothered the company with blossom ('I remember! I remember that drive!' she exclaimed), he had fled from Paris to escape from what he felt he was not yet ready for – *une grande passion*. 'Oh, but why – *why* – WHY!' cried Augusta. 'I might have married him!'

When we parted after three hours' ardent conversation, we embraced with fervour. I promised her I would bring or send Harry to see her – a promise I kept – and felt we really were friends. Just at the end there was a touch of symposium: *'Adieu, chère collègue,'* she said – a remark I pretended not to hear.

In November a sort of *Wald* Symposium took place in London at Mr Frank Schuster's, composed of members of the Covent Garden Opera Syndicate and a few real lovers of music. I was too bored and unwell – also too certain that nothing would come of it – to press the matter home; and though friendly musicians present, such as Korbay, were gratifyingly enthusiastic, I knew that things did not depend on feelings kindled in such as these – these musicians! Great therefore was my astonishment at getting a note from Mr Harry Higgins, chairman of the Syndicate, saying that if I had any intention of running over to Paris, would I show *Der Wald* to Monsieur Messager, who was to be their chief conductor next season, and discuss with him the possibilities of a production at Covent Garden.

The interview with Messager, whom I liked extremely, took place in December, and was very satisfactory. *Der Wald* really impressed him, and he said that if the orchestration was on the same level he would recommend the Syndicate to produce it (which, when the time came, he did). But I had been too thoroughly broken to operatic disappointments to lay much store by his words.

The next thing was a letter from Mottl saying that *Fantasio* was 'in study', that the performance was now fixed for 4 February 1901, and that whenever I came I should be welcome. Thereupon I and Harry (who was in England) had an expensive little farewell meeting at the Hotel Vendôme; after which I steered a more or less direct course for Carlsruhe, and he went back to Rome.

Before betaking myself to Carlsruhe I paid a visit to Count Seebach in Dresden. I have said that the Press at Weimar had been devastating, though it was a slight consolation to learn from old Lassen, who though a poor composer was a man of vast experience, that they never attacked mediocrities in this style. I knew Seebach had been present at the performance, and he had told his Weimar friend, Princess Lichtenstein, that if I would consent to certain cuts, he would give it at Dresden. So I thought it worthwhile to write to him about *Der Wald*, and was at once told to bring it along.

Seebach was friendly though guarded. Schuch was not in Dresden that day, but when I played *Der Wald* to him he was anything but guarded! I reminded him of what he had said to me years ago – that he always thought every new work he was conducting a masterpiece! 'Ah,' he said, 'but I'm not *conducting* this opera . . . *yet!'*

I think he must have expressed his opinion with emphasis to his overlord, for when, two days later, I saw Seebach again, I found a changed being – human, almost loving! In fact I could easily believe what I had been told, that when he chose this alarming personality could be a lady-killer! The failure of another work was referred to as the reason why he never again would sign a contract for producing an opera till Schuch had seen the score. Finally, he said, 'I give you my word of honour I *want* your opera; firstly because it pleases both me and Schuch; secondly, because I want an English opera for my English colony here; thirdly, because *Der Wald* will be inexpensive to mount.' And finally he added, 'I could put you off in a dozen ways – but you must believe me, if I don't sign a contract with you today it is simply for the reason I tell you. In fact the whole thing depends on what Schuch thinks of the instrumentation.' As he spoke it suddenly flashed across me, 'Perhaps he believes about *Fantasio* what Levi, until he came to know me, thought about the Mass – that I had probably got someone else to score for me; just as in yet earlier days Brahms jumped to the conclusion that Henschel had written my songs!' Such are the delights of being a woman!

The interview concluded, I went into the waiting-room, and in order to forget nothing I wrote at once to Harry, jotting down every word Seebach had said. After which, being absolutely certain about my scoring, and equally certain that Seebach was speaking sincerely, I gave up an idea I had had of trying my luck at Berlin. Having heard Schuch conduct a couple of operas in Dresden, I knew that *Der Wald* would be as safe with him as with any man alive.

The Boer War hatred of England, the expression of which had hitherto been kept more or less within bounds by the German Government, was now fanned to white heat by the Kaiser's well-meant but ill-judged presentation to Lord Roberts of the Order of the Black Eagle – the highest honour he could bestow. This act, which even the English thought rather premature, was evidently intended to efface the recollection of the Kruger telegram.* How often it happens that, thinking they have gone too far in one direction, people try to put everything right by going too far in the other. But it never succeeds!

* In January 1896 the German Emperor had congratulated Paul Kruger, President of the Transvaal, on the outcome of the Jameson Raid.

Needless to say, the idea that England was in disgrace would never have been gathered from the reception my friends and I met with from everyone connected with that delightful old-fashioned Court at Carlsruhe, which, though very unlike Weimar, had a charm of its own. The friendship of the Empress Eugénie was a special passport to the good will of the Grand Duchess, who was well posted in my musical affairs, so much so that I felt impelled to tell her about Dresden and *Der Wald*. 'After Dresden we must have it here!' she cried. And when I said that perhaps *Fantasio* would be a ghastly failure, she said, 'Well! if so we'll make good with *Der Wald*.'

Having described the Weimar première at length, there is no need to dwell on the Carlsruhe performance of *Fantasio*, of which I will only say that inasmuch as it was perfect, I was free to criticize my work without mercy, and as usual was more disgusted with weak spots than pleased with good ones, this being my unfortunate disposition.

The Press, as may be imagined, was more ferocious than ever, and we fancied the reviewers must have arranged a plan of campaign among themselves, as each chose a different feature for vituperation, although, here again, not one but gave grudging praise to the orchestration – in one or two cases adding, 'When Felix Mottl is conducting this effect can always be achieved!' His fury at that remark was almost comic.

After all was over, his considered opinion was that the libretto as it stood was weak, but he felt certain I could hit upon something to improve it, *and that to preserve the music was worth any trouble*. He insisted on the point again and again, and I promised to well consider the matter some day.

But 'some day' is a dangerous date, and even as every dressmaker would rather make a new gown than 'mess about' with last year's creation, so every artist prefers tackling a new job to recasting an old one. Then came the War, and about 1916 there arrived – via Kamchatka, or Singapore, or some such place – a ton of music from the German publisher of *Fantasio*.

Now my cottage is small, the soil hereabouts poor, and about a year later I learned from a famous gardener that the ash of well-inked manuscript is even a better manure for flowers than soot . . .

A decision was taken. Dragging forth from the mountain of 'material' a few beautifully printed vocal scores and the two volumes of full score (the former from sentiment, for I have never opened them since, the latter to remind myself what my manuscript used to be!) I conveyed them up to my loft where they still repose. All the rest of the material was ruthlessly put out of its pain; and to this day, glancing at my solitary flowerbed, I sometimes think tenderly and gratefully of my operatic first-born.

'Der Wald'

From Carlsruhe I went straight back to England, completed the full score of Der Wald, and sent it to Schuch. Almost immediately it came back with a letter from Count Seebach regretting that after all he found it impossible to produce the opera. In vain I asked why; did Schuch disapprove of the instrumentation, or what? (I knew this was impossible; even the Carlsruhe Press had grudgingly allowed the effectiveness of Fräulein Schmit's scoring, but I thought I would just put the question.) The reply was a curt note to say that in these cases explanations were never given. But a friend ferreted out that the authorities professed to be 'after all' doubtful as to the success of Der Wald.

Now Seebach was not an enthusiast; he was simply a hard-bitten, fairly musical Court official, with a certain flair, plenty of character, and a reputation for extreme caution. Above all one who prided himself on never launching failures at Dresden. Since we had met before Christmas, the anti-English feeling in Germany was increasing almost hourly, and I quite see now that to produce Der Wald might have brought a swarm of wasps about the intendant's head, who would accuse him of kowtowing to the 'English colony' he had spoken of. I realize too that to explain all this by way of justifying his action would have been a humiliation, as puncturing the proud claim inherited from Frederick the Great and Goethe, that in art and science Germany knows no frontiers.

This bolt from the blue – for I had absolutely counted on Seebach's being a gentleman – was not taken lying down, and the result of my protestations was that when, some few years later, my friend Princesse Edmond de Polignac (a great musician) met Count Seebach in Paris and thought to open up a pleasant conversation with this distinguished foreigner by asking him if he knew Miss Ethel Smyth, the distinguished foreigner replied that he did indeed know Miss Ethel

Smyth, and that if he spied her walking in the streets of Dresden he would leap into a droshky and leave the town by the next train.[34]

In spite of the Dresden rebuff, inasmuch as there was no outlet for English opera in England, I again turned my thoughts to Germany and decided to have a try at Berlin. There was no English colony there, and the Opera was not up to the Dresden level, but in England I had made great friends with Muck, the first conductor at the Opera House, whom I admired greatly as musician, who had dined frequently at my sister Mary Hunter's house, and who had been genuinely struck by such parts of *Der Wald* as I had shown him. Besides being a fine musician he was the straightest of men, and I knew his appreciation was genuine – not merely a form of acknowledgement for a good dinner.

In September 1901, therefore, I went to Berlin, and being well aware that in the opera world things are not as they seem, and that the real and the apparent potentates are seldom one and the same person, I proceeded to reconnoitre the situation. Sir Frank Lascelles, our then Ambassador, being a friend of my sister's, I was in luck as to my basis of operations, and will say at once that but for the kindness of himself and his daughter Florence I doubt if I could have put through the adventure that lay before me.

Three powers are concerned in the running of a Court Theatre. There is the *Hof Intendant*, generally one of the great nobles of the State, whose relation to the actualities of his opera are generally such as were, in old days, that of the Master of the Buckhounds to the Kennels. (There are exceptions to this rule – men like Count Seebach of Dresden and Herr von Hülsen of Wiesbaden who were really, and not only nominally, at the helm – but these were rare.) Then comes the business manager, I think he was called Director in those days, who, together with the third power, the leading conductor, is really responsible for all things.

I soon found out that the supreme power at Berlin was Director Pierson, a German Jew with an English strain somewhere. He was a deeply musical individual, a fine judge as to the worth, whether artistic or financial, of the operas submitted to him, and supreme of flair as regarded the capacities of young artists. He would pick out talent, however deeply concealed under the napkin of immaturity or shyness, and see that talent through. Every thread in the web of corruption and intrigue that then enwrapped the Berlin Opera was held by him, and I was informed that the *Hof Intendant*, Count Hochberg, a musical and most amiable *grand seigneur*, not unamenable to judicious flattery, was wax in Pierson's hands.

Count Hochberg was still in the country, so I forthwith went to Pierson and performed my opera at the piano in true composer's fashion, which includes a rendering of all the choral and orchestral effects as well as the solo parts. The main idea of *Der Wald* is that the short, poignant tragedy which for a moment interrupts the tranquil rites of the Spirits of the Forest is but an episode, the real story being the eternal march of Nature – Nature that enwraps human destiny and recks nothing of mortal joys and sorrows. I saw at once that this theme appealed to the dreaminess that pairs so wonderfully with acute business instinct in men of Pierson's race, and that the musical treatment of it delighted him.

He at once declared himself willing to produce *Der Wald* immediately after Christmas, at the same time telling me frankly that owing to the Boer War frenzy there would be difficulties – also that the Press would be merciless to an English opera written by a woman. I saw, however, that, quite apart from his estimate of the work itself, two things in the enterprise tempted him; firstly, the English blood that ran in his veins spoke for me, and secondly, the prospect of an uphill job appealed to the masterfulness of his temperament. His plan was that though of course a contract would duly be made out, the whole thing was to be kept dark till the moment came . . . then, suddenly, he, Pierson, would demonstrate to an astonished world what sort of work a woman, an *English* woman, could turn out!

'We will mount it splendidly,' he said; 'you will be satisfied!' He bade me play it to Count Hochberg directly he came back, send the full score to Muck 'now – at once', and go next day to Muck's house and interview him on the subject.

I did so . . . and a remarkable interview it was! One of the things I liked about Muck was the chiselled, Abbé-like profile, the frigidity, illumined now and again by a charming smile, that masked the fire he infused into the orchestras he conducted. I now found frigidity enough, Heaven knows, but no smile. 'Your work is good,' he said. 'I liked it in England in the rough; I like it now, and am willing to conduct it . . . But there can be no friendly personal relations between us, for when I hear the word "England" I see red.' His hands clenched convulsively and the veins stood out on his forehead . . . here was the fire, unmistakably ablaze! I knew that his wife adored England, but as if he guessed my thought he went on, 'My wife snatches the newspapers away from me . . . for reading about this horrible war of yours deprives me of appetite and sleep . . .' I then asked whether his views would prevent his doing his best for me? He calmed down a little and said certainly not, that art is art, etc. About the orchestration he was most satisfactory, and trusting to his dear kind wife to help me where she could (a trust that the event justified) I went away, less dismayed, on the whole, than one might expect.

These, and other negotiations which followed, can be dismissed in a few words, though they took some time to complete – also countless efforts of patience and diplomacy on my part, and again and again I thought all was lost. But in the meantime another source of delightful human intercourse became available in the person of Countess von Bülow, wife of the German Chancellor, who came back from the country early in October, bringing with her her mother, Donna Laura Minghetti – one of the great luminaries I have met in my life – whom I was accustomed to see every winter in Rome.

The first result of the return of these two ladies to Berlin was a message from Donna Laura to Count Hochberg. And lo! a meeting with him which I had been trying to achieve for three weeks instantly took place! But there were many details yet to be settled before I could return to England, and it gradually became an institution that I was to go and make music with Madame de Bülow every day at 6 p.m.; 'music is the one bit of real life I have in the twenty-four hours,' she once said. On one occasion the Chancellor looked in – I suppose to take stock of this protégée of his womenkind – and after that I was often asked to dine *en famille*, and thus had ample opportunity to form an opinion of the statesman who, they said, was responsible for the foreign policy of the German Empire rather than the Emperor.

In those early days I was not favourably impressed. Obviously a remarkable man, he was also a polished cynic, and I thought, rather overdid the part of villain of the piece; on the other hand he was too much of a professional charmer to inspire confidence – all of which impressions were to merge, under the influence of his extreme friendliness towards me, in qualified admiration and unqualified personal liking, if one may lay a humble tribute at so exalted a shrine. Meanwhile he struck me at once as being one of the few real gentlemen and men of the world it had been my fortune to come across in Germany, and whenever he either looked at his wife or spoke to his dog I loved him unreservedly.

Sir Frank Lascelles told me that ten or twelve years ago when he and the Bülows were at Bucharest, he had gained the impression which was to be mine later that Bülow lived on two things only, politics and his wife, and certainly I never saw a more devoted and adoring husband. And no wonder! Often, when I found her lying back comfortably in the corner of her sofa – lazy, sunny, dreamy, sincere, and yet so light-hearted and pagan – I thought what a repose it must be to him just to let his weary eyes rest on this intensely intelligent woman with a child's soul! Such was the burden carried by the Chancellor of such a master, that he seldom saw her for more than two hours in the day – often less. But one felt he could not have existed without those two hours; and she knew it, and was proud of the fact – as of her husband and his career generally.

Those were times calculated to put a strain upon English Ambassadors all over Europe, but especially on the one accredited to the Court whence the Kruger telegram had proceeded. Day by day the German newspapers were full of the supposed atrocities committed by the English troops in South Africa, and a faked photograph of an English soldier twirling a Boer baby on his bayonet went the round of them all. To this incident I owe one of those phrases that sum up a perennial state of mind, especially in the Fatherland, and haunt one amusingly to the end of one's life. 'Do you really believe,' I said to my old friend Johanna Röntgen, who had come over from Leipzig for the day – 'you, who have English friends, and know English literature – that our soldiers impale little children?' Johanna's excited and convincing reply was, '*Es steht ja in meinem Blatt!*' – that is, 'it is in my newspaper'! And I happened to know that her newspaper was one of the vilest, most heavily subsidized rags in Germany! Further, these stories were officially supported by a remark made in the Reichstag by some responsible person, to the effect that atrocities were only to be expected of undisciplined mercenaries such as our troops. Thereupon Mr Chamberlain replied in the House of Commons that our troops were as patriotic and highly disciplined as the German or any other army. Then the German Government threw the reins on its own neck, and Bülow begged, furiously and officially, that the German army be not mentioned in the same breath as what he implied were English savages.

All this will show among what shoals and quicksands the British Ambassador was called upon to manoeuvre . . . and my own navigation in the treacherous waters of the Berlin Opera House became hourly more difficult. Nevertheless the cast and the approximate date of the première were settled before I left Berlin at the end of October.

I went home by Copenhagen in order to make the acquaintance of the Benckendorffs, new and great friends of Maurice Baring, then attached to the British Legation at Copenhagen. After a few days there I returned to England, and spent a strenuous two months revising the orchestral parts of *Der Wald* and seeing to the thousand and one things that have to be seen to on these occasions; such as drawing plans of the stage, of the action, of the lighting required, etc., to think out which beforehand saves time. This, and training the infant mind of a sheepdog puppy of the Old English tailless breed, named Pan (successor to the beloved Marco, deceased), occupied me fully till the day dawned when I reluctantly packed up my scores and once more started for Germany.

I got back to Berlin on 29 December, to discover that after all there was no particular hurry, since *Der Wald* could not come out as soon as Pierson had hoped – the usual fate of new operas, except in admirably organized theatres like Dresden and Munich. I found the air tense with the anticipation of the opening of the Reichstag which was to be about 10 January 1902, on which occasion the Chancellor was expected to make a speech that would either lessen or increase the friction between Germany and England. Sir Frank, who was an old enough hand to gather information from all available sources, no matter how humble, cross-questioned me as to my impressions concerning the state of public feeling in England; and he also told me, a day or two before the opening of the Reichstag, that he had been unofficially assured that the tenor of the anxiously awaited pronouncement would be soothing and satisfactory.

I have reason to think he was as astonished and horrified as outsiders like myself, when that speech turned out to be one of the most offensive, even threatening utterances that had ever issued from the Chancellor's suave lips – the kernel of it being that if England tried to bully Germany she would find herself 'biting on iron'!

The day after the opening of the Reichstag I was due, as it chanced, to make music with Madame de Bülow at 5.30, and my astonishment may be imagined when, after a little desultory musical trifling, she suddenly asked me what I thought of 'Bernhard's' speech? I replied that of course England would be lashed to a greater pitch of fury than ever and that one could only imagine that this was the deliberate intention of the German Government. She listened quietly, and I am certain without the faintest surprise, to my elaboration of this theme, and then said, 'Will you come to dinner tonight, and repeat all you have said to me, to my husband? You know how large-minded he is . . . that anything anyone says to him is taken in good part . . .'

This was absolutely true; he listened, and listened well, even to amateur politicians like myself; no wonder, therefore, that my previous sentiments were rapidly turning into liking and admiration! She told me that no one was dining with them except Delbrück and one or two other people whose names I have forgotten, and that I need not do anything elaborate in the way of toilette.

That dinner was one of the most interesting experiences of my life. The Chancellor was a delightful talker – gay, shrewd, witty, light in hand and well read, though when he got the time for reading I cannot think, unless perhaps in his summer home at Nordeney. And, as I remarked before, every time he looked at, or spoke to, his wife, my heart warmed towards him. Presently he said, 'My wife tells me that you think my speech last night will inflame all England. Now *why should it?*'

Never having had occasion to plumb the depths of German ignorance of public opinion elsewhere, it seemed to me inconceivable that a child should not have known beforehand what the effects of that speech would be; and I listened in amazement while he explained what, in his opinion, it amounted to; why, given German feeling, he could say no less; and why a calm, judicial nation like the English should understand that nothing offensive was meant. I said my say, as before in Madame de Bülow's room, and I saw that the other guests, who occasionally threw in a word, were listening attentively.

Then came a dramatic moment: enter a servant with the first telegram from London, reporting the reception of the speech in the English Houses of Parliament! Bülow read it, and saying half jokingly, 'Well, you were right!', he passed it round to his colleagues.

There are limits to the histrionic powers of ever so clever actors. As that dinner went on and telegram after telegram came in and was passed round the table, faces lengthened, exclamations of astonishment and something like dismay escaped the readers; there was no doubting the fact that the effect of that speech had *not* been foreseen by these German statesmen!

When Madame de Bülow and I left the dinner table no allusion was made to all this, and we were discussing Donna Laura, who was in Rome, and other innocuous subjects when the gentlemen came in. I remember the Chancellor, his hand full of new batches of telegrams, coming straight up to the sofa where I was sitting and dropping down beside me like a tired and rather exasperated man.

'But what do you English want and expect?' he said at once. 'Do you want us to *like* this war of yours? To look on and applaud while you are crushing a small nation?'

One generally remembers one's own answers. Mine was to the effect that if France, or some other Latin people, plunged into this hysterical and abominable Press campaign, one would say it was merely their excitable fashion of treating public questions; but from the Germans, a nation kin by blood to ourselves, we at least expected justice.

'My own opinion,' said he, quasi-confidentially, 'is, that *all* armies commit atrocities . . . and there's not much to choose between them' (a slight revision of that other, publicly expressed theory that the German army was sacrosanct and must decline to be bracketed together with undisciplined mercenaries!). I must have reproached him, as master of the Press Bureau, for not putting a stop to the newspaper campaign, as I very well remember his remarking, 'The German Chancellor is not *der Herr Gott*! . . . he can't do everything . . . *I* can't muzzle the Press!'

At the time I took leave to doubt this although I hope I did not say so exactly, but I came to see it was the truth, though not in the sense he meant me to understand.

The English never seem to me to have realized how much more apparent than real was the power of the Kaiser – and consequently of his Chancellor. The Prussian Junkers, besides being the chief representatives of the agricultural interest, were, as the aristocratic party, chief bulwark of the State, and a far greater power than the Court; the Army was their instrument . . . and the Kaiser the puppet of the Army.

Meanwhile, as before Christmas, the needle of my fortunes veered hither and thither in sympathetic response to the political weather. One of Sir Frank's first actions when I came back to Berlin had been to ask Pierson to lunch – a thing few British Ambassadors would have done, for Pierson was not an official power, and as a certain junior secretary remarked with disgust, 'not quite up to Embassy form'. But Sir Frank was one of those great gentlemen who are equally at ease with crowned heads and understrappers. A little later on, Pierson informed me that for many reasons the production of *Der Wald* had better be postponed to the middle of March, but when I asked whether he would advise postponing the whole thing till calmer times, he answered, 'Certainly not; say nothing, and when the moment comes, it will be put through all right.' So I made up my mind to cultivate patience and see as much as possible of Berlin life.

I found it absolutely odious, and should never have believed that, even in military-mad Germany, human beings could consent to exist on terms of such abject subservience. The Kaiser was alluded to in an awed, hushed whisper, and I noticed that anyone who pronounced an unorthodox opinion, such as admiration of modern pictures or music – both of them among his abominations – would be marked 'dangerous' and avoided by the discreet. In fact, those two words, *'der Kaiser'*, swallowed up every other conception in the Berlin brain, and distilled a brew of servility, terror, snobbishness and moral cowardice that defertilized all surrounding regions. Conversation was not possible, but merely the interchange of guarded phrases, as among people surrounded with spies: if you asked your neighbour whether he liked his potatoes mashed, he would qualify the reply lest some hostess in the vicinity should recently have given him fried potatoes. I used to speak freely to the Bülows about all this and rather gathered that the Kaiser liked the idea of all Berlin trembling in its shoes, each man in terror of the man above him, and all in terror of him; a terror tempered with admiration in his case, but none the less mortal dread. In fact, Berlin seemed to me what it was, the capital of a huge slave-state rather than a centre of civilized society.

For one result of the Kaiser Cult I was wholly unprepared, and I confess it shocked me not a little. Apparently the disease was catching, and it became obvious that some of our own countrymen had caught it. One day at the Embassy I overheard a certain flower of the British aristocracy say to her daughter after several minutes passed in a trance – and her tone was strangely languishing and ecstasied – 'Alice, did he wave his hand to us in the Thiergarten *three* times, or was it *four*?' But Alice, who was of a different grain to her Mama, answered with extreme gruffness, 'I really didn't count.' Another day, after I myself had had the unhoped-for honour and delight of meeting the Kaiser, I remarked to one who was high up in the diplomatic career – and a gentleman too – 'By the by, the Emperor spoke of you.' '*What* did he say?' asked my interlocutor, with a face . . . but one must have lived in Berlin to realize what a transfiguration came over that face . . . melted, hopeful, anxious! 'He said,' I went on, ' "Jack is a real good sportsman!" ' 'Did he call me JACK!!' gasped my friend . . . and for very anguish of bliss his voice had a dying fall.

The unfortunate thing was that the Kaiser dominated, and wished to dominate, in all fields. His tastes in Art were reactionary beyond belief, and it was about this time that he publicly thanked Heaven for the Sieges-Allee – 'a monument pure of the modern Art-Spirit'. He would have abolished the 'Secession' if he had dared – that is, the part of the National Museum devoted to modern pictures and statuary – instead he caused these 'abominations' to be exhibited on the top floor, hoping that no one would face the endless stairs; and a magnificent Zuloaga was only saved from banishment by unheard-of efforts. Further, the leading German sculptor, Hildebrand, was in disgrace at Berlin because, on being summoned thither to discuss the erection of some public monument, he mercilessly criticized the design which was first in the running – which possibly was more or less the work of the only Art-Authority the Berlin sycophants recognized, namely, the Kaiser himself!

For the Kaiser really had pretensions as an artist, and I myself have seen his great picture *The Yellow Peril*, a reproduction of which he presented to Sir Frank. The idea is a monstrous yellow dragon, emerging in one corner from blue clouds and extending its claws over the landscape below. And if I do not venture to criticize it, it is because I remember Brahms's remark: 'One cannot be too careful in expressing an opinion of Royal compositions for you never know who they are by.' But there is one charming and authentic anecdote of what the Emperor said to Strauss, when that great composer, who everyone agrees is one of the most delightful of personalities, became first conductor at the Berlin Opera House: 'It is a pity your music is so detestable, for you are such a dear fellow!' (*ein so lieber Kerl*).

Though the anti-English Press campaign was toned down, Anglophobia waxed all the fiercer for being deprived of this outlet. Anti-English demonstrations were now a daily occurrence, and one day the windows of our Embassy were smashed by a mob, the Kaiser himself calling next day to express his indignation. As time went on, too, we English abstained from gazing into shop windows, lest our turned backs should present too convenient a target for the patriotic but cautious spitter! Finally, as finishing touch to the situation, my one rock of defence, the sole powerful friend I had connected with the Hof Oper, was swept away in the flood of misfortune that, like the giant wave Neptune sent hurtling against the shore to madden Hippolytus's horses, now threatened to engulf me.

Pierson was a bit of a blackguard, perhaps, but also a bit of a genius. A difficult man to deal with – shifty yet reliable, maddening yet likeable, ambitious yet disinterested. Still though I guessed that he 'took money' I never doubted but that he would see me through, and well through, albeit he realized that none would be forthcoming from me. About the middle of February, however, I thought the psychological moment had arrived for his being asked to *dine* (not lunch) at the Embassy to discuss matters . . . but just about then he suddenly began to look so desperately ill that I was terrified. And Sir Frank's sister Lady Edward Cavendish who, like the secretary I quoted, did not consider Pierson 'up to Embassy form', and had been casting about for a reason not to ask him, finally said in desperation, 'but from what you say he might die at table!'

Alas! that invitation was never dispatched. It may have been a judgement on poor Pierson for befriending me, for I afterwards heard that he was actually filling in the rehearsal sheets, with a view to the production of *Der Wald* on 16 March, when the pen fell from his hand! He was carried home unconscious and expired two days later. As I wrote to H. B., 'You will not be surprised to hear that I have killed Pierson.'

From that moment my position was desperate, for not only had Count Hochberg never been called upon to cope with the realities of theatre direction, or do anything except 'represent' Opera and the Drama at Court, but he was totally unaware of the intrigues and countless forms of corruption that underlay the whole system of management to an extent which I myself had only half realized, so far. I knew that certain singers had grumbled as loudly as they dared at having to incur unpopularity by taking part in an English work; but Pierson was a bold and clever man who had every sort of hold on his team, and did not brook opposition. Once he had disappeared from the scene of action, however, I became aware of nothing less than a fixed intention, on the part of the Company, to make the production of *Der Wald* an impossibility.

The role of Röschen's lover, Heinrich, was in the hands of a certain Herr Kraus, a stout, bellowing tenor of the Siegfried type, who had a fine voice capable of tender inflections and was not a bad actor; and he too was a great favourite with the public. This singer, unable for some reason or other to wriggle out of the part, confined himself to doing his best to make things unpleasant; and his best was pretty good, for besides being of a vanity that made him take the suavest suggestion as an insult, he was one of the greatest brutes I have ever had the ill luck to meet. During the nerve-racking weeks that followed I recall two Kraus incidents. The first was when at a given moment, in my anxiety to make him believe that no offence had been intended, I rashly laid a hand on his arm; thereupon, with a voice and attitude peculiar to the stage-Joseph, he exclaimed, *'Bitte mich nicht anzurühren!'* ('Please not to touch me!') The second was when, at some other crisis, he shouted, *'Das Frauenzimmer soll die Bühne verlassen!'* To translate this phrase, 'Remove the female from the stage' is the best I can do, but no word in our language conveys the abominableness of that much-used term *'Frauenzimmer'*.

And so, more or less, with the whole cast. They all had the length of Count Hochberg's foot, and would craftily ask and obtain leave, one after the other, at dates which practically wrecked a coming rehearsal or possibly caused its postponement. This I would find out, would rush to the bewildered Hochberg, show him the real 'plan of hours' as opposed to the one submitted to him, and myself suggest what should be done – for he was as helpless as a babe. Obstacle after obstacle was thus erected, discovered by me, and circumvented. I often thought it fortunate I was a woman; firstly because I could pretend, as foolish, ignorant *'Frauenzimmer'*, to believe that all this was the working of chance, whereas a man would have had to kick or shoot someone continually; and secondly because I am certain that only a woman could have stood the strain – and many another strain connected with similar enterprises.

If a question here suggests itself, 'Where was Muck all this time?', the answer is that a conductor is not bound to busy himself with the preliminary study of an opera he is producing. Schuch and Mottl invariably did so, and Muck was such a big man that I am sure his usual practice must have been the same as theirs; but on this occasion the idea was to see as little of the composer as possible. Also, to do him justice, he reckoned me among the opera writers who are able to drive their intentions into the souls of their artists, though, as I have shown, this gift was of little use to me here. I fancy, too, that knowing what I was up against, he may have considered it improbable that *Der Wald* would come up for performance at all – which, to tell the truth, it would not, but that the joy of battle now possessed me . . . and also a fierce desire that England should win in the end! Finally, he knew, and so did I, his power of coming in at the last moment and pulling things together. But the last moment was far off . . . and meanwhile I got little or no help from Muck.

I think had an angel revealed to me at the time of Pierson's death what the future had in store for me, I should have gone straight back to England with my score. But it was only by degrees that the situation developed, and there was a great deal at stake. Dresden, and one or two previous experiences connected with *Fantasio*, had taught me how hard it was as woman and foreigner to get one's work accepted at all; and without the leverage of an ice-breaking foreign performance I knew I might knock on the doors of Covent Garden till my knuckles were raw. For there is no money in a new English work produced in England. Again, my own financial position was a factor, for though I was generously helped by a rich sister, you can't live for months in an hotel for nothing. In fact I was in the situation of a mountain climber who, having reached a certain point, must either go on or else postpone that climb for an indefinite period . . . perhaps for ever.

True, there came a phase in this ceaseless tug-of-war when I spoke to Count Hochberg of throwing up the sponge, but this was a political move rather than anything else; for I knew that to let me do it would be to give himself away in the eyes of his dread master. He was aware, or course, that Madame de Bülow, the woman whom the Kaiser went more out of his way to honour than any other '*Frauenzimmer*' in the German Empire, was my friend – and whether or no the Battle of Berlin was worth fighting it never would have been won but for that fact. The immediate result, therefore, of my suggestion was that poor Count Hochberg now made it clear to his subordinates that *the thing had to be put through*. After which, though alas! at the eleventh hour, they settled down to their job . . . it can be imagined with what good grace.

One evening, on returning from golf, I found a note marked 'URGENT' from Madame de Bülow, begging me to come round early next morning on important business; which I did, and learned to my inexpressible joy and surprise that the Emperor desired to make my acquaintance, and that I was to dine with the Bülows that night to meet him!! I had heard of these informal dinners at the Chancellor's palace, commanded by the Kaiser, at which no woman except his hostess was present – only certain men whom he wished to meet in a friendly, unofficial way. And it was said that on these occasions he really enjoyed himself and was at his very best.

My wild excitement may be imagined, and also my anxious preoccupations as to clothes, which matter was discussed in theory with Madame de Bülow, and supervised in practice later by Florence

Lascelles. As to what happened that evening I will quote a letter of mine to my eldest sister, Alice Davidson:

Reichshof, Berlin
11 March 1902

. . . I have been ceaselessly plunged from uncertainties and worries of all sorts into the exactly opposite conditions; but then I had to forge straight ahead and deal with a hundred and fifty fidgety little things, which stopped my writing good letters to anyone. Thus it is now nearly a week ago that I had the celebrated meeting with the Emperor.

He sometimes announces himself to dine with the Bülows, *sans façon*, only ten or twelve men and no ladies present. A list is submitted to him, or sometimes he suggests people. But on this occasion I suspect that Madame de Bülow proposed me as a sort of man; for I've noticed that, without in the least making a demonstration, she has quietly and steadily done everything to lay the train in case I should want help from above – which however is not the case.

Well, I arrived, and found a galaxy of men; and the Chancellor (whom I'm rather under the spell of, which is odd, as he isn't at all the sort of man I generally like) told me I was to sit next to the Emperor, and *not* next Professor Harnack – a theologian and poet combined, with a head like a bird of prey, whom I delight in. Presently, with no sort of fuss, in came the Emperor. He was in a sort of black mess jacket, with aiguillettes, and looked extraordinarily like a Fifth Form boy. He is very like the Royal Family, but a much cleaner cut, harder, browner face, and a wonderful 'outlook', though his eyes are not as good as his mother's. His walk is splendid – just what you would expect – and the main effect is one of the greatest conceivable quickness of intelligence, and, strange to say, kindness and good manners. I don't know what else to call it, but it is the acme of naturalness and easiness. He said he heard I was doing great things – the usual sort of Royal beginning, only bereft of its pro forma delivery for once. When he went on to the next people Gräfin Bülow said I was to be with him exactly as with anyone else – that he liked it; so I was.

Dinner was pleasant, only he said such incredibly *borné*, stupid, *military* things about Art, to a horrible man, a certain Court Painter, Herr von W., that I wheeled round and talked to my other neighbour, feeling I should say something too awful if I listened.

After dinner he came straight up to me, and said he had just had a letter from the Empress Eugénie. We talked of her, of her nobility of character (which it surprised me his knowing about), and he told me much about the relations between Napoleon III and 'Grandpapa', which was news to me. It concerned the founding of the German Empire; how, at a given moment, 'Grandpapa', baffled by the want of patriotism on the part of the German Princes, whom he had warned of the Emperor Napoleon's designs, determined to unite Germany himself, and how much ascribed to Bismarck was really due entirely to the old Emperor.

After my interview, which I am told lasted exactly one and three-quarter hours, the Emperor joined the others, and, thank goodness, sat down at last.

The first Full Orchestral Rehearsal of *Der Wald* is a dramatic and appalling memory. Muck must have known, more or less, what to expect, but even he was surprised, and gratifyingly horrified, at the exact amount of 'preparation' achieved, few of the singers being note-perfect and the scenic arrangements chaotic! And after all, Muck was morally responsible for this particular opera! Count Hochberg, who by this time was at bay and in a satisfactory but belated state of wrathful zeal, went clambering about among the rafters to see for himself whether I was right in saying that the green lights he had ordered to be prepared a fortnight ago were still jammed; and at one moment his eyeglass came crashing down on to the stage, where its pieces were reverentially swept up by the stage charwoman.

Of the following rehearsals I remember nothing, except that at one crisis I dressed up a sack in a pillow-case (lent me by that same charwoman, who was a great friend of mine) and, swarming up ladders and across beams, hung it up aloft myself, and begged Muck and Hochberg to judge whether, illumined by the now-mended green lights, it did not represent to perfection a shadowy Spirit of the Forest sitting in a tree? . . . but a veil over these details!

When, at last, the evening of the première arrived – I think it was 21 April* – Count Hochberg said that of course, as composers are wont to do on such occasions, I was to sit in his box, whence there is easy access to the stage to take your calls. I remarked that there might be none to take! He laughed. 'We produce many operas here,' he said, 'and some of them have been anything but successes, but I can recall no single instance of a composer not being called to the front. It is part of the ritual.'

I have some experience of the opera public, and throughout that performance, which went better than one could have hoped, I could see that though there had been some hissing when the curtain went up, the audience were interested, attentive, and responsive to my intentions. So musical are the Germans that even if they wish to they

* It was 9 April, according to Alfred Loewenberg, *Annals of Opera 1597–1940* (Cambridge, 1943).

cannot close their hearts and intelligences to the musical appeal as long as it is sounding in their ears! But in cases such as the Boer War frenzy, the deep, corporate feeling of a people has the final word, and as the last notes were sounding, strong, well-organized hissing and booing broke out in three parts of the house. The curtain rose once or twice – pro forma and in spite of vehement opposition – on the artists, but if the composer had shown herself, which is the last thing she wished to do, there would have been a demonstration – possibly rotten eggs!

Five minutes later I went into the conductor's room. Poor Count Hochberg was in the state of mind you would expect in a *Hof Intendant* and a gentleman. But Muck was the strangest study. I had always liked his ice-sheathed violence, even when I myself was the sufferer; and now, there he sat at the table, white with rage, his chin resting on his hands. 'I never make a mistake,' he said. 'I know, I feel it in my back when the public is interested . . . and I swear this opera interested them from the first bar.'

No condolences with the composer, but what I appreciated a million times more, the outraged sensibility of a great musician! And I rather wondered – I still wonder – if he said to himself that but for this political bias things might have turned out very differently. For, as I truly wrote home, 'If Mottl, who is not a fanatic, had been first conductor at Berlin, all this could never have happened.'

On the morning following the première the usual *Strichprobe* or 'Cut Rehearsal' took place. Few operas are not the better for cutting, and few composers blind enough not to perceive the fact in the fierce light of a public performance. As regards this rehearsal, alas! even dear Madame de Bülow had rather let me down, by insisting that Muck should conduct the music at some grand entertainment (I think a bazaar) she was getting up. And although I told her that this would prevent his taking the *Strichprobe*, I saw that her mind was set, gently but tenaciously, on Muck. As, therefore, the pariah I was could not ask anyone else to take the rehearsal, there was nothing for it but to take it myself, though I had never conducted in my life!

With rather a beating heart I walked into the huge *Probesaal*, and as soon as I appeared, O wonder! there was a burst of applause! Orchestras usually say 'good-morning' by rattling on their desks, but there was such marked warmth in this particular greeting that I was emboldened to say, as I took up the stick, 'Well, gentlemen, I don't believe *you* think my opera is as bad as all that, in spite of the Press!'

Then came a tribute that redeemed the whole hideous Berlin business. The leader of the second violins, a very grumpy old gentleman as a rule, growled in accents of scathing contempt, 'Ach! DIE PRESSE!!'; and then at the back of the room, up rose the Bass Tuba, stout as are most tuba players, and added, 'Your opera is simply splendid (*einfach grossartig*) as people will gradually find out, in spite of the Press!'

I may add that they all helped my ignorance and incompetence in every possible way, and that the *Strichprobe* was got through more or less satisfactorily.

Alas! the season was now too far advanced for a run of *Der Wald* such as might induce other German theatres to take it up when the fury of Anglophobia should have spent itself; besides which, fortified by the Press verdict, the enemy within the gates now reared its head again with admirable audacity. Hochberg would fix a day for the next performance; someone would surreptitiously obtain leave of absence from Pierson's temporary and popularity-hunting substitute; postponement; renewed fixture; and the same thing *da capo*. In fact, it was the usual demoralization at the fag end of a season, complicated by special malevolence and lack of a strong hand on the reins. Among other agreeable details I recall that my friend Kraus was pleased, at the second performance, to take the love-scene at such railway-speed that I had to rearrange the score for his pace.

Then came the final disaster; it appeared that Muck had long since been promised a fortnight's leave in April . . . and a conductor's leave means remunerative work elsewhere!

Thus, day by day, week by week, my chances dwindled, and by this time poor Count Hochberg's position had become so desperate all round that I was reluctant to worry him. Nevertheless, a third performance, conducted by the second (or third) conductor, and at which the public began to testify to its interest, had been successfully achieved, and I was busy plotting and counter-plotting for a fourth and final performance when a second interview with the Kaiser took place.

On 2 May I was to dine *en famille* with the Bülows at 8.00 – just a boring female relation of theirs and five or six men. And as I was going to play golf that afternoon, and as we seldom got back till 7.15, I thought it wise to have my hair done beforehand by a hairdresser, the erections of professionals being as a rule solid, and likely to look better, in spite of the ravages of wind and bunker-thumping, than the hasty improvisations of an amateur. This proved to be nothing short of an inspiration; for when, precisely at 7.15, I re-entered my hotel, I found awaiting me an official letter, confirmed by various telephone messages, saying that dinner was at 7.30, and that I was to come half *décolletée* and in mourning – which I knew meant a Prince of the Blood at least. But it turned out to be the Kaiser himself, who was leaving Berlin that night at 11.45, and wished to come in after dinner and while away the time at the Bülows till his train started!

But for the letter I have ventured to quote, I should have remembered little about the first interview; but though the account sent home this time was brief, I recall a good deal about the second, probably because *Der Wald* was now off my mind:

He came straight up to me with 'Miss Smyth, I am *delighted* to meet you again!' and was most tremendously cordial. And again he stood talking to me for three-quarters of an hour, when Bülow came up and joined in. The conversation now became German, for Bülow doesn't speak English, and was all about politics and shipping trusts and so forth.

Presently – I think to prevent my telling the Emperor what I think of Berlin, for the talk was veering in that direction – Bülow manoeuvred us most cleverly into chairs among the general group, and then he, the Emperor, Renvers, Madame de Bülow, my beloved old General von Loë and I, talked . . . but mainly the Emperor and I. He was absolutely delightful and I made him laugh (not a difficult task) till his chair nearly gave way, and this is supposed to be the great thing to do!

In a postscript to this letter, addressed to my sister Mary Hunter (a wonderful portrait of whom, by Sargent, was then on view at the Winter Exhibition in the Museum), I add:

I amused myself by speaking of Sargent for a second to the Emperor, who loathes all modern painters, and told him there was a very fine Sargent portrait of one of my sisters, in a corner of the town I knew 'His Majesty did not think well of' . . . the Secession!! And he actually allowed that he had seen *one* splendid portrait by Sargent! I think it must have been the Chilean Minister.

When the Chancellor herded us into safety among the other guests the Emperor had just remarked, 'I want to make of Berlin a town like Paris or London – a place towards which every cultivated European gravitates naturally – not merely the little burgher capital which it would remain if most of its inhabitants had their way!' (Indeed one of his ordinances had been that, in the stalls and dress circle, ladies were to be 'ausgeschitten', that is, show their necks; and on the night after this edict – which escaped the notice of several theatre-goers – was published, wonderful scenes were enacted in the ladies' garderobe, gold-braided officials in cocked hats producing pins, and deciding whether a stuff gown turned in in a V would, or would not, satisfy requirements.)

'Can you tell me why more *English* do not spend the winter here?' the Kaiser went on . . . and Bülow no doubt saw the moment coming when I should say to his master what I had often said to him, that nothing would induce English people to pass months in a Barrack, under military discipline!

Another dangerous moment was already behind us; it was when the Emperor had said, immediately after shaking hands with me – and as one certain what the reply will be – that he hoped all had gone smoothly for me 'at my Opera House'. After a moment's hesitation, during which Madame de Bülow began to look anxious, I said that Pierson's death had been an unfortunate circumstance, explained a little, and wound up by remarking that if the coachman dies on the box, of course the horses are all over the place for a moment.

'That should not be so,' said the Kaiser with a touch of his photographic face – a very different expression to the charming, friendly one it wore in private life. 'If one of my Generals falls down dead on parade, his place is instantly taken by another, and everything goes on as before!'

To this I replied, as politely as I knew how . . . but as I spoke my hostess's cheek paled visibly, 'Unfortunately it is not like that in the world of opera!'

Great must have been her relief when the Kaiser burst out laughing, and turning round to her, said, 'Do you hear what she says? That my Opera is a pigsty!' (*Schweinestall*).

There is little to add to this story of an eventful Berlin winter, unless to record the fact that the fourth performance of Der Wald, which took place on 9 May (Muck still being absent on leave), was far and away the best, strange to say; and this time the audience undisguisedly showed its approval. Heart-rending reflection! for now it was too late! True, Count Hochberg had faithfully promised a fifth performance (to complete the number stipulated for in my contract) but . . . he had also given my friend Kraus leave till 7 June! I had written home that 'to put this sort of thing through requires iron health and maniac persistence', but to hang about in Berlin for another four weeks was more than I could face. So on the 10 May I packed up my scores and started for England where, to this day, the *Wald* performances have achieved the noble number of . . . three!

Strange to say I never saw dear Madame de Bülow again, though I and Donna Laura met once or twice afterwards in Italy. The Kaiser I only saw once afterwards. I was staying in Rome when he passed through on a two days' visit, and by an extraordinary bit of luck I was bicycling in the Campagna, when I saw a carriage approaching at break-neck speed, preceded by the well-known Imperial outriders. Hauling my machine on to a hillock at the side of the road, I stood there, and as the carriage passed made a profound curtsey, without the bicycle collapsing on top of me – no mean feat. The Kaiser made a formal acknowledgement, then stared, whirled round in his seat, half stood up, and waved his hand in the friendly fashion that had so utterly overwhelmed the high-born English lady in Berlin a few years ago.

And needless to say, I was as deeply flattered and gratified as would be ninety-nine out of a hundred readers of these pages if it had happened to them![35]

The Covent Garden performance of *Der Wald*, on 18 July 1902, was one of my few almost wholly delightful operatic experiences. I had a splendid cast, and a first-rate stage manager and producer rolled into one called Neilson, who contrived a charming décor on the lines agreed upon by Charles Furse and me when that dear neighbour and friend informed me he meant to do a design for the cover of the vocal score. I more or less trained all the principals myself, and of course the chorus, a job I always love. Anything like the keenness and fiery enthusiasm of the whole company I never saw; and then it was I acquired a conviction which time and the upspringing of Sadler's Wells have strengthened, that if England were given a chance, she would become the leading operatic nation in the world.

That *Wald* was the only real blazing theatre triumph I have ever had (except one thirty-seven years later which, unfortunately, I was too ill to see, and in any case should have been too deaf to hear!). The absolutely shameful fact about the glad event is that when I think of it only two recollections stand out vividly: Neilson's setting, and, a million times more vividly, a remark Henry James made to Mary about the profound curtsey I launched, when 'called', at the Royal Box! Talk of male vanity! I wish it were seemly to repeat his words here!

Of course, in the years that followed, shreds of detailed recollections of that night still clung to me; but whoever said 'sufficient unto the day is the evil thereof' must surely have been thinking of opera composers. No Don Juan can ever have been more wholly engrossed by the charmer of the moment than are we by the horrors attending the birth of whatever new opera is on the stocks, nor more forgetful of it as soon as the next comes along!

Towards the end of the autumn the printed vocal score of *Der Wald* (which I paid for myself, the beloved Empress giving me £40 towards it) was ready, all except the title page and cover, which, as I said, were being designed by Charles Furse. Early in December the rough proof of his beautiful sketch arrived, surmounted by this dedication:

> To Henry Brewster, the onlie begetter, I dedicate my part
> in this work.

By which I meant to indicate that though the actual story was mine, the spirit of it was a result of continual association with a mind like his.

Owing to exigencies of the pictorial design, this dedication was printed in two lines (as above), which again were some little way from each other; and the rapture of Charles Furse can be imagined at finding the printer had added an 's' to the last word of the first line, giving it the appearance of a comprehensive if somewhat unblushing statement!

Now just then Mary was in a disapproving mood as regards me; and her sense of humour being notoriously limited, Heaven knows what induced me in writing to her to pass on the above anecdote; probably I had been too much amused by it to keep it to myself. The result was the three following postcards.

1. From Mary to Ethel:

Even as correctly stated, I cannot say how I loathe your dedication. Hope you will not let it stand.

2. From Ethel to Mary:

Sorry you don't like my dedication, which happens to be taken from Shakespeare.

255

3. From Mary to Ethel:

If your dedication is taken from Shakespeare, all I can say is it smacks of modernity.

My friend Mary Crawshay, who was with me when No. 3 postcard arrived, and who well knew us both and our occasional scraps, instantly said, 'Probably she means *maternity*.'

Harry was deeply amused at all this and wrote a characteristic comment: 'I think the term of *begetter* is singularly appropriate to the librettist. His work is short and extremely pleasant, so in a way there is nothing meritorious about it at all, yet it is indispensable and strongly affects the offspring. Thank you, dearest, for mentioning it.'

To avoid misunderstandings I slightly changed the wording of the dedication which finally read:

> To Henry Brewster, its onlie Begetter, I dedicate
> my part in this work.*[36]

*

As a result of her success at Covent Garden, Ethel was invited by the Metropolitan Opera to superintend a production of Der Wald *in New York. Mary Hunter, who wanted to see the decorations which Sargent was doing for the Boston Public Library, offered to pay her sister's expenses. Ethel believed that by going she was encouraging women 'to turn their minds to big and difficult jobs'.*

Grau, the impresario for the Metropolitan, died suddenly before Ethel's arrival. Two mediocre performances were mounted by his successor. A further performance, at Boston, was a fiasco. Ethel felt that Der Wald *was 'as out of place in Americas as one of the Muses would be at a football match'. To her 'mingled relief and chagrin' she was treated by Mary's rich friends as a poor relation.*

There was one more performance of Der Wald *at Covent Garden in 1903. As a result of Mary's meddling in the managerial side, a row developed between the sisters 'that lasted on and off nearly two years and never really closed on her [Mary's] side. She honestly believed that no one knew their own affairs as well as she did, and could not understand why I was so furious. And I allow I had uttered some home truths that even a more generous nature would not easily have got over.'*

---

* The dedication as printed in the Schott vocal score of 1902 is: 'My part in this work I give to Henry Brewster, its only begetter.'

SIX
1903–9

THE WRECKERS
THE ILLNESS AND DEATH OF H.B.
THOMAS BEECHAM

'The Wreckers'

From now onwards nothing existed for me – nor I think for Harry – except the coming into being of the libretto of *The Wreckers* – the subject on which we had been meditating all this time. And in order to make clear what brought us to this point, I must go back some eighteen years.

In 1886 I and the Hippisleys, then a young married couple, had walked round a large part of the Cornish coast, incidentally visiting some of the many smugglers' caves along that seaboard, the mouths of which are submerged at high tide, access being still possible by secret passages from the cliff above. The weirdest and most fascinating of them is the Piper's Hole in the Scilly Isles. On entering it, just above high water mark, you go downwards rapidly and alarmingly by an ever narrowing passage illumined by torches, which are stuck at intervals in rings in the wall; the passage suddenly bends sharp to the left, and you become aware, by the growling of boulders apparently only a few inches above your head, that you are under the sea; presently, to your great relief, the passage takes another turn, the rumbling ceases, and squeezing between two rocks at what seems to be the end of the cave, you behold an unearthly-looking little fresh-water lake, on which floats Charon's boat, while the waving torch of the guide reveals to you that the lake is full of goldfish (put there by the owner of that island, Mr Smith-Dorrien) and that the goldfish are blind.

Ever since those days I had been haunted by impressions of that strange world of more than a hundred years ago; the plundering of ships lured on to the rocks by the falsification or extinction of the coast lights; the relentless murder of their crews; and with it all, the ingrained religiosity of the Celtic population of that barren promontory, which, at the end of the eighteenth century, became the scene of Wesley's great religious revival! And I knew that these Cornish savages had come to believe that like the Israelites in the Old Testament they were God's Chosen People, whose right, nay, whose duty it was to plunder and extirpate less favoured peoples. And I learned too that

Wesley had striven for ten years to wean his congregations from this hideous practice, and that the impossibility of doing so had eventually broken his heart.

Did I pick up down there a legend of two lovers who, by kindling secret beacons, endeavoured to counteract the savage policy of the community; the woman impelled by humanity, and perhaps hoping that her action might palliate her unfaithfulness to her husband, her lover because for her sake he was ready to take any risk; how they were caught in the act by the Wreckers' committee – a sort of secret court which was the sole authority they recognized – and comdemned to die in one of those sea-invaded caverns? Or did this story come to me in my sleep? I cannot say, but I fancy the hint of such a legend must have been given me by someone in Cornwall.

One day I had passed on my notes to Harry, as one might hand a palette to a painter and ask him whether he could evolve the picture of one's dreams. Harry found the subject magnificent and obviously predestined for music. He said he would try what he could do, and when he asked whether he might work in French, that being the language he preferred when poetically disposed, I joyfully assented; for Monsieur Messager of the Opéra Comique would be the next artistic director at Covent Garden; and that for *Louise*, by Charpentier, a novelty of which all the world was talking, and various other operas, he would bring over some of his principals from Paris. So perhaps to compose this opera in French would be the best chance of a performance in England of an English opera!

In the wonderful autumn of 1902 I had run down once or twice to Cornwall to cross-question 'oldest inhabitants', and glean tales told them by their forebears (which may or may not have been gospel, but certainly fitted well into the picture!). And one or two antiquarian-minded clergymen gave me more reliable accounts of incidents in the past, some of which reappeared in the completed libretto of *The Wreckers* – for instance the comic chorus after Chapel in Act I. Between whiles I would lie on the cliffs, buried in soft pink thrift, listening to the boom of the great Atlantic waves against those cruel rocks, and the wild treble cries of the seagulls. (Most of the themes they suggested were eventually summarized in the prelude to Act II, 'On the Cliffs of Cornwall', but they run through the whole woof of the music.) And any suggestions I picked up there, or found in books at the British Museum, were at once passed on to Harry, while I, with mouth open and shut eyes, waited to see what good fortune would bring me.

In November 1902 came a 'regardless of expense' wire from Maurice Baring, who was in Rome, that prepared me for Harry's manuscript, which arrived a few days later. So far it was only a synopsis, a dramatis personae and a psychological chart. But when he wrote, 'I only hope you recognize your palette and your choice of colours,' it was a very modest way of putting matters, for he had sublimated my vision.

His story was so devoid of conventional morality that some timid spirits wanted me to persuade him to soften things down a little; for instance to let the heroine, wife of the aged preacher Pascoe (who after all adored her, and had been indulgent to her), express remorse for having yielded to her lover, and even mention Pascoe's wrecking proclivities as explaining her aversion to him! But Harry would not hear of it. 'Of course she hated Pascoe,' he cried; 'never mind about his being the leader of the Wreckers, and whether all that is or is not an excuse. *He was old and amorous*, and she was young and madly in love with Mark; that's all there is to it!'

What specially appealed to me was the idea so strongly brought out in the ultimate text, that each of these people is, from his point of view, *doing right*: the Wreckers in wrecking; Thirza, Pascoe's wife, in trying to save their victims and using Mark's passion to make him turn traitor to his clan; Avis, her young rival, who is willing to blast her own reputation and even risk death in a wild attempt to save Mark's life; her father in casting her off as one lost beyond hope of redemption, and so on. Real life is thus. The conviction that your own line is the only admissible one is the philosophy of most of us, and without it many would not always know how to behave! But however they act, compromisers and sentimentalists like the English are all for protesting in theory against moral fluidities; aware of which, one of Harry's French friends, a great critic, asked if an 'all for love' figure like Thirza would not stick in Nonconformist English throats? Harry pointed out that Catherine in *Wuthering Heights* had gone down without difficulty, and that music is a great lubricant. Whereupon, to my undying honour bracketing me with Emily Brontë, this Frenchman hazarded the conjecture that it is perhaps the job of some creative women of these later days to sweep once for all into the dustbin the old-fashioned darling of the gallery – the heroine made of timidity, purity and pounded sugar. This had not occurred to me when Harry and I were discussing the character of Thirza, but I have nothing against it!

Alas! the easy and carefree correspondence with my friend – one of the great joys of my life – now degenerated into an endless discussion about *The Wreckers;* in fact, our letters were about nothing else. When I think of how I worked him I should feel a pang of remorse but for knowing that the task intoxicated him, and remained the chief occupation of his life till it was done. In the spring of 1903 I went to Paris to thank him for the wonderful work he was doing for me, discuss its continuance, and introduce him to no less than four remarkable women, with whom, in this for me strangely blossoming year, I had made friends! So far he had met none of them, and I never could really settle down to a new course at the banquet of life, unless he had a place at the table.

The four new friends I speak of were Princesse Edmond de Polignac, Madame Bulteau, Anna de Noailles the poetess, and her sister, Hélène de Caraman-Chimay.

I first met Winnie de Polignac just before I went to America, and discovered that all I had heard about her was true; that she was a first-rate musician, an excellent painter, and altogether a remarkable woman. As she is still a faithful and cherished friend of mine, I will only say here that of the new friends the new century brought me, none counted more in my life than she. Also she is one of the few people mentioned in the book (except of course great foreign musicians, such as Nikisch or Bruno Walter) who are capable of estimating the point and value of music regardless of how the Faculty judges it.

Earlier in 1903 Vernon Lee had introduced me by letter to her new friend, Madame Bulteau, whom her intimates called Toche. Maurice Baring, quoting from O. Henry, said of her when she died that she was one of the people who make you 'bet on yourself'. She had a great admiration for his writing, and a good many distinguished people, such as M. Briand, Monseigneur Duchesne, Henri de Régnier, etc., were among her devoted friends, and no doubt, like Maurice, found the weight of their respective burdens lighter thanks to her friendship.

Besides these – like Mrs Benson and what I used to call her 'patients' – a crowd of women of all ages, whose lives she more or less directed – hovered round Toche, who was as warm-hearted as she was appreciative. I delighted in her company, but never was of those she once described as '*mes vampires*' (which I thought was not quite fair when you enjoy and deliberately lend yourself to exploitation!).

The story of her brief friendship with Vernon is so characteristic of both that I cannot help just indicating it.

When Vernon fell a victim to a new *culte*, the first thing she set herself to do was to clear the new charmer's decks of the crew in possession, on the plea that they were unworthy of such a craft. Now a few years before, Toche had penetrated into the homestead of a mysterious new poet who wrote anonymously and was reported to be a young and beautiful foreigner. She was shown up into a bedroom, in the huge bed of which lay two young Romanian girls. It was long past midday and neither of them seemed ailing; it was just that they did not see why anybody who preferred lying in bed should get up – so at least the legend came to me. Soon after, these two immensely gifted and wealthy maidens respectively married Count Mathieu de Noailles and Prince Alexandre de Caraman-Chimay, brother of the lovely Comtesse Greffulhe, who I always think must have been twin sister of Helen of Troy. With one flap of her strong young wings Anna de Noailles reached the topmost twig of the Tree of Fame, and the sisters, who were long since known to and beloved by Prince Edmond de Polignac and his wife, soon became devoted friends of Toche's.

Vernon had told me about Madame Bulteau long before I met her, adding that the first thing to be done was 'to get rid of those two little hop-o'-me-thumbs who infest her drawing-room – for ever lying about on sofas, or just rushing away shrieking "*tendresses*" '! Such was Vernon's description of Hélène and Anna!

Between me and Anna – surely as amusing and brilliant a genius as ever appeared upon this planet – spells of keen friendship and almost daily interchange of letters alternated with spells of silence and indifference. And indeed I think that each of us was too busy wrestling with her own private daemon to mix happily with someone in a similar plight! But Hélène, whose intelligence was in certain ways greater than her sister's, and whose nature seemed to me of almost flawless beauty, became one of my nearest and dearest. Both died on the threshold of middle age, Hélène thanks to a drama of 'medical etiquette'; Anna, whose physique was always a mystery to herself and all who had to do with her, and who had never known what ordinary mortals call good health, of an illness none could diagnose. I thought it must have been that, like volcanoes, she had burned herself out. But one who was as near to her as anyone tells me she died chiefly from cessation of desire to live. In later years we seldom met. She was not a happy woman, and could probably have said with Goethe, whom the world believed to be the most contented of men – and certainly he was one of the most successful – that in all her life she had not known one really happy day. I am glad she did not live to be old.

I greatly admired Harry's patient acceptance of this new turn in my life. Not that he himself held aloof from humanity nowadays – far from it; but his human relations were of a graceful and pleasantly superficial nature, not serious absorbing affairs like mine. Sometimes he reminded me of one with a small appetite obliged to look on, day after day, while his friend eats straight through the menu of the Grand Hotel. But he was glad to see me making friends with France and coming to understand French ways; besides which he delighted in, and was charmingly received by, three of my four – quite a good percentage!

Anna, and the adulatory group of men by whom she was always surrounded, were less in his line. And I think that his silent criticism of relations based on exuberant mutual admiration was probably divined by Anna. Again, it seemed to him morbid to carry worship of and sensitiveness to beauty to such a pitch. 'Madame de Noailles is half Greek,' he said; 'how comes it that she can throw moderation overboard like that?' One day I incautiously read him the following passage in a letter from Anna, who had spent two of the four days she was in Venice in bed: *'pour ne plus voir cette ville terrible tourmentée par Vénus, dont les cris me tiennent éveillée la nuit!'* ('this Venus-tormented town, whose cries rob me of sleep at night!'). He was acutely provoked, complained of these 'vibrating ladies', like Anna and Eleonora Duse, whose 'vibrations' got into their brains in everyday life, and said he thanked Heaven that I played 'hockey and golf and tennis and hopscotch'. (I never asked what hopscotch might be.)

The full story of Ethel's irruption into the Parisian circle of the Princesse Edmond de Polignac is told in The Food of Love *by Michael de Cossart (Hamish Hamilton, 1978). Ethel wrote tactfully of the warmth of her feelings for her younger contemporary, the daughter of the American millionaire, Isaac Singer. Winaretta, a generous, knowledgeable and discriminating patron of music, was as independent and forthright as Ethel. Though they continued to meet occasionally, in extra-musical matters discord was inevitable. Years later, during the Second World War, when the Princess took refuge in England, harmony between the two old ladies was restored.*

*

In the spring of 1905, with the score of The Wreckers *completed, the first phase of Ethel's new battle began. The soprano Emma Calvé signified that she would like to sing the role of Thirza (in French), but she and the conductor Messager 'had a terrific quarrel and were now deadly enemies'. Calvé's proposal to sing the role at Monte Carlo instead also fell through. Meanwhile the Princesse de Polignac suggested the Théâtre de la Monnaie in Brussels, more enterprising than most French opera houses. Ethel went to Brussels to play and sing her score. Her performance made the usual impact, but the*

264

management pleaded previous commitments and lack of money as excuses for not accepting the work.

Herewith perished the last hope of saving Harry's exquisite words alive, and my thoughts turned to the only other available quarter, Germany. The Boer War fury had died down, and I remembered having heard that Nikisch, with whom I had made friends at the Herzogenbergs' more than twenty years ago, was doing wonders as director of the Theatre at Leipzig. He was a large-hearted, lovable man, absolutely without prejudice, and I knew he would not refuse to examine my work nor let my sex affect his judgement.

I sent him the libretto, told him that I should be in Leipzig by such and such a date, and was at once given an appointment for the following day. 'The libretto is magnificent,' he wrote. 'If the music is as good I congratulate you.'

It was an amazing experience when we met, like the moment in the fairy tale when the evil spell is broken and all difficulties melt away. He made me play all three acts straight through, and then and there signed a contract with me, the pledge being for production before the end of the season 1906–7. But he told me he wanted to bring it out in the second half of *next* season (1905–6). Could I let him have the material immediately after this next Christmas so that he could then begin to study at once?

This was something that had never happened to me before – that a great conductor should simultaneously get to know an opera of mine and name the day! The only question was, could it be got ready in time? The immense difficulty of turning the text of an already composed opera into some other language can be judged by the appalling English translations we had to put up with before Professor Edward Dent's day. But the firm Peters recommended a certain Herr B. whose knowledge of French was profound, and who was a real musician. And the test pieces from *The Wreckers* which I gave him to try his hand on revealed the fact that he was also a real poet, with a peculiar genius for this particular work. Moreover, he was an extremely taking fellow, not ashamed to say how fine he thought the libretto and what luck it was for him to be given the job of turning into German such wonderful poetry!

In fact, it was without the faintest misgiving that I left a piano score with him and started for England. When I got home the first shock to my faith in Herr B. was finding that the promised first instalment of his work had not yet arrived. By the middle of October I had come to the conclusion that he was not very reliable; by the middle of November it was obvious that my collaborator was a scoundrel. He would send ten really exquisite lines followed by half a dozen of such absolute balderdash that I imagined he must be a drug-addict. And some of his actions, such as threatening to burn all the rest of his work unless I instantly sent him three pounds (evidently a classical copyist move) were bordering on the criminal. The adorable Empress Eugénie having come down with one hundred and forty pounds to defray the expenses of lithographing the German piano score, I felt the least I could do was to yield to her urging and promise a substantial extra tip should the work be delivered at the appointed time. It was, but the whole thing was a prolonged nightmare.

Arrived at Leipzig, I learned that as sometimes happens if a genius is in the place Nikisch occupied, he had exceeded the sum guaranteed by the Town Council to such an extent that after June 1906 his services would be dispensed with. His successor was to be the second Kapellmeister, a youngish and very rising man called Hagel, and all arrangements concluded with Nikisch would be honoured, 'for a contract is a contract'. Alas! as we now know, in Germany it is sometimes only a scrap of paper, and Nikisch advised me to safeguard myself elsewhere if I could, 'though', he added, '*if he chose* Hagel could give a very fair account of *Strandrecht*' (an admirable Germanizing of the title suggested by a lawyer friend).

But from what I heard of Hagel, it seemed unlikely that he would do his best for an opera chosen by Nikisch. His temper was said to be bad, one cause (or effect?) of which was the permanent skin disease which disfigured his countenance. 'That poor man,' I said to myself, 'can have had little or no success in love, is doubtless a woman-hater in consequence, and will vent his spleen on me!' Meanwhile there was no time to be lost, and I took my goods to three (or was it four?) other theatres, but without success. The most hopeful seemed to be Prague, where the director was the celebrated impresario Angelo Neumann. Twenty years ago he had been director at Leipzig and had produced *The Ring* there, which all the old Mendelssohn group considered equivalent to introducing the can-can at the stately Gewandhaus Balls. He had practically made Nikisch, who was then a quite unknown young man, and the two had remained great friends. Of course Nikisch now wrote to him about *Strandrecht*, but alas! in a letter direct to me Neumann said that though this was evidently, as our common friend said, 'a beautiful work – powerful and original', no one knew better than Nikisch that such qualities do not necessarily spell financial success. For next season he had already too many commitments; therefore with sincere regret (and I felt this was genuine) he could but send back the score.

At this point Harry took charge of the situation. He urged me to come at once to Rome for a rest, and discuss with him a new *Wreckers* scheme he had conceived. If it pleased me I should take the necessary steps, and then go on with him to Salso Maggiore, the stimulating effect of which on sluggish circulations Mary, who had just left Rome, was for ever extolling. 'And what could be better,' he asked, 'for chilly people like you and me? . . . Afterwards, *nous verrons.*'

I obeyed, set off for Rome, and found that his scheme was truly staggering. He had set his heart on a performance at Prague, and was prepared to reinforce his desire with a cheque of £1,000 for Neumann! If Leipzig wished after all to do it, well and good, but in every sense he put his money on Prague. Neither of us were versed in the annals of bribery and corruption, and it was not till years after that Henschel told me Neumann must have thought Harry mad, for £500 would have been ample, and eagerly jumped at!

After Salso I went to Prague, perceived Neumann's quality at once, and liked him. I heard most of the singers suggested for my cast, and was told that the first Kapellmeister, who was on sick leave, was 'fire and flame' for the opera (as Nikisch had told me he would be). Then, having settled everything, I went on to Leipzig, where, according to a telegram forwarded from Rome, *The Wreckers* was already billed for 15 November!

Hagel was quite mild and friendly, and had adopted the cast selected by Nikisch. All the same I determined to walk warily. Now Neumann had shown such a masterly grasp of the whole subject, and was so obviously looking forward to his £1,000 job, so full of the magnificent thing he would make of it, that half from policy, half from pusillanimity I thought I could take a risk at Leipzig. The best chance for the performance might perhaps be to let the conductor work it upon his own lines and not interfere at all. If he made a hash of it, everything would be redeemed at Prague, where the date had been fixed so that I could attend all the later rehearsals after the Leipzig performance. So after Hagel and I had looked at one or two risky places, I told him I should not reappear till the general rehearsal unless summoned. My only stipulation, to which he at once assented, was, that *no cuts* were to be made unless with my consent. Whereupon, after a few joyful meetings with the Wachs and Limburgers and other old friends, back I went to England, in my pocket a note from Harry highly approving my plan of staying there for the present.

In November, as prearranged, I arrived at Leipzig the day before the dress rehearsal, and found that Hagel had broken his word and cut the third act into an incomprehensible jumble. As every note of the opera had been studied, the cut being a recent happy thought, there was yet time to remedy matters. But my expostulations were rudely brushed aside. The new director, a really good fellow just promoted from the drama department to his present exalted position, was much distressed, but felt he could not interfere with Hagel, who had worked under Nikisch for two years. I said very well, but that rather than witness the mutilation of my work I should depart at once to stay with friends in the country, though the director's piteous plea, 'But I have a big supper party in your honour!', rather wrung my heart.

When the moment came, far from leaving Leipzig, as I had threatened to do, I hid myself in the audience; and O, wonder! not only was the performance very fair – specially the orchestra – but approval was so generously bestowed that I began to wonder whether I was not in for a big success. After the prelude to the second act the applause came with such a burst, that Hagel, half turning to the audience, instead of the usual bow shrugged his shoulders!

When the curtain went down on the third act, success became a certainty, noting which a brilliant idea, inspired by fury, revenge and *Macbeth*, rushed into my brain. My seat was in the third gallery on the right side of the house, and when people were 'called' it was always from the left wing that they emerged; but there must be some sort of way of getting on to the stage on the right side. Down I went, flight after flight, opening one iron door after another, and at one moment finding myself in a place that certainly will have been *verboten* to ladies. Apologizing hastily to the two men in possession, of whose horrified faces I have a blurred recollection, I sped on downwards, and presently, met by a blast of clapping, I found myself at the goal – that is in the front wing on the right side of the stage. Tumultuous applause was raging, and opposite me, just about to come on (I was told for the fourth time) beaming and beckoning the principals to do likewise stood the director and Hagel!

If ever men looked as if they saw a ghost it was those two as they caught sight of me in the opposite wing. I advanced quite quietly; the good director, quickly recovering himself, rushed forward and took one of my hands, signing Hagel to take the other, and though I was not dressed for the occasion, the public grasped who I was, and displayed what the widow of the former director styled 'southern warmth'. It appears that all in all there were thirteen curtains – an ominous number.

The director, who was evidently in the Seventh Heaven, then entreated me to come to his supper where I should meet most of the principals; I explained that eight or ten of my country people who had come over for the occasion were being entertained by my sister at Hotel Hauffe, but if he would allow me I would come along later as soon as I could. I did so, and anything more friendly than the general atmosphere cannot be imagined! Champagne corks ceased not to pop, and I told Hagel, next whom a place had been reserved for me, and who knew I was an expert, that I had thought it all out, and that half an hour's 'sitting rehearsal' with the principals, and perhaps quarter of an hour with the band, would suffice to make the third act plausible. 'O, of course, we can manage that!' said the director, and I suggested calling at the office next day at 10.30 to explain matters, adding that of course I would see to the material being put straight, and if Hagel liked would take the reopened cuts through with the soloists myself. And so good-night all round in happiest mood.

Early next morning two short notes were delivered by hand; one a curt word from Hagel saying that the opera must either be played exactly as last night or not at all; the other was a very shifty pencil note from the director saying that Hagel absolutely refused to do what I wanted, and that he himself was obliged to start in half an hour for Berlin but hoped to see me after the second performance on Thursday next!

I sent express notes to both men, saying that unless my suggestion was adopted I should withdraw the opera, and waited till evenfall for a reply. As far as I remember neither of them replied; I expect they thought this was an idle threat. I then wrote, and showed to Wach, a letter to the *Leipziger Tageblatt* explaining the reason of my action, and on the third day went down early to the empty orchestra, removed every scrap of *Wreckers* material which was still lying on the desks, including the full score, and departed by the midday train for Prague.

I cannot to this day decide whether it was wise to take a step that would make every theatre director in Germany my enemy, and increase, if possible, the virulence of the Press; and I do not say that I should have taken it but for having Prague there to set things right. But Harry who was always for 'no compromise' backed with all his heart an action which I am told is unique in the annals of operatic history; and so I fancy did Wach. But today, when I think of those singers, none of whose names I can recall now, who had been working for me for weeks and who would presently learn that there would be no 'next time', my heart rather fails me.

Shortly before I arrived at Leipzig the newspapers had spoken of a slight indisposition which prevented Herr Angelo Neumann of Prague from attending a certain important theatrical congress. Arrived at Prague, I learned that the 'slight indisposition' was a carefully hushed-up paralytic stroke, and that since the seizure he had been in bed, unable to move or speak and most of the time unconscious!

I tried to see his wife, but was told she was prostrate and could not see anybody. I went to the theatre meaning to speak to the Kapell-meister for whom Nikisch had so much regard; but it appeared he had left Prague – some people said for good – and that one of the other conductors was carrying on meanwhile. Everything was wrapped in mystery, and what I picked up I have forgotten. But, roughly speak-ing, there was no one in charge. It was a replica of the position at Berlin when Pierson died.

I will not exasperate the reader by describing, for it is easy to imagine, what it was like trying to bring order into a situation of which everyone was expecting the proximate dissolution, and endeavouring to make sure of a berth under the new dispensation. Of the perform-ance I fortunately remember nothing but that even the English Press correspondents (who by the by had been very gracious about Leipzig) were astonished that such appalling orchestral playing could be heard in a city that had the reputation Prague enjoyed. Considering that the players were practically reading at sight, it was not astonishing. (In the German Press, one specimen of which has by chance survived, it was put down to bad scoring!) Of course, Neumann knew the value of first-rate subordinates, and had there been any coordination, and respect for the work, and a strong man at the head of things who wished to make a success of it, we might have had a fine performance at Prague. For as far as I remember the ensembles were well studied, and the décor, had it been finished, would have been excellent. But everyone thought when Neumann had his stroke that he could not last three days, and all hands seem to have downed tools. Maurice, who came all the way from Petersburg for that one night, said he had never heard a more disgracefully under-prepared public performance. But he knew the music thoroughly, and being endowed with a vivid imagination seems to have had an impression of the thing all the same.

By this time a new *Strandrecht* plan was fermenting in my brain. It was impossible to be blind to the fact that the only chance for *The Wreckers* was to find a man who could care enough about it, and be big enough, to stand up against the really terrific onslaught the Press felt itself bound to make on the work of a female Anglo-Saxon.

I knew there was one man big enough to serve my turn, Gustav Mahler, now in charge of the Viennese Opera. But how get his ear? for I had not met him since the old, old Leipzig days, when I was slightly known to him as one of the reactionary anti-Wagner Herzogenberg group! I wrote to him boldly, however, and when Harry and I arrived at Vienna I found I had been given an appointment. But it appeared that, full of distrust of this composing Englishwoman's opera, Mahler had deputed his second-in-command to hear it and report; and thus it was that I first came together with one who instantly became as warm a friend of myself and my music as I have ever met – Bruno Walter.

He has often told me with what extreme reluctance he obeyed his chief's behest, but before I had played him two pages all was well. He advised me, for reasons he was not at liberty to divulge, not to press the matter with Mahler just then; I instinctively trusted him absolutely, said I would come again as soon as he summoned me, and feeling that my affairs were in the best hands I went back then and there to One Oak.

If in the Empress and my sister Mary my music-strivings had faithful supporters, I must now mention the most wonderful of them all. I do not know when first I met Mary Dodge, a rich American friend of my sister Violet. At that time she was able to play croquet, though rather stiffly, on the lawn of beautiful Loseley, near Godalming, where she then lived, but in the year I am now writing about – 1907 – she was already almost crippled with arthritis, and lived most of the time at Warwick House, St James's, the beautifully panelled and exceedingly acoustic room of which, on the first floor, was often put at my disposal for musical purposes. The performers were paid by her, and the invitation of such guests as I wanted to come, and the subsequent plying of them with tea and cakes, was also left to me, while their real hostess, hidden behind a locked door in a contiguous chamber, 'enjoyed the music', as she said, 'in peace'.

Among the services she rendered me was the gift, when One Oak came to an end, of enough money to purchase a plot of ground and build upon it the little house in which I have lived ever since;* the paying of the deficit (£600) on a *Wreckers* week I gave about the same time (1909) at His Majesty's; and the establishment of an annual subsidy to be paid me till my death. And though since her own death, in 1933, a new American law does not let such legacies go scot free (and O! if she had foreseen such a contingency how carefully she would have guarded against it!) that subsidy makes a blessed difference to my income. Later she became an ardent and most generous subscriber to the Militant Suffrage Society, but this matter was worked with extreme caution, for she naturally did not wish her connection with a body that waged ceaseless war on the Government to be generally known. She was one of the noblest characters I have ever met, and one of the very few people who contrive to come relatively unscathed out of the ordeal of possessing great riches.

Meanwhile, upsetting news reached me from Harry's friend, Mr Wickham Steed, who was now foreign correspondent of *The Times* at Vienna, and with whom I had eagerly made friends. It was rumoured, he said, that, disgusted with the penny-wise pound-foolish policy of the committee responsible for the financial side of the business, Mahler had determined to throw up his post of director of the Opera House and devote himself wholly to composition. It was impossible to get reliable information on the subject, for Mahler had made the Viennese Opera the leading Opera in Europe, and all Vienna was shrieking at the idea of losing him. But until the matter was settled it was useless to worry him with questions. I knew Walter would make a sign when the moment came, so I went on quietly with other work, and in June, both Harry and I being in need of invigorating air, we met and stayed for three or four weeks at Briançon.

In November, with Walter's approval, I went again to Vienna and saw Mahler, who was perfectly delightful and said he would tell his successor, Weingartner, that if he had not been leaving Vienna *Strandrecht* would certainly have been performed there. Alas! I met Weingartner in London in December and ascertained that Mahler had not said one word about me or my opera!

Of course this was a disappointment, but early in life I came to the

* Coign, in Woking.

conclusion that you cannot expect one composer to be so mad keen about the work of another as to face willingly opposition and odium in order to produce it. It is nothing but natural that your own children should have the first claim on any bread and butter that may be going, and the opera-writer's field of action is desperately crowded. Therefore, though Walter wanted me to reappear in Vienna, once Weingartner was in the saddle, after having heard him conduct, and ascertaining that he too was an opera composer, I felt he was the last person to take any interest in my work, and preferred to rest in the certainty that as soon as Walter had a theatre of his own he would certainly create *Strandrecht* for me (which in the event he contracted to do on 15 February 1915, before which date arrived the Great War had broken out!).

As Harry said, 'Where's the hurry? *Strandrecht* will arrive some day by its own weight.' So I eased off the ropes of my endeavour, believing that if I let the river flow quietly underground a bit in Germany it might come up again some day, and I actually began wondering what – if anything – could be done in England.

The Illness and Death of H. B.

By April 1908 all sorts of plans for a mild attack on the English music world had come into being. A performance of my chamber songs in London had been what is called in friendly newspapers 'a triumph'; and honestly I think the music created a genuine impression. Anyhow it formed the basis of my relation to the harpsichordist Violet Woodhouse. Our friendship did not dig itself in till some months later, but I think we made friends at once, as children do; as Pauline Trevelyan and I had done nearly twenty years ago, and for the same reason, because of music. Harpsichord-playing such as Violet's, comprising of course the whole conception and re-creation of whatever comes under her hands, is but one manifestation of a natural, effortless kinship with beauty in every form – art, literature or nature.

While I was in Vienna, Violet and a Spanish friend of hers, Gomez, who was a member of the London Symphony Orchestra, put their heads together and brought about the appearance on the prospectus of that band an announcement that on May 2 Nikisch would conduct the Prelude to the Second Act of *The Wreckers* ('On the Cliffs of Cornwall'), the first time an orchestral work of mine would have been performed in England. And as one thing leads to another, out of this new warm little centre on interest in my music, a bold decision on my part emerged – namely to give a performance of the First and Second Acts of *The Wreckers* in a concert-room. Needless to say, the conductor of my choice, if I could get him, would be Nikisch, and the orchestra the LSO, which would thus already have rehearsed some of the most difficult pages of the score at their own concert on 2 May.

As it turned out Nikisch was quite content with the fee I was able to offer him, and if the concert seemed unlikely to cost more than £400, of which I might get half back, it was partly owing to the refusal of Madame Blanche Marchesi – one of the largest-souled artists I have known – to accept a fee. The role of Thirza appealed to her profound musicality and great dramatic gifts, and she created it according to my dreams. She also suggested that the chorus difficulty might be overcome by training a bevy of her pupils, stiffened with a few old hands, to turn themselves into a set of bloodthirsty savages; '*ce qui leur fera du bien,*' she added, and I quite agreed. For the other solo characters, artists with voices and a dash of dramatic blood in their veins were quickly found, and Queen's Hall booked for 28 May.

At the same time yet another concert was looming. In London and in Paris I had made great friends with various French musicians, among them Gabriel Fauré, Léon Delafosse and Louis Fleury – the exquisite flautist who had already played the flute part of my songs in London – and Hélène's heart was set on a Smyth Chamber Music Concert in Paris, to take place before the afterwash of the London concert had subsided. As Harry and I were bent on a care-free expedition to the Greek Islands in the very earliest days of June, Hélène begged me to leave everything to Fleury, herself, her mother and Fauré; all they asked was that I should come over to rehearse the day before the concert. To this I gratefully assented, secretly agreeing with Harry that music of that character might perhaps take root in the soil that had produced men like Bizet, Delibes, Ravel, Debussy and Fauré himself.

I did not tell them or anyone else that my chief reason for insisting on a change and a spell of quiet, once these alarums and excursions should be over, was that by degrees I was getting rather troubled about

Harry's health, and I ascribed it partly to over-intensive work on his new play, *Buondelmonte*. In February he had an attack of deafness, and a mysterious inflammation in his mouth. The nerves of a tooth or two had been killed, as it seemed to me rather at random; but he said this was less unpleasant than living with a poultice between his jaws. We had been counting on going to Greece not later than April, but as had so often happened before, my music commitments had squashed that idea. Still we could do something else later.

After a while these strange symptoms subsided. When Anna was in Rome he had been, as she told me afterwards, in great form; and to me he wrote that he now had an attack of worldliness and was enjoying it greatly.

In March, when dear Frau Hirsch and her two daughters, Marie Lewis, and the beautiful Ella Joshua, whom Harry greatly admired and whose company he delighted in, had been in Rome, they had told me how well he seemed, and how full of the idea of my giving a *Wreckers* concert. Indeed I had already had a letter from him that he should call upon his 'cheerful money-box' to disgorge at least £200 towards expenses, and that he would lend me as much more as I wanted at three per cent. But not long afterwards he confessed that he had been feeling 'ill and miserable' and had been doctoring himself for three weeks with Epsom salts, in consequence of which his liver felt like an open wound! He now spoke of the châteaus and cathedrals in the Loire district as an expedition we had always vowed to do together, but in a postscript he added, 'If the worst came to the worst, could you bear to go to Carlsbad with me?' to which I truthfully replied that I was always enchanted to go to Carlsbad, as it was one of the few cures I believed in.

Somewhere in the midst of this uneasy time came the performance of 'The Cliffs of Cornwall', Nikisch conducted divinely, and I now knew, once for all, that if properly conducted my music would always sound exactly as I had meant it to. And in complete sincerity I told Harry that I believed my foot was on one of the lower rungs of the English ladder at last!

Then came another pause, followed by a letter from him saying that though he was 'now' all right again, the liver symptoms had recurred; that it had felt as though a litter of kittens with extra-sharp claws and exceedingly strong teeth had set up a nest under his waistcoat, which kittens were succeeded by a wolf his doctor called 'Rheumatism', that went marauding about and devoured all that the kittens had left. But luckily these visitors had now repaired to some other Zoo.

Not unnaturally I took all this for a *boutade*, and being deep in the usual cross-currents of musical enterprise, I said with some irritation that I wished he would not execute fantasias on his ailments just now, for not knowing how much of it was sober truth it made me nervous. This letter called forth a penitent reply, assuring me that it was more than half fun; that, however, he was not very fit, and was thinking of calling in Marchiafava, a very great Italian physician, in whom he had absolute faith.

A letter from me, imporing him to do so at once, elicited a line from his son Christopher to say that Marchiafava, who had been out of Rome, was calling tomorrow morning, and had requested his father to stay in bed till he arrived, and keep as still as possible till he had examined him. Hence Christopher was doing amanuensis. 'I am to tell you,' he said, 'that he feels quite all right now, and that there is nothing to worry about; that he has often had similar attacks and that they mean nothing. That is the message, but I must tell you that I never saw him like this. He has suffered great pain and I think he is very ill. Of course, I will at once let you know, under seal of secrecy, what Marchiafava says, but I fear you must prepare for very, very bad news.'

Two days later came the verdict. 'Cancer of the liver, and at no time would operation have been possible.' By the same post arrived a very cheery letter from Harry, saying there was nothing wrong except 'a congested liver with some angry spots'. Of course, he added, Marchiafava had been at first against the excursion to London, but was now reconciled to it and giving him strychnine to get up his strength, which he confessed was 'not much to boast of'. Marchiafava had wanted him to go straight to Carlsbad now, but allowed that English physicians know a lot about the liver 'which', the doctor had added, 'is only natural in such a climate!'. And the letter wound up with laughing at me for proposing to put off the concert till the autumn. 'You must indeed not let yourself worry about me,' he said. 'It is only a case of *pazienza*, and I am sure I am right to come. The disappointment would have weighed on me.'

At the same time Christopher wrote that postponement of the concert would be a death warrant, so intensely was his father's heart set on its being now; Christopher was coming with him, and his father persisted on arriving on 26 May so as to see the performance of Maurice

Baring's first play, *The Grey Stocking*. All Marchiafava was now aiming at was to forestall pain and keep up strength, which, so far, was being successfully accomplished.

I met them at Victoria. He could walk fairly well and was his usual serene self, continually saying with a touch of triumph, 'Now wasn't I right to come?' But if after seeing him I had one grain of hope left, it was because the optimistic cling automatically to hope as the drowning clutch at the tiniest bits of floating wreckage; for on his face was the unmistakable look of those who are under orders. He liked the rooms I had taken for them at the Hotel Cecil, from the balcony of which he could watch the river, and he made no objection to seeing a great London physician whose verdict was 'exactly the same as Marchiafava's', so he told me. But to me the doctor said it seemed incredible that a man in that condition should have accomplished such a journey. Neither Maurice nor I remember if he saw *The Grey Stocking*, but I think all he was aiming at by then was to be well enough to go to the concert. Had he seen the play I am sure we should remember it.

I think the person he was most anxious to see as soon as possible was Maurice, being consumed with desire to hear what he thought of *Buondelmonte*. Many years afterwards I asked Maurice to write down for me all he remembered about the two conversations they had in London. Here is what he wrote.

The first time I went to H. B. he told me he had finished his French play. 'So it *is* finished now?' I said. 'Yes,' he answered, and then he added with a smile; 'and so am I.' This was no surprise or shock to me, because some little time before he arrived, I met you at St James's Palace where we lunched with Aunt M'aimée and you took me into the little room near the dining-room and told me you were afraid H. B. was dying. This was before anyone dreamt of it.

He then told me he had his play with him and was very anxious for me to see it. He went into his bedroom and fetched a small travelling-bag; I saw it was a little too heavy for him, and tried to help him, but he wouldn't let me and took out of it a typescript; I said I'd read it at once and bring it back directly I'd done so. After that we talked exactly as usual of one thing and another, and I think he may have said that after your concert he meant to go to Carlsbad. Anyhow, the conversation got on to remedies and cures, and I said that nowadays cures sometimes happened in cases that seemed desperate. Then, quite lucidly and impersonally but very firmly, he gave me to understand that for him there was no hope of any such thing. It was only one sentence but there was nothing more to be said. I remember thinking he looked desperately ill.

I read his play that night and took it back two days later, and when I told him I liked it he was very pleased. I said the verse probably needed some correction for French ears, but I thought the subject magnificent.

There are bits of life that we live through as in a dream. Such was everything connected with those days. Toche Bulteau and Hélène had come over for *The Grey Stocking* and the concert. The band was obviously under-rehearsed, and they said '*ils ont joué comme des cochons*', notwithstanding which there was no question of the effect upon the public and the Press. Harry sat next me in the balcony without moving. Evening clothes had always been very becoming to him, and now, the dignity of his dead white face, which had grown a good deal thinner, seemed unearthly. His head looked like a marble Donatello bust; Sargent told Mary he had never fully realized its beauty before.

Ever generous on such occasions, Mary gave the artists and a few great friends of Harry's and mine a gorgeous supper. But, of course, Harry went straight back to the hotel with Christopher who told me (when he had seen his father into bed) that he was not in pain, and intensely happy at the way everything had gone. Also that he was not too tired, and seemed likely to have a good night. Of course all his friends saw how terribly ill he was, but at his wish we told them he was looking forward to seeing them at the hotel, and that on 4 June he was going down to the country and afterwards probably to Carlsbad.

It was of course impossible not to go to Paris for the chamber music concert, got up as it was by the zeal of a handful of friends who considered I ought to get known there. All these, including Princess Brancovan, Madame Greffulhe and Fauré were organizers. Some of them who knew Harry were aware of the tragic circumstances in which the concert took place, and I think I was sorrier for them than for myself; especially for Hélène, the prime mover in it all, who cared so deeply about my musical destiny-to-be. One thing I was able to tell them. When the reviews came out, so happy did they make him, that had one not known there was no cure for his disease, one would have said the enthusiasm of those reviewers was working a miracle! Never had music written by me been understood *en bloc* by a whole Press in this fashion! (Lalo and Brussel are the only two names I recollect); and upon one accustomed as Harry was to the sneers and really incredible unfriendliness of the German Press about my work, the vivifying effect was amazing. Not only had these French reviewers profound knowledge of music and views of their own, but they expressed themselves like literary artists. Without exaggeration, I think I never saw the Francophile Harry happier about anything.

The day of my return from Paris (5 June) we took him down to Clotilde's house, The Rushes.* I had asked my housekeeper, Mrs Faulkner, to bring my bike in a fly to the station; also Pan, for Harry loved him. But today he scarcely noticed him – a significant fact that gave me a sharp pang. And Mrs Faulkner was so shocked at his appearance that she could hardly respond to his greeting. One Oak was three miles from The Rushes, and I had decided that the best plan would be to sleep at home and bike over daily to spend the day there. This would make things easier for Clotilde (whose cottage was small) and also break the monotony of the day for her father. And never can I say how deeply I was touched at the way those children took my presence as a matter of course.

Just at first, the fatigue of the journey from London over, and the reviews arriving, you would have thought but for his looks that nothing was wrong. He spent the day downstairs, dressed much as usual, and once he suddenly almost rushed up the stairs as a *tour de force*, saying, 'You see, there's plenty of strength to go on with!' But drops of perspiration were on his forehead . . .

Presently came the time when pain, or at any rate discomfort, began; and, possibly owing to the action of the drug prescribed by Marchiafava, there was less talk; but the quality of it – amusing, witty and wise – was unchanged. What Christopher was as nurse I shall never forget. One morning when I arrived Harry was sitting on a chair with a shawl over his shoulders, and ever so gently Christopher was rubbing his back. His father had once said to me that intercourse with his son was like biking down a gentle slope with a silken flag fixed upright on your handlebars! At the sight of his present occupation I quoted these words, and both of them laughed. But I thought with a pang, 'Could *I* ever be as gentle as that?'

During the last twenty-four hours the doctor kept him practically unconscious, and he died quite quietly on 13 June, at 8.30 a.m. I had always believed, until the day before, when Christopher told me he had whispered, '*C'est fini! Tant pis,*' that he did not guess what his disease was. But after reading Maurice's account of their talk at the Hotel Cecil it became obvious that when he left Rome he must have known he was dying.

At the end I sat beside his bed holding his hand; he seemed hardly

* In South Farnborough.

breathing, and whether he was conscious or not I do not know; but when I said his name softly I seemed to feel a slight answering pressure. Presently, as I am told often happens, the death-stupor suddenly lifted. Raising his head a little, he opened his eyes, wide, wide, and on his face was a look I had seen once before on the face of a dying man – that of my father; a look so glad, so confident, as of one who has just caught sight of a long looked-for goal. Then his head sank again and his eyes closed.

Sargent, dear man, at once offered to come down and draw him. But it could not be done till next day; there was no light, and the result was not successful. Portraits after death seldom are.

Christopher and Clotilde brought the coffin to Brookwood Crematorium, where Mary and I joined them and took part in the little religious service. And in due course Christopher received the ashes.[37]

The closing years of what was not a long life had been uneventful and happy. Worshipped by his friends, there was something quietly impressive about him that made itself felt even among strangers. In society he never took the floor, but people would stop talking in order to listen to what he was saying. If, for instance, the conversation turned on politics, if literature, philosophy, the taxes, the main sewer, or anything else came under discussion, whatever the contribution of the experts he always seemed to delve a yard deeper than they. People talked of his culture, his humour, his distinction, his courtesy, his appearance, but I think the magic lay chiefly in the fact that he was kind, kind, kind. He was able at a touch to ease even a stranger's burden. This was literally true; and one asks oneself what greater miracle a man can work for his fellow-creatures than to make the aches and pains of life seem bearable after all – to find instinctively the word Thackeray speaks of 'that brings angry, poisoned blood to its natural flow'.

Maurice Baring thus records his impression of him in *The Puppet Show of Memory*:

His external attitude was one of unruffled serenity and Olympian impartiality, but I often used to tell him that his mask of suavity concealed opinions and prejudices as absolute as those of Dr Johnson. He had the serene, rarefied, smiling melancholy of great wisdom, without a trace of bitterness. He took people as they were, and had no wish to change or reform them. He was catholic in his taste for people, and liked those with whom he could be comfortable.

Any assumption of moral or intellectual superiority could rouse him to fury, and the only people I ever saw him deliberately rude to – sometimes without the slightest provocation – were Roman Catholic priests, for instance a dear, inoffensive old Abbé at the hotel at Briançon! . . . But the subsequent game of chess was quite peaceful, the Abbé murmuring ceaselessly, as his hand hovered now over this piece now over that, *'Dunque facciamo così . . . Dunque facciamo così'* – a phrase H.B. used for evermore as a sort of incantation in moments of hesitation. More than once I had minor scenes with him about a trait so strange in one of his meticulous courtesy. He could not deny the charge, but pleaded as excuse his New England blood; in fact the Johnsonian absolutism of which Baring accused him resented absolutism in others. Had he been a professing Christian, no doubt the fold of his choice would have been Rome. But he looked on adherence to any specific creed as the sign of a feeble, or undeveloped, religious instinct, and the only religion I ever heard him extol was Mohammedanism, partly no doubt because of the houri element, to which men of a certain stamp never fail to do homage.

He was the best correspondent in the world – Henry James used to say almost the last of an extinct race. Although his letters are personal, they might, with very few excisions, be laid before and enjoyed by any cultivated stranger, explanatory notes being as unnecessary as in the correspondence of famous epistolarists of the eighteenth century. Written with the lightest of pens and saturated in what we are still obliged to call culture (however the word may have become cheapened, there is no other that conveys the idea) one feels certain that a faithful impression of the writer, his fun, wisdom, gentleness, violence, prejudices, large-mindedness and other qualities, would infallibly imprint itself on the retina of any sensitive reader.

Here I cannot do more than give a few extracts, merely to show the compass of his instrument:

OF COUNTESS BENCKENDORFF: When one talks with her it is always fresh molten bronze, and not old putty accustomed to take any shape or none.

OF WOMEN'S INSIDES: How women can live and go about and be animated with twins inside them is a mystery to me. They seem to be constituted like Gladstone bags; a pair or two of top boots more or less makes no difference.

OF A PROLIFIC AUTHOR: Baring has got another subject now – preparing another litter of rabbits to scamper on the Elysian fields.

ON UNREQUITED LOVE: The fact is it takes two to make a passion. One can't do it alone. It is a child; and one can let oneself cheerfully be devoured by one's own children – not by hobgoblins hatched in solitude. 'Strangle the goblin and move on,' is the only advice for such cases.

OF WIDOW'S WEEDS: My cousin cultivates her widow's weeds as if they were black tulips; unheard-of flowers seen for the first time in Europe.

The relations between H.B. and his servants were patriarchal, as was then traditional in Italy, and highly confidential. Once when I was commenting to the manservant, Palmizio, on the interminable time it took his master (who, by the by, was extremely particular about his personal appearance) to get together a hat, a stick and a greatcoat, I was informed with pride that the *signore* could not perform his morning toilette under two hours. 'Let the lady imagine to herself,' he added, with a smile of one who related an amusing trait in a quaint child: 'He sits in his tub and soaps and scrubs every one of his ten toes separately, and even dries them separately!' His staff were liberally paid and full of respectful devotion, but puzzled by his refusal to go into details of house management. The cook once informed Christopher with tears that his father refused even to indicate what were his favourite dishes, declaring that it was the cook's business to find that out. 'The proof of the pudding is in the eating,' said H.B.

Sir George Henschel tells a uniquely characteristic story of him as *padrone*, a story I had forgotten. After a prolonged stay at Palazzo Antici Mattei, Christopher came regretfully to the conclusion that the trusty and well-beloved Palmizio, knowing full well that the house books were never checked, had for years been cheating his master on a scale larger than is permissible even in Italian households. Whereupon the culprit was summoned and thus addressed by H.B.: 'I find that you, whom I believe to be an honest fellow at bottom, have been systematically robbing me, so I can only conclude that I have been under-paying you. From this day your wages will be doubled.'

The thoroughly Italian scene that followed, Palmizio down on his knees, seizing, kissing, bathing with tears the hand of this terribly incomprehensible *padrone*, is said to have rather amused his master for once and a way. But he will have withdrawn into his Olympian fastness pretty quickly, for scenes and H.B. was an unnatural blend. The daughter of my great friend Lady Ponsonby relates that one day when the two of them were in the midst of a violent altercation in the garden, her mother's demeanour suddenly became so chastened that Maggie thought she must be feeling ill; but it was only that 'Mr Brewster's serene hat' had been caught sight of advancing behind the hedge.

Philosopher though he was, the prospect of old age filled him with unmitigated horror. And when, as member of a long-lived family, I would urge that one might take getting old as a kind of sport, and contrive to knock fun out of it somehow, as you do out of playing a losing game, he would reply that he was not a sportsman; further that he shared the opinion of one of my sisters who, on being asked to guess how many trees the octogenarian Mr Gladstone felled per week, remarked that nothing in life is more tiresome than an inverted infant prodigy.

Early in the century, riding with a friend, his horse slipped up sideways on the greasy Roman pavement and rolled on him. He was a heavy man and I always think that accident was indirectly responsible for the illness of which he died a few years later at the age of fifty-seven. It seemed hard that one whose life meant so much to his children and his friends should slip thus prematurely out of their reach, but I often think what a relief it would have been to him could he have known for certain that he would escape old age.[38].

One of our favourite spots near Rome – one to which we often biked – was the Protestant cemetery in the Campagna, which Shelley thus describes in a letter to Thomas Love Peacock:

. . . The English burying-place is a green slope, near the walls, under the pyramidal tomb of Cestius, and is, I think, the most beautiful and solemn cemetery I ever beheld. To see the sun shining on its bright grass – fresh, when we first visited it, with the autumnal dews – and hear the whispering of the wind among the leaves of the trees which have overgrown the tomb of Cestius, and the soil which is stirring in the sun-warm earth, and to mark the tombs – mostly of women and young people who were buried there – one might, if one were to die, desire the sleep they seem to sleep.

Here Keats and Shelley were buried, and here Harry's ashes now lie. Since his death I have only once been in Rome, but having always shrunk from graveyards of which anyone I love is a tenant I did not go there. But in 1925, finding himself in Rome for the first time since he left the Embassy over twenty years before, Maurice sought and found Harry's grave, and spoke about him to the *custode*, who remembered him well. He was seldom forgotten even by those who had only known him slightly.

I love to think of his ashes lying there; also that if the casket has yielded a little, they may already have mingled with the 'stirring, sun-warm soil'.[39]

Thomas Beecham

To return to June 1908 when I had succeeded in pulling off an enterprise which I hoped might lead to bigger things, namely, a concert performance of two acts of my opera, *The Wreckers*, at Queen's Hall, it is unnecessary to say that what I had in view, but only as one envisages obviously unachievable bournes, was an eventual stage performance of the whole work in England. And in order to let present-day readers understand what an English opera composer was up against I will quote the following passage in a letter from the Covent Garden Syndicate, to whom I eventually submitted the score; not with much hope of a favourable issue, but knowing the matter would receive fair and sympathetic consideration under the then directorship:

Frankly there is no chance of our being able to produce it. To announce a new work by a new composer is to secure an absolutely empty house, and in future no opera will be produced here that has not established its success abroad. I feel sure you will understand that we are not justified in embarking on expeditions into a *terra incognita* at the expense of our shareholders.

The logic of this statement seemed to me then, as it does now, unanswerable.

Meanwhile the incredible was happening. Thomas Beecham, whose father in the year 1911 was to bring over the Russian Ballet to London, started a series of concerts the programmes of which consisted wholly of new or totally unknown works. Henry Wood, in spite of protests from whoever was backing his concerts financially, had often suc-ceeded in slipping novelties into his programmes, but young Mr Beecham believed in a frontal attack on Philistinism. In vain did his manager, Quinlan, wring his hands and implore for one single popular favourite – *'just one decoy duck'* – in each programme. Beecham was inexorable.

The results of the concerts, attended of course by a mere handful of enthusiasts, must have been depressing from a financial point of view, but to some of us they were a revelation. Never in England, indeed only in Vienna under Mahler, had I heard music rehearsed to such a pitch of perfection.

Transported with admiration, I and my friend Violet Woodhouse forthwith made the acquaintance of the intrepid spirit who, with pinions wide extended, had flown straight in the faces of our concert paladins, nearly causing them to jump out of their skins. Violet and I made great friends with Beecham, who of course was ravished by her harpsichord playing. And he, on his side, amazed us not only by the richness of his musical gift but by his knowledge of classical literature, especially poetry, and his phenomenal memory. And it goes without saying that, what with his wit and the grace of his mind, he was then, what he has always been, the most delightful of companions.

One point I should like to stress at the outset. Thomas Beecham is a figure that appeals peculiarly to the imagination, and a necessary element in a portrait that shall resemble him is a strong infusion of fantasy. In the course of this portrait that infusion may now and then spill over and colour the subject too strongly. But thus the present writer sees life – a grim, or at least a stern reality, illumined by ever-recurring flashes of comedy, extravagance and inconsequence; in fact all that the word *'fantastic'* implies. And nowhere are these elements more inextricably knit together than in the career of a man of genius who is trying to work out his destiny in spite of what St Paul calls 'principalities and powers'; by which he means, I take it, inimical spirits of all kinds, from within and without, whose business it would seem to be to hold up such a one from the cradle to the grave.

In Goethe's *Tasso* is embedded a glittering splinter of wisdom that one who has come across it never forgets. How, asks the poet, could one stand up against the inexorable cruelty of life, were it not for *'der holde Leichtsinn'* – which may be approximately translated *'adorable Levity'*. And note that Goethe speaks of this principle as gravely as a medieval saint might speak of Renunciation, Acceptance or Sacrifice. I wonder what would remain of Thomas Beecham today had not that blessed goddess kept an eye on him, waiting round the corner as she always waits for and succours those among whose christening gifts some good fairy has contributed an unfailing sense of humour.

In 1909 the generosity of my friend Mary Dodge enabled me to hire His Majesty's Theatre for six performances of *The Wreckers*. Of course it was impossible to aim at anything more ambitious than what one may call a *duodecimo* edition of 'grand' opera; the scenery could only be hinted at, and, notably in the last act, was more a matter of faith than of sight. But the cast, which included John Coates and Madame de Vere Sapio, was first rate, and so was the little chorus. The orchestra had been selected by Beecham himself: Albert Sammons was the leader of the band and Lionel Tertis led the violas, and with characteristic generosity Beecham conducted for nothing. His dream had always been to form an opera company, and inasmuch as he was in a certain sense a stranger, that is, not a product of any of our musical colleges and of a singularly different type to the ordinary run of conductors, he maintained it would be quite worth his while to present himself to a somewhat distrustful music world in a new light . . . which is just the way he puts things when doing someone a kindness.

But there was more to it than that – only mind, the following remarks are not framed to challenge the microscopic lens of a future biographer; I am merely handing on current legends as conveyed by irresponsible lips to probably over-credulous ears.

The position of our hero was rather a critical one. It was an open secret that he and his father were not on speaking terms, in fact, the situation was such as may be expected when, on the one hand, you have a rich and disgruntled parent and, on the other, a gifted, rebellious and altogether fantastic son; and one guessed that the son, gloriously far from taking up the role of shorn lamb, was equally incapable of discreet and submissive conduct such as might induce an irate father to temper the wind of his wrath. Rumours of bailiffs, of hairbreadth escapes, of desperate expedients, were for ever circling round the name of this brilliant portent in the musical firmament, to ascertain whose address was a problem not even his own business manager – if for a moment there was such a person – was always able to solve.

I remember once hearing he was laid up and dead lame, having hurriedly left a friend's house by a window that was twenty-five feet above ground level. When bodies are seen hurtling, Icarus-like from upper windows, it generally implies the unexpected appearance of someone else – perhaps a detective with a warrant . . . perhaps a husband or his temporary equivalent.

Now, as usually happens in cases such as we have described of a breach between father and son, various people were interested in devising some sort of bridge between the parties. One of the difficulties being, so it was said, the father's doubts as to the reality, or at least the steadfastness, of his son's musical projects and ambitions, it occurred to me that if the exact state of the case could be breathed tactfully into Royal Ears; if it could be hinted that here was a man of genius ready to do wonderful things for English music, yet held up by his father's lack of faith in his seriousness – a scepticism which, though formerly excusable, was no longer justified; if King Edward would consent to honour this all-English venture with his presence, and ask that Thomas Beecham be presented to him afterwards, why, then a very great step in the direction of reconciliation would have been taken.

Thanks to a friend of mine at Court, who, like his father before him, never raises a finger to claim credit for a service he has been able to render you, everything came off according to plan. We were even permitted, under seal of secrecy, to let the impeding honour be mentioned in the right quarter. Thus it came about that during one of the rehearsals, with a touch of something that almost, but not quite, amounted to excitement, Beecham whispered to me, 'Look . . . the left hand man of the two men hiding behind the pillars at the back of the stalls *is my father!'*

As the rehearsals wore on I discovered that in more respects than one my new friend was a disconcerting person to work with. For one thing he was never less than half an hour late, a habit which in that department of music life bears cruelly on all concerned. I also noticed that not only was it an effort to him to allow for the limitations of the human voice, to give the singers time to enunciate and drive home their words, but that *qua* musical instrument he really disliked the genus singer, which seemed an unfortunate trait in an opera conductor. In short, my impression was that his real passion was concert rather than opera conducting.

Today Beecham denies that this was ever the case, and maintains that he had been interested in opera since he was five! and his first step in active music life was to present himself at the office of an opera company with two operas of his own composition. But this seems to me quite compatible with an angle towards the human voice which, at the time I am speaking of, struck me as lacking sympathy. I dare say that at times all conductors are apt to wish singers at blazes; but to make allowance for their vagaries and sore throats and headaches, and accompany them accordingly, must surely come less naturally to unfortunates who only get a chance of conducting opera for a few weeks in the year – and that under scratch conditions – than to the great German conductors who have been up to their eyes in opera all their lives, and deal with it all the year round in decent and stable conditions. Anyhow, the only point that matters is, that today he accompanies the human voice as sympathetically, as lovingly, as he would accompany the leader of his band playing the solo in a symphonic poem.

Then there were other things that to my mind betrayed a disquieting lack of familiarity with the whole business of opera producing; and though I plead guilty to what the Germans discreetly call 'nervousness' – that is, unreasonableness, and the all round detestableness of that most trying of God's creatures, the composer of the opera then on the stocks – after all, I had had prolonged experience abroad of the operatic problem, and really knew practical things about rehearsal planning and so on, the neglect of which must infallibly lead to disaster. Or if not to disaster at least to terrible waste of time, and that means less polish than with proper organization the timetable would easily permit.

These views must of course, to put it mildly, have oozed through my skin and made themselves felt. And though from the first I had always liked Beecham, and do not believe he disliked me, it must be remembered that in those days I had not yet learned to pitch my voice on the suave mellifluous note that tempestuous people would do well to acquire as early as possible if they are dependent on the goodwill of others, and desire to tread the musical arena with comfort to themselves and all concerned! On the whole, I think it is immensely to Beecham's credit that, in spite of marked divergencies, both on this and similar occasions later on, he never ceased to be my friend. *That is at least when I could get hold of him!!*

Meanwhile I cannot admit that my doubts and fears were either imagination or hysteria. For instance, here is an incident that grievously shocked my serious, Germanically thorough, opera-composing soul.

The second act of *The Wreckers* – a prolonged duet between the lovers – was that day to have its one and only orchestral rehearsal, and as there was a terrible fog – a real London particular – one thought with dismay of probable conditions on the railway. True enough, after rehearsing the orchestra alone for about half an hour, neither of the principals having turned up yet, a telegram arrived for Beecham, and as he read it I caught a rather joyful gleam in his eye. 'Mr Coates is held up at Bedford by the fog,' he announced, 'and can't get any farther. Go on, gentlemen, please!' Not five minutes later came another telegram. *'Glorious,'* he remarked to me in an undertone; 'Madame de Vere Sapio says no trains are starting from Willesden and not a taxi is to be had!' And then aloud, very cheerfully, to the band, 'Alright! Go on, gentlemen!' Of course to bewail this fatality would not have mended matters, but one could not help perceiving his only feeling was gratitude to the elements that enabled him to conduct the orchestra in peace without those tiresome spoilsports the soloists!

When the great day arrived, the result, I believe, was very fair, and of course as the week went on the performances got better and better. Indeed, on the penultimate evening I remember thinking *The Wreckers* was quite a good opera; but then I had had a pint of champagne at dinner, therefore was all philosophy and optimism. Anyhow, those concerned seemed to think that, on the whole, everything had been 'werry capital', and nothing could have been more gracious than the King's reception of both Beecham and myself. I believe that the reconciliation between father and son took place shortly afterwards.[40]

Peace having been established between father and son, a sort of Beecham season was mounted at Covent Garden the following year. Ethel's opera was included, but according to her account Beecham's main energies went on the Village Romeo and Juliet *of Delius and Strauss's* Elektra, *leaving* The Wreckers *'to go to the wall'.*

A few years later an offer came from a quarter for which Ethel felt particular regard and affection – Lilian Baylis and Sadler's Wells. Thus it was that in 1939, Ethel having 'long ago given up all hope of what I may call a real performance taking place in my lifetime, such a one came to pass, though I was not only too deaf to hear, but by evil chance too ill just then even to see what Mr Sumner Austin [the producer], Mr Warwick Braithwaite [the conductor] and a splendid cast had brought about! But I knew that wonderful Miss Baylis had been justified in her faith!'

One way and another the later operas were all produced. Beecham gave the first performance of The Boatswain's Mate *at the Shaftesbury Theatre in London in 1916, and the Old Vic staged it again in 1922. Fête Galante was produced at the Birmingham Repertory Theatre in 1923, Covent Garden following a few days later in a coupling with a revival of* The Boatswain's Mate, *Percy Pitt and Eugene*

Goossens the respective conductors. *Of her last opera,* Entente Cordiale, *the first public performance took place at Bristol in 1926, the Royal College of Music having the previous year produced it in a double bill with* Fête Galante.

SEVEN

1910–25

WOMEN'S SUFFRAGE

Women's Suffrage

Emmeline Pankhurst (1858–1928), leader of the Suffragette movement and a founder in 1903 of the Women's Social and Political Union (WSPU), was married to Dr R. M. Pankhurst, a Manchester barrister of radical views, twenty years her senior. There were three daughters, Christabel, Sylvia and Adela, and a son, Frank. Frederick Lawrence and Emmeline Pethick (after marriage they combined their surnames) were committed supporters of the movement. He edited Votes for Women. *Other supporters mentioned are Annie Kenney, a former mill-worker from Oldham; Mrs Mabel Tuke, joint honorary secretary of the WSPU; and Lady Constance Lytton, daughter of the Viceroy Earl of Lytton and sister of another friend of Ethel's, Lady Betty (later Countess) Balfour.*

It was in the year 1910 that Mrs Pankhurst came into my life, changing, as contact with her was apt to do, its whole tenor. At first she was indignant, but later on amused, that the full significance of the Suffrage movement and more particularly of militancy should have been brought home to an English woman by an Austrian novelist, who, together with the presently to be enlightened one, was extended, wet but rapidly drying, on an Italian beach.

Hermann Bahr, Anna Mildenburg his wife – the most superb of Isoldes as all who saw her agree – and the present writer had forgathered in Venice, and seizing our letters had embarked for the Lido at what passes in Venice for cock-crow. The degree of honorary Doctor of Music had recently been conferred on me by the University of Durham, and one of my letters was from an old acquaintance, Lady Constance Lytton, member of the Women's Social and Political Union (the militant society founded by the Pankhursts), inquiring, as was their habit when any woman received a distinction, what my views were on the Suffrage in general and militancy in particular.

Presently Bahr, fresh from England, was listening with astonishment to a confession of indifference tinged with distaste and, Heaven forgive me, ridicule. 'Why!' he said, 'the militant movement is the one really alive issue in England . . . perhaps in Europe, and your Mrs

Pankhurst is in my opinion the most astounding personality that even England – a country that is for ever turning out new types of genius – has yet produced.' He told me that he had lately listened to political talk of every description, from debates in the Houses of Parliament to meetings in Trafalgar Square, and had never once heard a poor speech from these so-called wild women . . . 'the only people', he repeated, 'who are dealing with realities'.

I was deeply impressed, and at once cancelled a projected reply to Lady Constance Lytton which it still makes me hot to think of.

A fortnight later I went to a meeting at Lady Brassey's to hear Mrs Pankhurst and be introduced to her. A graceful woman rather under middle height; one would have said a delicate-looking woman, but the well-knit figure, the quick deft movements, the clear complexion, the soft bright eyes that on occasion could emit lambent flame, betokened excellent health. She knew I was an artist of sorts and connected with no Suffrage society, hence my reception was, if anything, chilly. But a very short time afterwards, at the fiery inception of what was to become the deepest and closest of friendships, she was told how, at that first confrontation, the words addressed by the disguised Duke of Kent to Lear instantly came into my head:

KENT: You have that in your countenance which I would fain call master.
LEAR: What's that?
KENT: Authority.

Before a fortnight had passed it became evident to me that to keep out of the movement, to withhold any modicum it was possible to contribute to that cause, was as unthinkable as to drive art and politics in double harness. At the moment I was deep in certain musical under-takings. These liquidated, I decided that two years should be given to the WSPU after which, reversing engines, I would go back to my job.

Of those years no record exists. I kept no diary, and between people who meet constantly and are engaged in that particular sort of activity there can be no correspondence worth the name. She was a woman who had by nature certain instincts characteristic of royal personages, and which, if they have them not, it is necessary for them to cultivate in self-defence. From intimate friendship she had hitherto held aloof, her boundless love and admiration for her eldest daughter satisfying all the needs of her heart. I imagine it is unnecessary to dwell on the devotion a magical personality like hers was able to kindle when she chose; but apart from that it was possible during these two years to gain insight into parts of her nature of which few, I think, except myself were aware.

She had no home and at that time was living at the Lincoln's Inn Hotel, close to the WSPU offices, and sometimes I would occupy the second bed in her room. She was not a religious woman in the ordinary sense of the word, nor addicted to metaphysical speculation. But there was in her a deep sense of what in my Carlyle-ridden youth people used to call the Immensities; the things that lie beyond life and death, effort and fruition, success and failure, love and the dying away of love.

I remember one night – Census night it was – when she and I, standing in our dressing-gowns at the window, watched the dawn rise beyond the river and fight its way through the mist. She was on the eve of some terrible venture that would end in rough usage and prolonged imprisonment, thinking perhaps of the inevitable hunger-strike, while I, for my part, was tasting the bitter anguish of one fated to look on powerless. Our foreheads pressed against the window pane staring silently into the dawn, gradually we realized that her love for down-trodden women . . . her hope of better things for them . . . my music . . . our friendship . . . that all this was part of the mystery that was holding our eyes. And suddenly it came to us that all was well; for a second we were standing on the spot in a madly spinning world where nothing stirs, where there is eternal stillness. It was a curious experience. Not a word passed between us, but we looked at each other, wondering why we had been so troubled . . . Neither of us ever forgot that dawn.

Sentimentalists have a fatal predilection for the chocolate-box style of portraiture, and cling to tags like 'The Lady of the Lamp' – supposed to sum up adequately that fiercest and most glorious of reformers, Florence Nightingale. By the same token a tendency to impassioned hero-worship seldom goes with a comprehensive sense of the humorous. Hence I fear some of Mrs Pankhurst's devoted companions of past days may be rather shocked at the relation of an incident that delighted me at the time and will always be a perpetual joy to think of.

In spite of occasional violence and bad relapses of many kinds, I always fancied the people who really understood us best were the police. Accustomed to cope with habitual drunkards and genuine criminals, these men of the law, whose wives were of the people, were quick to discern the difference between ordinary law-breakers and gentle, delicate, often elderly women who invited every kind of outrage (and some suffered unnameable things in the crush and hustle of a held-up raid) rather than acquiesce in injustice. But the young roughs of London only saw in militancy an excuse for hooliganism, and at the time I am thinking of the crowd had reached danger point.

There was a great meeting at the Albert Hall, one of those astounding money-making efforts so often put through by the WSPU, and on this occasion Mrs Pankhurst and Annie Kenney – most irresistible of blue-eyed beggars – were the chief protagonists. Sometimes as much as £6000 to £7000 – on one occasion, late in the fight, £10,000 – would be raised in a couple of hours, but as 'money talks', these painful facts found no mention in the Press!

Militancy was a costly business and much depended on these Albert Hall meetings; hence it is not surprising that as the day approached the faces of the leaders grew grave. On the way to the hall Mrs Pankhurst's silence seemed to me to betoken a touch of nervousness, and as the Union car, flaunting its purple, white and green colours, passed slowly down Piccadilly, booing and jeering men and women lined the pavement, only held back from more active demonstrations by the presence of the police.

Suddenly the car pulled up with a jerk; a woman was down, caught by our mudguard; there was hatred and menace in the air and loud execrations. In a twinkling Mrs Pankhurst was on the pavement, her arm round the blowzy victim of Suffragette brutality, while with the innate authority that never failed her she ordered a policeman to fetch an ambulance. And so manifest was her distress, so obviously sincere her bitter regret that because of the meeting she could not herself take the injured one to the hospital, that in less time than it takes to tell the story it was the crowd that was comforting Mrs Pankhurst, assuring her (which was the case) that no harm had been done, that the lady was quite all right. And all this time Mrs Pankhurst's face, soft with pity, radiant with love, was the face of an angel, and her arm still encircled the lady, who was now quite recovered and inclined to be voluble. Finally the crowd of late enemies urged her to get back into the car, 'else you'll be late for the meeting!' Half-crowns passed, and we drove off, cheers speeding us on our way. But as she settled down somewhat violently in her seat, Mrs Pankhurst might have been heard ejaculating in a furious undertone, 'Drunken old beast, I wish we'd run over her!'

As I think of my last Suffrage year picture after picture rises in my mind, one replacing the other like magic-lantern slides. Of the order of these events I can give no connected account, nor does it matter; let that be the business of the future biographer.

In those early days of my association with the WSPU occurred an event which, in her pride, the writer must recount ere the pace becomes such that a personal reference would be unthinkable; namely the formal introduction to the Suffragettes of *The March of the Women*, to which Cicely Hamilton fitted words after the tune had been written – not an easy undertaking. A Suffragette choir had been sternly drilled, and I remember Edith Craig plaintively commenting on the difficulty of hitting a certain E flat. But it was maintained that the interval is a peculiarly English one (which is true) and must be coped with. We had the organ, and I think a cornet to blast forth the tune (a system much to be recommended on such occasions), and it was wonderful processing up the centre aisle of the Albert Hall in Mus. Doc. robes at Mrs Pankhurst's side, and being presented with a beautiful baton, encircled by a golden collar with the date, 23 March 1911.

As time passed, events followed on each others' heels more and more quickly: arrests of the leaders; then, after their release, a week of comparative calm but really of intensive preparation; meetings at which, though the doors were watched by the police, the speaker they were after managed not only to get in and speak, but afterwards to effect a mysterious exit, leaving no clue to guide would-be pursuers. The infamous 'Cat and Mouse' Act had not yet issued from the brain of Mr McKenna, but hunger-striking was becoming rather the rule than the exception; and there was a growing feeling of uneasiness in the air which Ministers' perpetual assurances that they were 'getting the militants on the run at last' did little to allay. People had heard that tale too often. It was three years since gentle Marion Wallace-Dunlop, the first hunger-striker, had shown the way; two years since Lady Constance Lytton as 'Jane Wharton, Seamstress', and two others had been forcibly fed – the former never having recovered from the incidental heart shock – and 'the cry was still, "they come! they come!" '

The Conciliation Bill, a private, thin-end-of-the-wedge measure supported by all the Suffrage societies and by all our friends in both Houses of Parliament, had passed its second reading by large majorities in two successive Parliaments and had every likelihood of

becoming law in 1912.* Seeing which, Mr Lloyd George (who professed to be in favour of the vote, but wished, so the Pankhursts
averred, to reap all the glory himself) and our unreconcilable opponent
Mr Asquith decided that a red herring was urgently called for. Adult
Suffrage had always been, of course, a chief plank in the Labour platform, consequently the Government had proceeded in November 1911
to launch an Adult Suffrage Bill, for men only, with a 'possible' amend-
ment in favour of women should it pass. The idea was to detach the
Labour vote from the Conciliation Bill and ensure its defeat, and our
false Labour friends in the House of Commons, quite aware that this
Adult Suffrage Bill had not the ghost of a chance of becoming law, but
too afraid of their constituencies not to vote for it, now began pointing
out that some quite other Women's Bill, to be launched on some
unspecified date, a Bill giving women the vote on equal terms with
men, was surely worthier our noble aspirations than a limited 'aristocratic' measure like the Conciliation Bill?

Of course the trick was a complete success. The Adult Suffrage Bill
was thrown out, Mr Lloyd George was soon boasting openly of having
'torpedoed' the Conciliation Bill, and Mrs Fawcett, the least excitable,
most level-headed leader that ever steered a political party, wrote, 'If
it had been Mr Asquith's object to enrage every woman to the point
of frenzy, he could not have acted with greater perspicacity.'

It was, I think, in connection with this monstrous piece of trickery –
for Mr Asquith had ceased not to promise that in this Parliament the
women were going to have a square deal – that a great window-
breaking raid was planned. It was to be timed so as to lodge some 150
of us in Holloway simultaneously, which we knew would put the
Government to considerable expense and inconvenience; and one of
the most enchanting, certainly the most comic of my magic-lantern
slides, shows Mrs Pankhurst training herself to break a window. As
dusk came on we repaired to a selected part of Hook Heath – a far
from blasted heath; indeed, owing to the golf course, a somewhat
over-sophisticated heath that lies in front of my house. And near the
largest fir tree we could find I dumped down a collection of nice round
stones. One has heard of people failing to hit a haystack; what followed
was rather on those lines. I imagine Mrs Pankhurst had not played
ball games in her youth, and the first stone flew backwards out of her

---

* The Bill proposed votes for women householders and occupiers of business premises over a certain rateable value. Though not excluding married women as such, it
did not allow husband and wife to vote for the same property.

hand, narrowly missing my dog. Once more we began at a distance of about three yards, the face of the pupil assuming with each failure – and there were a good many – a more and more ferocious expression. And when at last a thud proclaimed success, a smile of such beatitude – the smile of a baby that has blown a watch open – stole across her countenance, that much to her mystification and rather to her annoyance, the instructor collapsed on a clump of heather helpless with laughter.

Alas! the lesson availed nothing! The Downing Street window selected by Mrs Pankhurst was duly bombarded – I think she had two shots at it before they arrested her – but the stones never got anywhere near the objective. I broke my window successfully and was bailed out of Vine Street at midnight by wonderful Mr Pethick-Lawrence, who was ever ready to take root in any police station, his money bag between his feet, at any hour of the day or night.*

The subsequent trial I thoroughly enjoyed and rather fell in love with our Judge, Sir Rufus Isaacs, in whose eye I detected a gleam of amused sympathy. At one moment he nearly got me into a hole and I was electrified by the way Mrs Pankhurst sprang up and with a lightning leading question showed me the way out. Thus might an experienced fish with a swish of its tail sweep a novice away from the mouth of the net. But Mrs Pankhurst declared it was far too simple a matter to make such a fuss about, and I dare say it was, to such as her.

The ensuing two months in Holloway, though one never got accustomed to an unpleasant sensation when the iron door was slammed and the key turned, were as nothing to me because Mrs Pankhurst was in with us. The merciful matron put us in adjoining cells, and at exercise, in chapel and on such other occasions as a kind-hearted matron can make for a prisoner, we saw more of each other than the protocol permitted. For instance she would often leave us together in Mrs Pankhurst's cell at tea-time 'just for a moment', lock us in, and forget to come back and conduct me to my own. But, as with policemen and detectives, Mrs Pankhurst refused to be softened by these favours, or by obviously sincere protestations of the 'it-hurts-me-more-than-it-hurts-you' order. And when, with an accent of cold scorn, she said, 'I would throw up any job rather than treat women as you say it is your *duty* to treat us,' the worst of it was that everyone knew this was

* Ethel's missile, variously described as a rock, a stone and a brick, smashed a window in the house of the Colonial Secretary, Lord Harcourt, on 4 March 1912. Of the prison sentence this led to ('two months') she served only three weeks (see Collis, *Impetuous Heart*, p. 115).

nothing but the truth. Newcomers like myself were charged to forget hereditary ideas as to *esprit de conduite* (there is no English term to express it) and make the most of our ailments; O! the ravages of prison fare on delicate digestions could hardly be exaggerated! We were also charged not to submit meekly to 'silly' rules, commanded to rage against the dubious complexion of bath water, and generally render the lives of the Governor and his visiting magistrates intolerable. The other tactics had been tried at first, but suited the authorities far too well to be continued, and newcomers like myself soon came to see the point of jettisoning traditional behaviour, whether we enjoyed doing so or not. I for one rather liked the Governor, I think because he reminded me of a favourite brother-in-law ('What! like that *brute!'* Mrs Pankhurst would cry in disgusted amazement), nevertheless I successfully concealed my love, and endeavoured to make his life a burden to him.

The athletic sports in the prison yard, inspired and organized by the younger prisoners to the delight of Mrs Pankhurst, were capital fun. How we got the materials – calico, purple, white and green tissue paper and so on, not to speak of hammer and nails – I cannot remember, but designs and mottoes breathing insult and defiance would embellish the courtyard walls for hours before they were discovered and torn down. Evidently some of the wardresses were afflicted with blindness – also on occasion with deafness.

I have often reflected that during those two months in Holloway for the first and last time of my life I was in good society. Think of it! more than a hundred women parked together, old and young, rich and poor, strong and delicate, one and all divorced from any thought of self, careless as to consequences, forgetful of everything save the idea for which they had faced imprisonment. Among them were elderly gentlewomen – Mrs Brackenbury was seventy-eight! – unfit for the rigours of prison life; young professional women who were deliberately snapping in two a promising professional career, made possible by God knows what heavy sacrifices; countless poor women of the working class, nurses, typists, shop-girls and the like, who had good reason to doubt whether their employers would ever take them back again. But of that they never spoke, perhaps never even thought, in Holloway. No wonder if some of us look back on that time with thankfulness and with awe, for where else on earth could we have scraped acquaintance with the Spirit that in those days had pitched her tent in Holloway Prison?

Meanwhile things had been going on from bad to worse. The so-called 'Cat and Mouse' Act, of which the murderous, cowardly, pseudo-humane refinement is to my mind more revolting than any torture invented in the Middle Ages, was now in full swing. The authorities dared not let the women die, so would release them, sometimes half-dead, to be rearrested as soon as they were judged fit to serve the remainder of their sentence. Whereupon the whole hideous business would begin again, the idea being that by degrees bodies and wills would be broken past mending. How a group of civilized Christian men could lend themselves to this proceeding rather than perform a simple act of justice already fifty years overdue is inconceivable – but so it was.

In April 1913 Mrs Pankhurst was once more arrested, and embarked on a hunger- *and* thirst-strike. Years afterwards she found among old papers, and gave me, two bescribbled little cards dated 9 April 1913, written on the ninth day of this ordeal which she believed she would not survive. The matron had mercifully put her in the charge of a wardress she was much attached to, and to her these farewell lines were secretly confided, to be posted to me in case of her death.

When hunger-striking she always refused with such terrible violence – mainly I think from personal fastidiousness and sense of dignity – to be forcibly fed, that no doctor dared attempt it, and in this little scrawl her handwriting is, if anything, more legible than usual, as if to show me her will was unbroken. She begs that in case of her death the old invalid mother of her dear wardress, Miss Harper, may be looked after. The next day she was let out and the wardress gave her back the letter; after which she forgot all about it, including her intention of destroying it; and not till nine years afterwards did I even know it had been written! The whole incident is typical of this strange woman, who lived less in the past and more wholeheartedly in the present and future than any one I have ever known.[41]

After Holloway and the end of the two years' political activity promised to the WSPU, Ethel went on her travels again, to Paris, Stuttgart and Vienna where she heard Bruno Walter conduct some of her music. Although inactive politically, she was in close touch with Mrs Pankhurst. With the intention of making an opera out of J. M. Synge's Riders to the Sea *she went to western Ireland and the Aran Islands. The Synge idea was dropped in favour of a comic opera based on W. W. Jacobs's story* The Boatswain's Mate.

But it was a complete change of scene that she needed. The diplomat Ronald Storrs, a keen music-lover, at the time on Lord Kitchener's staff in Cairo, recommended Helouan where there was a 'harum-scarum but sympathetic and not too ruinous hotel' – the converted Palace of the Khedive Tewfik – with a desert golf course near by.

My chief golf companion was a rather pompous old Scotsman who lived at Helouan and went into Cairo two or three times a week on business – something to do with a bank, I fancy. He also was Director General of something, I never knew what, and had a great idea of his own importance. In our little world he was referred to as 'the DG', and when I went up to him without having been introduced and suggested a match, he glared as though I were taking an indecent liberty; but the match came off and he beat me on the eighteenth green. We played very equally, and eventually struck up quite a friendship which lasted till nearly the end of my time out there, when it was wrecked on the rock Ulster and his discrimination between different brands of law-breakers. He was a shrewd old boy, with great culture and sense of humour, and I all but converted him to militancy, particularly after a friend of his in Cairo, a barrister, informed him that nothing but that would win us the vote; that Mrs Pankhurst was, as speaker, in a class by herself, and that a speech of hers, defending herself at the Old Bailey was one of the finest forensic efforts he had ever heard. After which he went on to extol her charm, her speaking voice, and so on ad lib.! Anyhow, the DG took to studying my weekly *Suffragette* (the militant organ), and was reported, so Ronald said, to talk of nothing but Women's Suffrage in Cairo. Given which, I forgave him for always calling my good strokes flukes, and worse, for producing an album of snapshots of his wonderful child, aged five, beginning with one at the font. I wondered what he would say if I produced an album of snapshots of my beloved sheepdog, Pan, whom I certainly loved as much as he loved his infant, and who was far handsomer.

Then there was a very pretty woman, a friend of my sister Mary Hunter, who lived in the smart hotel on the hill. Her husband was a great hotel boss in Egypt, and thanks to her kindly offices the Tewfik took me in on very easy terms. Her line was 'will-power' and 'self-development' and all sorts of psychic preoccupations, and when the Suffrage was mentioned she would murmur, 'O, I am coming to it . . . my spiritual strength is developing owing to the breathing exercises . . . wait . . . you'll see!' No doubt those two Suffrage years, and contact with an elemental being like Mrs Pankhurst, had increased an almost insane impatience of sentimentality and fluffiness of brain to which I had always been prone; and I was provoked, too, that this lady, who though emphatically a man's woman was really a very kindly soul, was apt to indulge in little digs at any woman one praised – only a habit I am certain, but to my mind an irritating habit. Her manner was very gentle, in fact unruffleable, and when I told her what I thought of 'all that psychic stuff', and then apologized, saying I feared she would think me very unsympathetic, she merely raised her pretty eyebrows and said most sweetly, 'O . . . *no!*' Whereupon I am afraid I almost bellowed, '*But I am!*', after which the conversation, which had been on the everlasting Suffrage theme, rather languished. Eventually it was settled that we both should refrain from dragging in our respective King Charles's heads, the Suffrage and psychic talk, after which things went better.

On New Year's Day, 1914, a marvellous prospect opened itself out before my eyes. I had by now made great friends with the George Hunters, and Mrs Wild, the friend who had been spending the winter with them, was one of my most cherished golf companions. Captain Hunter, a particularly delightful man, was Director General of the Egyptian Coastguard Service; among his duties was to attend the big yearly camel fairs down in the Sudan and pick camels for the Coastguard, and it was settled that I and Mrs Wild who, like myself, loved adventure, should accompany him and his impromptu aide-de-camp, Mr Gordon Morice of the Camel Corps, on the ensuing trip. We were to start on 16 January, travelling by train to Suez; then forty-eight hours in a small cruiser to a place called Mersa Halib, and then, mounted on camels, to proceed some miles into the interior where we would camp out for ten days and be back in Cairo by 1 February. No money on earth could have helped me to see the interior in this ideal fashion, for of course Hunter Pasha was a great swell, and the whole thing would not cost more than about seven or eight pounds – less than I should spend in the time on full pension at the Tewfik!

The date fitted in miraculously with my personal circumstances. First of all Mrs Pankhurst was safe in Paris, and would not be taking up her fight again till Parliament met – that is to say, well after my return to Helouan – so that I need not mind being completely cut off from civilization and beyond even the reach of a telegram for a couple of weeks. Secondly, my work had been going so well that I had hope of finishing the First Act of *The Bo'sun* before we started (a hope that was realized). Our luggage was to consist of two camel bags apiece, stuffed with sheets, blankets, a few medicines and masses of books.

Captain Hunter and Edythe Wild, both good shots, would take rifles, and I and Mr Gordon Morice golf clubs, for we did not see why we two should not knock up a nine-hole golf course somewhere.

The night before my departure the DG, who was said to be 'near' in money matters, belied this reputation by giving a grand dinner to me and his barrister friend. This lawyer, considered over-blunt in Cairo, was a charming fellow, and so hot on militancy, so convinced that nothing else would win us the vote, that, perhaps to get a rise out of me, the DG at last said, 'Well, I don't *like* their getting the vote that way.' Whereupon I, for once rising superior to an habitual and painful weakness, *esprit de l'escalier*, retorted, 'Do you think we *like* men being so obstinate, so lost to sense of justice, that there is no other way? We wish to God you were different; *but you see you aren't,* so we have to take you as you are!'

The barrister was delighted, laughed, and said, 'Bravo! One sees you have been trained in the Pankhurst school!' I am glad to say the DG took it with great good humour, and we parted in all peace and love.

Next day I joined my party at Cairo, and in deep but controlled excitement boarded the train for Suez.

Mersa Halib looked less like a 'capital' than any place I have yet struck. It was simply a tiny Arab fort about the size of my woodshed (eighteen feet by thirteen feet), inhabited by a Sudanese sergeant and another soldier, both splendid looking fellows; and near at hand were five or six Arab tents grouped round a well – the only one for hundreds of miles. The little bay, a natural harbour, is completely shut in by coral reefs, save for one tiny opening through which our cruiser could slip; but only in daylight, for the reefs are just below water level. No traffic ever comes near that lonely little station; how should it? why should it? Trade there is none, and except our cruiser once a year, none ever threads the passage into that bay. While the camels were being laden I sat in a boat marvelling at the fantastically brilliant colouring of the fishes; one could hardly believe they were real. We then rode inland for about six miles, heading for a magnificent chain of mountains. Here we made our camp – four roomy little tents for our four selves, one for the cook and the Egyptian orderly (an amazing fellow – valet, waiter and ladies' maid all in one), and a bigger tent for meals and lounging. We brought deck and other chairs from the cruiser, and behind a screen of canvas rigged up on oars was our kitchen.

Between us and the mountains was a huge amphitheatre of low hills; the flat white sand was dotted with thorn bushes, and as we were on the fringe of the rain district to the south, nature ran to a few blades of grass and even to tufts of little yellow flowers. In this region are bred the finest camels in Africa. To compare them with the animals you see elsewhere is like comparing ordinary draught horses with thoroughbreds exercising on Epsom Downs. Here, year after year, the Coastguard make good the wear and tear in camels for half what they would have to pay in Cairo, and the camel owners, who are scattered about all over the desert farther inland, were always told when to expect us. But to Arabs dates are as nought, and the first duty of Mr Gordon Morice, who was running the whole show, was to chase around and make sure that the hurrying-up process was well in hand. Edythe Wild and Captain Hunter at once sallied forth with their rifles to try for gazelles. I, equally at once, mounted my camel, a marvellously smooth-paced beast after those I had ridden hitherto, and accompanied by an orderly on another camel, who carried staves, flags and tin pots (not quite of regulation size perhaps), went off in search of a suitable place for a nine-hole golf course; which was found without difficulty, and, as laid out, covered about two and a half miles.

Of course, like most people, I fell passionately in love with this life, the only drawback being, at least during the daytime, the everlasting wind. But at sunset it suddenly fell and then began the real life, the life with the stars.

I had already discovered one reason why their dominion is so absolute in Egypt. Elsewhere, at sea for instance, on the horizon they are always dim; here the smallest star steps over the edge of the earth in full glory, as radiant a presence as it will be a few hours later halfway up the sky. Even at Helouan, a relatively sophisticated place, night after night one succumbed to the richness, the profusion of that jewellery, but how shall one who is not a poet speak of such things as seen in the desert? I believe the veriest atheist – and when I came to Egypt I had been in rather in atheistical mood – would find himself falling back on the old psalmist and his rhapsody about the heavens declaring the glory of God and the firmament showing His handiwork. There seems no other way out of it.

We all slept with our tent doors open and the stars seemed only just outside. A first sight of the Southern Cross is a thing I fancy no one ever forgets, even if less impressed than they had expected; but my own introduction to that beautifully named constellation could not have been planned more effectively by Reinhardt himself. I had been told it got up about 3.30, chanced to wake at that hour, and lying quietly on my bed glanced through the open door. On the horizon facing me was a range of mountains, and lo! framed in the opening, poised aslant on a slope of the range, there was the Cross – a vision that must surely for ever haunt one who has had the luck to see it for the first time in that particular presentment. Then and every succeeding night I threw on a light dressing-gown and walked out into the deadly still desert; sometimes, if you listened sharply, the sea could just be heard, and in gratitude for that wonderful duet, the silence and the soft distant roar, you blessed the wind that you had been cursing all day.

The camel owners had been told that seventy camels would be wanted, and presently they began coming in two or three at a time – no one in the slightest hurry – and congregated about half a mile off. Meanwhile Mr Morice and I were having thrilling golf matches, generally at cock-crow and both of us in pyjamas, gigantic Sudanese soldier-caddies handing us our clubs (and they were wonderfully quick at guessing which club one wanted) in the style of acolytes handing the sacred vessels to the priest at High Mass. The other two were out shooting most of the time, though how anyone could fire at those exquisite shy little gazelles I could not conceive. As I told Edythe Wild, I should as soon think of shooting my dog Pan. But these are the feelings of one who, not being a good shot, has no passion for slaying; and I confess they did not prevent my gloating over gazelle soup at dinner, nor thinking with rapture of the shoulder of gazelle we should have for luncheon next day – very pleasant variants on our usual tinned diet.

After about one hundred camels had arrived, the most wonderful exhibition of camel riding began, and among all the performers none was more daring and more graceful than one rider, learning whose history my interest rose to fever pitch.

Considered by her family to be a woman, she had been married to an elderly and wealthy sheik, but two years later the marriage was dissolved. The sheik and his relations maintained that he had been 'deceived', and that she wasn't a woman at all. She and her relations maintained that if nothing to speak of had been achieved matrimonially, the fault lay with the sheik. Anyhow, whether because she fancied this bad start would compromise her career as a woman, or because the greater freedom of male life attracted her, she decided to be a man, clad herself in turban and loincloth, armed herself with shield, sword and spear, and became 'Mohammed, camel owner and herdsman'.

Her appearance was delightful: a magnificent port, face strong, clean cut, and for a Bisharin not ugly; bright, intelligent eyes, a lovely smile, and the ghost of a curly beard. I should have judged her a very attractive man of about thirty, but the men told our men she was a hermaphrodite – somewhat on the mannish side, as she was apt to give young girls five shillings for letting her kiss them, though merely in an open-air, harmless way. Knowing nothing about the sexual pro-clivities of the Bisharin I wondered if this deduction – that as she liked kissing girls she must probably be a man – was sound, and determined to go into the matter myself. So George Hunter was begged to invite her to come to my tent one day for that purpose.

Under the circumstances it was not quite an easy conversation to carry on. First of all, putting modesty aside, I had to tell Mr Morice – our Arabic expert – what to say to the Arab who always acted as intermediary between the Camel Corps and the Bisharin, and who now explained matters to Mohammed and her uncle (I always think of the former as 'her'). Of course, a liberal fee was promised and an undertaking given that no one but myself should be in or near the tent. It was conveyed that I wanted to photograph her in a state of nature, and that unfortunately I was not a photographer. Hunter Pasha would therefore have to arrange the camera and explain to me what to do, after which he would go away as far from the tent as she desired.

No difficulties whatsoever were raised, but what intrigued me was her insisting that before the seance took place I must see her camel riding – which I did. Her contention being that *she really was a man*, perhaps she thought that once I had seen her galloping madly about, hanging by one toe to her camel and performing various similar feats, I should support this claim, no matter what conclusion one might otherwise have come to in the tent, it being obvious that no *woman* could do such deeds! If that was the idea, plainly the Bisharin had not yet heard of the Suffragettes nor guessed what some women think of their sex's capabilities!

By degrees we pieced together bits of her story. Her uncle began by relating with a touch of pride that her sister was wife of the Omdar (which means Governor – maybe of a village, maybe of a district). Mohammed, he said, was thirty; she had left her husband twelve years ago, at once taking to sheep and camel breeding of which she had made a great success, apart from being considered the finest camel rider in the country. She insisted that she was a man, habitually shaved, and was very popular with both sexes, but 'wouldn't let a man touch her'; nor, beyond the blameless five-shilling kisses, was there any talk of connections with women – so our inquirer understood.

It was arranged that the visit to my tent should come off last thing, when business was over and done with; but we occasionally met, and if on camel-back she would indulge in a little bit of innocent show-off, winding up with one of her lovely smiles, and I felt we had made friends. Often did I wonder whether her betwixt-and-betweenness had made life hard for her – anyhow till she had lived down the disgrace of having been sent home to her mamma without a character and had pulled up to her present position. And perhaps these reflections set up a little current of sympathy between us, for if I liked her, I felt she liked me.

At length the great day came, but for some reason I cannot recall the seance had to take place in a cabin on the cruiser just before our departure. We descended to the cabin, Mohammed and the uncle having satisfied themselves that there could be no peeping through the portholes. The light, alas! was far from ideal, but Captain Hunter worried out a possible place for the camera and instructed me as to what I should do, and how long the exposure was to be. Then the uncle explained everything to Mohammed, who fully grasped that this was to be a study in the nude, after which the gentlemen withdrew.

My sitter's first action was to inquire by aid of gestures that left nothing to the imagination whether I was . . . shall we say *married*. She then undressed, and a thorough inspection began. Being, alas, only a Doctor of Music, not of Medicine, I do not venture to put the result into words, but will only say that if not a complete man, still less was she a complete woman, which, one would think, the sheik must have found out not in two years but in two minutes. There is an institution in the Midlands where mentally deficient children training for domestic service are unable – so I was told – to memorize and describe the difference between a poker and a cushion, whereas bananas and pancakes – similar objects yet demanding 'merely *natural* perceptiveness' as the teacher put it – present no difficulty to these simple minds. Evidently the sheik's 'natural perceptiveness' was less than that of a mentally deficient infant; or else – which I expect was the case – he was an old rip and knew all about it beforehand, but thought it would be whatever is Bisharin for 'rather fun' to have a wife of a new type in his Harem. Then perhaps, the novelty wearing off, he got tired of her – who shall say?

The examination concluded, she took her place on the chalk mark and stood like a rock while I carefully followed instructions and took three or four photographs; after which she dressed and we said good-bye.

No sooner was she gone than Captain Hunter began developing the negatives, but without much hope, for the light had been really impossible; and though perhaps an expert photographer, operating in that cabin, might have done something to mend matters, all I could do of course was to follow instructions.

Alas! to the speechless disappointment of us all, when the films were developed, absolutely nothing was to be seen! Nor is that all. The film of my memory, even after registering matters as unique, as exciting as on that day, is apt to become blurred and dim in less than no time. Aware of which, I carefully wrote down every possible patho-logical detail I had gathered, quite prepared to send it on to the British Medical Society. But on my way home, while travelling across Europe, war broke out and that paper got lost, though there is still a good deal that I remember and could tell a doctor . . . or even record in these pages if only the censor were a disembodied spirit!

Still, I have one or two aftermath recollections it amuses me to think of. One was George Hunter's remark that, owing to my munificence (for thus they considered it), next time he visited those parts the western shore of the Red Sea would be strewn with hermaphrodites.

But best of all were three written comments on my proceedings that reached me later at Helouan. The first, an extraordinarily characteristic one, was from Mrs Pankhurst, who merely remarked, 'How very like you to have been so thorough and businesslike about the hermaphro-dite.' The second was from my beloved eldest sister who was very religious, and though a great sport, occasionally liable to whiffs of early Victorian sentimentality. 'O, my dear,' she wrote, 'how *could* you examine that *poor* hermaphrodite!' To this I replied, 'Why "poor"? You don't talk of *poor* Rossetti because he was not only a painter but also a poet? "Lucky" hermaphrodite would be more like it, *I* should say!' (a flourish that my sister took in the proper spirit, as I knew she would!).

But supremest was my youngest sister's comment, and to my delight she tells me she is still of the same opinion. To summarize her letter (and I am sure that no reader who is also a human being will resent the long-suffering word 'genius' being used in this connection) it runs thus: 'I suppose geniuses are always like that. In some ways capable of the most noble and beautiful feelings, they so very often do *perfectly beastly* things.'

This, to borrow a term from music, seems to me such a 'perfect close' to my trip, that I am thankful nothing interesting happened on the homeward journey, and that all one need say is that by 1 February I was back at the Tewfik.

Having gone star-mad in the desert, it may be imagined what happened when at tennis I met the young fellow who was in charge of the Helouan Observatory! A few nights afterwards, for the first time in my life, and in that gorgeously clear atmosphere too, I looked through a big telescope . . . saw the moon, Saturn, and the centre star of Orion's sword, which is really countless millions of starlets in a huge gas cloud. I was more stunned by these sights than by anything hitherto vouchsafed me in the way of earthly glories.

We have all seen unforgettable sunsets; others remember storms at sea – even I, a person of no marine experience, once came in for a terrific one on the way to America, fortunately latish in the voyage when the stage of seasickness was over. And all mountain climbers have seen peaks and glaciers suddenly turned into things no longer earthly by those rapid changes you get in the mountains. Here, again, in spite of my limited experience, the gods have been kind. Once I was weather-bound in the hut at the top of Monte Rosa, and around us was the heavy stillness of fog; then, quite unexpectedly, the mist parted and behold, a stone's throw distant, there stood the Matterhorn, bathed in sunlight. Half a minute later up rushed clouds that would have been coal black were they not alive with lightning, and hurled themselves against the Matterhorn, instantly annihilating it. Then our rift closed and we were left gaping. I little thought that an experience still more overpowering could ever befall me, but so it was.

Alas! unless you are an astronomer, and consequently a mathematician, the star-passion is bound to die of malnutrition in a climate like ours; but meanwhile I was in Egypt, and the sometimes oppressive heat I was beginning to grumble at was favourable to getting up at all hours of the night (the best things generally happened about 4 a.m.), lying flat on your back on the flat roof of the Tewfik, and gazing Heavenwards. My new friend lent me a star atlas, and now I not only knew what to look for in the Heavens, but was able to identify on it the wonders I had seen in the desert – constellations that are invisible north of Suez. I had made homely but very careful jottings of my own – and a very long time it took an amateur like me to do, though it only requires a good eye and a certain twist for map-making. And when I compared these efforts of mine with the real star map, and ascertained that they were trigonometrically correct, wave upon wave of conceited satisfaction coursed through my veins. So far Orion had impressed me more than anything else in the Heavens, but the great excitement was the prospect of at last seeing Scorpio, which looked magnificent on the star map, would be visible late in March, and of course is never visible at all – at least only a tiny bit of it low down on the horizon – in our latitudes.

My heart being set, if possible, on finishing the Overture of *The Boatswain's Mate*, and still more on seeing that unknown bit of the Milky Way in spite of the moon, I hung on too long at Helouan for pleasure. But both my ends were accomplished, and the new bit of the Milky Way, and a big terrifying blank area in it where there was nothing at all, were well worth a stiff neck I did not get rid of till ages after I had left Egypt. You now did well not to open a window till an hour after sunset, and on the roof at 2 a.m., clad in a single linen wrapper, some nights you were dripping, others obliged to creep noiselessly downstairs again and fetch a shawl. It seemed impossible in one's bedroom to know what it would be like up there. Hence the stiff neck, and I registered a vow that next time I came here, not all the stars in the firmament should persuade me to prolong my stay beyond 15 April.

When I said goodbye to the beloved Tewfik Hotel, so absolutely certain was I that the following winter would see me back again, that I even pointed out the room I hoped they would reserve for me; this after due consultation with my friend at the Observatory as to what would be 'on', so to speak, in the Heavens in November and December.

First I went to Vienna, and O, how smoky, how sordid, how noisy did this town, which I had always considered so beautiful, seem after the desert! My publisher, a deeply musical man, was most satisfactory about *The Bo'sun*, and Walter, I knew, intended to produce it at Munich during the coming season (1914–15), so the immediate preoccupation was to place *The Bo'sun* – now ready to be reeled off to any opera director who would listen to it.

There were details about printing, etc., to be seen to, and I stayed on a few days in Vienna, partly to meet Arthur Schnitzler, the dramatist, whose work I much admired; and we decided we could and would pull off something together. I then went out into the country to see Hugo von Hofmannsthal, Strauss's librettist, to whom I had got much attached when I had wintered in Vienna a few years ago, besides considering him a true poet. He was eloquent on my hard and healthy appearance, declaring I looked like a cavalry officer just home from a campaign against the Mahdi . . . Strange, strange, to reflect that in three weeks' time the Sarajevo assassins would be starting the most terrible war ever known, and here at Vienna, the hub of it all, not a soul I met had the faintest premonition of the coming tragedy! . . .

From Vienna I went to Munich, then to Frankfurt-am-Main armed with *The Bo'sun*, and by the middle of June the goal was touched towards which I had been stealthily moving for eight years. The work by which I stand or fall, *The Wreckers*, was to be dragged out of the pit again, and would, as produced by Bruno Walter after Christmas in the finest opera house in Europe, be safe – so I believed – for all time. And without hesitation the director at Frankfurt-am-Main had accepted and fixed the première of *The Bo'sun* for fourteen days after *The Wreckers'* production at Munich! My wild dream had come true; in the coming winter two of my operas would be running simultaneously at two of the first opera houses on the Continent! Both contracts in my pocket I left Frankfurt, not unnaturally in a state of delirium, and O! how the gods, seated up aloft and looking on, must have split their sides!

Arrived in Paris I learned from Christabel Pankhurst that terrible things of which I knew nothing had been happening, all letters having missed me. Her mother had been terribly hurt while trying to present a petition at Buckingham Palace – half crushed to death in the grip of a huge policeman who lifted her off the ground when he arrested her. She had lost a stone during the ensuing three days' hunger- and thirst-strike, and had been sent home more dead than alive. And I, owing to my own folly, could not go to her! The Government were now taking strong measures against all who encouraged or even defended the law-breaking of Suffragists, and . . . I had written a certain article, approving of the destruction of property, that appeared in *The Suffra-gette*! Asked for his opinion, my friend George Lewis wrote that it might be wiser for the writer of that article not to put in an appearance in England yet awhile!

Now I had not the faintest intention of risking imprisonment at this particular moment, *The Bo'sun* not being even scored yet, and the usual engraving horrors still ahead of me. But there was an alternative plan that had been warmly supported by Mrs Pankhurst, who wanted, when the hour of one of her miraculous escapes should strike, to be near the sea. At St Briac, not far from Dinard, there was a capital cliff golf course and a golfers' hotel; also a tram line to St Malo, where, when recovered, she could indulge her passion for shopping, so I wrote suggesting a meeting there.

I spent two or three days in Paris and had a game of golf at St Cloud with Winnie de Polignac. Then the Empress Eugénie, who was on her way to her villa at Cap Martin, turned up and told me that if, when I should think it safe to return to England, my cottage should still be let, I might camp out at her house, Farnborough Hill. The caretaker and his wife would manage a bed and meals for me somehow, she said.

On 28 June came the news of the murder of the Archduke Franz Ferdinand and his wife at Sarajevo, and people began to look grave. On 1 July I established myself at St Briac.[42] And at last came the happy day, when, supported by two of the militants, the ghost of what had been Mrs Pankhurst tottered on to the quay at St Malo. All precautions for concealing her departure had been taken as usual, but I dare say the enemy was only too thankful to wink at her leaving our shores, particularly as she was too broken just then – after a *tenth* hunger-strike – for anything but a prolonged course of bed. In an incredibly short time, however, she was bathing in the sea for the first time since twenty-five years, discovering that she could still swim, and giving me lessons in arts I have never been able to acquire – swimming with my mouth *above* water, and floating on my back. 'You're very good at *diving*,' she commented, 'but so very helpless when you come up again.'

Then followed what were the most terrible days of my life – and I am sure it was the same with Mrs Pankhurst – when, in spite of our reassuring reply to the everlasting question, '*Mais les Anglais ne vont pas nous lâcher, n'est-ce-pas?*' we were none too certain that England would come in; and I remember feeling that if she didn't, there would be only one thing for an English woman stranded in France to do – leap off those cliffs into the sea.

Eventually, though it was not so easy, we both got back to England. Mrs Pankhurst declared that it was now not a question of Votes for Women, but of having any country left to vote in. The Suffrage ship was put out of commission for the duration of the war, and the militants began to tackle the common task.

Hardly had we all settled down to whatever war work suited us best, than the ghost of the rift which seven years later was to silence the music between Mrs Pankhurst and myself, peeped over our shoulders, though so far only as a ghost. It was a question of differences of opinion on various subjects into which there is no need to enter here – many of them being of little importance in themselves, yet indicative of divergent temperaments.

In 1915 I joined one of my sisters on the Italian front, returning to Paris to pass my examination as radiographer, and eventually got attached to the XIIIth Division of the French army as voluntary 'localizer' in the huge hospital at Vichy.

Mrs Pankhurst meanwhile was addressing recruiting meetings in Trafalgar Square and all over the country, going later to Wales where there was much unrest and a constant threat of strikes among the miners. Her letters exude fury at the pacifist activities of some former militants in America, particularly of a certain childless couple who had declared England was 'decadent' and that they meant to live in America. 'Decadent indeed!' she remarks. 'Well, it comes badly from them to talk about decadence – married people who have failed in the real purpose of marriage!' (A very Pankhurstian gibe!)

Early in January 1918 the vote was at last given to women, and as Mrs Pankhurst remarked, we all took it very quietly, being under the shadow of the war. At that time I was still in France, and after the pushing back of the British line in March 1918, it was only with difficulty that I managed to get back to England. In April I saw Mrs Pankhurst fresh from Manchester, where the day before she had addressed four open-air meetings of munition workers and others. She was very tired but once more glorying in the loyalty of the women, who she told me were disgusted with the men. In some places, not daring because of public feeling to strike openly, these men, so the women informed her, were having what they called 'indoor strikes', i.e. working, but carefully doing exactly a quarter of what might be done in the day. She told me the whole 'skilled labour' cry was rubbish; there was nothing in it that any woman could not learn in three weeks; only the men wouldn't teach them, and were trying to get them out of the factories, because they, by their loyalty, had prevented strike upon strike. At Crossley's works, not having had a special wire from Winston Churchill to ask them to forgo their Easter holiday, they stopped work, and the women to their fury could not go on without them. Mrs Pankhurst addressed the women, and the men made a grievance of not being addressed too, so she curtly said she'd give them ten minutes when she had done with the women. They were seated at tea and she was helped on to a strong table to speak, whereupon they began banging (*and breaking*) their plates on the table! She stepped straight off again and marched out of the room, remarking, 'I'm not going to waste my breath and try my voice for people like you.' She said there was instant silence and everyone looked astonished and crestfallen and entreated her to stop, but she was adamant and departed. The decent elder men were cowed by the young Bolsheviks, and their wives and children insulted; a reign of terror in short. Yet all her scathing remarks are applauded *by the majority*! The old story; a disloyal minority runs the whole thing.

Now that the fierce flame of the Suffrage was no longer there to dissolve, or at least render them unimportant, one became increasingly conscious of temperamental differences. For instance, my Memoirs, *Impressions that Remained*, had just appeared, and the second volume tells the story of the broken friendship between the writer and her German foster-mother, Elisabeth von Herzogenberg. It was one of those events that give a new and tragic turn to a girl's life, and as such was treated in the book. When, therefore, as sole comment, Mrs Pankhurst remarked, 'Won't people say "*what a storm in a teacup*"?' one thought of the man who said *Hamlet* would be an interesting play if only that bore the Prince of Denmark could be cut out. And though I laughed, it was impossible not to realize that between reader and writer a gulf was fixed.

My story has now arrived at what, given the dramatis personae, was probably a foredoomed crisis. Suddenly, for the time being anyhow, the friendship between me and Mrs Pankhurst came to an abrupt end. The rock of offence was a letter I wrote round about an effort that was being made by certain of her old friends to raise a Testimonial Fund in recognition of her incomparable services to women. The letter was not offensive; it was a plain unvarnished statement of facts and opinions which I think were bound to gall her, even if put in a more diplomatic, roundabout way. But I wrote it because I considered it my duty, have nothing to retract or regret, and should do the same in a similar case.

The result was . . . my own letter returned, and on a covering half-sheet the following words:

March 10, 1921

MY DEAR ETHEL – I return your letter. You may wish to destroy it. I would if I were you.

EM.

I got one more letter from her, maintaining that the effort of her old friends in the matter of this Fund was taking a form that could but wound her pride, and so on. I considered this letter unreasonable, and as she was arguing from incorrect premises, it was no use pursuing the correspondence.

One day, towards the end of 1925, to my great surprise I got a letter from her announcing that she was in London, staying with her sister Mrs Goulden-Bach. I went there to see her and learned that Christabel and their old WSPU friend Mrs Tuke had embarked on what looked like, and eventually turned out to be, a wild scheme for starting a tea-shop at Antibes. Mrs Pankhurst had just come from there, said it was more bitterly cold than words could say (it was a very hard winter everywhere), and I had a distinct impression that the other two had wanted to get rid of her while they were settling in.

My only feeling on seeing her again was . . . that I didn't really want to resume relations, for between us lay a silence – the subject of the breach. It was then I learned what doubtless many people are aware of, that when a profound and warm relation comes to what may be called an unnatural end, it can attain a quite surprising degree of dead-ness. How Mrs Pankhurst felt about it I do not know; but it was not given to her to form new ties, and I think she would have liked us to be on affectionate terms. Alas, I had nothing to give! This she felt, and it made her shy and uncertain in her manner . . . which again made my manner grim. Result: little American laughs and increased shyness on her side; no little laughs whatever and increased grimness on mine. And when the visit was over I was glad, realizing with a sort of macabre amusement how much more comfortable I was talking to her sister than to her! Looking back into the past one often says to oneself, 'If that time could come again, I wonder if I should be less hard and uncompromising than I was then?' And Echo replies, as well as it may, 'I wonder!'[43]

In 1930, two years after Mrs Pankhurst's death, the statue of her near the Houses of Parliament was unveiled by Stanley Baldwin. During the ceremony Ethel had the 'supreme privilege' of conducting her March of the Women *and the* Chorale *from* The Wreckers. *'The instrumentalists engaged,' she noted, 'were the Metropolitan Police Band, who, it was said, had craved the privilege, and I quite believe it; for none honoured the militant leader more than "the Force".'*

*

Impressions that Remained *had been written during the war while Ethel was working as a radiographer in France. Isolation from normal surroundings, musical or otherwise, may explain the spontaneity with which she was able to recall and recreate events and feelings of half a long lifetime. The two volumes were published in 1919, the year of her meeting with the object of her next passionate friendship, the Anglo-Irish writer Edith Somerville, co-author with her cousin 'Martin Ross' of* Some Experiences of an Irish R. M. *Edith, whose humour, vitality and imaginativeness Ethel found irresistible, travelled with her to Sicily. Little writing came of this, but a walking-tour in Greece in 1922, at the age of sixty-five, with her great-niece Elizabeth Williamson, produced the characteristic* A Three-Legged Tour in Greece. *In the same year Ethel went to Paris for an unavailing consultation with an aurist about her increasing deafness, and then to Salzburg to hear her* Odelette *from the 'chamber songs' at a music festival. Here she was introduced to post-war developments in music; Webern she loathed but liked Hindemith.*

She also spent some weeks in Germany. In a letter to Lady Balfour quoted by Christopher St John she described the miserable condition of old Leipzig friends like Johanna Röntgen: 'O Betty, they live on soup . . . 3 times a day soup!' Wach, now aged seventy-eight, told her that Hildebrand's bust of Lisl von Herzogenberg was in the Museum. Ethel 'went there at once'. 'It is Lisl herself just as she was in the last year of our friendship . . . O! the hair – how can he have caught the texture and colour of that soft gold hair!' The wound was healed, the German wheel had come full circle.

EIGHT

RECOLLECTIONS OF THE EMPRESS EUGÉNIE

Recollections of the Empress Eugénie

The death in 1920 of the ex-Empress Eugénie of France removed 'one of the most precious, the most engrossingly interesting figures of my world'. Eugenia María de Montijo de Guzmán (1826–1920), a Spaniard with Scottish blood on the maternal side, married the Emperor Napoleon III in 1853. Their court was the most splendid in Europe. Paris, transformed by the Baron Haussmann into a modern city, became a capital of pleasure. Eugénie was virtuous as well as beautiful, an achievement in a lax society. Towards the end of her by then ailing husband's reign her political influence was unhappy. She is thought to have encouraged Napoleon to swallow the bait of the Spanish succession trailed by Bismarck who wanted to smash France without being seen to take the initiative. In private (she scorned public self-justification) Eugénie firmly refuted the view that she or the Emperor wanted the war.

On 15 July 1870 France declared war on Prussia. After some initial successes the ill-prepared French Army collapsed, and by the end of August Napoleon had capitulated at Sedan and was taken prisoner. On 4 September the Empress escaped, just in time, from the Tuileries Palace in Paris and fled to England. She found temporary refuge at Chislehurst where she was joined by the ex-Emperor, who died there in 1873. Their only child, the Prince Imperial, was killed in Zululand in 1879, fighting as a volunteer with the British Army.

In the following pages no attempt will be made to speak of the Empress as historical personage, unless incidentally, when recording things she said that struck one so much that they found their way into private letters, or into a diary which, alas! was only started in 1917. This is merely a record written by one who saw her constantly, travelled with her, stayed in her houses, lived practically next door to her for more than thirty years, and who eagerly sought her company because, quite apart from her story, she was one of the most interesting, original, remarkable and delightful people in the world.

When she came to live at Farnborough Hill after the Prince Imperial's death, my parents were among the neighbours occasionally invited to tea or dinner; and my mother's French upbringing, which included an easy command of the language, was a point in her favour in a house where no one but its mistress had any English. In those days the

Empress had more or less of a household: the old Duc de Bassano; Madame le Breton – once *Lectrice*, now *Dame d'Honneur*, sole companion of the flight to England in 1870; and Monsieur Pietri, the Empress's secretary, who was one of the few people connected with her in the old days of whose deep personal devotion there could be no doubt. The Empress went nowhere except on occasional visits to Queen Victoria, and at such times was attended by Madame Arcos who was a *persona grata* at Court.

I first came into personal contact with her at a meet of the harriers which took place, at her special request, at Farnborough Hill. She came out on to the gravel sweep in front of the house, and her manner was more gracious and winning than any manner I had ever seen as she bowed right and left to the awe-struck field, saying repeatedly, 'Put on your 'ats; I pray you, put on your 'ats.' The Master was then presented, and she really and truly did remark to him – as, if you come to think of it, she naturally would – 'I 'ope the 'ounds will find the 'are near the 'ouse' – all of which was my first intimation of a fact which surprised me in later years, her lack of gift for languages; for well I knew that her education had included a prolonged sojourn at a boarding-school at Clifton.

In due course I and my sisters were presented, and instantly were lifted into the Seventh Heaven by the warmth of our reception, for even then she had the delight in young people that became such a marked characteristic in after years. A little later my mother was bidden to tea, and thus began the relation that was one of the great joys and burning interests of my life up to the day of her death.

When my father died in 1894 my public career as musician was just beginning, and I want to lay stress on the fact that never had a beginner a more wonderful friend to look to. She had always been keen on women's work, and told me how furious it had made her during the Empire when they decided that, inasmuch as women were not eligible as members of the *Légion d'Honneur*, that distinction was to be conferred upon Rosa Bonheur's *brother*, who, it appears, was a very middling painter! I now learned, too, that it was at the Empress's instigation that women were first employed in the French P.O., and how fierce the opposition had been.

Such being her views, it will be believed that all it was possible to do was done by her to help me. But alas! too soon she came to the conclusion that in some ways I was a bad horse to back – too uncompromising and bent on having things properly done, too averse to diplomacy and the use of the soft sawder! *'Vous n'êtes donc jamais lasse de vous faire des ennemis!'* she would say.

This, according to her own account, was not a matter she herself had considered negligible. I remember her once relating how at Biarritz she had been at infinite pains to shower civilities upon an imposing gentleman whom she believed to be the editor of *The Times* – a journal that had been inimical to the Empire from the first – and how it gradually became manifest that the object of her amenities was not connected with *The Times* at all, but owner of a racing stable! I suppose Sovereigns are obliged to do this sort of thing, but I wondered how such a conspicuously sincere, upright nature could thus stoop to conquer. It was, however, one of the peculiarities of her complex character that, in spite of a sense of honour so delicate that at times one felt as if all other nations were crawling worms compared to the Spaniards, she could not conceive why any reasonable being should shrink from opportunism in cases such as one's 'career'.

In the same way she would advise me to be specially civil to so-and-so, because he or she was very rich; and I must admit that though she was pre-eminently the friend of the unfortunate, riches appealed to and impressed her. I remember saying in the case of a certain Dives, that, apart from his being a cad and antipathetic to me, I hated rich people. Whereupon she remarked with some violence, *'Dieu, que c'est bête!'*

In those early days I used in my innocence to urge her to write her Memoirs, and even maintain it was a duty. She said it never would be done by her – mainly because the idea of reliving her past filled her with horror. And there were other reasons. 'In such cases,' she remarked, 'one is surrounded by St Peters – people who in a moment of infidelity failed you, but later on in their remorse did their best to atone – sometimes at heavy cost to themselves. Who could show up such penitents? Yet if Memoirs are not to be useless it must be done' – which was unanswerable.

Many years later she spoke one day of the folly of supposing that she and the Emperor, who had little to gain by success and everything to lose by defeat, had pressed for war. As for the role of the firebrand attributed to herself, she said she had not even been present at the Councils of that period, the Emperor having informed her, on her return from opening the Suez Canal, that M. Ollivier desired her attendance should be dispensed with, 'which', she remarked characteristically, 'I found quite natural. Former Ministers had requested my presence, this one requested my absence. Why not?'

She added that so far were she and the Emperor from conviction that France would be victorious, and so convinced that in the opposite case they themselves would be driven from the Tuileries, that as soon as war was declared she made over the Crown Jewels to the Ministry on her own responsibility – *and got a receipt!* – 'for I knew,' she said, 'that if it came to a revolution, I should be accused of having stolen them.'

As the Emperor was very ill at the time, and in constant pain, he may not have always been able to conceal his forebodings. If so, and indeed in any case, it would be like her to do her best – her violent best, one may say – to profess enthusiastic confidence; hence perhaps the legend of her crying, *'C'est ma guerre à moi!'* and so forth.

She would have been less than human, however, if Bismarck's revelations concerning the Benedetti telegram* which were published about that date had left her indifferent, and next time I saw her she cried, almost triumphantly, *'Vous voyez comme on a raison de ne pas se défendre!'* Yet I think what gave her as much gratification as anything in connection with that affair was the joy of our own Royal Family at seeing her and the Emperor vindicated at last – thanks to the cynicism of Bismarck's confessions – from the charge of having brought about the war.

I think no one can ever have had greater natural violence of temperament than the Empress. Age may be supposed to have mitigated it, but as late as 1918 I have seen her possessed by a passion of wrath and pouring forth a torrent of magnificent invective such as few young women could emulate. We had been discussing the future of Serbia, and gradually worked round to the murder of King Alexander and Queen Draga. None have ever disputed the proposition that these unfortunate Sovereigns were puppets of Austria, and I had been contending that this fact should count, to a certain extent at least, in defence of a people struggling for independence. But the Empress hated and disbelieved in the Slavs. Moreover Austria was one of her sacred subjects, owing chiefly to the romantic attachment she cherished for the aged Emperor Francis Joseph.

This cult found expression in a visit she had paid him some years previously, and her fond belief was that one as sorely stricken in his

---

* Sent by the King of Prussia to Bismarck, the telegram described a conversation at Bad Ems with the French Ambassador, Benedetti, who pressed the king for assurance that the unwelcome candidature for the Spanish throne of Prince Leopold of Hohenzollern-Sigmaringen, already withdrawn, would not be renewed. The king declined to give this assurance and would not grant Benedetti further audience. By judiciously pruning the version given to the Press, Bismarck contrived to magnify the king's polite refusal into something more ominous. (Also known as the Ems telegram.)

domestic affections as she herself would inevitably share the emotion she felt at the thought of their meeting again. Pathetic illusion! Blatant instance of her lack of intuition as regards character! I do not suppose that in the whole world you could have found another Monarch who, on being informed of her desire to visit him, would merely have said, as did that cold-hearted old cynic, *'Was will denn eigentlich die alte Eugenie?'** This supremely characteristic remark went the round of Vienna, and greatly amused the Viennese who rather admired, but had no illusions concerning, their venerable Sovereign.

To return to the murder of the unfortunate Alexander and Draga, the Empress's contention was that the horrible circumstances of the crime, though carried out (as she must have known) by a Court cabal, proved the Serbians to be a race of barbarians, unworthy to take rank among civilized nations. Thereupon I could not refrain from pointing out that no nation, civilized or otherwise, had gone the lengths of the French in the unnameable charges brought by a more or less regularly constituted tribunal against Marie Antoinette. It was not a bad retort, for Marie Antoinette was a still greater idol of hers than the Emperor Francis Joseph, and for the moment she could not think of an adequate rejoinder.

Nobody likes being cornered, and one could not expect a woman of ninety-three, and an ex-Empress, to like it more than another. As a matter of fact, large-minded as she was, and far from demanding other deference than that due to her age, she was not accustomed to her *dicta* being opposed. Pietri was of course a privileged person, though she did not always endure his bluntness with equanimity; otherwise I think young Count Clary, son of her former Master of the Horse, and myself were the only two people who ever ventured to contradict her, for which reason she bracketed us together as *'mauvais caractère, tous les deux!'*

Long, long ago I remember a splendid onslaught of hers. Something I said infuriated her to such a pitch that she suddenly seized me by the shoulders, and, with an *'allez-vous-en pour vous calmer!'* ran me bodily out of the smoking-room, dragging one half of the double swing-door to with such violence that I found myself involuntarily plagiarizing the young lady of Norway.† I cannot remember ever

* What does old Eugénie want? (E.S.)

† There was a Young Lady of Norway,
  Who casually sat in a doorway;
  When the door squeezed her flat,
    she exclaimed 'What of that?'
  This courageous Young Lady of Norway.
  Edward Lear

hearing of a similar outbreak on her part, and fear I must have begun by showing temper, or at least unseemly zeal, myself. Anyhow, to continue the plagiarism, if the door squeezed me flat, well may I exclaim 'what of that!' for I never think of that scene – the Empress's swift concentrated fury and the Herculean strength it gave her – without laughing.

There was one particular manifestation of annoyance that could only be studied at meals. The Empress had told me that toothpicks, together with a certain over-thorough, not to say dreadful, use of finger-bowls, were forbidden by the Emperor at the Royal Table. But in my day the toothpick had come back again, and at certain critical moments you might watch it turn into a weapon of warfare in the Empress's hands. Brandished right and left, it gave point and emphasis to her argument; put to its proper purpose, the while she listened with simulated patience to your reply, nothing but the reflection that never was a human body made of more magnificent material than hers, relieved your anxiety as to the outcome of so furious an onslaught. Meanwhile her eye would be fixed on you sideways, darting such disgust and aversion that you were thankful it was only a toothpick and not a stiletto she held in her *crispé* fingers.

I must add that sooner or later after these little scenes she would be at special pains to soften down the impression – perhaps put her arm round the offender's shoulder as the party trooped down the corridor. On one such occasion, quite in early days, I remember her saying to me, *'vous n'êtes pas commode, ma chère'*! It was said chaffingly and in all friendliness, but she meant it!

Association with her was like a stroll on the upper slopes of Vesuvius; a chance stumble cracks the cool lava . . . and lo! the sole of your boot is smouldering! It was this eternal ardour, combined with a powerful brain and unlimited intellectual curiosity, that kept her so young, and guaranteed her against boredom. An advance in science, a new discovery in medicine (which I trust one is not expected to class among the sciences) was a fortune to her bookseller, for no scientific or technical book was too recondite for her. She was a great and wise doctor herself, and thanks to her medical instinct and knowledge, also no doubt to her magnificent constitution, was able to tackle with impunity certain Spanish dishes – high explosives, swooning in languorous oil – that daunted even her own compatriots. Her firm intention to go up in an aeroplane was crossed by the war, and her only consolation was to reflect that her growing blindness would have taken away half the pleasure. 'But if, when peace comes, I recover my sight,' she said, 'then . . . *nous allons voir!*'

I fancy hers was one of those natures that love danger for its own sake. Old as she was, and surrounded by people who felt it to be their duty to say 'don't', if there was any danger going she wanted to be in it. At one period of the war the Germans were said to be planning to bomb Aldershot, and one objective would certainly be the Royal Aeroplane Factory, just beyond her park. '*S'ils viennent,*' she said, her whole face lighting up with excitement, '*au moins nous serons au premier rang!*', and I could not help fancying that the presence in her house of a guest who made no secret of her own extreme dread of air raids rather enhanced her delight in the prospect.

To one whose physical courage was so flawless, whose sense of honour was so passionate, it must have been torture that among the cruel things said of her in 1870 was the attributing of her flight to fear. As Empress she had walked the cholera hospitals. Those who at the time said 'don't' – and there must have been plenty – were not listened to. But the French would seem to have forgotten the incident. I never heard her allude to that monstrous imputation of cowardice, but in the early days of the late war one was to learn how it had rankled.

When the French Government removed to Bordeaux, Paris became a desert. A former *Dame du Palais* of hers was among those who took refuge in England, and though, when I saw her in Paris two years later, she did not comment on her reception by the Empress, I can well imagine it! What she did tell me, however, was, that the Empress had instantly announced her own determination to start for Paris then and there. 'If I left after Sedan,' she said, 'it was in order to save bloodshed, but some said it was from fear! Now I will prove to them that that was not the reason!' My informant added that if, after unexampled efforts, she and the rest of the 'don't' party carried the day, it was by insisting that if the Empress were to go to France it might make difficulties for the French Government, which she would rather have died than do.

One of the strangest things about her was that, notwithstanding this unquenchable fire within, you felt instinctively that love can never have played a great part in her life. People have said that her skill, as Caesar's wife, in avoiding the breath of scandal, is a great proof of her 'cleverness', but I suspect it was still more a case of absence of temptation from within. She was not tender, for one thing, nor imaginative; and imagination plays a great part, I think, in women's love-

327

affairs. Above all, not to beat about the bush, there was no sensuality in her composition. Age has nothing to do with it. There are old women who are far from being that *bête noire* of the Empress, '*de vieilles folles*', in whom you none the less feel how great a part that element must have played in their youth. Without their realizing it, to the end of their days their whole outlook is thereby coloured. But in her case you felt convinced that it must have been the feeblest string of the lyre from the first.

She was anything but lacking in romance, however, and given a temperament so passionate in other respects, it would be strange indeed had there been no love episode. Even the least amorously gifted should be able to fall in love once in a lifetime, and that much she accomplished. Unfortunately this was not a subject it was possible to broach with her, and her contemporaries, among whom the story was no secret, are dead long ago. But it is well known in the inner circle, and I think there is no indiscretion in repeating it as it was told to me by a relation of hers – one deep in her confidence, a faithful, ardent admirer, to whom, in a rare and fortunate moment of expansion, she communicated the details.

One must begin by saying that the Empress idolized her sister – in my humble opinion this was the strongest emotion of her life – and after the Duc d'Albe married that sister their house became her home. A certain Duc de S. became deeply enamoured of the Duchess, and in order to gain easy access to the house made love to Mademoiselle de Montijo, who, suspecting nothing, fell desperately in love with him. The truth having dawned upon her she did exactly what one would expect her to do under the circumstances – took poison; and when the fact was discovered, nothing would persuade her to swallow an antidote. Finally, as a last resource, the man she loved was brought to her bedside to break her resolution, and as he bent over her he whispered, '*Where are my letters?*' Well can I imagine that his victim's love thereupon perished in the blaze of her contempt! 'You are like Achilles' spear,' she exclaimed, 'that healed the wounds it had made!' . . . and forthwith she swallowed the antidote.

Even if the story had not come to me from an indisputably reliable source, one would be certain that it must be true. She herself was probably proud of only having loved once; myself, I wish she could have had the experience of a second and happier passion. But to wish that is to wish the Empress had been someone else – which is inadmissible.

The anomalies of her mental equipment were nowhere more baffling than on the field of politics. I am not venturing to speak of her political action in France; nothing save the lapse of time can decide how far it went, and as I have hinted, there were documents in her possession which, to my certain knowledge, would reverse many a settled conviction.

Judging by her character, and in spite of a qualified sympathy with democratic ideals, I imagine she must always have been an absolutist at heart. I remember her saying that though the English monarchical system was undoubtedly the only one suited to England, to be a ruler bereft of real power would not appeal to her personally, nor did she think the position dignified *au fond*. At the same time she allowed that to fill it adequately required a rare combination of qualities – especially in wartime; 'and if you were to search history,' she added, 'you could not find a more ideal wartime monarch than *le Roi Georges*'.

As for the verdict of history on herself, a very sympathetic cover-notice in the *Revue des Deux Mondes* for August 1920 quotes a bitter remark I have heard her make more than once: '*Ma légende est faite: au début du règne, je fus la femme futile, ne s'occupant que de chiffons; et, vers la fin de l'Empire, je suis devenue la femme fatale, qu'on rend responsable de toutes les fautes et de tous les malheurs! Et la légende l'emporte toujours sur l'histoire!*'* One day, in the last summer she was to spend at Farnborough (1919), she said, '*Je déteste les gens qui ont peur de la responsabilité. On veut me rendre responsable pour les événements; bien! j'en accepte la responsabilité! . . . au moins j'ai l'air de l'avoir acceptée, puisque je me tais!*'† Then, after a pause, she added, '*C'est l'orgueil,*'‡ and I shall never forget her accent as she said it – the proud magnificent expression that was on her face . . .

Nevertheless, towards the end of her life, when the Great War, monstrous epilogue of the Bismarck revelations, opened all eyes to Germany's designs of world-dominion, I think she came to believe in the silent depths of her heart that that legend of '*la femme fatale*' might some day fade out of existence. I would often urge – only one had to put these things very carefully, so intolerant was she of anything that

---

* 'My legend has taken shape: at the beginning of the reign I was the frivolous woman only interested in clothes; towards the end of the Empire I became the *femme fatale*, responsible for everything that went wrong! And legends always get the upper hand of history!'

† 'I detest people who are afraid of responsibility. They want to make me responsible for what happened – very well, I accept . . . at least, I appear to accept, because I remain silent!'

‡ 'It is a matter of pride.'

329

might be construed into flattery – that the self-restraint exercised by her since the fall of the Empire must shed a reflex light on the past. And she herself was surely too sensible, too just, to believe that such testimony could be swept aside as worthless. So, at least, I hope.

I think the Empress cared for politics more than anything, and if you take passionate interest in a subject, it is hard not to believe yourself specially equipped for it. One day I had been asking her who were the most *fascinating* personalities she had met, and among them, greatly to my surprise, she mentioned Bismarck! 'When it was worth his while,' she added, with a peculiar look on her face, 'no one could be a more adroit courtier.' To extol her beauty would have left her indifferent, and suddenly it was borne in upon me that he must have laid himself out to flatter her on the score of her political flair! It was late in the sixties when last he was in Paris, and such flattery would have been well 'worth his while'!

Another vivid recollection of mine is the account given me in Paris by her friend and dentist M. Hugenschmitt, of the celebrated letter written to her after Sedan by the King of Prussia, which letter she passed on during the late war to the Archives of France. It was in reply to one from her, in which she had implored him, for the sake of future peace, not to make the mistake of annexing Alsace-Lorraine; and the point is that, far from looking on these provinces as ancient German territory, which was the claim put up in later years by the Germans, the King wrote that if they should decide to *annex French territory* it would not be from any desire to enlarge Germany, 'which', he adds, 'is large enough already', but in order to guarantee themselves against future attack by France. Knowing that Clemenceau was one of M. Hugenschmitt's patients, the Empress bade him show the Minister a copy of the letter. Whereupon M. Clemenceau begged that the original of so important a document might be deposited in the Archives.

Together with that letter were others from the Emperors of Russia and Austria which M. Hugenschmitt was also permitted to read; and in returning the packet to the Empress he asked if he might take copies of these as well. 'They are wonderful justification of Your Majesty,' he added. But the Empress snatched the parcel from him, saying, 'I will have nothing said or done in my own justification. I have long ceased to care about that.' And nothing that M. Hugenschmitt could say would move her from that position.

When I came home I spoke of all this to the Empress who confirmed it in every detail, adding, 'I told Hugenschmitt to impress upon M.

Clemenceau that I gave up the letter, not to the *Government*, but to *France*; that I wished it put in the Archives, and that if he chose to use it I could not prevent him!' Watching her proud face, the flash of her eyes that at such moments seemed undimmed, the incredible transformation of an old into a young woman that always happened when she was deeply moved, I could not help wondering if M. Clemenceau would catch the nuance of that message . . .

Afterwards the conversation veered in the direction of the Kaiser, who had paid her a surprise visit in her yacht years ago, somewhere in the North Sea. She remarked that he had obviously taken pains to make that visit an agreeable one, and succeeded. I reminded her of what she once told me she had said to him, almost as farewell word, 'For the sake of the principle of monarchy *don't upset any more thrones!*', and we spoke of the downfall of his own throne, utterly without what the Germans call *Schadenfreude* on her part – that is, pleasure in the misfortunes of others. Speaking of revolutions in general, not of 1870 in particular, she said, 'It is not that your enemies dethrone you, *c'est que le vide se fait autour de vous*'; and I thought of what Napoleon had written about the battle of Waterloo – *'tout d'un coup je me trouvais seul sur le champs de bataille . . .'* That same day she had been reading the account of the cheering of our King at Buckingham Palace: 'It is the most intoxicating sound mortal ears can hear,' she said, and then her face changed suddenly, 'and no one who has not heard it can realize the horror of its *pendant*, the roar of a crowd that has only one desire – to tear you to pieces.'

Sometimes, but not often, the Empress would talk about the Prince Imperial, and no one who ever heard it can forget the piteous fall of the phrase by which she always referred to him, *'mon petit garçon'*. The last time I remember her speaking of him was when I came back from Paris in 1919 and told her that at that moment every one in France was saying the country was ripe for a Dictator. Rather to my surprise, I noticed she had been meditating this point with reference to her dead son. 'If he had lived,' she said, pausing between the phrases, '. . . he had every quality they needed . . . now might have been his chance . . . but I often say to myself I would rather he is dead than think of him as Emperor . . .'

Then she began speaking of her past experiences, telling me among other things that when, after the fall of the Empire, Gambetta came to the front, he informed the Government that he had known nothing whatever about Metz being in danger, whereas the Empress herself had gone into every detail of the investment with him, day by day! But of course the blame was to be hers, and while dragging her in the mud he knew her well enough to count on her silence! It has always made me ache to reflect that many of those who betrayed her must have known her true fibre; but in the moment of danger the legend of the *femme fatale* lay conveniently to hand, and was used to destroy her. 'Not for one second have I ever regretted losing my throne,' she went on; 'to think of *his* perhaps going through it all – *de passer par là où j'ai du passer . . . ah!*' and her face contracted with an indescribable pain and horror it pierced one to witness. *'Je remercie Dieu que cela, au moins, lui a été épargné!'*

If the Empress loved England, England loved her with an intensity of sympathetic understanding which, I think, would astonish many old French friends of hers who had seen her in the possibly fierce, but above all artificial, light that beat about that particular throne, and met her but seldom in the later decades of her life. I used to notice that all who had known the Emperor spoke of him with that particular inflection of voice that conveys the idea of personal affection more unmistakably than many an asseveration; but no such inflection would accompany their reference to his consort, who seems, in those days, to have lacked the quality of inspiring personal devotion. I have heard her say that, in her position, anything in the nature of favouritism would have been inadmissible; and I have no doubt that the same exaggerated conception of the correct official attitude that was to trouble her relations with her son later on, hampered her unnecessarily during her reign.

Certainly the one exception she made was unfortunate. One can well understand that the brilliant Princess Pauline Metternich – *grande dame*, and exponent of that ancient Austrian Court which had so much prestige for the Empress – would be paramount in the favour of the newly promoted Sovereign; when the crash came, however, among those who dropped her without hesitation – who, even in later years, studiously avoided any marked show of attachment and sympathy – was her former great friend. But neither on this point nor on any other did the Empress show bitterness: *'Étant donné les circonstances c'était tout à fait naturel,'* she would say . . . And all the time one knew that she herself would have suffered torture and death rather than even *seem* to fail the fallen.

The human, adorable side of her seems but scantly appreciated out of England, and yet I must own that in early days, when she had a

Household, more or less, she was not at her happiest in her relations with her Ladies. Here there was nothing human. I do not think that she and Madame le Breton really liked each other – rather the reverse, though one's impressions were of course indirect. When the latter died, and in her will made absolutely no mention of her Sovereign Lady, the Empress was deeply wounded – and for years there was no mention of Madame le Breton. But I, who was devoted to both, said to myself that though to omit that name was a strong measure, the testatrix probably had her reasons. And certainly had I been the Empress it would not have surprised me, for if it came to violence of temperament one was a match for the other.

Of course the Empress was an ardent Suffragist. During the fight for the vote I saw little of her; I think she took two of her long voyages in successive years. Being ostentatiously law-abiding in her sentiments, she disapproved, theoretically, of militant methods. All the same, I cannot but suspect that certain chords in her nature must have responded sympathetically to militancy. People have said that women's services during the war would have won them the vote without violent methods: the answer to that is that one could not base one's tactics on an event which none of our most sapient statesmen foresaw. This the Empress allowed, but none the less continued to say, '*Moi, je suis contre la violence, vous savez.*' And meanwhile she expressed a strong desire to make the acquaintance of the Militant Leader!

Never have I seen the Empress more utterly bowled over, if I may use the expression, than by Mrs Pankhurst. The gentle manner, the quiet authority, the immense radical good sense that veils the violence of that fiery spirit, and, I must add, the daintiness and good taste of her clothes, captivated the Empress at first sight, and I was entreated to bring her to luncheon as often as possible. On labour questions she was the Empress's last Court of Appeal, and a dozen times she has said how fantastic it was that under our Constitution no use could be made of so statesmanlike a brain. I said that Ministers would doubtless shrink in horror from the idea of anti-compromise incarnate seated at the council board; whereupon she shrugged her shoulders and remarked that responsibility begets moderation only too rapidly; '*Eux-mêmes mettent assez d'eau dans leur vin, il me semble!*' she said.

I must add that her feelings of respect and admiration were fully reciprocated, and once or twice when she emitted some view that I knew her visitor disagreed with, I was surprised that Mrs Pankhurst held her hand from ever so gentle a slaughter. 'I couldn't dispute with her,' she explained afterwards. 'She is large-minded and generous enough in argument as it is.' And, indeed, I never saw the Empress more utterly adorable with anyone than she was with Mrs Pankhurst.

And all this time a shadow worse than death hung over her, for she was called upon to face the probability of total blindness. She had been one of the most assiduous readers I have known – not of novels, for which she had a contempt as unreasonable as it was adamantine, but of stiff books which most people would have thought twice about tackling. True, she was immensely fond of conversation and of company; but the relations and intimates she was accustomed to receive as guests, year after year, were now out of her reach. For one thing, Governments discouraged private travelling; for another, there was now no room for guests at Farnborough Hill. Even from such distraction as casual English visitors might have afforded her she found herself debarred, for who had time or petrol for visiting in those days? It may be imagined, therefore, what it meant to her to be deprived of books, and unfortunately she could not bear to be read to; yet no one ever heard her grumble.

Once, when a cold confined her upstairs, I found her and her old maid, Aline, who had been with her at the Tuileries, busy pasting ancient cuttings from newpapers into huge scrapbooks. The maid, far more shaky than the mistress but at least in possession of her eyesight, was on all fours on the floor; the Empress, seated in her chair, was pointing with a stick to the cuttings she wished pasted into a particular place – occasionally, under the influence of an attack of mistrust, insisting on having the whole monstrous book lifted on to the table and seizing the paste brush herself. But gently, firmly, with Tuileries courtesy, Aline would intervene: '*Non, Majesté . . . pas comme cela . . . c'est tout à fait de travers;*' and with the same gentle firmness the book would be removed, the brush extricated from the Empress's obstinately clutching fingers, and the former operator would resume operations. Whereupon the Empress would shrug her shoulders. '*Aline croit toujours qu'il n'y a qu'elle pour bien faire les choses!*' she would say, and resign herself to the inevitable. The relation between those two always touched and amused me deeply.

Only once do I remember the Empress seeming to pity herself. She had always detested needlework but now took to knitting comforters and cholera belts for her wounded officers. I cannot say these efforts progressed very quickly, and the aid of Aline and her other maid was invoked at the finishing-off parts and other crises. One day when I went into her sitting-room she was busily rolling into a ball a skein of wool that was stretched across two chair-backs: '*Vous voyez à quoi je suis réduite*,' she said. It stabbed one's heart to hear her. She knew that, and that is why she never complained.

Up to a few years ago time had left but little mark on her, and there was no diminution of her beauty – the touching majestic beauty of a once supremely beautiful woman who, if I may quote Lord Rosebery, had 'lived on the summits of splendour, sorrow and catastrophe with supreme dignity and courage'. The face was of the pallor of ivory, the figure full and gracious, and in spite of her rheumatism she was erect and active. But within the last five or six years she became smaller and thinner, also rather deaf, and with the oncoming of blindness she began to stoop; but one always felt it was because she chose to rather than because it was inevitable. And, strange to relate, in spite of her blindness, if some small catastrophe happened, a tiny crack in a huge plate-glass window, for instance, which it was hoped would escape her notice, the event proved the vainness of that hope. To the last, in moments of fire – and at least one such occurred whenever one saw her – forty years would fall from her like a garment. Forty? That is to understate the case. Let us rather say sixty! Personally, I never got accustomed to this transfiguration, and was amazed afresh whenever it happened.

The very last time I saw her, in November 1919, it was a bright sunny day and she had just come in from the garden. She had on a new hat, and looked so magnificent that I stood astonished on the threshold. Whereupon she cried out, '*Qu'avez-vous donc? Entrez – entrez!*' It would have been impossible to give the real reason of that pause, for to her the association of old age and beauty was ludicrous, but an allusion to the loveliness of the hat was well received. That vision was so striking that I recorded the impression in my diary, little thinking it was to be the last. And when in June 1920 news came of the success of an eye operation, I had been counting as never before on seeing her again in a week or two, younger and more radiant than ever in the triumph of her recovered sight!

There are two conditions, I think, which determine fitness to survive: your own interest in life must be unimpaired, and further, you must possess the certainty that your company is still eagerly desired by your friends. Such was more emphatically the Empress's case, surely, than that of other mortals who have reached so great an age. One felt convinced, too, that as she had been, so she would be to the end; that there would be no gradual failing – no sad period of death in life, which is the fate one most dreads for the old.

And so it turned out. Well in health, back in Spain again, after years of absence, and among her own people; her sight painlessly and, as it seemed, miraculously restored; congratulating herself on having faced an operation that if painless was formidable; glorying in the fact that it was a Spanish doctor who invented the method, behold her one day walking in her nephew's garden, discussing the details of her imminent return to England – and the next, after a few hours of pain and distress, sinking gently into death. As one who loved and was beloved by her has told me, 'her heart gradually ceased to beat, as it might be a little bird that dies in your hand'.

Such was her end; and who shall say it was not the happiest one could wish for her?[44]

NINE

WOMEN IN MUSIC
PAN THE FOURTH
A LIFE SUMMED UP

Women in Music

The themes of the inferior status of women in a male-dominated land and the need for a revitalizing of music, especially opera, in Britain, were intertwined in Ethel's mind and in her polemical writings. Much has changed for the better since her day (the first of the following extracts was written in 1920), but the voice remains trenchant.

I know few places more depressing nowadays than concert rooms, apart from their being too often half empty when the free list is suspended. Programme after programme is reeled off with scarce a semblance of fervour (even the critics, the least critical beings in the world, are beginning to notice it), and judging by appearances the audience are derelicts putting in time till something more interesting happens – a tea-party perhaps, or, if it is an evening concert, bed. Of course there are exceptions, but as a rule this is the situation.

It may be partly owing to war fatigue, and I fancy another factor is the disappearance of the Germans and German Jews who, whatever their faults, really do love music and disseminated an attitude towards it that counteracted our own fundamental indifference. But I also believe that the commercial principles we carry into everything, and which result in as many performances and as little rehearsing as possible, bring their own Nemesis. Spiritual aridity, the mead of all who industrialize sacred things, has overtaken languid performer and bored listener, and people who once cherished illusions on this subject are beginning to ask themselves whether we are a musical people – in the sense that we certainly are a sporting and an adventurous people. The exterior equipment, perhaps a heritage of the past, is there still – beautiful voices, exquisitely fine ears, and great natural technical facility; but the fire within burns low and capriciously.

The one element of hope lies, I think, in the gradual interpenetration of the life musical by women. I say this in no fanatical feminist spirit, but in all calmness, as the result of quiet and, I trust, sane observation of things in general, and of what is going on under my nose in particular. What is more, many thoughtful, knowledgeable men I know are saying the same; not openly, for moral courage is, I think, the rarest virtue in the world, but in corners!

Generally speaking I find women more capable of enthusiasm and devotion, readier to spend and be spent emotionally than men – as I noticed in my dealings with stage choruses long before the war. Their nerves, too, seem nearer the surface, more responsive to appeal, less deeply buried under that habitual resistance to the emotional appeal which is surely a post-Elizabethan trait. I cannot conceive of music being an Englishman's religion – that is, a thing pure of financial taint – but in the case of an Englishwoman I can conceive it. At this moment, too, women are the keener, the harder-working sex. All the world over men seem disinclined to put their backs into the job – war-weariness, it is called – and the responsible statesmen of Europe are unanimous in ascribing the slackness of trade in large measure to the slackness of the workers. But during the war woman *found out her powers*, glories in them now, and only asks to go on using them.

During the war it became impossible to carry on without admitting women into the orchestras, and few things more deeply impressed such as were capable of dispassionate judgement than the increased brilliance and warmth of tone. A new and refreshing spirit, too, was perceptible – in part the result, no doubt, of sex rivalry of the right sort. Well do I remember the transfiguration of a certain elderly violinist who seldom used more than half his bow, and who now was making it bite into the strings as it had not bitten for years in honour of the extremely capable maiden who was sharing his desk. But I think the main gain was the infusion of un-war-wearied feminine vitality, the 'go' of keen young talents for the first time allowed scope.

It was generous-minded Sir Henry Wood, I think, who first started mixed bathing in the sea of music, and so successful was the innovation that many other orchestras followed suit. True, the London Symphony Orchestra, much to its disadvantage, in my opinion, still remained an all-male body, except of course as regards the harp (an immemorial concession, I imagine, to aesthetic promptings . . . this solitary, daintily clad, white-armed sample of womanhood among the black coats, as it might be a flower on a coal dump). One hoped however that in time the LSO would come to see the error of its ways and that one more selfish monopoly was a thing of the past.

But now, a bolt from the blue: it appears that the Hallé orchestra at Manchester, true to its Hun origin I suppose, has suddenly sacked its women members. Not in order to make way for fighting men whose places they had been occupying – no woman that breathes but gives way gladly in such case – but merely because of their sex!

Asked to justify this proceeding, the Committee give two reasons that remind one of the wonderful excuses put forward for opposing female Suffrage – excuses so feeble, so transparently bogus, that one almost pities the gentlemen who, unequal to higher flights of invention, imagine that this sort of thing will do!

The first excuse is that when on tour it is not always easy to find suitable hotel accommodation for 'the ladies'. Very sad – yet dramatic companies have not yet reverted to the Elizabethan practice of entrusting women's roles to men on that account!

But the second excuse is the supreme effort – as fine an instance of solemn pretentious humbug, in other words cant, as I have ever come across. It is in the interests of 'Unity of Style', we are told, that the women have been shown the door!

Now will anyone bind a wet towel round his head (yes, *his* head, for only a man can expound the deeper workings of the male mind) and tell us what on earth this means? What, pray, is 'unity of style' in this sense? When Joachim and Lady Hallé played the Double Concerto in the very town whence issues this precious pronouncement, did the fathers and uncles of the members of that Committee hand in their resignation? Did Bach turn in his grave with horror (although it is his own fault for not mentioning the sex question in his score)? Do the soprani and alti interfere with the 'unity of style' in a chorus? Does the English Quartet, that is led by Miss Hayward, lack it?

No! You can talk of unity of style between static things, such as Italian violins, verses of a poem, houses in a street, bank clerks, priests, etc., but not in the case of a fluid force. Sex will not give it to forty men of different talent, temperament, habit, digestions and schools; that is the conductor's office. And two first-class artists of different sexes who respond subtly to his intention can more easily be welded by him into the 'unity' he wants than a first-rate and fourth-rate male.

But a truce to poking about in the unsavoury dust-heap of man's disingenuous reasons for doing an ugly action. Let us rather see what that action leads to.

Apart from the more spiritual element which I know women will bring, as performers, to the making of music, their admission on equal terms with men to our orchestras has another aspect. As I am never weary of pointing out, orchestral playing is the finest training a young composer can have, and the cheapest. The whole of musical literature passes across your desk; you are learning form and instrumentation automatically; and even though much of your time be spent in what must be the hateful work of giving lessons, you are on the crest of the wave of music, where strong breezes refresh your spirit and keep it buoyant.

Finally, to wind up with a consideration of a practical order, once you are member of a well-known orchestra, you are entitled to ask good fees for private lessons.

All this was hitherto denied to woman; no wonder the sacred flame that burned in her bosom throughout her student years too often flickered out. I have always maintained that until we are in the rough and tumble of musical life as men are, there cannot possibly be many women composers worth talking about. Competition, environment, and the sort of chance you get all round, are to talent what sunshine and the less poetical activities of the gardener are to a flower. In a word, the general level of human circumstance determines what stature one particularly gifted being can be expected to attain, and if you have to hurl yourself upwards from the sea-level you may become a Tenerife, but improbably a Mount Everest.

Bullying and cowardice, meanness and jealousy, are not pretty qualities, and I wonder if men have a notion with what contempt women view these attempts to prevent them from earning their livelihood in any sphere for which they can prove themselves fitted? Meanwhile, as finishing touch, a certain group of young intellectuals are busy shedding crocodile's tears in any newspaper that will act as blotting paper over the paucity of female stars of the first magnitude, *the equality of their chances with men notwithstanding*! . . .

I believe Englishmen to be congenitally incapable of judging a woman's work at all. They may try, but this sex-bogey is between them and it. If Selma Lagerlöf and Anna de Noailles, whom the whole civilized world acclaims as two of the greatest living writers, had been Englishwomen, every notice about them would have carefully described them as 'among our greatest *women* writers'! And such men as recognized their true dimensions would keep the awful knowledge to themselves. ('The old girl's a wonder,' said Mr Bagnet, 'but I never tell her so. *Discipline must be maintained*.')

An instance in our own literature occurs to me. *The Irish R.M.* having notoriously girdled the globe with laughter, no man, I am glad to say, attempts to patronize that work (unless by alluding to these pages, in which an absolutely new type of humour with an illimitable background to it has been evolved and perfected, as 'Sketches'). But how many English *men* realize the staggering dimensions of these authors' supreme masterpiece, *The Real Charlotte*?

Some few dimly feel it, perhaps, but concluding that since it is the work of two women it can't be so epoch-making as all that, they confine themselves to pointing out that it is not as 'pleasant reading' as the R.M.!

As I write these lines I see on page 768 of *The Times Literary Supplement* that there is 'a vein of feminine irresponsibility' in a book by a certain Major General, and two contemporary Press cuttings praise a certain musical composition as being 'of a strength we do not expect to find in a woman's work'.

My comment on this last remark is that Art is constructive action, that no one can build without strength, and that the qualities of men and women of this breed are probably identical. Anyhow all first-line artistic or literary work by women has exactly the characteristics of remarkable women all down history. And whether names such as Caterina Sforza, S. Teresa, Catherine of Russia, Florence Nightingale, Elizabeth Tudor, Queen Victoria, Joan of Arc, Edith Cavell, Elsie Inglis and Mrs Pankhurst suggest strength, or 'feminine irresponsibility', let man ask himself. For he is 'quite a fair beast if he gives himself time', as a small boy I know said of his house-master.

To sum up, there is a slight discrepancy between the theory and practice of men on the subject of such women as in any way compete with them for bread and butter, for honours or emoluments. Theoretically we are inferiors; practically we are, one would imagine, superiors, or at least formidable competitors, judging by the lengths men go to keep us out of the arena. For as Mrs Besant once said, to build barriers is to show you are afraid.

Now as long as the public life in your country, which includes its sanctioned outlook, is unsound, there can be no artistic renaissance; I will go further, and remind my readers that when Socrates was pondering the possible regeneration and survival of Greece, one point that deeply troubled him, as containing the germ of inevitable decadence, was the attitude in the Grecian state towards women.

During the Great War it looked as if the axe had been laid to the root of a certain Prussian tree that flourished in our midst – determination to permit women to do such work only as man did not wish to do himself.

But I see signs of another spirit, a spirit of which the incident of the

Hallé Orchestra is an illustration. Men are not only slacking themselves, but are combining to prevent women from earning their livelihood in this and that sphere, notwithstanding the fact that if
prosperity is to be restored to this country, every ounce of its working
power must be utilized.

I do not blame men too severely for clinging to what have hitherto
been considered male monopolies; alas! it is human nature, though an
ignoble part of it. But since, as regards the questions we have been
considering, it is a dangerous anachronism, there must be no meek
acquiescence on our part. Whether the Grecian women had it in their
power to arrest, by asserting themselves, the downward trend of civilization that so painfully preoccupied Socrates, I do not know. But I *do*
know that in resisting tyranny, jealousy and selfishness, in refusing
to take the dog-in-the-manger action of these Trade Unions lying
down, we are only doing our duty to ourselves and *to our country*.

In conclusion here is what Sir Henry Wood, who has had a more
varied experience than any conductor in England, recently said:

> I will never conduct an orchestra without women in the future, they do their
> work so well. They have great talent for the violin and wonderful delicacy of
> touch. They are sincere; they do not drink, and they smoke less than men. In
> the Queen's Hall *they have given a certain tone to our rehearsals and a different spirit
> to our performances*.

That is good enough! Thanking Heaven for this champion, who says
straight out what others, perhaps, feel, but have not the courage to
proclaim, I think we may leave it at that.[45]

*

*An unexpected trait in her character was Ethel's childlike pleasure in worldly rituals –
'I think we must all allow that being given a degree or a decoration is not only a
gratifying but an enchanting experience.' But she ruefully suspected that the reasons
for the honours she received were not solely musical.*

My first honour came to me through lawn tennis. In the nineties I used
to play tennis a good deal in the Quadrangle of Durham Castle with
the nephews of a shy bachelor Canon who liked to watch our games
from behind the curtain of his study window. When, in 1910, the
Durham University decided to confer degrees on women, this Canon,
who was musical, and had followed my career, such as it was, with

kindly interest, suggested my name – so I learned later; and I was invested in Dr Walford Davies's gown, a fact to reflect on which gives me quite particular pleasure!

The second honour I owe to golf. In 1922 there was a rumpus at the Woking Golf Club, which is really a man's club, women being what is called 'temporary members', though treated with greatest consideration. Certain ladies would persist in using a certain short cut from the General Rooms to their own quarters which we are requested *not* to use, because it leads past the Men's Dressing Rooms. Once or twice the secretary had remonstrated with our captain, but the delinquents persisted in their shocking conduct, and it came round to me through a golfing man-friend that there was some talk of our being forbidden to play at all during weekends. This was a terrible thought. Getting wind of an impending meeting of the Ladies' Committee, I, who had never done such a thing before, turned up and made a speech, in which the short cut business was specially dwelt on. For if, as I confessed to my colleagues, people who have lived much abroad are seldom squeamish about these matters, none could doubt, given the modesty of the British male, that herein lay our chief crime. The meeting broke up in laughter, but I got my resolution carried (three valiant 'noes' still clinging passionately, in theory at least, to the short cut), and the crisis was over.

Now many of our members are married women, and no doubt the tenor of my remarks was passed on to husbands. Anyhow when Lord Riddell, a distinguished London member with strong literary proclivities, came down to spend a weekend with his friend Mr Stuart Paton, known as the Mussolini of the Woking Golf Club, he expressed a gratifying wish to make the acquaintance of the author of *Impressions that Remained*. And a twinkle in the visitor's eye, when he referred to a recent tumultuous meeting in the Ladies' Room, showed that he was well posted in the inner history of the dispute.

Soon after this New Year came round. At that time Lord Riddell and our then Premier, Mr Lloyd George, were inseparables, and if the question of Honours turned up ('We've got to do something for the women!'), and if my name was eventually put before His Majesty as one suitable for the letters DBE after it, I am morally certain it was thanks to that scene at the Woking Golf Club.

As regards the final honour conferred upon me by the University of Oxford at the Encaenia, 23 June 1926, I believe the present Chancellor is more literary than musical. And since I learned that my inclusion in the list was his own, unprompted idea, I cannot help hoping, just to complete the tale, that if it is now my privilege to wear the handsomest of all the Oxford doctors' gowns, my books may have been a contributory cause. D.Mus., via tennis, golf and literature, is a splendid and quite normal instance of causation as it really is, though not perhaps as it should be![46]

Pan the Fourth

The 'incomparable Marco', having grown 'nerve-rasped and ferocious' in old age, had been put down in 1899 at the age of fifteen. To console his mistress, an acquaintance recommended to her an Old English Sheepdog puppy ('Once you've had one of these,' he said, 'no other dog will suit you'), which she named Pan. He became the head of a dynasty, the most beloved of them being Pan the Fourth.

Not long ago, when putting old letters together for a new volume of autobiography, I lit upon one from myself which was included in the collection because of a bit of special pleading which I thought rather ingenious.

Probably all young people who have felt deeply about religion, and at the same time were conscious that human affections played a somewhat overweening part in their lives, will have deeply scored, as I did, the many warnings in their *Imitation of Christ* against 'Inordinate Affection'. But in this letter I argue that a desperate longing for the presence of those to whom, because you love them, it is given to stimulate, raise the temperature of your soul, and set the wheels of your life spinning as no other agency can, is as healthy and legitimate as your desire that the best tennis-player on the lawn shall play in your set – if possible opposite you, thereby drawing out every ounce of skill and resource you have up your sleeve. And as I re-read that forty-year-old plea, which greatly amused me, the thought flashed through my mind, 'That's all very well about human beings . . . but what about the part a dog plays in some lives?'

Little as I knew it, while that book was in the Press, what I unhesitatingly call the most overwhelming grief of this, the last stage of my life, was raising its head above the horizon and creeping towards me. If I write about it, it is (I confess) partly in the hope of thereby drawing a few sharp thorns out of my own heart – a merciful service the pen sometimes performs for a writer – and partly because I want to join hands with those who are travelling the same road, and make them feel that they are not alone in their sorrow.

Pan IV was a grand puppy, huge of bone; and though his spirits were tearing and his need of affection practically insatiable, from the very first he was no trouble, seeming for instance to know by instinct that certain actions are not permissible indoors, or over flowers. And on all such private occasions he learned, after next to no instruction, to betake himself to the very farthest corner of that end of my little property which I am pleased to call 'the wood'.

His one wish was to please you – a wonderful trait in a being literally bursting with ideas and initiative; and when, as adult, he committed some small crime, such as resting his chin on the flower border while lying on the gravel path, I believe he did it just for the pleasure of being caught *in flagrante delicto* and then twisting himself into a comma and sidling about with an absurd expiatory grin that got him his laugh as certainly as any grimace invented by George Robey. When we spoke to him we never raised our voices but addressed him exactly like any other human being: 'Don't get so close to the fire, Pan' . . . 'Go and see if the butcher's coming' . . . 'A friend of yours is coming today . . . no . . . *not now*; you must wait,' and so on. And so literally did he understand every word that in his last illness we dared not discuss his state in his presence.

In a hundred ways he was oddly unlike other dogs. For instance most of them adore meat and bones, not to mention unpleasantly tasty morsels met with on the roadside; but Pan's innocent master-passion was white bread. Not really greedy and a most fastidious feeder, when my servant, Mary, was preparing something for my dinner that he liked – fish, a bird, or anything involving fried breadcrumbs – he would lie under the kitchen table so dead still that often she never knew he was there. But lynx eyes were watching her every move; the very tiniest bits of anything that fell on to the floor were noted, and the moment she moved into the scullery he would quickly slip out, pick up the treasures – one . . . two . . . three – and be under the table again before she came back. This not from slyness, but because he knew better than to get under a cook's feet when she's cooking.

Since it was these countless little ways of his that so utterly enthralled me – each one planned in passion and carried out as quietly

347

and methodically as the clock strikes when some cog has released the hammer – I cannot refrain from relating how, when booted, hat on head, and just going out, if at the last moment I paid a safety visit to a little apartment in the hall, there he would stand, his nose glued to the chink under the door, not moving a muscle even if, for fun, Mary called and tempted him with a bit of bread. But the second he heard the bolt sliding back, with one bound he was in the garden. Having I suppose a coarse mind, I confess that this particular indiscretion, born of frantic dread lest he should be left behind after all, deeply amused me.

But otherwise, in every sense he was the soul of delicacy. My friend and neighbour Lady Balfour has only one fault, a dislike of dogs; and once she unjustly suspected him of eating her chickens' food, which he perhaps overheard and must have mildly resented. Anyhow though she never was unkind to him, when he heard her coming he would rise from his place under my writing-table and at once enact the role of Dead Sheepdog in the farthest corner of the room. And this year, when another friend of mine who adored him stuck her head in with 'May I use your telephone?' and ran down the hall to do so, instantly his wild welcome was checked and a Slumber Scene staged at the other end of the passage till he heard her hang up the receiver, whereupon the wild welcome was resumed.

When sure of his ground there was no reticence, even with comparative strangers. The Henry Woods were very rare visitors, but Muriel Wood adores dogs, and I remember that in quite early days, after a little hesitation, he deliberately clambered up her armchair and sat down – that huge monster – on her lap, looking at me as much as to say, 'It's all right, I assure you.' And so it was, for this surprising demonstration greatly delighted and flattered Muriel – though perhaps 'flattened' would be a more appropriate word.

Two or three years ago when I confessed to Mary that I loved Pan IV more than all my dogs put together, the memory of Pan II (who I think remained her favourite) was, and still is, so vivid, that a twinge of conscience assailed me. But such is the truth. He was unusually big, and no doubt his extreme beauty had something to do with my adoration – the rich colour, quantity and fabric of his coat, the nobility of his head, and above all the big melting brown eyes that were in a certain light of an almost unearthly quality – so deep, so calm, so steady, so loving were they. As character he not only had all the traits I chiefly care for in humanity but had them more abundantly than

348

most humans. His intelligence, as I think I have indicated, was almost alarming, yet it never interfered with the restful, rather massive qualities we look for in animals. Full of fire, yet temperate as a saint; mad keen to do this, that, or the other – to go out with you for instance – yet if told it could not be, behold him instantly and cheerfully resigned; no sneaking after you, no profiting by a latch that had not caught. Maurice Baring says somewhere 'the second best is intolerable'. But unfortunately it is too often all that can be squeezed out of Providence, and Pan's ready acceptance of it is a lesson I try not to unlearn.

An image of bounding health, he was never ill that I remember for a single day, and to all the neighbourhood he gradually became a permanent part of the landscape; and no wonder – for though of course he had his favourites he was friendly to all. Mad keen on life in its every manifestation, yearly growing more beautiful, more adorable, and a more incredibly perfect companion, for seven and a half years we walked down the calendar together, step by step. And as this year (1936) on 9 May he would have been eight years old, which is no great age for a sheepdog, I used to reflect with satisfaction that in all probability he would outlive me, and in my Will left the following instruction: 'If you think it the kindest thing to do, please put Pan down.'

Today I sit here, my eyes on the shady bit of garden where on 7 May, two days before his eighth birthday, after I had fought for his life for two and a half months, he was put into his last sleep. How did it come to this? That we shall never know. One can only tell the story of the preceding months.

During the latter part of the past year I was working furiously to get that book I spoke of ready, and immediately after Christmas I ran up to Cromer for three days and there acquired a serious cold on my chest. But being one of those people who dislike throwing over engagements, not to speak of possibly forfeiting fees, on 27 December I went back to London to broadcast.

Retribution followed, and early in February, when fit to go out again, I noticed that Pan was not assimilating his food properly, whereupon Mary informed me that he was picking the meat out of the dish and leaving the rest. We changed his diet but the symptoms continued. On 22 February I took him to Camberley to see Mr Ambrose, the vet who eleven years ago had put down Pan II. He examined him carefully, found nothing wrong, prescribed for him, and remarked that so far his condition was good. Later on, as the symptoms persisted and his appetite became more and more unreliable, another remedy was tried but again without success.

As time went on his thinness got alarming. His nose was always cold and his spirits good, but . . . he wouldn't eat; so at last we had to make up our minds to feed him forcibly.

Now in spite of his temperateness, common sense, and an unfailing readiness to do any mortal thing you asked of him, like all high-couraged, hyper-intelligent animals he was desperately nervous, and I think I shall never lose the agonizing memory of seeing him tremble – still apologetically wagging his stump of a tail – when from afar he caught a glimpse of the feeding cup. One day I spoke to a strange vet, a kindly dog-loving man, of my distress at this sight, and his cheerful reply was, *'Let him tremble'*! But amateurs cannot improvise a spirit that doctors and nurses are obliged to cultivate if they are to get through their job; and more than once I said to myself, 'All this may or may not help Pan, but if it goes on long enough it will kill me!'

As a last resource, early in April I took him to the great veterinary surgeon Mr A. Cornish Bowden. He was puzzled, but did not think the case necessarily hopeless and carried him off to his clinic at Beckenham. Of course I paid no visit there lest it should upset Pan, and in answer to phoned inquiries was told they did not think he was pining. But I felt it must be so, though given his wisdom, gentleness and exquisite manners he would not be making a fuss. After ten days Mr Cornish Bowden said he was still unable to diagnose the disease; that nothing tempted his appetite, that he fought desperately against the forcible feeding, and was visibly weakening . . .

I could hold out no longer and started for Beckenham to discuss the next step.

To my dying day I shall be haunted by that first glimpse of him. He was sitting up rather expectantly on a low window-sill, beautifully clean, and I knew that he had been treated with all kindness and wisdom. But he seemed half dazed, and save for a feebly wagging tail appeared hardly to know me. A taxi was ordered and I took him straight back to Coign; if he had to die it should be in his own home. And though, in the kindness of his heart, Mr Cornish Bowden allowed that all things are possible, that perhaps, in the joy of finding himself once more with Mary and me, he might take a turn for the better, I knew full well that the great vet believed he was doomed.

By next morning he was more like himself, came into breakfast with me, and afterwards went straight up to a certain deal table in the hall called 'Pan's table' where he was always combed, and on which he loved to lie, thereby commanding the kitchen, sitting-room and front door, for the idea of missing anything was more than he could bear. He stood there a moment, decided that he couldn't make the jump, and quietly walking away lay down on the doormat – an act of acceptance that wrung my heart as the whining and struggling of another type of dog could never have wrung it. Mentally he was the same as usual, except that the tail that used hardly ever to stop wagging seldom wagged now; and when at luncheon he took a few slices of duck from my hand, and afterwards a mouthful or two of dressed fish, for a moment hope flickered . . . only to die down again, for he could not digest and refused to try again.

I then evolved a way of getting food down his throat that he didn't too much object to, one of us opening his mouth and the other poking down balls of Allenbury, Brand's Essence, medicine and brandy. But he came to dislike this proceeding more and more, so I took to subcutaneous injections of the same ingredients. Unfortunately hairs kept getting into the syringes, which caused them to burst; and when this too began to worry him, there remained only one thing, rectal feeding, which I think he rather liked; and now that I know what was wrong I see why. The only thing he partook of naturally was water with glucose in it; this he drank copiously, but only if it was given him in the spare-room jug, for which, as it was forbidden, he had always had a predilection.

All these days, until he got too feeble to react much, he was like the ghost of his former self, with all the same queer adorable little ways . . . but *con sordino*.

Yet there was one curious indication of a subtle change somewhere. I never let dogs lick my face, or even my hands – an incomprehensible whim he respected with great difficulty; for though never a bore with it, he was extraordinarily affectionate and I never could dissuade Mary from allowing that particular demonstration. Strange to relate, during the whole course of his illness he never once attempted it, though otherwise clinging tenaciously to every old habit that could still be pulled off. Almost to the end he struggled up to the bathroom when he heard me turn on the water, and once or twice, but only just at first, when I settled down in my armchair, following his usual custom he contrived to heave up one wasted hip and hind leg on to the seat and squeeze up beside me; or he would do the same thing in the opposite armchair – what I used to call 'sitting like a husband'. And to the last, if Mr Stevens the butcher, a great ally of his, or Audrey Taylor, whom he adored, came round to the mat outside the garden door to see him, he was so pleased that one could not realize he was dying. Again and again Mary and I felt almost certain he would pull through after all, and when Audrey saw him five days before the end she was of the same opinion.

Yet looking at his body from which the coat was gradually falling, once could not but face the truth. His great strong neck, once over twenty inches round, was now the size of a fox-terrier's, and so emaciated was he, that to pass your hand along him broke your heart. How he kept his spirit as he did I shall never understand; the day he died the vet marvelled: 'You wouldn't say he's *ill*,' he remarked, '. . . merely wasting away!'

Twice in those sixteen days I had settled within myself to ring down the curtain. One morning at 5.30 after an almost sleepless night I went downstairs to see how he was, for all the previous day he had seemed failing. Evidently he had heard me coming, for he was wide awake, lying on his stomach, his head up like a bird sitting on its nest. I knelt down in front of him. 'Why, Pan,' I said, 'you're better!' And as I stooped to kiss his forehead, to my pain and amazement he, who knew it was forbidden, licked the tip of my nose! I had meant to ring up the vet later on; now I felt I couldn't. As a matter of fact that day was one of his best, and it was not till two days later, on 6 May, when he could hardly struggle on to his feet and I felt that his weakness had begun to distress him; when, to his still greater distress (for a more meticulously clean, decent-minded dog never was born), he could no longer keep down the glucose and water, then at last the decision was taken.

That night, his last on earth, Mary let him out as usual at 9 p.m., and presently came into my sitting-room asking if he was with me; she had called and called him, she said, but with no result. It was a pitch-dark night; along one side of my garden runs a dry bounds ditch, and we both had the same dreadful thought that he might have fallen in and been unable to get out. Methodically searching my half acre with torches – she on one side, I on the other, calling and calling – at last my light flashed on his white head quietly turned my way. There was a heavy dew; he was lying in the long sopping grass, again reminding me of a bird on its nest. Whether he had settled down there, for he always loved wet grass, or had stumbled and couldn't get up again, who shall say? I helped him on to his legs, which to the last remained straight and strong, and he followed me into my room and dropped down on his mat. I think few experiences in my life have equalled the strange indescribable anguish of that search in the dark.

Next day he walked quietly after the vet and me to a spot in the garden he had always favoured. 'Lie down, Pan,' I said, and down he lay in the position he had always taken up of late, his head resting on the ground between his forepaws, probably because his neck was now too weak to support it. Being accustomed to injections he never even looked up when the morphia was administered, while I, stroking his head, was telling him the old, old news that he was a beautiful dog. Which was nothing but the truth, for terribly fallen in though it was, his head had never lost its noble outline, nor his face the matchless sweetness and dignity of its expression. Presently the pad of chloroform was laid against his nose; he made no sign and I went away. Later came the lethal injection, of which of course he knew nothing . . . and all was over.

The post-mortem and pathological analysis revealed that he had a disease of the mesenteric (intestinal) gland called lymphosarcoma. Akin to soft cancer it is incurable, but in his case it is safe to say there was no pain, only deadly lassitude. All the rest of his organs were amazingly sound and how he got this thing who shall say? His life was guarded, nothing left to chance, and one can only suppose he picked up a germ. There never was a dog more addicted to what Harry Brewster used to call 'reading the newspapers', that is, eagerly sniffing every blade of grass by the wayside; wherein of course lies danger. But who has the heart to deprive a dog of this unfailing source of pleasure and excitement? Anyhow I have not. His number was up, and there is no more to be said.[47]

A Life Summed Up

In the year 1933 fell my seventy-fifth birthday, which event drew forth a very charmingly worded letter, signed by most of our leading musicians, suggesting that a Festival be given in honour of a colleague who was, I believe, the eldest extant specimen of the British

Composer, and who, according to the Psalmist, should have been put down painlessly five years ago. (One of the signatories would, I fancy, have been quite ready to drop the 'painless' part, but that is a detail.)

Spontaneous tributes are usually worked up in the sweat of their brows by single individuals. In my case the moving spirit, to mention whose name would be the one thing he would never forgive, was the sole person who had spiritual weight, practical leverage, and friendship enough for me and my work to put such an enterprise through. And the underlying idea was that after this projected display of specimens of forty years' work – most of it practically unknown – an English composer, who so far had been relegated to operations in backwaters, might at long last find herself happily travelling the main line of traffic.

In order to meet expenses £400 had to be raised privately, and this four wonderful friends of mine undertook to do – and did. Thinking back to the year 1889 when I had first stepped into the musical arena, 'This Festival,' I said to myself, 'will be like the final flare-up at the end of a display of fireworks'; and indeed there is a striking analogy between a prolonged pyrotechnic display and the career of a composer, damp squibs and all.

I ask readers to imagine what it means to a composer if, at the eleventh hour, among other things her first and her last big choral works, the Mass and *The Prison*, are held up in the blazing sunlight by one of the most astounding personalities that this or any country has produced – my old friend Thomas Beecham. Not only had he offered to conduct the two big choral and orchestral concerts – a graceful, gracious and kindly act such as we are accustomed to from him – but he rendered the music as I had never hoped to hear it; and what is more, as if he himself loved it!

Now apart from his confession that nearly all music bores him, I had fancied from what I know of his preferences regarding modern work that he could not care much about *Smyth* music, however warm his friendship for the composer. If that be so, his inspired rendering of it is one more proof of the diabolical cleverness of that authentic but exceedingly bewildering genius, Thomas Beecham.

How I would like to extend myself over various details of that Festival, particularly the final concert at the Albert Hall, including my proud sojourn in the Royal Box. This was a surprise honour for which the recipient was so inadequately equipped, that at the close of Part I, returning, after the usual platform acknowledgements, to the upper ether, she realized that all this time a certain woolly under-garment must have been clearly visible through the gauze sleeves of an almost new best gown. Needless to say if Royal eyes marked what was amiss not a quiver of Royal eyelids betrayed the fact; and, without reference to that particular incident, while in that box I noted many little touches of human sympathy and intuition which explain why the Queen's popularity, though never directly sought, permeates all classes; trifles that increase one's sense of what the great ones of the earth can give other mortals, providing their souls are so tempered that the fierce ordeal of occupying a throne leaves them unscathed.

After the concert came the improvised 'Mad Tea Party' at an adjacent Lyons, where the guests paid for their own tea and buns, and whence one patroness of music, finding herself for the first time in her life in such a low place, fled *a prima vista* – in other words 'did a bunk'. O what fun it was, though we of the family, Nina, Nelly, Bob and I, were thinking of three sisters who during their lifetime had faithfully followed my musical fortunes year after year, and of whom two, Alice and Mary, had died only a few months ago. And I am certain many besides us were thinking of Mary, who had always undertaken my post-concert entertaining, and done it so splendidly. Of course if she had been alive Lyons would never have taken place, but it made us laugh to think how she would have loathed it and its suggestion of a new sort of harum-scarum school feast at which the unfortunate children pay for their own victuals. That wonderful collection of friends new and old – Joyce Wethered, Laura Lovat, Thomas Beecham, Hugh Allen, Violet Gordon Woodhouse, Virginia Woolf, Duncan Grant, Vanessa Bell, Maud Warrender, Diana Cooper, Vera Brittain, Winifred Holtby, Ethel Steel of the Royal School, Bath – greatest of head-mistresses (seated on an umbrella stand full of umbrellas) and many who are less well known but equally cherished by me – all these might doubtless have been got together elsewhere, but at the price of forgoing a memory the comic value of which Time will, I fancy, be powerless to efface.

It may have puzzled certain readers when I said my friend hoped by this Festival to get my output at long last into the mainstream. 'But *aren't* you in the mainstream now?' such a one might ask.

Ah! it's a queer business! Because I have conducted my own operas and love sheepdogs; because I generally dress in tweeds, and sometimes, at winter afternoon concerts, have even conducted in them; because I was a militant Suffragette and seized a chance of beating time to *The March of the Women* from the window of my cell in Holloway Prison with a toothbrush; because I have written books, spoken speeches, broadcast, and don't always make sure that my hat is on straight; for these and other equally pertinent reasons, in a certain sense I am well known. If I buy a pair of boots in London, and not having money enough produce an envelope with my name, the parcel is pressed into my hand: 'We want no reference in *your* case, madam!'

This is celebrity indeed! – or shall we say notoriety? – but it does not alter the fact that after having been on the job, so to speak, for over forty years, I have never yet succeeded in becoming even a tiny wheel in the English music machine; nor did this fantastic latter-day notoriety even pave the way – that much it really might have done! – to inclusion in programme schemes! Today, when, as a beautiful phrase of T. S. Eliot's puts it, 'age and forgetfulness have sweetened memory', it is possible, without one single grain of animus, to examine the cause of what Bret Harte calls 'this thusness'.

Discussing the situation which my powerful friend hoped the Festival might modify, one sympathetic and highly intelligent well-wisher, Constant Lambert, ascribed it to my having taken to opera and concentrated on Germany. Luckily for Mr Lambert he and most of the younger men who count in music today were not even in their cradles in the nineties. But not till I had knocked my knuckles raw on the closed doors of England's concert halls did my eyes swerve back again across the Channel. For I had always loved England as passionately as I do today when patriotism is at a discount. (And well it may be, seeing what is being done in its name!)

Now it may be said that hundreds of artists are called on to endure the like, but in my case was a disheartening element no man has to cope with – that only men of great imaginative power and intellectual integrity can picture to themselves – an instinct borne out later by our struggles for the Suffrage (which J. S. Mill believed to be won in 1860), that given my sex, my foreign musical education, and the conditions of English music life as I was coming to know them, if I were ever to win through at all it would not be till I had one leg in the grave. And there was I, crotchets and quavers racing round and round in my head like mice in a barn, seething with musical desire, and knowing that unless a composer tried out his work in public he is like a painter who should paint in the cellar. I believed I had something to say, but as far as my countrymen went was seemingly alone in that opinion.

Then I revisited haunts in Germany where years ago I had been considered a promising neophyte, bringing with me two ripe works – the Mass and the pianoforte score of a three-act opera. I will not elaborate the effect produced, beyond saying that if I had ever lacked self-confidence that little composers' tour would have made good the deficiency. None the less, of those foreign performances of the Mass, believed by me to be as certain as the arrival of Christmas, *not one materialized*; and in each case the reasons, as reported by faithful friends on the spot, were the same: (1) my sex; (2) the fact that apparently I was quite unknown in England. CHECKMATE!

The difficulty has been that from the very first, for some reason or other, what I call 'the Machine' was against me. If you ask me 'What *is* the Machine?' I can only answer, 'I don't know,' but apparently it is a complex construction, made up, say, of units from every section of our music life: heads of Musical Colleges, leading publishers, dominant members of music committees throughout the country, the Press, and so on. Of course this is the wildest guesswork, but though the motions of its spirit are so veiled and mysterious that to try and follow them makes you giddy, once you are up against it there is no doubting its existence.

Another materialization of the same idea – collective responsibility – functions today at the BBC, though an attempt to describe its nature is, again, rather like describing China when you have never been there and have to depend on the tales of other travellers. There, again, you have a mysterious complex composed of various units, a collection of chefs who are responsible for England's musical meals; some for the joints, some for the entrées, and some (far the most important people on the staff) for the kickshaws; in sort a *Società anonima* summed up under the generic term 'Music Director' (or in the provinces 'Conductor'). But in all these cases you will be doing somebody grave injustice if you mix up active agents and connecting links – the child with the umbilical cord.

It is possible that modern industrialized music – and particularly a huge concern like the BBC – cannot be run on any other system, disquieting though the reflection may be in a country like England which is more interested in money-making than in art. You think this is an exaggeration? Then listen to the considered opinion of Sir Landon Ronald, a very clever man who knows what he is talking about, and who recently in genial after-dinner mood spoke the following words: 'I feel that in this country nothing succeeds like *financial* success, and that artistic ideals and aims count for little *unless they happen to pay;*' the nation of shopkeepers, you see, following Shakespeare's advice and remaining true to itself, but unfortunately in the wrong place. For when machines, committees and groups decide these matters, do not hope to turn out mighty figures in music such as many we have known: Levi, Mahler, Nikisch, Richter, Muck, Mottl, Bruno Walter and the like – flaming torches of men raised in the land where the greatest of all musical traditions was built up by composers who penetrated deeper into the heart of music then those of any other nation. Whether on Parnassus or at Jerusalem you cannot serve Mammon and God.

In one thing I was fortunate. Opera being no part of our regular music life it was outside the sphere of the Machine's operation. Here Society had a say; Royal Ladies whose princely relatives had enabled me to produce my operas in Germany had a say; and a very remarkable woman, Miss Lilian Baylis, had a say. The *Wreckers* week in 1909 was financed by a noble-hearted American woman who was £600 out of pocket on the venture . . .

In all other respects the situation of one tabooed (or ignored) by the Machine is pretty hopeless. Publishers decline to print your full scores and orchestral parts, and you yourself have to pay for their execution in manuscript – a desperately expensive and most unsatisfactory affair. Again, conductors hate hiring half a hundredweight of manuscript for a single performance, and O! the revolting aspect those MS parts gradually assume . . . torn, bescribbled and in some cases assuming no aspect whatsoever, having been lost on various transits! And when, about a year before my Festival, I reproached the once faithful Henry Wood for not doing something or other, he remarked, 'Well, I'm the only one of them who ever plays your music at all!' – which was true, always excepting the independent-spirited Dan Godfrey.

But the story of an outsider's disabilities is so ugly and boring, even to think of, that I pass with relief to a more amusing theme – that of my own sins of omission and commission.

Life has taught me one thing: when people fail to get over (or round) obstacles, it is never wholly the fault of other people. True, what with the terrible tenacity of the English – a quality one thanks Heaven for, since it played a great part in winning the war – combined with our less admirable tendency to nurse our own prejudices; what with my sex and my foreign musical education, I do think the odds against winning through were overwhelming. Still I could doubtless have played my cards better, specially if, to quote Mrs Poyser, I could have been 'hatched again and hatched different'.

There is a passage in a letter Vernon Lee wrote me in July 1924, of which I felt the truth even then – and now I feel it still more strongly:

> I can't help wondering whether, as much as being a woman, what makes a comparative vacuum round some of your work is not, perhaps, that you sometimes scatter people's feeble wits – which of course come back to console themselves by pooh-poohing – with the tremendous *attack*, in the Italian musical sense, of your personality and your West-wind 'sausing and brausing' (*storming and stressing*).

This is fair comment, but, as I used to point out to people who complained of the 'sausing and brausing' of the Suffragettes, to swim gracefully downstream is easy; but if the current is against you, or even trying like Uncle Klingeborn in *Undine* to draw you under, it is not so easy!

To quote a very pertinent remark of Julius Röntgen's: that though professional life brushes the bloom off your spiritual independence, still *to live by music, you must live in music*. This I never did in England. I was country bred, couldn't sleep or work in London, and for my particular job needed quiet, the company of a big dog, and, I confess, the satisfaction of an insensate passion for games to which I have already pleaded guilty. Sitting in my garden, bicycling and walking across the heather with Marco and his successors, I peacefully worked as hard as slow workers have to work, and slept like a top.

But the chief reason why I did not live in, but outside music was that the atmosphere of music life in London was one I could not breathe with comfort. Quite apart from personal difficulties, and for subtler reasons than sex, I felt like a stranger; I, who even as half-baked neophyte had associated with people for whom music was a sacred thing – people like Frau Schumann, Levi, Nikisch, Brahms, the Herzogenbergs, the Röntgens, the Griegs, Tchaikovsky, Dvořák, Kirchner and the rest; I, who had won cognizance of the part played by music in the lives of average Germans, from mediatized Princes to hotel porters; who had learned the meaning of passionate, unqualified devotion to the ideal of which music is the soul and the vestment.

Of this spirit I perceived scant traces in England. But for a few foreigners domiciled here, like the von Glehns, August Manns, or Henschel, no one seemed aware that music is religion, mathematics, passion, tragedy, comedy, what you will; not a clumsy machine knocked up for semi-industrial uses, and disguised in the cast-off clothes of some down-and-out fifteenth cousin of the Muses. And feeling thus in every fibre of my body, I doubt not that in contact with other musicians it worked up to the surface, and did not conduce to their making a pet of the fierce white crow that had flown uninvited into their peaceful black midst.

Then there were many occasions on which the interloper deliberately queered her own pitch; for instance, by leaving the field of action in order to devote two years to the cause of Women's Suffrage at that critical moment of a musician's career when headway is being made at last. Need I say that I do not regret my action, and should do the same again? But we know that *'qui va à la chasse perd sa place'*, and the further Nemesis for this lapse was, that no sooner was I back from Egypt, whither I had fled in the winter of 1913 in order to write *The Boatswain's Mate*, than war broke out . . . and therewith my carefully built up connection with Germany (which was to have culminated in February 1915 with *The Wreckers* at Munich and the première of the *Bo'sun* at Frankfurt) collapsed for ever and ever!

Finally, to conclude the *mea culpa* list, attention to business was sometimes interrupted, as readers of this autobiography will have guessed, by an inordinate flow of passion in three directions – sport, games and friendship.

It would be useless and falsely modest to make a mystery of what most readers will have read between the lines of this story – that all my life, as regards the worth of my contribution to music such as it is, I have been confronted by two opposing estimates – one made in Germany, the other in England. And even as one single blameless citizen was not enough to save Sodom and Gomorrah from a fiery doom, so one single voice chiming in with Germany from the pages of *Grove's Dictionary** was powerless to change a consistent cold trickle of neglect, for which, as we have seen, the Press has not been invariably responsible, into the other thing. Time can generally be trusted to show which of two divergent judgements is correct, but what chance has Time in the case of perishable manuscripts rotting on the upper shelves of various music shops?

That moment of . . . not indifference exactly, but of acceptance, and of understanding how all this was inevitable, has now arrived, and as

* In an enthusiastic article by J. Fuller Maitland, editor of the 1908 edition.

most of the reviews are in German my unfortunate heirs won't feel obliged from loyalty and affection to read them! Meanwhile it amuses me to think that someday after my death, when all traces of sex have been reduced to ashes at the Woking Crematorium (so handy!) some-one will very likely take me up as a stunt – no extravagant assumption, seeing what subjects attain Stunt Rank in these days! Then, together with the assembling of my musical remains, this Annex will be avail-able, and the Stunt Raiser, lifting his eyebrows, can either burst out laughing ('O, come! you can't put that across in England!') or he can have those pages made into a fan and therewith fan the flame of the Stunt. And thus, someday, I may make friends, musically, with those I cannot get at in my lifetime.

Yes, reader . . . even now, at an hour when perhaps all passion should be spent, it sometimes saddens me to think that during my lifetime I have had no chance of making myself musically known to my countrymen and women as I have done in books – more or less. Yet rather less than more. Knowing nothing of astronomy I have boldly affirmed that it is the burning core of planets that differentiates them from dead moons, and composers like other creators can tap at will that fiery furnace which is their own heart. But in letters I only profess to be a humble autobiographer, equipped with a bucket which I let down as far as it will go into my private well of truth.

This being part of the story of a prolonged effort some of which was apparently fruitless, is it possible that a feeling of anything dimly approaching sadness should have been conveyed to the mind of the reader? If so, this book is a fraud and should be shot into the first dustman's cart that passes. But fantastic as the idea of its producing such an impression seems to the writer, to be on the safe side may I refer readers to a fable about an old man who, dying, bequeathed to his three sons a field in which was buried, so he said, a treasure. No sooner was he dead than they all started digging, the consequence of which was that every year the ground yielded richer crops. And that was the treasure.

So it is with most lives, I believe; so it has been anyhow with mine. Blessed with friends, with health, spared the most wearing, the most disheartening form of the inevitable struggle for existence, whatever has or has not been achieved the days have been gloriously spent in the open. And if, digging from morn till eve, one has not unearthed exactly what one expected, all the while the treasure was being found.

I do not pretend there have not been times of sadness, of frustration, even of despair. But as Harry Brewster writes in one of his letters, 'I walked all the way back, sad and happy. Never mind the sadness, *it is always about the perishable self and therefore does not exist'* . . .[48]

Epilogue

In 1930 Virginia Woolf had succeeded and surpassed Edith Somerville as reigning passion. The friendship between the two women, the one vigorous, outspoken, domineering, generous, the other frail, shy, elusive, undependable, lasted for over a decade until it was cut short by Virginia Woolf's suicide in 1941. During this time, with Virginia's encouragement, Ethel wrote six of her ten books. A sentence in the short memoir 'Ethel Smyth, the Writer', contributed by Victoria Sackville-West to Christopher St John's biography, sums up the exasperation caused to friends by successive passions: 'Blinkered egotism could scarcely have driven at greater gallop along so determined a road. But although often a nuisance, Ethel was never a bore.'

The curse of deafness, which had set in before 1914 and gradually led to distorted hearing, finally disrupted Ethel's career as a composer but did not extinguish her vitality. ('I think I had always been rather slow of hearing,' she wrote, 'though my friend Harry Brewster once said, "It's merely that you are deafened by what you are going to say next." ') She could no more hear the concerts given in 1934 to mark her seventy-fifth birthday than she could the Sadler's Wells revival of The Wreckers in the same year. In her memoirs, The Goldfish Bowl (Cassell, 1972), Ethel's colleague Elisabeth Lutyens, her junior by nearly fifty years and a niece of her old friends Betty Balfour and Constance Lytton, gives a vivid picture of the 'battling Dame' at this period: 'She was vastly entertaining, with enormous, vociferous vitality for which one needed to be in exceedingly rude health. In later years her shouting through the wrong end of the ear trumpet, necessitated by her deafness, doubled the volume of her voice and shut off all incoming sound. As hers was, anyhow, the only voice to be heard in her presence, this seeemed unnecessary.'

The admission in 'A Life Summed Up' that her musical career had been interrupted by 'an inordinate flow of passion in three directions – sport, games and friendship' shows that she remained well aware of the dangers spotted years before by Lisl von Herzogenberg. That the pull worked in both directions is suggested by an incident noted (at an earlier period) by Sylvia Pankhurst in The Suffragette Movement: 'She had a passion for ships. I stood with her on the quay at Southampton, bidding goodbye to Mrs Pankhurst, on board for America. At the moment of parting the siren blew hugely. The adored Mrs Pankhurst, smiling and waving to us from the deck, was forgotten by the musician, who snatched a notebook from her pocket and scribbled eagerly, exclaiming in her ecstasy, "A gorgeous noise!" '

When her tenancy of One Oak had come to an end before the 1914–18 war, Ethel *had moved to Coign, near Woking, the small house she built with money provided by Mary Dodge. Coign was her home for the rest of her life. Here she spent the greater part of the Second World War, fighting tenaciously against total deafness and the gradual failure of her body, cheered by glimpses of family and old friends, saddened by the illness and death of many of them and by the early accidental death of Pan VI, the last of her sheepdogs. 'I think I shall die soon, and I intend to die standing up,' she told her nurse-companion, Miss Brook. She did not quite do that, but she insisted on dressing and coming downstairs every morning until her last illness carried her off on 8 May 1944, at the age of eighty-six.*

Biographical Notes

ALEXANDER, KING OF SERBIA (1876–1903) Assassinated with his wife, Queen Draga, in Belgrade.

ALLEN, SIR HUGH (1869–1946) Organist, conductor, administrator. Conductor, London Bach Choir, 1907. Director, Royal College of Music (London), professor of music at Oxford, 1918.

ARCHER, FRED (1857–86) Champion jockey, 1874–86. Won the Derby five times.

AUSTIN, SUMNER (1889–1981) Baritone. Opera producer at the Old Vic and Sadler's Wells between the wars.

BAHR, HERMANN (1863–1934) Austrian writer and dramatist. Married Anna von Mildenburg (Bahr-Mildenburg) (1872–1947), Austrian singer.

BARING, HON. MAURICE (1874–1945) Writer and diplomat. Author of *Landmarks in Russian Literature*, *'C'*, *Cat's Cradle*, etc.

BARNBY, SIR JOSEPH (1838–96) Composer and choral conductor. His own choir was amalgamated with the Royal Choral Society.

BARRÈS, MAURICE (1862–1923) French writer, politician and patriot. Author of *La Colline inspirée*, *Les Déracinés*, etc.

BASHKIRTSEFF, MARIE (1860–84). Russian diarist and painter. Wrote in French. Lived mainly in France.

BATTENBERG, PRINCE HENRY OF (1858–96) Married Princess Beatrice, youngest daughter of Queen Victoria.

BAYLIS, LILIAN (1874–1937) Theatre manager. Developed the Old Vic and later Sadler's Wells theatres, presenting drama, opera and ballet at modest prices.

BEECHAM, SIR THOMAS, BT (1879–1961) Conductor, founder of orchestras, operatic entrepreneur. Beecham Opera Company, 1915–20. Chief conductor and managing director, Covent Garden, 1932–9.

BISMARCK, COUNT (later PRINCE) OTTO VON (1815–98) Prussian statesman. Architect of German unity. Prime Minister of Prussia, 1862. Chancellor of German Empire, 1871. Resigned, 1890.

BONHEUR, ROSA (1822–99) French painter, notably of animals.

BOULT, SIR ADRIAN (1889–1983) Conductor. Birmingham Symphony Orchestra, BBC Symphony Orchestra (of which he was also founder).

BRAITHWAITE, WARWICK (1889–1971) Conductor. Sadler's Wells, 1933–40.

BRODSKY, ADOLPH (1851–1929) Russian violinist, professor at Leipzig, 1880. Moved to Manchester, 1895. Leader of Hallé Orchestra.

BRUSSEL, ROBERT (1874–1940) French music critic (*Le Figaro*, etc.) and administrator.

BUCHOLZ, FRAU WILHELMINE Fictional character in Berlin stories of Julius Stinde (1841–1905).

365

BÜLOW, COUNT (later PRINCE) VON (1849–1929). German statesman. Chancellor, 1900–1909.

CALVÉ, EMMA (1858–1942) French soprano, a famous 'Carmen'. Covent Garden, 1892–1904.

CAVELL, EDITH (1865–1915) Hospital nurse. In charge of Red Cross hospital in Brussels during First World War. Arrested, tried and shot by Germans.

CHAPPELL & CO. Music publishers. Founded in London, 1810. Also piano manufacturers and concert promoters (Promenade Concerts, Queen's Hall, 1915–26).

CHRISTIAN, PRINCESS (1846–1923) Third daughter of Queen Victoria. Married Prince Christian of Schleswig-Holstein.

CHRYSANDER, FRIEDRICH (1826–1910) German musicologist. Authority on Handel.

CLEMENCEAU, GEORGES (1841–1929) French statesman. 'The Tiger'. Mayor of Montmartre during the Commune. Prime Minister, 1906 and 1917, when he was also War Minister. Played dominant role in negotiating Treaty of Versailles, 1919.

COATES, JOHN (1865–1941) Tenor. Beecham Opera Company, etc. Wagnerian roles, oratorio, recitals.

COMTE, AUGUSTE (1798–1857) French philosopher, founder of positivism.

CONNAUGHT, DUKE OF (1850–1942) Third son of Queen Victoria. Commanded in Aldershot, 1893–8. Married Princess Louise of Prussia.

CRAIG, EDITH (1869–1947) Theatrical producer and designer. Daughter of Ellen Terry. Sister of Edward Gordon Craig.

DAVIDSON, RANDALL (1848–1930) Former Dean of Windsor, Bishop of Rochester, Chaplain to Queen Victoria. Archbishop of Canterbury, 1903–1928. Brother-in-law of Ethel Smyth's elder sister, Alice Davidson.

DAVIES, FANNY (1861–1934) Pianist. Pupil of Clara Schumann. Played chamber music with Joachim. Toured widely abroad.

DAVIES, SIR WALFORD (1869–1941) Organist, composer, educator. Master of the King's Musick, 1934. Celebrated broadcaster.

DELAFOSSE, LÉON (1874–1955) French pianist. Noted interpreter of Fauré. A model for Proust's 'Morel'.

DENT, EDWARD J. (1876–1957) Musicologist, writer, administrator. Professor of music at Cambridge. First president, International Society for Contemporary Music. Much concerned with development of opera in England.

DUCHESNE, LOUIS (1843–1922) French ecclesiastic and historian.

DUSE, ELEONORA (1858–1904) Italian actress, as famous abroad as in her native country. To the normal repertory of her time she added Ibsen and d'Annunzio.

EDEN, SIR WILLIAM, BT (1849–1915) Landowner and amateur watercolourist. Sued by Whistler. Father of Anthony Eden.

EDINBURGH, DUKE OF (1844–1900) Second son of Queen Victoria.

FIEDLER, CONRAD (1841–95) German writer on art. Patron and collector.

FLEURY, LOUIS (1878–1926) French flautist, much admired in England. Debussy dedicated *Syrinx* to him.

FRANZ JOSEF, EMPEROR OF AUSTRIA (1848–1916) Defeated by Prussia at Sadowa, 1886. Declared war on Serbia, 1914.

FURSE, CHARLES (1868–1904) Painter, especially of portraits and horses.

GERMANY, CROWN PRINCE OF (1831–88) Succeeded his father as Emperor Frederick III in 1888. Married 1858 Victoria, the Princess Royal, elder daughter of Queen Victoria (known during her widowhood as the Empress Frederick).

GLEHN, W. G. DE (1870–1951) Painter. Member of New English Art Club. Son of German painter Oswald von Glehn. Married Jane Erin, also a painter.

GODFREY, SIR DAN (1868–1939) Founder of the Bournemouth Municipal (later Symphony) Orchestra. Loyal supporter of British composers.

GOOSSENS, SIR EUGENE (1893–1962) Conductor and composer. Russian Ballet, British National Opera Company, Covent Garden, etc.

GROVE, SIR GEORGE (1820–1900) Writer on music, civil engineer, etc. First director, Royal College of Music (London). Conceived and edited first edition of *Grove's Dictionary of Music and Musicians*.

HAGEL, RICHARD (1872–1941) German conductor. Leipzig Opera, 1900–1909.

HALLÉ, LADY (Wilma Norman-Neruda) (1838–1911) Austrian violinist. Married first Ludwig Norman, second (1888) Sir Charles Hallé.

HARTE, BRET (1836–1902) American writer of stories and verse. Author of *The Luck of the Roaring Camp*, etc. Lived latter part of his life in England.

HAYWARD, MARJORIE (1885–1953) Violinist, taught at RAM, London. Distinguished chamber music player.

HENSCHEL, SIR GEORGE (1850–1934) Baritone and conductor. Born Breslau, Silesia. Studied Leipzig Conservatoire. British nationality, 1890. Knighted 1914. Married Lilian Bailey, American soprano (d. 1901).

HESSE, GRAND DUKE LUDWIG IV OF (1837–92) Married Princess Alice, second daughter of Queen Victoria.

HILDEBRAND, ADOLF (1847–1921) German sculptor. Wittelsbach Fountain in Munich, equestrian statue of Bismarck at Bremen, portrait busts, etc.

HOCHBERG, COUNT BOLKO VON (1843–96) German composer. General administrator, Prussian theatres, 1886–93.

HOFMANN, JULIUS (1840–1910) German theatre administrator. From 1881 to 1903 ran Cologne Stadttheater (opera and drama) as the last independent director operating at his own financial risk. Later intendant in Mannheim.

HOLMÈS, AUGUSTA (1847–1903) French composer of Irish extraction. Pupil of César Franck.

INGLIS, ELSIE (1864–1917) Physician and surgeon. Founded Scottish Women's Suffrage Foundation.

ISAACS, SIR RUFUS (later Marquess of Reading) (1860–1935). Lawyer and statesman.

JADASSOHN, SALOMON (1831–1902) Composer and conductor. Taught at Leipzig Conservatoire.

JOACHIM, JOSEPH (1831–1907) Hungarian violinist. Based in Berlin but toured widely. His opposition to the 'new music' of Liszt and Wagner endeared him to conservative tastes. Married the contralto Amalie Weiss.

KIRCHNER, THEODOR (1823–1903) Organist and composer. Held many posts in Germany and Switzerland. Leipzig, 1875–83.

KLENGEL. Prominent Leipzig musical family. Julius (1859–1933) was principal cellist of Gewandhaus Orchestra for forty-three years.

KORBAY, FERENCZ (Francis) (1846–1913) Hungarian tenor, pianist, composer and teacher. Settled in London. Arrangements, in English, of Hungarian gypsy songs.

KOWALEWSKI (KOVALEVSKAYA), SOPHIE (1850–91) Russian mathematician and novelist. Studied in Heidelberg and Berlin. Professor of higher mathematics, Stockholm.

KRAUS, ERNST (1863–1941) German tenor. Berlin Court Opera for many years, also Bayreuth, Covent Garden, Metropolitan Opera.

KUHE, WILHELM (1823–1912) Pianist, composer and teacher of Czech origin. Settled in England.

LAGERLÖF, SELMA (1858–1940) Swedish writer. Nobel Prize, 1910. Author of *The Saga of Gösta Berling*, etc.

LALO, PIERRE (1866–1943) French critic (*Le Temps*, etc.). Son of composer Edouard Lalo.

LAMBERT, CONSTANT (1905–51) Composer, conductor, critic.

LASCELLES, SIR FRANK (1841–1920) British Ambassador to Russia, 1894; Berlin, 1896–1908.

LASSEN, EDUARD (1830–1904) Danish composer and conductor. Court Kapellmeister, Weimar, 1858.

LEE, VERNON (1856–1935). Real name, Violet Paget. English writer. Lived in Florence. Author of *Studies of the Eighteenth Century in Italy*, etc.

LEVI, HERMANN (1839–96) German conductor. Principal conductor, Munich Court Opera, 1872–96. Conducted first *Parsifal*, Bayreuth, 1882. Married Ethel Smyth's friend Mary Fiedler as her second husband.

LIND-GOLDSCHMIDT, MADAME (Jenny Lind) (1820–87) Soprano. 'The Swedish Nightingale.' British nationality, 1859. Married her accompanist, Otto Goldschmidt.

MAAS, LOUIS (1852–89) German pianist and composer. Taught piano at Leipzig Conservatoire from 1875.

MACKENZIE, SIR MORELL (1837–92) Physician. Specialist in heart disease.

MANNS, SIR AUGUST (1825–1907) Conductor. Born in Germany. Settled in England, 1854. Appointed permanent conductor, Crystal Palace Concerts, 1855. British nationality, 1895.

MARCHESI, BLANCHE (1863–1940) French singer. Settled in London. Daughter of singing teacher Mathilde Marchesi.

MCKENNA, REGINALD (1863–1943) Statesman. Home Secretary, 1915–16.

MENDÈS, CATULLE (1841–1909) French writer and poet of Parnassian school. Became a leading Wagnerite. Married Judith Gautier.

MESSAGER, ANDRÉ (1855–1929) French composer and conductor. Musical director at various times of Paris Opéra and Opéra-Comique. Covent Garden, 1901–1907.

METTERNICH, PRINCESS PAULINE (1836–1921) Granddaughter of the Austrian statesman, married his son (her step-uncle) Prince Richard Metternich, Austrian Ambassador to France during the Second Empire.

MOTTL, FELIX (1856–1911) Austrian conductor. Carlsruhe, Bayreuth, Munich, etc. A Wagnerian of catholic tastes.

MUCK, KARL (1854–1940) German conductor. Neumann's Wagner Co., then long associations with Berlin Court Opera (1892–1912) and Bayreuth (1901–30).

NEILSON, FRANCIS (1867–1961) Author and actor. Stage director, Covent Garden, 1900–1903.

NEUMANN, ANGELO (1838–1910) Austrian baritone and impresario. Organized Wagner Company for touring outside Germany. German Theatre, Prague, 1885–1910.

NIKISCH, ARTUR (1855–1922) Austrian conductor. Leipzig Opera, 1879. Gewandhaus and Berlin Philharmonic Orchestras, 1895.

NOAILLES, COMTESSE ANNA DE (1876–1933) French poet of Romanian-Greek descent.

OLLIVIER, EMILE (1825–1913) French lawyer and statesman. Prime Minister at outbreak of Franco-Prussian War. Married Liszt's daughter Blandine.

PARRATT, SIR WALTER (1841–1924) Organist, St George's Chapel, Windsor, 1882–94. Private organist to Queen Victoria. Master of the Queen's Musick, 1893.

PARRY, SIR HUBERT, BT (1848–1919) Composer, teacher, administrator. Director, Royal College of Music (London), 1894. Professor of music at Oxford, 1900. A leading figure in the English musical renaissance.

PATTI, ADELINA (1843–1919) Italian soprano. Born in Madrid. Educated in New York. The most celebrated prima donna in her time.

PIERSON, GEORG (1852–1902) *Intendanturdirektor* at Prussian Court Theatre, Berlin.

PITT, PERCY (1870–1932) Conductor, associated with Beecham Opera Company, BNOC and BBC.

RÉGNIER, HENRI DE (1864–1936) French symbolist poet.

REINECKE, CARL 1821–1910) German composer and administrator. Director, Leipzig Conservatoire, 1897.

REINHARDT, MAX (1873–1943) Austrian actor and director (Vienna, Berlin, London, etc.). A radical reformer who became famous for large-scale spectacular productions. Co-founder of Salzburg Festival.

RICHEPIN, JEAN (1849–1926) French poet, novelist, playwright.

RIDDELL, LORD (1865–1926) Newspaper proprietor. Chairman, *News of the World*, 1903–1934.

ROBEY, SIR GEORGE (1869–1954) Music-hall comedian. 'The Prime Minister of Mirth.'

RONALD (formerly RUSSELL), SIR LANDON (1873–1938) Conductor, pianist, composer. Principal, Guildhall School of Music, London, 1910–38.

RÖNTGEN. Prominent Leipzig musical family of Dutch origin. Engelbert ('Papa') was leader of Gewandhaus Orchestra. His son Julius (1855–1932), composer, conductor and pianist, became director of the Amsterdam Conservatoire.

ROSEBERY, EARL OF (1847–1929) Statesman and author. Foreign Secretary, 1892. Prime Minister, 1894–5.

RUBINSTEIN, ANTON (1829–94) Russian pianist and composer. Brother of pianist Nikolai Rubinstein.

SAMMONS, ALBERT (1886–1957) Violinist. Leader of Beecham and Philharmonic Society Orchestras, also of London String Quartet. A noted soloist.

SARASATE, PABLO DE (1844–1908) Spanish violinist and composer. Saint-Saëns, Lalo and Joachim were among the composers who wrote for him.

Biographical Notes

SCHUCH, ERNST VON (1846–1914) Austrian conductor. Long associated with Dresden Court Opera, of which he became *Generalmusikdirektor* in 1882.

SCHUMANN, CLARA (1819–96) German pianist and composer. Survived her husband Robert by forty years.

SCHUSTER, FRANK (1852–1927) Financier and music lover.

SCOTT-GATTY, SIR ALFRED (1847–1918) Amateur composer, notably of musical plays for children. Authority on heraldry.

SEEBACH, COUNT NIKOLAUS VON (1854–1930) German theatre administrator. Intendant, Dresden Court Opera, 1894–1919.

SHANKS, EDWARD (1892–1953) Writer. First winner of Hawthornden Prize, 1919.

SPITTA, PHILIPP (1841–94) German musicologist. Authority on Bach.

SPURGEON, CHARLES (1834–92) Baptist preacher. His sermons, delivered in London and published weekly, were famous.

STANFORD, SIR CHARLES VILLIERS (1852–1924) Dublin-born composer, conductor and teacher. Wrote seven operas. Professor of music at Cambridge, 1887. Taught composition at Royal College of Music (London). With Parry, a leading figure of the English musical renaissance.

STAVENHAGEN, BERNHARD (1862–1914) German pianist and conductor. Pupil of Liszt. Court Kapellmeister, Weimar, 1895.

TAUCHNITZ. Leipzig publishers who issued a numerous 'Collection of British and American authors for sale on the Continent'.

TERTIS, LIONEL (1876–1975) Viola player. By persuading many composers to write for him, making transcriptions and designing a large, resonant model, he achieved acceptance of the viola as a solo instrument.

TONKS, HENRY (1862–1937) Painter. Taught at Slade School, London.

TOSTI, SIR PAOLO (1846–1916) Italian song and ballad composer. Singing teacher to Royal Family. British nationality, 1906.

TOVEY, SIR DONALD FRANCIS (1875–1940) Writer on music, conductor, pianist, composer. Reid Professor of Music, Edinburgh University.

VOLKLAND, ALFRED (1841–1905) German pianist and conductor. A founder of the Leipzig Bach Verein.

WAGNER, COSIMA (1837–1930) Daughter of Liszt. Married to Hans von Bülow and then (1869) to Richard Wagner. After Wagner's death she ran the Bayreuth Festival for many years.

WALTER, BRUNO (originally Schlesinger) (1876–1962) German conductor. Mahler's assistant in Vienna. *Generalmusikdirektor*, Munich, Berlin Municipal Opera, Vienna State Opera.

WILHELM II, EMPEROR OF GERMANY (1859–1941) Succeeded 1888. Grandson of Queen Victoria through his mother, the Empress Frederick. Known as 'the Kaiser'.

WOOD, SIR HENRY J. (1869–1944) Conductor. Presiding genius of the Promenade Concerts during their first half-century.

WOODHOUSE, VIOLET GORDON (1872–1948) Harpsichord and clavichord player. Pioneer of the revival of early instruments.

ZULOAGA, IGNACIO (1870–1945) Spanish painter of genre scenes, portraits, etc.

Sources

Numerical references in the text indicate the conclusion of an extract or group of extracts from a single volume of Ethel Smyth's memoirs. The page on which each reference occurs in the text is given here in brackets; the pages on which the extracts can be found in their original editions are given after each volume title.

1. (p. 59) *Impressions that Remained*, vol. 1, pp. 7–127
2. (p. 99) *Impressions that Remained*, vol. 1, pp. 152–260
3. (p. 102) *Female Pipings in Eden*, pp. 57–63
4. (p. 103) *Impressions that Remained*, vol. 1, pp, 263–4
5. (p. 103) *Female Pipings in Eden*, p. 64
6. (p. 104) *Impressions that Remained*, vol. 1, p. 264
7. (p. 104) *Female Pipings in Eden*, pp. 64–6
8. (p. 108) *Impressions that Remained*, vol. 1, pp. 266–77
9. (p. 113) *Impressions that Remained*, vol. 1, pp. 281–4
10. (p. 159) *Impressions that Remained*, vol. 2, pp. 5–227
11. (p. 161) *As Time Went On . . .* , pp. 26–30
12. (p. 166) *Impressions that Remained*, vol. 2. pp. 227–53
13. (p. 166) *Impressions that Remained*, vol. 1, p. 54
14. (p. 167) *Impressions that Remained*, vol. 2, p. 253
15. (p. 167) *Impressions that Remained*, vol. 1, p. 54
16. (p. 173) *Impressions that Remained*, vol. 2, pp. 254–64
17. (p. 183) *As Time Went On . . .* , pp. 83–99
18. (p. 192) *Streaks of Life*, pp. 95–108
19. (p. 193) *As Time Went On . . .* , pp. 139–41
20. (p. 193) *Streaks of Life*, p. 109
21. (p. 193) *As Time Went On . . .* , p. 109
22. (p. 193) *Streaks of Life*, p. 109
23. (p. 199) *As Time Went On . . .* , pp. 143–79
24. (p. 200) *What Happened Next*, pp. 63–119
25. (p. 205) *As Time Went On . . .* , pp. 198–270
26. (p. 206) *Streaks of Life*, p. 69
27. (p. 207) *What Happened Next*, p. 6
28. (p. 207) *Streaks of Life*, p. 71
29. (p. 207) *What Happened Next*, p. 7
30. (p. 209) *Streaks of Life*, pp. 71–89
31. (p. 209) *What Happened Next*, p. 33
32. (p. 215) *What Happened Next*, pp. 8–13
33. (p. 215) *As Time Went On . . .* , pp. 270–71
34. (p. 236) *What Happened Next*, pp. 13–176

35. (p. 254) *Streaks of Life*, pp. 142–205
36. (p. 256) *What Happened Next*, pp. 204–214
37. (p. 280) *What Happened Next*, pp. 233–315
38. (p. 283) *Female Pipings in Eden*, pp. 108–112
39. (p. 284) *What Happened Next*, pp. 315–16
40. (p. 289) *Beecham and Pharaoh*, pp. 4–41
41. (p. 301) *Female Pipings in Eden*, pp. 190–213
42. (p. 313) *Beecham and Pharaoh*, pp. 104–180
43. (p. 317) *Female Pipings in Eden*, pp. 235–259
44. (p. 336) *Streaks of Life*, pp. 4–66
45. (p. 344) *Streaks of Life*, pp. 232–46
46. (p. 346) *A Final Burning of Boats Etc.*, pp. 39–41
47. (p. 353) *Inordinate (?) Affection*, pp. 15–78
48. (p. 362) *As Time Went On . . .* , pp. 284–308

List of Works

Compiled by Jory Bennett

This chronological works list of Ethel Smyth's music, authenticated as far as possible by reference to primary sources, supersedes Kathleen Dale's classified catalogue in the fifth edition of *Grove's Dictionary of Music and Musicians* (1954). It incorporates revisions, extracts and arrangements which characterize Ethel Smyth's output, and excludes only a few inconsequential student exercises and some unidentified fragments of early string parts. Care has been taken to establish an accurate chronology for the early German period works, but it is by no means conclusive: the few published opus numbers, discontinued after Opus 8, are erratic and appear to follow the order of publication rather than composition. A more detailed thematic catalogue will form part of my thesis.

All autograph scores are in the Department of Manuscripts of the British Library, and all first performances and publication of scores took place in London, except where otherwise stated. In the case of publishers that have ceased trading or have been amalgamated with others, a separate note states where parts can be obtained. The scoring of orchestral works is given in standard abbreviated form, e.g., '2(1) 2 2+1 2/4 2 3 1/str timp cym' indicates 2 flutes (one doubling piccolo), 2 oboes, 2 clarinets plus a bass clarinet, 2 bassoons; 4 horns, 2 trumpets, 3 trombones, 1 tuba; strings, timpani and cymbals. Timings and details of scoring derive mainly from the composer's inventory of music (British Library MS Add. 49196). Recordings cited can be found in the British Music Information Centre and the National Sound Archive.

The lack of detail in some entries is compensated for in part by the inclusion of previously unlisted works: an early Cello Sonata, a Fanfare for brass and the *Fête Galante* ballet, as well as reference to a printed edition of the original version of *The Wreckers* in French. The location of the Mass in D autograph, in an unidentified London bank vault, remains unknown.

1876 'We Watched her Breathing through the Night' (T. Hood), part-song, S A T B

c 1877 *Lieder und Balladen*, Op. 3, mez. and pf. 1 'Vom Berge' (trad); 2 'Der verirrte Jäger' (Eichendorff); 3 'Bei einer Linde' (Eichendorff); 4 'Es wandelt was wir schauen' (Eichendorff); 5 'Schön Rohtraut' (Mörike). *Ded 'Frau Livia Frege gewidmet'. Edn*: C. F. Peters, Leipzig, 1886

Lieder, Op. 4, mez. and pf. 1 'Tanzlied' (Büchner); 2 'Schlummerlied' (E. von Wildenbruch); 3 'Mittagsruh' (Eichendorff); 4 'Nachtreiter' (K. Groth); 5 'Nachtgedanken' (P. Heyse). *Ded*:

List of Works

'Meiner Mutter gewidmet'. Edn: C. F. Peters, Leipzig, 1886
Eight songs (Ger. anon), texts illegible

1877 Sonata No. 1 in C, pf. 'Dedicated to *la Madre'*
Sonata 'Geistinger' No. 2 in C sharp minor, pf
Sonata No. 3 in D, unfin., 2 movts only

1877–80 Theme and Variations in C, pf, unfin., solo and duet versions
Four Canons by Inversion, pf, unfin., no. 2 titled 'Nocturne'
Four-part Dances, pf. 1 Minuett (sic) in D; 2 Sarabande in C minor;
3 (lost); 4 Minuet in A minor; 5 Sarabande in C minor
Two-part Invention in D, pf
Two-part Suite in E, pf. 1 Gavotte; 2 Bourrée; 3 Gigue; 4 Minuet
Aus der Jugendzeit!! (study) in E minor, pf. *Ded*: 'E[lizabeth] v[on]
H[erzogenberg]'
Symphony No. 2 in D by Brahms, pf transcr., 1st movt only

1878 String Quartet No. 1 in A minor, unfin.
Variations on an Original Theme (of an Exceedingly Dismal Nature) in
D flat, pf. Theme, 8 Variations (no. 4 ded. *'À la Phyllis'*) and
Finale

1878–84 Nine Rounds (Ger. texts, unidentified)
'Denke, denke mein Geliebter' (?), song, vce and pf, sketches only
'Sur les lagunes' (Gautier), song, vce and pf, unfin., 41 bars only
Prelude and Fugue in C, pf
Symphonie für kleines Orchester in D, unfin., 1 movt only. *Orch*:
2 2 0 2/2 0 0 0/str
Trage-komische Oüverture in F, orch, unfin., short score sketch, 117
bars only

1880 String Quartet in D minor. *Fp*: Röntgen family, Leipzig, 2 June
1880
Sonata in C minor, vc and pf. *Fp* (public): John Franca, Eric Ste-
vens, Wigmore Hall, 16 Feb 1981. *Timing*: 23'
Prelude and Fugue in F sharp, pf
Trio in D minor, vn, vc and pf. *Fp* (public): Kenneth Goldsmith,
Terry King, John Jensen (Mirecourt Trio), Grinnell College,
Iowa, 30 Aug 1985. *MS*: Durham Univ. (Edn in prepa-
ration.) *Timing*: 35'

1882–4 String Quartet in E flat (2nd movt identical to 3rd movt of 1883 Str
Qt in C minor, below)
String Quartet in E flat, unfin., 1 movt only
String Quartet in E minor, unfin., 203 bars only
String Quartet in C, unfin., 167 bars only
String Quintet in B minor, 2 vn, va, 2 vc, unfin., 2 movts (Prelude
and Fugue) only
Fugue à 5, org, 2-stave (B flat minor) and 3-stave (B minor) versions
Study on 'Wie selig seid Ihr Frommen', org
Five Sacred Part-Songs Based on Chorale Tunes, SATB. 1 'Komm

süsser Tod'; 2 'Kein Stündlein geht dahin'; 3 'Gib dich zu-
frieden und sei stille'; 4 'O Traurigkeit, O Herzeleid'; 5
'Erschienen ist der herrlich' Tag'. (Published, edn not traced)
Short Chorale Preludes (rev. 1913), org. 1 'Du, O schönes Weltge-
bäude!'; 2A 'O Gott du frommer Gott'; 2B (canonic version); 3
'Schwing dich auf zu deinen Gott'; 4 'Erschiene ist der
herrlich' Tag'; 5A, Prelude and 5B Fugue on 'O Traurigkeit, O
Herzeleid'. *Ded*: 'To my friend Sir Walter Parratt, MVO'. *MS*:
BL (orig. version nos. 1, 2B, 3, 5A); RCM (rev. version nos.
1, 2A, 4, 5A, 5B). *Edn*: Novello, 1913
arr. as *Four Short Chorale Preludes for Strings and Solo Instruments*
(orig. title *Short and Solemn Interludes for Sectional Orchestra*;
rev. 1913). 1 'Du, O schönes Weltegebäude!' (str, tpt, timp);
2 'O Traurigkeit, O Herzeleid' (str); 3 Erschienen ist der
herrlich' Tag' (str, tpt, tb, timp); 4 'Schwing dich auf zu
deinem Gott' (str, solo fl or vl). *Fp*: Queen's Hall Orch, E. S.,
Queen's Hall Prom, 29 Aug 1923. (MS of rev. version lost.)
Edn: Novello, 1913(?). *Timing*: 12'

c 1883 *Prelude and Fugue for Thin People*, pf. *Ded*: Clara Schumann. (MS
lost)

1883 String Quartet 'Hildebrand' in C, unfin., 58 bars only
String Quintet in E, Op. 1, 2 vn, va, 2 vc. *Ded*: 'To the memory of
Rhoda Garrett'. *Fp*: Engelbert Röntgen, Carl Bolland, Carl
Thümer, Julius Klengel, Johann Pester, Gewand-
haus, Leipzig, 26 Jan 1884. (MS lost.) *Edn*: C. F. Peters,
Leipzig, 1884
arr. as *Suite for Strings*, Op. 1A, str orch and pf duet versions.
(MS lost.) *Edn*: E. Hatzfeld, Leipzig, 1891
String Quartet in C minor, 4 movts and a discarded set of vari-
ations on *Horbury* (3rd movt identical to 2nd movt of 1882–4
Str Qt in E flat, above). *MS*: Durham Univ.

1886–8 String Quartet in C

1887 Sonata in A minor, Op. 5, vc and pf. *Ded*: 'Herrn Julius Klengel
freundschaftlich zugeeignet'. *Fp*: May Fussell, Kathleen Long,
Court House, Marylebone Lane, 8 Dec 1926. (MS lost.) *Edn*:
C. F. Peters, Leipzig, 1887
Sonata in A minor, Op. 7, vn and pf. *Ded*: 'Frau Lili Wach geb.
Mendelssohn-Bartholdy in alter Freundschaft gewidmet'. *Fp*:
Adolph Brodsky, Fanny Davies, Gewandhaus, Leipzig, 20
Nov 1887. *Fp* London: Edith Robinson, Fanny Davies, Wig-
more Hall, 19 Nov 1923. *Edn*: J. Reiter Biedermann, Leipzig,
1887; Universal Edn, Vienna, 1923. *Rec*: BMIC, 1977.
Timing: 22'
String Trio in D. *MS*: Durham Univ.

1888 *The Song of Love* (Song of Songs, adapted in Eng. and Ger. by

E. S.), Op. 8, cantata for sop. and ten. sol., ch. and orch. *Orch*: 2 2 2 2/3 2 0 0/str timp. *Timing*: 45'

1889 *Serenade in D*, orch. *Orch*: 2(1) 2 2 2/2 2 0 0/str timp. *Fp*: Crystal Palace Orch, August Manns, 26 Apr 1890. *MS/hire*: Universal Edn. *Timing*: 30'
Overture to Shakespeare's Antony and Cleopatra, orch. *Orch*: 2 2 2 2/ 4 2 3 0/str timp. *Fp*: Crystal Palace Orch, August Manns, 18 Oct 1890. *MS/hire*: Universal Edn. *Timing*: 13'

1891 Mass in D (rev. 1925), S A T B sol., ch. and orch. 'Written for Pauline Trevelyan'. *Orch*: 2+1 2+1 2 2+1/4 2 3 1/str hp timp s.d.b.d. cym tr org. *Fp*: Esther Palliser, Belle Cole, Ben Davies, Watkin Mills, Royal Choral Soc, Albert Hall Orch, Sir Joseph Barnby, Albert Hall, 18 Jan 1893. *Fp* rev.(?): Caroline Hatchard, Mme Marsland, Joseph Green, Roy Henderson, Sheffield Musical Union, Leeds S O, Dr Henry Coward, Victoria Hall, Sheffield, 12 Nov 1925. *MS*: (lost; sketches, Lady Boult); R A M (incomplete vocal score). *Edn*: Novello, 1893, 1925; Da Capo (reprint), New York, 1980. *Timing*: 65'

1892–4 *Fantasio*, *'Phantastische Komödie'* (opera) in 2 acts after the play by Alfred de Musset. (rev. 1898–9). Lib. in Ger. by Henry Brewster and E. S. *Orch*: 2(1) 2 2 2/4 2 3 1/str hp timp s.d. b.d. cym tr. *Fp*: Agnes Stavenhagen (Danila), Anna Hofmann (Countess Anna), Heinrich Zeller (Fantasio), Rudolf Gmür (Count of Croatia), Leonard von Szpinger (Marinoni), Herman Bucha (King of Herzegovina), Bernard Stavenhagen, Hoftheater, Weimar, 24 May 1898. (M S two versions.) *Edn*: C. G. Röder, Leipzig, 1899. *Rec*: B M I C, 1984 (excerpt)

1899–1901 *Der Wald*, 'Music-Drama' in 1 act with Prologue and Epilogue, after an idea by Henry Brewster. Lib. in Ger. and Eng. by Henry Brewster and E. S. *Ded*: 'My part in this work I give to H. B. Brewster, its only begetter'. *Orch*: 2+1 2(1) 2+1 2/4 3 3 1/ str hp timp s.d. b.d. cym tr tamb. *Fp*: Marie Deitrich (Röschen), Ida Hiedler (Iolanthe), Ernst Kraus (Heinrich), Baptist Hoffmann (Rudolf), Carl Nebe (the Pedlar), Dr Carl Muck, Königliches Opernhaus, Berlin, 9 Apr 1902. *Fp* London: Katharina Lohse, Olive Fremstad, Alois Pennarini, David Bispham, Robert Blass, Otto Lohse, Covent Garden, 18 July 1902. *Edn*: Schott, Mainz, 1902. *Hire*: Boosey & Hawkes. *Rec*: B M I C, 1984 (excerpt). *Timing*: 65'
A Spring Canticle (or *Wood Spirits' Song*), ch. and orch, adapted from the Prologue to *Der Wald* (Chorus of Spirits of the Forest). *Orch* (3rd version): 2 2 2 2/3 1 2 0/str hp timp cym (ad lib). *Fp*: pupils of Blanche Marchesi, Crystal Palace Choir, LSO, E. S., Queen's Hall, 29 June 1911. (M S lost.) *Edn*: Schott, Mainz, 1903; Curwen, 1923, 1927. *Timing*: 8' 30"

c 1900 *Wedding Anthem*, ch. and org. (M S lost.)

1902/12 String Quartet in E minor (movts 1 and 2, 1902; movts 3 and 4, 1912). *Ded*: 'To the London Quartet'. *Fp*: Albert Sammons, Thomas Petre, H. Waldo Warner, C. Warwick Evans, Aeolian Hall, 3 Dec 1914. (MS lost.) *Edn*: Universal Edn, Vienna, 1914. *Hire*: Universal Edn. *Timing*: 30'

1902–4 *The Wreckers*, 'Lyrical Drama' in 3 acts after an idea by E. S. (rev. 1909–16). Lib. in Fr. (*Les Naufrageurs*) by Henry Brewster and E. S.; Ger. tr. (*Strandrecht*) by H. Decker and J. Bernhoff; Eng. tr. by A. Strettell and E. S. *Ded*: '*À la mémoire du grand musicien Prince Edmond de Polignac*'. *Orch*: 2+1 2+1 2+1 2+1/4 2 3 1/str hp timp s.d. b.d. cym tr tamb gong glock org; (*on stage*) alto saxhorn tpt hn tuba bell cannon. *Fp*: Frau Doenges (Thirza), Fräuln Fiadnitzer (Avis), Jacques Urlus (Mark), Walter Soomer (Pascoe), Richard Hagel, Neues Theater, Leipzig, 11 Nov 1906. *Fp* London: Mme de Vere Sapio, Elizabeth Amsden, John Coates, Arthur Winckworth, Thomas Beecham, His Majesty's Theatre, 22 June 1909.* *Fp* rev.: Enid Cruickshank, Odette de Foras, Francis Russell, Philip Bertram, John Barbirolli, Covent Garden, 24 Sept 1931. (MS of overture lost.) *Edn*: Breitkopf & Härtel, Leipzig, 1906 (Fr. and Ger.); Universal Edn/Forsyth, 1916 (Eng. and Ger.). *Rec*: NSA, c 1920 (excerpt), 1982 (complete). *Timing*: 135'

    Overture to The Wreckers, orch (conc. end). *Fp*: Philharmonic Soc., Bruno Walter, Queen's Hall, 3 Mar 1909. (MS lost.) *Edn*: Breitkopf & Härtel, Leipzig, 1911. *Hire*: Universal Edn. *Rec*: NSA, c 1930, 1946; BMIC/NSA, 1968. *Timing*: 9'. (Also arr. for military band by A. Stretton, Universal Edn, 1922, and by Sir Dan Godfrey, Chappell, 1924.)

    On the Cliffs of Cornwall, the Prelude to Act 2 of *The Wreckers*, orch. *Ded*: '*À la Princesse Edmond de Polignac*'. *Fp*: LSO, Artur Nikisch, Queen's Hall, 2 May 1908. MS (autograph proof): Dr Robert Pascall. *Edn*: Novello, 1909. *Timing*: 10'. (Also arr. for military band by Sir Dan Godfrey, Chappell, 1927.)

1907 *Songs*, mez. or bar. and chamber ensemble. 1 'Odette' (Régnier); 2 'La Danse' (Régnier); 3 'Chrysilla' (Régnier); 4 'Ode Anacréontique' (anon, tr. Leconte de Lisle). Eng. tr. by A. Strettell (nos. 1–3) and E. S. (no. 4). *Ded*: 1 'To Madame Bulteau'; 2 'To Mary Hunter'; 3 'To H. B. Brewster'; 4 'To Madame la Princesse Alexandre de Caraman Chimay'. *Orch*: vn va vc fl hp s.d. cym tr tamb. *Fp* nos. 1–3: Elsie Swinton, Principals of New Symphony Orch, Emil von Reznicek, Queen's Hall, 12 Nov 1907. *Fp* (?) no. 4: Emile Engel, Philip Cathie Quartet, Albert Fransella (fl), Gwendoline Mason (hp), E. S., Bechstein Hall, 11 Dec 1908. *MS*: RAM (no. 4; nos. 1–3 lost). *Edn*: Novello, 1909. *Timing*: 20' 30"

* *Fp* Acts 1 and 2, concert (in Ger.): Queen's Hall, 30 May 1908

Songs, arr. for solo instr. and large orch. (MS lost). Also no. 3 arr. mez. or bar., vn and pf. (MS lost.) *Edn:* Novello, 1909. *Ode Anacréontique,* arr. for orch. *Orch:* 2+1 2 2 2/3 2 0 0/str hp timp s.d. cym tr. *Fp:* Herbert Heyner, BBC SO, E.S., Queen's Hall Prom, 4 Sept 1930. (MS lost.) *Timing:* 4' 30"

1910 *Hey Nonny No* (anon, Ger. tr. L. Kirschbaum) (rev. 1920), ch. and orch. *Ded:* 'To Violet Woodhouse'. *Orch:* 2+1 2+1 2+1 2+1/ 4 2 3 1/str hp timp s.d. b.d. cym tr. *Fp:* London Choral Soc., LSO, Arthur Fagge, Queen's Hall, 26 Oct 1910. *Fp* rev.: Hull Vocal Soc., E.S., Hull City Hall, 19 Jan 1921. *MS/hire:* Fentone Music, Corby. *Edn:* Breitkopf & Härtel, Leipzig, 1911. *Timing:* 7' 30"

Sleepless Dreams (Rossetti), ch. and orch. Ger. tr. *(Nacht)* by F. Schreker. *Ded:* 'To Maurice Baring'. *Orch:* 2+1 2+1 2+1 2+1/ 4 2 3 1/str hp timp s.d. b.d. cym tr. *Fp* details as *Hey Nonny No,* above. *MS/hire:* Universal Edn. *Edn:* Universal Edn, Vienna, 1912; Curwen, 1929. *Timing:* 9'

The March of the Women (Cicely Hamilton), unison song with opt. pf acc. 'Dedicated to the Women's Social and Political Union'. *Fp:* Suffrage Choir, E.S., Suffolk St Galleries, Pall Mall, 21 Jan 1911. (MS lost.) *Edn:* The Women's Press, 1911; Curwen, 1929. *Rec:* NSA, 1937 (excerpt). *Timing:* 4'

The March of the Women, arr. for pf solo, published in *King Albert's Book* (for Belgian relief), 1914. Also arr. for orch. by F. Collinson *(Orch:* 1 0 2 1/1 2 1 0/str hp timp s.d. b.d. cym tr. *MS:* BBC). An arrangement for military band (MS lost) was first performed by the Metropolitan Police Band, E.S., Victoria Tower Gardens, Westminster, 6 March 1930.

Songs of Sunrise, unacc. ch. (opt. orch. in nos. 2 and 3). 1 'Laggard Dawn, based on a melody by the late Prince Edmond de Polignac' (E.S.); 2 '1910, being a faithful chronicle of remarks frequently heard and liable to repetition *ad lib.* on a current question' (E.S.); 3 'The March of the Women' (Cicely Hamilton). 'Dedicated to the Women's Social and Political Union'. *Orch* (opt): 2(1) 2 2 2/4 2 3 1/str timp s.d.b.d. cym tr. *Fp:* pupils of Blanche Marches: Crystal Palace Choir, LSO, E.S., Queen's Hall, 1 Apr 1911. (MS of no. 1 lost; no. 3, parts only.) *Edn:* Breitkopf & Härtel for The Women's Press, 1911; Curwen, 1929 (nos. 1 and 3)

1913 *Three Moods of the Sea* (Arthur Symons), songs, mez. or bar. and orch. 1 'Requies'; 2 'Before the Squall'; 3 'After Sunset'. Ger. tr. by R. S. Hoffmann. *Ded:* 'Meinem Übersetzer, Dr R[udolph] St[ephen] Hoffmann, dankbar gewidmet'. *Orch:* 2+1 2+1 2+1 2+1/4 3 1/str hp timp s.d. b.d. cym tr glock. *Fp* Herbert Heyner, LSO, Artur Nikisch, Queen's Hall, 23 June 1913. *Edn:* Universal Edn, Vienna, 1913. *Timing:* 9' 30"

Three Songs, mez. or bar., pf (nos. 1 and 2) and orch (no. 3). 1 'The Clown' (Maurice Baring); 2 'Possession' (Ethel Carnie); 3 'On the Road: a marching tune' (Carnie). Ger. tr. by R. S. Hoffmann. *Ded*: (1 no dedication); 2 'To E[mmeline] P[ankhurst]'; 3 'To C[hristabel] P[ankhurst]'. *Orch*: 2+1 2+1 2+1 2+1/4 2 3 1/str hp timp s.d. b.d. cym. *Fp* no. 3: details as *Three Moods of the Sea*, above. (*Fp* of nos. 1 and 2 not traced.) (MS lost.) *Edn*: Universal Edn, Vienna, 1913. *Rec*: NSA, 1978 (nos. 1 and 3)

'The Clown' and 'Possession', arr. for mez. or bar. and chamber ensemble. *Orch*:vl va vc fl hp tr. *MS*: Universal Edn

1913–14 *The Boatswain's Mate*, Comedy (opera) in 1 act after the story by W. W. Jacobs (rev. 1921). Lib. by E.S. Ger. tr. (*Der gute Freund*) by R. S. Hoffmann. *Orch* (1921): 1(1) 1 1 1/2 1 1 0/str timp s.d. b.d. cym tr tubular bell; (*on stage*) banjo concertina harmonium. *Fp* Overture: Queen's Hall Orch, E. S., Queen's Hall Prom, 26 Aug 1915. *Fp*: Rosina Buckman (Mrs Waters), Courtice Pounds (Harry Benn), Frederick Ranalow (Ned Travers), Beecham Opera Co., E. S., Shaftesbury Theatre, 28 Jan 1916. *Fp* rev.: Muriel Gough, Robert Curtis, Sumner Austin, E. S., Old Vic, 30 Mar 1922. *Edn*: Universal Edn/Forsyth, 1915; Universal Edn, Vienna, 1921. *Rec*: NSA, c 1930 (excerpts), 1945 (excerpt), 1950 (complete), 1985 (excerpts). *Timing*: 89'

Overture to The Boatswain's Mate, arr. *Orch*: 2(1) 2 2 2/4 2 3 1/ str hp timp s.d. b.d. cym tamb. *Fp*: BBC SO, Sir Henry Wood, Queen's Hall Prom, 13 Sept 1930. *MS*: RAM. *Timing*: 6'

Intermezzo (Mid Briars and Bushes), arr. of the Introduction to Part 2 of *The Boatswain's Mate*. *Orch*: 2(1) 2(1) 2 2/3 2 3 1/str hp timp s.d. b.d. cym. *Fp* (?): Guildford SO, E.S., Guildford, 26 Nov 1924. *MS*: Universal Edn. *Timing*: 5'

1920 'Dreamings' (Patrick Macgill), part-song, SSA. (MS lost.) *Edn*: Year Book Press (H. F. W. Deane & Sons), 1920. *Timing*: 4' 30"

1921–2 *Fête Galante*, 'Dance-Dream' (opera) in 1 act, after the story by Maurice Baring. Lib. by E. S. and Edward Shanks. *Orch* (2nd version): 1(1) 1 1 1/tpt *or* tb (opt)/str hp (opt) timp s.d. b.d. cym; (*on stage*) fl picc banjo concertina. *Fp*: Dorothy Orsay (the Queen), Muriel Gough (Columbine), Joseph Yates (the King), Sumner Austin (Pierrot), Harry Sennett (Harlequin), Geoffrey Dams (the Lover), British Nat. Opera Co., E. S., Birmingham Rep. Theatre, 4 June 1923. *Fp* London: Enid Cruikshank, Doris Lemon, Andrew Shanks, Raymond Ellis, Browning Mummery, Tudor Davies, British Nat. Opera Co., Percy Pitt, Covent Garden, 11 June 1923. *MS*: Universal Edn. *Edn*: Universal Edn, Vienna, 1923. *Timing*: 40'

Fête Galante, arr. as a ballet with additional music. *Orch*: 2(1) 2(1) 1 1(1)/2 1 1 0/str hp timp s.d. b.d. cym; (*on stage*) coconut. (Unstaged.) *Fp* (concert): Liverpool Philharmonic, E.S., Philharmonic Hall, Liverpool, 26 Nov 1932. *Fp* London (concert): BBC SO, E.S., Queen's Hall Prom, 10 Jan 1933. MS: Universal Edn. *Edn*: Universal Edn, Vienna, 1933. *Timing*: 23'

Fête Galante, suite for orch. *Orch*: 1(1) 1(1) 1 1/2 1 1 1/str hp timp s.d. b.d. cym tr. *Fp*: Bournemouth SO, E. S., Winter Gardens, Bournemouth, 8 Aug 1924. *Fp* London: British Women's SO, E. S., Nov 1924. *MS*: Universal Edn. *Edn*: Universal Edn, Vienna, 1939. *Rec*: NSA, *c* 1940 (excerpts), 1943 (excerpts). *Timing*: 15'

Soul's Joy (Donne), madrigal from *Fête Galante* for unacc. ch. *MS*: Universal Edn. *Edn*: Curwen, 1923. *Timing*: 2' 30"

1923–4 *Entente Cordiale*, 'A Post-War Comedy' (opera) in 1 act, 'founded on fact' by 'Bengal Military Orphan'.* Lib. by E. S. *Ded*: 'To my own branch – the Army'. *Orch*: 2(1) 1 2 1/2 2 cornet (2 tpt) 1 o/str timp s.d. tr. *Fp* Overture and Intermezzo: Queen's Hall Orch, E.S., Queen's Hall Prom, 3 Oct 1925. *Fp* (student prod.): Gwyneth Edwards (Jeanne Arcot), Winifred Burton (Emma Iggins), Robert Gwynne (Erb Iggins), Dunstan Hart (Bill Baylis), Charles Draper (Charles Arcot), E. S., RCM, 22 July 1925. *Fp* (public): Judy Skinner, Dorothy d'Orsay, Robert Gwynne, Sumner Austin, Edmund Davies, Bristol Opera Co., City of Birmingham SO, E. S., Theatre Royal, Bristol, 20 Oct 1926. *MS/hire*: Faber Music. *Edn*: Curwen, 1925. *Timing*: 50'

Entente Cordiale, suite for orch. *Orch*: 1+1 1 1 1 1/2 1 1 o/str hp timp s.d. tr. *Fp*: BBC SO, Sir Henry Wood, Queen's Hall Prom, 3 Jan 1935. *MS*: Faber Music. *Timing*: 15'

Two Interlinked French Folk Melodies, arr. of the Intermezzo (no. 8) from *Entente Cordiale*, orch. *Orch*: 1 1 1 1/2 1 0 o/str hp *or* pf timp s.d. tr. *Fp*: Lincoln Mus. Soc., E. S., 27 Nov 1929. *Fp* London: London Chamber Orch, Anthony Bernard, April 1930. *MS*: Philharmonic Library. *Edn*: OUP, 1929. *Rec*: NSA, *c* 1940, 1952. *Timing*: 3' 30"

Two Interlinked French Folk Melodies, arr. for large orch. *Fp*: BBC SO, E.S., Queen's Hall Prom, 4 Sept 1930. (MS lost)

Two Interlinked French Folk Melodies, arr. for fl, ob (vn *or* va) and pf. Also arr. for vn *or* va and pf. (MS lost.) *Edn*: OUP, 1936. *Fp*: Albert Fransella, Helen Gaskell, Bertram Harrison, Wigmore Hall, 11 Feb 1928. (MS lost.) *Edn*: OUP, 1928. *Rec*: NSA, 1982

1926 Double Concerto in A, vn, hn and orch. *Ded*: 'To the best friend of English Music, Henry Wood'. *Orch*: 2(1) 2 2 2/2 1 0 o/str hp timp s.d. b.d. cym tr tamb xyl. *Fp*: Jelly d'Arányi, Aubrey Brain, Queen's Hall Orch, Sir Henry Wood, Queen's Hall, 5 Mar 1927. *MS/hire*: Faber Music *Rec*: BMIC/NSA, 1975. *Timing*: 25' 30"

*see *Memoirs*, p. 29

Double Concerto in A, arr. for vn, hn (va *or* vc) and pf. *Fp*:
Marjorie Hayward, Aubrey Brain, Kathleen Long, Wigmore
Hall, 11 Feb 1928. *Edn*: Curwen, 1928. *Hire*: Faber Music.

1927 *Variations on Bonny Sweet Robin (Ophelia's Song)*, fl, ob (vn *or* va)
and pf. *Ded*: 'To Albert Fransella'. *Fp*: Albert Fransella, Helen
Gaskell, Bertram Harrison, Wigmore Hall, 11 Feb 1928. *Edn*:
OUP, 1928. *Rec*: NSA, 1972. *Timing*: 9'

1929–30 *The Prison*, symphony for sop. and bass sol., ch. and orch. Lib.
compiled by E.S. from the book by H.B. *Motto*: 'I am striving
to release that which is divine within us, and to merge it in
the universally divine'. *Orch*: 2+1 2+1 2+1 2/4 3 3 1/str hp
timp s.d. b.d. cym tr tamb cel org (opt); (*offstage*) tpt. *Fp*: Elsie
Suddaby (the Soul), Stuart Robertson (the Prisoner), Reid
Chorus, Reid SO, E. S., Usher Hall, Edinburgh, 19 Feb 1931.
Fp London: Elsie Suddaby, Stuart Robertson, Bach Choir, Dr
Adrian Boult, Queen's Hall, 24 Feb 1931. *MS/hire*: Faber
Music. *Edn*: Curwen, 1930. *Timing*: 65'

Two Orchestral Preludes, arr. from *The Prison*, orch. 1 'The First
Glimmer of Dawn'; 2 'Organ Music in the Chapel'. *Orch*: 2+1
2+1 2+1 2/4 2 3 1/str hp timp s.d. b.d. cym tr tamb cel org.
MS/hire: Faber Music. *Timing*: 7'

1930 *Hot Potatoes*, fanfare, 4 tpt, 4 tb, timp, cym, tr. 'Written in aid of
the Musicians' Benevolent Fund'. *Fp*: Royal Military School
Bandsmen (Kneller Hall), H. E. Adkins, Musicians' Benevolent Fund Annual Dinner, Savoy Hotel, 8 May 1930. (MS lost.)
Rec: NSA, *c* 1930. *Timing*: 1' 15"

1938 *Prelude on a Traditional Irish Air*, org. 'Written for E[dith] Œ[none]
Somerville'. *Edn*: Boosey & Co., 1939. *Timing*: 3' 30"

Index

E. S. = Ethel Smyth; H. B. = Henry Brewster;
Lisl = Elizabeth von Herzogenberg

Addington, 144, 147, 196
Agra Bank, failure of, 29
Aibling, 122, 124–5
Alba, Duchess of, 328
Alba, Duke of, 328
Albert Hall, 184, 296, 297, 354
Aldershot, 10, 31, 39, 45, 50, 52, 54, 177, 207, 214, 327
Alexander, King of Serbia, 324–5
Alexander II, Emperor of Russia, 330
Allen, Sir Hugh, 355, 365
Ampthill, Lady, 186, 187
Archer, Fred, 178, 365
Arcos, Madame, 177, 186, 189, 192, 322
Asquith, Herbert, 298
'Aunt M'aimée', see Ponsonby, Hon. Lady
Austen, Jane, 43, 114
Austin, Sumner, 289, 365
Austria, 66, 72, 96, 324

B., Baroness, 220, 222
Bach, J. S., 64, 70, 93, 95, 98, 101, 104, 105, 106, 107, 112, 146, 341
Baden, Grand Duchess of, 234
Bahr, Hermann, 293, 365
Bahr-Mildenburg, Anna, 293, 365
Baldwin, Stanley, 317
Balfour, Lady Betty (later Countess Balfour), 293, 317, 348, 363
Balmoral, 185, 187, 188, 193
Baring, Hon. Maurice: E. S.'s tribute to, 8; on H. B. (The Puppet Show of Memory), 9, 280–81; relations with Lady Ponsonby, 181; first meeting with E. S., 196; 214, 230; attaché at Copenhagen, 240; 261, 262; travels to Prague for The Wreckers, 270–71; The Grey Stocking, 276–7, 278; visits dying H. B. in London, 277–8, 279; H. B.'s comment on, 282; 283, 349, 365

Barnby, Sir Joseph, 184, 193, 194, 197, 365
Bashkirtseff, Marie, 113, 365
Bassano, Duc de, 322
Bassano, Marquis of, 192
Battenberg, Prince Henry of, 185, 193, 365
Baudelaire, Charles, 122
Baylis, Lilian, 289, 358, 365
BBC, 357
Beaconsfield, Lord, 190
Bechstein Hall, 273
Beecham, Sir Thomas, Bt.: his admiration of The Wreckers, 12; 184; the Beecham Concerts, 284–5; approached by E. S., 285; his fantasy and levity, 285–6; undertakes The Wreckers at His Majesty's, 286; relations with his father, 286–7; his rehearsal methods, 287–9; The Wreckers at Covent Garden, 289; The Boatswain's Mate, 289; conducts The Prison at Smyth Festival, 354; to tea at Lyons, 355; 365
Beethoven, Ludwig van, 36, 45, 48, 51, 57, 66, 73, 93, 99, 105, 152–3
Bell, Vanessa, 355
Benckendorff, Countess, 281
Benckendorffs, the, 240
Benedetti, Count, 324
Benson, Mrs, 8; her 'patients', 144–5; her tactful handling of the Archbishop, 146–7; reaction to E. S.'s 'conversion', 164; loses daughter Nelly, 165; 166; meets Lili Wach, 168; 262
Benson, A. C., 144, 145
Benson, E. W. (Archbishop of Canterbury), 8, 144; his awesomeness, 145–7; 163; welcomes Lili Wach, 168; on E. S.'s Mass, 196
Benson, Maggie, 144, 146, 165
Benson, Nelly, 144, 145, 146, 156, 157, 165, 168

383

Benson family, the, 144

Berlin, 79, 84, 85, 106; musical personalities in, 112–13; 127, 136, 138; Cosima Wagner in, 150; 226, 233; the Court Theatre (Opera), 236–8, 239–40, 244–5, 253; the Chancellor's speech, 240–42; the Kaiser Cult, 243–4; National Museum, 244; Anglophobia in, 244; the 'Battle of Berlin', 247; rehearsals and performance of *Der Wald*, 249–51; 252, 254, 269, 270

Besant, Annie, 343

Birkhall, 185, 186, 189, 190

Birmingham Repertory Theatre, 289

Bismarck, Count von (later Prince), 249, 321, 324, 329, 330, 365

Bizet, Georges, 106, 274

Blanche, Jacques-Emile, 198

Boer War, 230, 233, 237, 250, 265

Bonheur, Rosa, 322, 365

'Bonnemaman', *see* Struth, Emma

Booth, 'General' William, 146

Boult, Sir Adrian, 197, 365

Brackenbury, Mrs, 300

Brahms, Johannes, 7, 56, 66, 67, 71; in Leipzig to conduct Second Symphony, 79–80; 86, 87, 89, 95, 98; rudeness, 99–100, 101–2; love of food, 100–101; attitude to women, 102–4; as pianist, 104–5; 106; defends Frau Joachim, 112*n*; 113, 139, 142, 149, 228, 233, 244, 359

Braithwaite, Warwick, 289, 365

Brancovan, Princess, 278

Brandt, Frau, 80

Brassey, Countess, 294

Brewster, Christopher, 10, 276, 278, 279, 280, 282

Brewster, Clotilde, 10, 202, 218, 220, 225, 279–80

Brewster, Henry (Harry, H. B.): Baring describes him, 9, 280–81; influence on E. S., 10; 11; as librettist, 12; *The Prison*, 13; on Lisl von Herzogenberg, 89; first meeting with E. S., 119–20; anti-German bias, 120–21; 122; dawning of love for E. S., 130–31; 161; views on religion, 164; correspondence with E. S., 165, 169, 172; comes to London for the Mass, 194; meets E. S.'s father, 195–6; 197; rebuffs the Hildebrands, 202–3; joins E. S. at North Berwick, 204–5; refers Lady Ponsonby to Montaigne, 205; helps at One Oak,

206, 209; 213; becomes E. S.'s lover, 214–15; illness and death of Julia Brewster, 216; question of re-marriage, 217; reconciliation with the Hildebrands, 217; 219, 220; at Weimar for *Fantasio*, 225; defeats bulldog, 226; 230; remembered by Augusta Holmès, 231–2; meets E. S. in Paris, 232; 245; dedication of *Der Wald*, 255–6; *The Wreckers* libretto, 260–62, 265; meets E. S.'s French friends, 262; subsidizes *The Wreckers* in Prague, 267; 268, 270, 271, 272, 273, 274; writing *Buondelmonte*, 275; signs of liver trouble, 275–6; cancer diagnosed, 276; travels to London, 277; visited by Baring, 277–8; attends *Wreckers* concert, 278; nursed by son Christopher, 279; his death, 279–80; his personality, 280–83; his generosity to staff, 282; burial in Rome, 283–4

Brewster, Henry and Julia: their views on marriage, 119, 121, 122–3, 130

Brewster, Julia, 88, 119, 120, 121, 122, 130, 131, 133, 135, 172, 202, 203, 215; illness, 216; death, 216–17

Briand, Aristide, 262

Brittain, Vera, 355

Brockhaus, Dr, 74

Brockhaus, Frau Dr, 74, 78, 80, 83, 94

Brockhaus (publishers), 67

Brodsky, Adolph, 139, 140, 365

Brontë, Emily, 261

Brook, Miss (E. S.'s companion), 364

Brussel, Robert, 278, 365

Buchholz, Frau, 99–100, 365

Bülow, Count (later Prince) von, 238–9, 240–42, 252, 253, 365

Bülow, Countess von: makes music with E. S., 238; her husband's devotion to, 239; 240–41; influence with the Kaiser, 247–9; 250, 252, 253, 254

Bülow, Count and Countess von, 239, 243, 247, 248, 251, 252

Bulteau, Madame ('Toche'), 262, 263, 278

Byron, Lord, 32, 169

Cairo, 302, 303, 304, 305

Calderón de la Barca, Pedro, 75

Calvé, Emma, 264, 366

Cap Martin, 184, 201, 213–14, 230, 313

Caraman-Chimay, Prince Alexandre de, 263

Caraman-Chimay, Hélène de, 262, 263, 274, 278
Carlsbad, 229, 275, 276, 277, 278
Carlsruhe: E. S. negotiates with the Opera at, 219, 220–21,, 228, 229; performance of Gluck's *Orpheus* at, 228–9, 232; the Court at, 234; 235
'Cat and Mouse' Act, 297, 301
Catherine, Empress of Russia, 343
Cavell, Edith, 343, 366
Cavendish, Lady Edward, 245
Chamberlain, Joseph, 239
Chappell (publishers), 57, 366
Charpentier, Gustave, 260
Chopin, Frédéric, 28, 52, 106
Christian, Princess, 186, 190–91, 193, 366
Chrysander, Friedrich, 112–13, 366
Churchill, Sir Winston, 315
Clary, Count, 325
Clemenceau, Georges, 330–31, 366
Coates, John, 286, 289, 365
Coign (Woking), 272, 350, 364
Cologne, 218, 219, 220
Comte, Auguste, 53, 366
Conciliation Bill, 297–8
Connaught, Duchess of, 185, 221
Connaught, Duke of, 148, 185, 365
Cooper, Lady Diana, 355
Cossart, Michael de (*The Food of Love*), 264
Covent Garden, 12, 232, 236, 247, 253, 256, 260, 289
Covent Garden Syndicate, 232, 284
Cradock, Sheldon, 196
Craig, Edith, 297, 365
Crawfurd, Nancy, 96
Crawshay, Mary, 256
Cross, Viscount, 191
Crostewitz, Lake, 113, 129, 132, 137
Crystal Palace, 24, 162
Crystal Palace Concerts, 113, 150

Davidson, Alice, 22, 23, 24, 25, 28, 36, 43; engagement, 48; marriage, 49; 148, 160, 165, 167, 225, 248, 309; death, 355
Davidson, Edith, 144, 177–8
Davidson, Harry, 48, 59, 63, 64, 65
Davidson, Randall (Dean of Windsor, Bishop of Rochester, Archbishop of Canterbury), 144, 146, 163, 186
Davies, Emily, 179
Davies, Fanny, 140, 366
Davies, Sir Walford, 345, 366
Delafosse, Léon, 274, 366

Delius, Frederick, 227, 289
Dent, Edward J., 14, 265, 366
Dodge, Mary, 271, 286, 364
Draga, Queen of Serbia, 324–5
Dresden, 74, 84, 94, 132, 133, 140, 218, 219, 223, 226; E. S. proposes *Der Wald* for Court Opera at, 232–3; 234; *Der Wald* turned down by, 235; 240, 247
Duchesne, Monseigneur, 262, 366
Durham, University of, 293
Duse, Eleonora, 264, 366
Dvořák, Antonin, 101, 105, 359

Eastwood, Colonel Hugh, 161
Eastwood, Nelly, 23, 33, 49, 151, 161, 355
Eden, Sir William, Bt., 200, 366
Edinburgh, Duke of, 184, 193, 366
Edward VII, King, 287, 289
Egypt, 302–5, 310, 311, 360
Elgar, Sir Edward, 8
Eliot, George, 57, 180
Eliot, T. S., 356
Elizabeth I, Queen, 343
Empress Frederick, *see* Victoria, Crown Princess of Germany
Ernle, Lady, *see* Hamley, Barbara
Eugénie, ex-Empress of France, 8, 11; first meeting with E. S., 125; her beauty, 177; 182; invites E. S. to Scotland, 184–5; visited by the Queen, 186–8; dinner at Balmoral, 188–92; agrees to attend performance of E. S.'s Mass, 193, 196; 197, 201; at Cap Martin, 213–14; advises E. S. against marriage, 217; 223, 234, 248, 255; subsidizes *Wreckers* publication, 266; 271, 313; entertains at Farnborough, 321–2; her interest in women's work, 322; impressed by wealth, 323; on the Franco-Prussian war, 323–4, 329–31; her affection for Austria, 324–5; her strength in anger, 325–6; her table manners, 326; her fiery temperament, 326–7; her lack of sensuality, 327–8; her one romantic episode, 328; her refusal of self-justification, 328–30; on the Prince Imperial, 330; her Household, 332–3, 334; receives Mrs Pankhurst, 333–4; blindness, 334; sight restored, death, 336
Ewing, Alexander, 50–52, 54, 55, 56, 66, 105
Ewing, Juliana, 50–52, 54, 55

Farnborough, 39, 54, 125, 329; South
  Farnborough, 279
Farnborough Hill, 46, 126, 177, 227, 313,
  321–2, 334
Faulkner, Mrs (E. S.'s housekeeper), 279
Fauré, Gabriel, 11, 227, 274, 278
Fawcett, Mrs (later Dame Millicent), 114,
  116, 298
Feilding, Percy, 10
Fiedler, Conrad, 111, 112; intervenes
  with Lisl, 137–8; attitude to Wagner,
  149; 157–8; accidental death, 168; on
  Lisl, 172; 217–18, 366
Fiedler, Mary, 111–12; interview with
  Lisl, 138; as 'the voice of Cosima
  Wagner', 149; kindness to E. S. in
  Munich, 156–8; 169; Lisl's letters to
  E. S., 201; marries Levi, 217–18
Fiedlers, the, 137–8, 149, 150, 156, 201
Fitzwilliam, Earl and Countess, 40
Fleury, Louis, 274, 366
Flinsch, Herr, 93
Florence, 89, 116, 118–19, 122, 130, 137,
  197, 202, 230
Ford (E. S.'s housekeeper), 207–9
France, 9, 28, 34, 35, 36, 120, 242, 314,
  317, 321, 329
France, Anatole, 122
Frankfurt-am-Main, 91–2, 312, 360
Franz Ferdinand, Archduke, 313
Franz Joseph, Emperor of Austria, 324–5,
  330, 365
Frederick, Crown Prince of Germany
  (later Emperor Frederick III), 43, 221,
  366
Frederick the Great, King of Prussia,
  235
Frege, Livia, 85–7, 91, 92, 168
Friedländer, Thekla, 56, 57, 59, 64–5, 67,
  68
Frimhurst, 39, 41, 43, 45, 51, 53–4, 58, 67,
  68, 74, 122, 125, 128, 129, 147, 158, 160,
  166, 193, 206–7
Frimley, 39, 160, 183
Furse, Charles, 254–5, 366

Gambetta, Léon, 331
Garrett, Agnes, 114–16
Garrett, Edmund, 115
Garrett, Rhoda, 114–16, 168
Garrett Anderson, Dr Elizabeth, 114
Geistinger, Marie, 76–9
George III, King, 102
George V, King, 329, 331

Germany, 10, 51, 59, 63, 66, 68, 70, 71,
  72, 81, 88, 94, 98; German views on
  women, 102; 120, 121, 128, 139; a
  strange case of Anglophobia, 143; 147,
  150, 152, 157, 161, 164, 196, 197, 201,
  213, 217, 225, 226, 227, 228, 230;
  increase in anti-English feelings, 235;
  236, 238, 239, 240; military fervour,
  243; the Kaiser on 'Grandpapa', 248–9;
  265; German attitude to contracts, 266;
  269, 273; after the war, 317; 329, 356,
  358, 360
Gladstone, W. E., 31–2, 144, 283
Glehns, the von (de), 359, 367
Gleichen, Lady Helena, 161
Gluck, C. E. von (*Orpheus*), 228–9
Godfrey, Sir Dan, 358, 367
Goethe, J. W. von, 42, 70, 75, 91, 120,
  137, 221, 225, 235, 263, 285
Goossens, Sir Eugene, 290, 366
Gordon, General, 127
Goulden-Bach, Mrs, 316
Grant, Duncan, 355
Grau (impresario), 256
Greece, 124, 275, 317, 343
Greffulhe, Comtesse, 263, 278
Grey, Earl, 179
Grey, General, 180
Grieg, Edvard, 101, 104, 105, 141–2
Grieg, Nina, 141
Griegs, the, 105, 141, 359
Grove, Sir George, 113, 367
Grove's Dictionary of Music and Musicians,
  360

Hagel, Richard, 266–9, 367
Hallé, Lady, 341, 367
Hallé Orchestra, 340, 341, 344
Hamilton, Cicely, 297
Hamley, Barbara, 58, 114
Hamley, Sir Edward (later Lord Ernle),
  58
Hammond, Miss, 42
Harcourt, Viscount, 299
Harnack, Professor, 248
Harper, Miss, 301
Harte, Bret, 356, 367
Hauptmann, Helene, 170
Haussmann, Baron, 321
Haydn, Joseph, 195
Hayward, Marjorie, 341, 367
Heathcote, Gilbert, 168
Heimbach, Frau Professor, 59, 63, 64–5,
  67, 68, 70, 71, 80

Helouan, 302–3, 305, 309, 310, 311

Henry, O., 262

Henschel, Sir George: as singer, 13; 22; at St James's Hall, 56; 66–7; presents E. S. to Brahms, 79; stays at Frimhurst, 165–6; preparations for E. S.'s Mass, 193–4; gives dinner party for E. S., 195–6; 198, 218; in Weimar for *Fantasio*, 225; advice on Germany, 225; 233, 267; on H. B. and Palmizio, 282; 359, 367

Henschel, Helen, 225

Henschel, Lilian (Mrs), 166, 367

Henschel, Mr and Mrs, 165, 193, 194, 195, 367

Herzogenberg, Elisabeth (Lisl) von, 10; deplores distractions in E. S.'s musical career, 11, 363; 79, 80, 85; appearance, personality, musicianship, 87–9; fear of conflicts, 90; nurses E. S. through breakdown, 94–6; E. S. 'semi-detached member of family', 98–9, 100, 135; talent for cooking, 100–101, 102–3; managing Brahms, 101–3; 104; her parents, 107–8, 117–18; 112, 113, 116; admiration for her sister Julia, 119, 122–3; 120, 121; dislike of French poetry, 122; with Frau Schumann, 124; with E. S.'s mother, 128; her farewell to E. S., 129; informed about E. S. and H. B., 130; 131; severance of relations with E. S., 132–8; 149; praised by Cosima Wagner, 150; 155, 162, 168, 169; death of her mother, 170; death at San Remo, 170; her nature summed up, 170–73; E. S.'s letters to her returned, 201; 202, 203, 215; an act of perfidy, 217; Mrs Pankhurst's comment, 315; the Hildebrand bust, 317

Herzogenberg, Heinrich von, 79, 90; undertakes E. S.'s tuition, 93, 99; 97, 98, 105; on Bizet, 106; as orchestrator, 106; 108, 117; appointed to Berlin Hochschule, 127, 136; 128, 170, 172, 201, 202, 216

Hesse, Grand Duke Ludwig IV of, 191, 367

Higgins, Harry, 232

Hildebrand, Adolf, 10, 108, 118–19, 149, 170, 201, 202, 244, 317, 367

Hildebrand, Frau, 118, 121, 123, 132, 202, 217

Hildebrands, the, 118–19, 126, 202, 217, 218

Hindemith, Paul, 317

Hippisley, Colonel R. L., 161

Hippisley, Violet, 23, 161, 162, 225–6, 226, 230, 271

Hippisleys, the, 214, 259

Hirsch, Berta, 227–8, 275

His Majesty's Theatre, 272, 286

Hochberg, Count von, 236–7; receives E. S., 238; placed in difficult position concerning *Der Wald*, 245–6, 250, 251; asserts authority, 247, 249; 253, 367

Hofmann, Julius, 218, 220, 367

Hofmannsthal, Hugo von, 312

Hohenzollern-Sigmaringen, Prince Leopold of, 324

Hollings, Herbert, 160

Hollings, Nina, 23, 43, 148, 160–61, 355

Hollings family, the, 148, 160, 227

Holloway Prison, 298, 300, 301, 356

Holmès, Augusta, 10, 230–31, 367

Holtby, Winifred, 355

Hugenschmitt, M., 330

Hülsen, von, 236

Hunter, Charles, 48, 81, 160, 198, 200

Hunter, Charles and Mary, 229

Hunter, Captain George, 303–9

Hunter, Kitty, 225

Hunter, Mary, 10, 23, 24–6, 33, 43–5, 46–7; engagement and wedding, 48–9; helps E. S. with career, 114, 160, 196, 271, 355; 152; friendships with artists, 198; attitude to husband and changing relations with E. S., 199–200; financial difficulties and death, 200–201; 206; in Bayreuth and Munich with E. S., 220; in Weimar, 225–6; 227, 229, 236; Sargent's portrait of, 252; 254; lack of humour, 255–6; falls out with E. S. over *Der Wald*, 256; 267, 278, 302

Hunter, Sylvia, 225

India, 23, 30, 36, 45, 159, 161, 162, 167

Indian Mutiny, 21, 45

Inglis, Elsie, 343, 367

Ireland, 52, 301

Isaacs, Sir Rufus (later Marquess of Reading), 299, 367

Italy, 116, 122, 126–7, 220, 254, 267

Jacobs, W. W., 13, 301

Jadassohn, Salomon, 71, 367

James, Henry, 9, 254, 281

James, Lord Justice, 58

Joachim, Amalie, 101, 112

Joachim, Joseph, 57, 101; home life, 112; divorce, estrangement from Brahms, 112n; declines E. S.'s Violin Sonata, 140; 341, 367
Johnson, Dr Samuel, 167, 280
Jonquière, 28
Joshua, Ella, 227, 275
Joshua, Mr, 227

Kaiser, the, *see* Wilhelm II, Emperor of Germany
Keats, John, 27, 283
Kenney, Annie, 293, 296
Kent, Duke of, 294
Kirchner, Theodor, 101, 105, 359, 367
Kitchener, Earl, 302
Klengel, Julius, 70, 367
Klengel family, the, 69, 80, 94, 367
Korbay, Ferencz (Francis), 232, 367
Kowalewski, Sophie, 113, 367
Krall (music critic), 196
Kraus, Ernst, 245–6, 251, 253, 367
Kruger, Paul, 233
Kruger telegram, the, 233, 239
Kuhe, Wilhelm, 48, 367

Lagarde, Mademoiselle de, 35
Lagerlöf, Selma, 342, 367
la Grange, Henry Louis de, 141
Lalo, Pierre, 278, 368
Lambert, Constant, 356, 368
Lambeth, 11, 83, 144, 145, 146–7, 163, 168
Langbein, Dr, 97
Lascelles, Florence, 236, 247
Lascelles, Sir Frank, 236, 238, 240, 241, 244, 245, 368
Lassen, Eduard, 222, 226–7, 232, 368
Lawrence, Frederick, *see* Pethick-Lawrence
Lear, Edward, 325
le Breton, Madame, 182, 214, 322, 333
Leconte de Lisle, Charles, 13
Lee, Vernon, 262–3, 359, 368
Leipzig, 10, 11, 12, 36; Conservatorium, 45, 66, 71–2, 93; 51, 58; Leipzig in 1877, 64–5, 69–71, 80–81, 93; Thomas Kirche, 64; Thomas Schule, 64; Gewandhaus Concerts and Orchestra, 67, 68, 72, 79, 91, 92, 102, 106, 107; *Thomaner Chor*, 107, 127, 169; new hall, 73; 'little' hall, 73; Stadttheater (Opera), 73, 106, 139, 140, 265, 266–70; social life, 74–5, 78, 82–4, 91, 94, 104, 140; 'old theatre',

75–8; Saxons and Prussians, 84–5; 87, 88; Gewandhaus balls, 91, 266; Bach Verein, 92, 93, 106; 96, 97, 101, 105, 127, 128, 131, 132, 136, 137, 141, 168, 170, 203, 219, 223, 224, 239, 265, 266, 267, 268, 270, 271, 317
Levi, Hermann: encourages E. S. to write operas, 12, 213; 150, 151, 153, 197; advises E. S. to enter *Fantasio* for competition, 213; marries Mary Fiedler, 217–18; recommends *Fantasio* to Mottl, 219, 220; 223, 227, 230, 358, 359, 368
Lewes, G. H. 57
Lewis, Ella, 227
Lewis, Sir George, 227, 312
Lewis, Lady, 227
Lewis, Marie, 275
Lichstenstein, Princess, 232
Limburger, Consul, 91, 102, 127, 168
Limburger, Ella, 127, 128, 138–9
Limburger family, the, 92, 219, 268
Lind, Jenny (Lind-Goldschmidt), 47, 73, 368
Liszt, Franz, 105, 222
Lloyd George, David, 298, 345–6
Loë, General von, 252
London Symphony Orchestra, 273–4, 340
Longman, Mrs, 46
Lovat, Lady, 355
Lutyens, Elisabeth, 363
Lytton, Earl of, 293
Lytton, Lady Constance, 293–4, 297, 363

Maas, Louis, 71, 368
Mackenzie, Sir Morell, 143, 368
McKenna, Reginald, 297
Mahler, Gustav: in love with Baroness von Weber, 140–41; as conductor, 141; in Vienna, 271, 272, 285, 358
Mainz, 227, 228
Mannheim, 227, 228, 229
Manns, Sir August, 150, 161, 359, 368
Marchesi, Blanche, 274, 368
Marchiafava (physician), 276–7, 279
Marco (E. S.'s dog): discovery of, 138; his character and temperament, 139; terrifies Tchaikovsky, 142; in Munich, 151, 156, 157; journey to England, 159; the staghounds, 206–7; relations with Ford, 207–8; and the Highlander, 209; 224, 226; death and successor, 240, 346, 359
Marie-Antoinette, Queen, 325

Mary, Queen, 355
Mary (E. S.'s housekeeper), 347–8, 349, 350, 351–2
Maupassant, Guy de, 70
Melba, Dame Nellie, 112
Mendelssohn, Felix, 71, 84, 86, 87, 107, 168, 266
Mendès, Catulle, 231, 368
Mérimée, Prosper, 140
Mersa Halib, 303, 304–6
Messager, André, 12, 232, 260, 264, 368
Metcalfe, Sir Theophilus, 29
Metropolitan Opera House, 256
Metternich, Princess Pauline, 332
Meyendorff, Baroness Olga von, 221–4
Meyer, Amanda, 70, 75
Mildenburg, Anna von, *see* Bahr-Mildenburg, Anna
Militant Suffrage Society, 272
Mill, J. S. 356
Milner, Lord, 115
Minghetti, Donna Laura, 126, 220, 238, 241, 254
Mohammed (the hermaphrodite), 306–10
Montaigne, Michel de, 205
Moore, George, 200, 230
Moran–Olden (singer), 139
Morice, Gordon, 303–7
Mottl, Felix; taken with *Fantasio*, 219–20; Levi's advice on, 220–21; 223, 227; prevarications, 228; his *Orpheus*, 228–9; date promised for *Fantasio*, 229; postponement, 230; E. S. summoned to Carlsruhe, 232; *Fantasio* performed, 234; 246, 250, 358, 368
Mozart, W. A., 105, 106
Muck, Karl, 236, 237; elusiveness, 246; 249; anger at bad reception for *Der Wald*, 250; 251, 253, 358, 368
Munich, 12, 111, 138, 148–9; E. S.'s reactions to, 150–51; lodging difficulties in, 151, 155–6, 157; at the opera, 151–2; *Missa solemnis* 152–3; 159, 162, 201, 202, 218, 220, 240, 311, 312, 360
Musset, Alfred de, 12, 213

Napier, Mrs, 58
Napier, General William, 58
Napier, Sir Charles, 58
Napier of Magdala, Lord, 78
Napoleon I, Emperor of France, 331
Napoleon III, Emperor of France, 248, 321, 323–4, 326, 332

Neilson, Francis, 254, 368
Neumann, Angelo: director at Leipzig Opera, 73; director at Prague, 266; accepts *The Wreckers*, 267; has paralytic stroke, 270–71; 368
Nightingale, Florence, 295, 343
Nikisch, Artur, 228, 262; accepts *The Wreckers* for Leipzig, 265; leaves Leipzig unexpectedly, 266; recommends *The Wreckers* to Neumann, 266–7; 268, 270; conducts excerpt from *The Wreckers* in London, 274, 275; 358, 359, 368
Noailles, Comtesse Anna de, 262, 263–4, 275, 342, 368
Noailles, Count Mathieu de, 263
Norman Tower (Windsor Castle), 177, 178, 192

Old Vic, 12, 14, 289
Ollivier, Émile, 323, 368
Opéra-Comique (Paris), 230, 260
Oxford, University of, 53, 160, 345–6

Palestrina, G. P. da, 113
Palmizio (H. B.'s manservant), 282
Pan (E. S.'s dog), 240, 279, 302, 306, 346
Pan II, 348, 349
Pan IV, 346, 347–9, 350–53, 364
Pankhurst, Adela, 293
Pankhurst, Dame Christabel, 293, 312, 316
Pankhurst, Mrs (Emmeline), 8, 9; her family, 293; praised by Bahr, 293–4; personality, 294–6; 297; lessons in throwing stones, 298–9; in Holloway Prison, 299–300; hunger- and thirst-strike, 301, 312; 302; in Paris, 303; 309; in Brittany, 313; war work, 314–15; rift with E. S., 315–16; their last meeting, 316–17; meets the Empress Eugénie, 333–4; 363
Pankhurst, Frank, 293
Pankhurst, Dr R. M., 293
Pankhurst, Sylvia, 13, 293, 363
Paris, 10, 27–8, 34, 215, 230–32, 235, 252, 260; E. S.'s four women friends in, 262–4; concert of E. S.'s music proposed, 274; favourable reviews for concert, 278–9; 301, 303, 312, 313, 314; E. S. consults aurist in, 317; under Napoleon III, 321; in the First World War, 327; 330–31
Parratt, Sir Walter, 177, 368–9

Parry, Sir Hubert, 116, 369
Pater, Walter, 118
Paton, Stuart, 345
Patti, Adelina, 48, 72, 369
Paul, St, 285
Peacock, Thomas Love, 283
Peters (publishers), 265
Pethick, Emmeline, 293
Pethick-Lawrence, Frederick, 299
Picot de Peccaduc, Vicomte, 90
Pierson, Georg, 236–7, 240, 242–3, 245, 247, 251, 253, 270, 369
Pietri, Monsieur, 322, 325
Pitt, Percy, 289, 369
Polignac, Prince Edmond de, 263
Polignac, Princesse Edmond de, 235, 262, 264, 313
Ponsonby, Betty, 177, 178, 183
Ponsonby, Sir Henry, 178, 180, 192, 193
Ponsonby, Hon. Lady ('Aunt M'aimée'), 11, 85, 177–8; her homes at Windsor Ascot, 178–9; speaking voice and movements, 179; 'a modern woman', 179–80; her appearance, 180–82; violent temperament, 182–3; rows with E. S., 183; 192, 193, 195, 198, 205; on E. S.'s relations with H. B., 215; captivated by H. B., 217; 219, 277, 282
Ponsonby, Maggie, 177, 183, 283
Prague, 266, 267, 269–70
Prince Imperial, the, 230, 231, 331
Punch, 47, 63, 191
Pursey, Mr (cobbler), 31

Queen's Hall, 344

Redeker, Fräulein, 56, 57, 66
Reece, Mr, 28
Régnier, Henri de, 13, 262, 369
Reinecke, Carl, 71, 72, 105, 369
Reinhardt, Max, 306, 369
Richepin, Jean, 42
Richter, Hans, 358
Riddell, Lord, 345
Rivoli, Duchesse de, 214
Roberts, Earl, 233
Robey, Sir George, 347, 369
Rodin, Auguste, 118, 198
Rome, 9, 126, 197, 202, 217, 220, 230, 232, 238, 241, 254, 261, 267, 275, 279, 283
Ronald, Sir Landon, 356, 369
Röntgen, Engelbert: admirer of Brahms, 79; teaches E. S. the violin, 99; allows

her to play in Bach *Passion*, 106–7; dies, 169; 369
Röntgen, Frau, 69, 75, 79, 103
Röntgen, Johanna, 69, 70, 169, 239, 317
Röntgen, Julius, 69, 70, 75, 359, 369
Röntgen, Line, 69
Röntgen family, the, 69–70, 73, 74–5, 79, 80, 86, 359
Rosebery, Earl of, 335, 369
Rossetti, D. G., 24, 124, 215, 309
Royal Choral Society, 184, 193
Royal College of Music, 290
Rubinstein, Anton, 112, 369
Ruskin, John, 118
Russian Ballet, the, 284

Sackville-West, Hon. Victoria, 363
Sadler's Wells Theatre, 12, 14, 254, 289, 363
St James's Hall, 56, 57
St John, Christopher, 7, 8, 201, 317, 363
Saint-Saëns, Camille, 224
Salisbury, Marquess of, 145
Sammons, Albert, 286, 369
Sand, George, 113
Sandhurst, 39, 58, 207
San Remo, 170, 201
Sarajevo, 312, 313
Sarasate, Pablo de, 139–40, 369
Sarawak, Ranee of, 183
Sargent, J. S., 10, 198, 200, 214, 227, 229, 252, 256, 278, 280
Sayn-Wittgenstein, Princess, 222
Schiller, F. von, 75, 120
Schnitzler, Arthur, 312
Schott (publishers), 227, 229
Schubert, Franz, 48, 57, 66, 73, 208
Schuch, Ernst von, 218, 219, 223; listens to E. S. play *Der Wald*, 232–3; *Der Wald* turned down, 235; 246, 369
Schumann, Clara, 56, 63, 71; mishap at concert, 73; 101; Brahms's respect for her, 104; her character, 123–4; 359, 369
Schumann, Robert, 48, 85
Schuster, Frank, 232, 369
Schwabe, Madame, 74, 140
Schwabe, Mary, 56, 58, 59, 74
Scott, Dr Charles, 41
Scott-Gatty, Sir Alfred, 55, 369
Sedan, 321, 327, 330
Seebach, Count Nikolaus von, 219, 232–3, 235, 236, 369
Selaby, 198, 199
Sermoneta, Duchess of, 126

Shaftesbury Theatre, 289
Shakespeare, William, 70, 75, 120, 163, 255, 358
Shakespere, Mr, 56
Shanks, Edward, 13, 369
Shelley, P. B., 283
Sickert, W. R., 198, 200
Sidcup, 21, 23, 27, 36, 39, 41
Singer, Isaac, 264
Sitwell, Lady Louisa, 7
Sitwell, Sir Osbert, Bt., 7
Smith-Dorrien, Mr, 259
Smyth, Alice (E. S.'s sister), *see* Davidson, Alice
Smyth, Edward (E. S.'s grandfather), 34
Smyth, Dame Ethel, 7–14 *passim*; birth, 23; relations with father, 32; first attempts at composing, 44–5; decides to study at Leipzig, 45; composition lessons from A. Ewing, 50–52; engaged to W. Wilde, 53–4; on ballroom dancing, 54–5; first hears music of Brahms, 56; confirms intention of going to Leipzig, 56; leaves for Germany, 59; arrival in Leipzig, 63; presented to Brahms, 79; meets Livia Frege and Lili Wach, 86–7; description of Lisl von Herzogenberg, 87–90; and Herzogenberg, 90–91; joins Bach Verein, 93; nursed by Lisl during illness, 94; convalesces in England, 96; returns to Leipzig, 98; gets to know Brahms, 100–105; plays violin in Bach *Passion*, 106–7; disliked by Lisl's mother, 108; Christmas in Berlin, 111–12; on friendships with women, 113–14; friendship with Rhoda Garrett, 114–16; mountaineering, 116–17; visit to Venice, 117–18; meets the Hildebrands in Florence, 118–19; meets Julia and Henry Brewster, 120–22; joins the Herzogenbergs at Berchtesgaden, 122–3; makes friends with Clara Schumann, 123–4; mud-cure at Aibling, 124–5; holidays at Frimhurst, 125; first meeting with Empress Eugénie, 125–6; on the Italians, 126–7; her mother visits Leipzig, 128; Lisl's withdrawal from friendship, 129–36; adopts Marco, 138–9; her Violin Sonata performed, 140; meets Mahler, the Griegs and Tchaikovsky, 141–2; friendship with the Benson family, 144–7; to Munich,

148; friendship with Pauline Trevelyan, 153–5; illness and return home, 155–9; description of her sisters, 160–61; August Manns performs her Serenade, 161–2; surprise visit from H. B., 162; bicycling, 163–4; spiritual crisis, 164; composition of the Mass, 164; correspondence with H. B. resumed, 165; death of her mother, 167; deaths of many friends, 168–9; death of Lisl, 170; reflections on the broken friendship, 170–73; meets Lady Ponsonby, 177, invited to Scotland by the Empress Eugénie, 185; presented to Queen Victoria, 186; at Balmoral, 188–91; the Mass accepted by Barnby, 193; her father meets H. B., 195–6; performance of the Mass and aftermath, 196–7; hunting at Selaby, 198; relations with Mary decline, 199–200; her letters to Lisl returned, 201–2; golf at North Berwick, 204–5; moves to One Oak, 206–7; *Fantasio* entered for competition, 213; at Cap Martin with the Empress, 213–14; H. B. becomes her lover, 214–15; illness and death of Julia Brewster, 216; result of opera competition, 218; 'round journey' to sell *Fantasio*, 219–20; *Fantasio* accepted at Weimar, 224; *Fantasio* performed, 226–7; on Mottl's *Orpheus*, 228–9; *Fantasio* booked for Carlsruhe, 229; visits Augusta Holmès, 230–32; Messager approves *Der Wald*, 232; to Dresden, 232–3; *Fantasio* at Carlsruhe, 234; buries *Fantasio*, 234–5; Dresden turns down *Der Wald*, 235–6; to Berlin, 236–8; meets Countess von Bülow, 238–9; rehearsals and performance of *Der Wald*, 245–6, 249–51, meets the Kaiser, 247–9, 251–3, 254; *Der Wald* at Covent Garden, 255; in New York and Boston, 256; row with Mary, 256; origin of *The Wreckers*, 259–60; H. B. writes libretto, 260–62; makes four new French friends, 262–4; begins battle to stage *The Wreckers*, 264; *The Wreckers* billed for Leipzig, 267; performed, 268; performance in Prague, 270–71; plays *The Wreckers* to Walter in Vienna, 271; Mary Dodge provides money for Coign (house in Woking), 271; trouble in Vienna, 272–3; 'chamber songs' performed in

London, 273; friends plan chamber concert in Paris, 274; concern for H. B.'s health, 274–6; Nikisch conducts 'On the Cliffs of Cornwall', 275; Acts I and II of *The Wreckers* given in concert form, 278; Paris concert, 278–9; H. B. moved to his daughter's house, 279; death of H. B., 280; his burial in Rome, 283–4; Covent Garden turns down *The Wreckers*, 284; meeting with Beecham, 285; plans for *Wreckers* season, 286–7; Beecham in rehearsal, 287–9; performances at His Majesty's, 289; further history of *The Wreckers*, *The Boatswain's Mate*, *Fête galante* and *Entente cordiale*, 289–90; first meeting with Mrs Pankhurst, 294; performance of *The March of the Women*, 297; window-breaking, 298–9; trial and imprisonment in Holloway, 299–300; to Vienna, Ireland, etc., 301; to Egypt, 302–11; interest in Mohammed, the hermaphrodite, 306–10; *The Boatswain's Mate* accepted by Viennese publisher, 311–12; Walter accepts *The Wreckers* for Munich, 312; *The Boatswain's Mate* booked for Frankfurt, 312; Mrs Pankhurst joins her in Brittany, 313; they return to England, 314; to Vichy as radiographer, 314; publication of *Impressions that Remained*, 315, 363–4; cooling of friendship with Mrs Pankhurst, 315–17; unveiling the statue, 317; friendship with Edith Somerville, *A Three-Legged Tour in Greece*, music at Salzburg, increasing deafness, return to Leipzig, 317; the Empress Eugénie described, 321–36; on women in English musical life, 339–44; receives honours, 344–6; on the Pan dynasty (Old English Sheepdogs), 346, 364; Pan IV, 346–53; Festival for her seventy-fifth birthday, 353–5; 'mad tea-party', 355; qualified celebrity, 355–6; the English music machine, 356–9; disruptive effect of sport, games and friendship, 360, 363; friendship with Virginia Woolf, 363; the curse of deafness, 363; last illness and death, 364

Smyth grandparents, 21–2

Smyth, Major-General J. H. (E. S.'s father), 10, 21, 22, 23, 24, 25–6; loss of savings, 29; Army experience, 29–30;

civilian activity, 30–32; his *'coq-à-l'âne'*, 32–3, 193; marriage, 34, 35; commands Artillery at Aldershot, 39, 43, 45–6; opposes E. S.'s plans for Germany, 49–52, 56, 57–8; 64, 66, 80, 96, 97, 125, 148, 162, 165, 166, 167, 168, 193; meets H. B., 195–6; 206, 280, 322

Smyth, Johnny (E. S.'s brother), 22, 24, 25, 26, 38, 41, 48–9, 124, 206

Smyth, Mary (E. S.'s sister), *see* Hunter, Mary

Smyth, Nelly (E. S.'s sister), *see* Eastwood, Nelly

Smyth, Nina (E. S.'s mother), 10, 24, 25, 26, 28, 31, 32, 33; marriage, 34; her un-Englishness, 35, 38; accomplishments, 36–7; 'Morning Calls', 37; illness of Johnny, 38, 41, 42, 43, 45, 46, 47; death of Johnny, 48–9; 50, 52, 57, 58, 78, 95, 96, 97, 121; her extravagance, 125; visits Ethel in Leipzig, 128, 131, 136; 137, 147–8, 159, 162, 163, 165; her death, 166–67; 183, 207, 224, 321, 322

Smyth, Nina (E. S.'s sister), *see* Hollings, Nina

Smyth, Brigadier-General Robert ('Bob') (E. S.'s brother), 21, 32–3, 41, 47, 148, 158, 162, 167, 179, 230, 355

Smyth, Violet (E. S.'s sister), *see* Hippisley, Violet

Socrates, 343, 344

Somerville, Edith (E. Œ), 9, 317, 363

Spitta, Philipp, 101, 112, 369

Spurgeon, Charles, 147

Stanford, Sir C. V., 12,, 369–70

Stavenhagen, Bernhard, 220, 221, 222, 370

Steed, Wickham, 272, 370

Steel, Ethel, 355

Stockhausen, Baroness von, 108, 117, 118, 147, 169, 217

Storrs, Sir Ronald, 301–2

Stracey, Sir Edward, 34

Stracey family, the, 28, 163

Strauss, Richard, 244, 289, 312

Struth, Emma ('Bonnemaman') (E. S.'s grandmother), 27–9, 34

Suez, 303, 304, 311, 323

Sydney, Lord and Lady, 26, 36

Synge, J. M., 301

Tauchnitz (publishers), 78, 370

Taylor, Audrey, 352

Tchaikovsky, P. I., 142, 147, 359

Tertis, Lionel, 286, 370
Thackeray, W. M., 280
Thomas à Kempis, 163
Thuringia, 66–7
Tonks, Henry, 200
Tosti, Sir Paolo, 188, 192, 370
Tovey, Sir D. F., 11, 370
Trevelyan, Sir Alfred, 152
Trevelyan, Beatrice, 153
Trevelyan, Lady, 152, 153, 154–5, 164
Trevelyan, Pauline, 152, 153–4, 156, 161, 168, 220, 273
Trevelyan family, the, 152–6
Tuke, Mabel, 293, 316

Vaughan Williams, Ralph, 11
Venice, 66, 116, 117–18, 122, 147, 264, 293
Vere Sapio, Madame de, 286, 289
Verlaine, Paul, 122
Victoria, Crown Princess of Germany (later Empress Frederick), 143, 178, 188, 219, 221
Victoria, Queen, 8, 11, 177, 178, 180, 184, 185; calls on the Empress Eugénie, 185–8; dinner at Balmoral, 188–92; the Shah's carpet, 192–3; sends message about E. S.'s Mass, 197–8; visits Empress Eugénie at Cap Martin, 213–14, 322
Vienna, 138, 141, 170, 271, 272, 285, 301, 311–12, 325
Vizthum, Count Paul, 140
Volkland, Alfred, 101, 370

Wach, Adolf, 87, 104; as mountaineer, 116–17; his patriotic outburst, 143; 269, 270, 317
Wach, Adolf and Lili, 91, 116, 128, 143, 268
Wach, Lili, 85, 87, 103; with Brahms, 104, 117; interview with Lisl, 136–7; 143; visits Lambeth, 168; 169; on Lisl, 172
Wagner, Cosima, 149–50, 219
Wagner, Richard, 12, 51, 55, 72, 86, 104, 106, 149–50, 213, 217, 271
Wallace-Dunlop, Marion, 297
Walter, Bruno, 262; deputed to report on *The Wreckers*, 271; 272; agrees to mount *The Wreckers*, 273, 312; 301; 312; 358; 370
Warrender, Lady Maud, 355
Weber, Baron von, 140–41
Webern, Anton von, 317
Weimar: Levi recommends Weimar for *Fantasio*, 220; a Grand Ducal capital, 221–5; 226, 227, 232, 234
Weimar, Grand Duke of, 220, 221, 222, 223, 224, 225, 226
Weingartner, Felix, 272, 273
Wesley, John, 260
Wethered, Joyce, 355
Wild, Mrs Edythe, 303–6
Wilde, Oscar, 52–3
Wilde, William, 52–3
Wilhelm I, Emperor of Germany, 248
Wilhelm II, Emperor of Germany, 102, 233, 238; the Kaiser Cult, 243; his views on art, 244; his admiration for Frau von Bülow, 247; his 'naturalness and easiness', 248; 251, 252; his ambitions for Berlin, 252–3; 254, 366
William I, King of Prussia (later Emperor of Germany), 324, 330
Williamson, Elizabeth, 317
Woking Golf Club, 345
Women's Social and Political Union (WSPU), 293, 294, 295, 296, 297, 301, 316
Wood, Field Marshal Sir Evelyn, 52, 53
Wood, Sir Henry J., 284, 340, 344, 358, 370
Wood, Lady (Muriel), 348
Woodhouse, Violet Gordon, 273, 285, 355, 370
Woolf, Virginia, 8–9, 355, 363

Yacco, Sada, 69

Zuloaga, Ignacio, 244, 370